STATES AND PEOPLES IN CONFLICT

D1528262

This volume evaluates the state of the art in conflict studies. Original chapters by leading scholars survey theoretical and empirical research on the origins, processes, patterns, and consequences of most forms and contexts of political conflict, protest, repression, and rebellion. Contributors examine key pillars of conflict studies, including civil war, religious conflict, ethnic conflict, transnational conflict, terrorism, revolution, genocide, climate change, and several investigations into the role of the state. The research questions guiding the text include inquiries into the interactions between the rulers and the ruled, authorities and challengers, cooperation and conflict, accommodation and resistance, and the changing context of conflict from the local to the global.

Michael Stohl is Professor of Communication, Political Science, and Global Studies, and the Director of the Orfalea Center for Global and International Studies at the University of California–Santa Barbara.

Mark I. Lichbach is Professor of Government and Politics at the University of Maryland–College Park.

Peter Nils Grabosky is Professor Emeritus at the Australian National University School of Regulation and Global Governance (REGNET).

Praise for *States and Peoples in Conflict*

In this brilliant volume, the world's leading conflict researchers have contributed their latest theoretical and empirical findings regarding terrorism, crime, civil conflict, and revolutions, including their underlying causes. Examining the nature of the state, the role of religion, and the dynamics of the international system, this collection will be of immense value to both senior researchers and their students. No single volume tells more about what we know, and need to learn, in analyzing conflict.

Jack A. Goldstone, *George Mason University*

States and Peoples in Conflict is a rare synthesis of where we are in conflict studies, its methodologies, theories, and the way forward. A summary of this vast and expanding field of research is provided on the forms and reasons behind political and religious violence by some of the best academics of the discipline. Making the state the focal point of analysis, the book manages to shed new light on why the Hobbesian bargain is breaking down. The terror, crime, and military conflict we see around us highlight the need for this book.

Hans-Henrik Holm, *Danish School of Media and Journalism*

States and Peoples in Conflict is unique in its scholarly breadth and depth regarding the varied forms of deadly violence we face in the globe today. Each chapter in this volume presents an encyclopedic treatment of existing knowledge, while also engaging the puzzles that on-going violence poses to researchers. This is an indispensable compilation for any serious analyst of peace and conflict.

George A. Lopez, *University of Notre Dame and United States Institute of Peace*

This outstanding collection of essays provides a state-of-the-art overview of the conceptual pillars and controversies that constitute behavioral conflict studies.... In all, the book is a must-read for those interested in where behavioral conflict studies stands after a half-century of systematic empirical research.

Raymond D. Duvall, *University of Minnesota*

STATES AND PEOPLES IN CONFLICT

Transformations of Conflict Studies

Edited by Michael Stohl, Mark I. Lichbach, and Peter Nils Grabosky

Routledge
Taylor & Francis Group

NEW YORK AND LONDON

Published 2017
by Routledge
711 Third Avenue, New York, NY 10017

and by Routledge
2 Park Square, Milton Park, Abingdon, Oxon, OX14 4RN

Routledge is an imprint of the Taylor & Francis Group, an informa business

Library of Congress Cataloging in Publication Data
A catalog record for this book has been requested

ISBN: 978-1-138-65372-6 (hbk)
ISBN: 978-1-138-65373-3 (pbk)
ISBN: 978-1-315-62363-4 (ebk)

Typeset in Bembo
by Sunrise Setting Ltd, Brixham, UK

Visit the eResource: www.routledge.com/9781138653733

CONTENTS

Conclusion   **273**

FIGURES

TABLES

CONTRIBUTORS

Victor Asal is Chair of Public Administration and Associate Professor of Political Science at the State University of New York-Albany.

Colin J. Beck is Associate Professor of Sociology at Pomona College.

Halvard Buhaug is Research Professor at the Peace Research Institute (PRIO) in Oslo and Professor of Political Science at the Norwegian University of Science and Technology (NTNU) in Trondheim.

Benjamin R. Cole is Assistant Professor of Political Science & International Relations at Simmons College.

Kathleen Deloughery is Assistant Professor of Public Administration and Policy at the State University of New York-Albany.

Scott Englund is a Postdoctoral Fellow at the Orfalea Center for Global and International Studies at the University of California-Santa Barbara.

Jonathan Fox is a Professor of Political Studies at Bar Ilan University in Ramat Gan, Israel, and Director of the Religion and State project.

Nils Petter Gleditsch is Research Professor at the Peace Research Institute (PRIO) in Oslo and Professor Emeritus of Political Science at the Norwegian University of Science and Technology (NTNU) in Trondheim.

Peter Nils Grabosky is Professor Emeritus at the Australian National University School of Regulation and Global Governance (REGNET).

Ted Robert Gurr is Professor Emeritus of Government and Politics and formerly a Distinguished University Professor at the University of Maryland-College Park.

Barbara Harff is Professor Emerita of Political Science at the U.S. Naval Academy.

Keith Jaggers is Professor in the Honors College at Colorado State University.

Mark I. Lichbach is Professor of Government and Politics at the University of Maryland-College Park.

Monty G. Marshall is Director of the Center for System Peace and President of Societal-Systems Research, Inc.

Pamela Martin is Professor of Politics and International Relations at Coastal Carolina University.

Marc V. Simon is Associate Professor and Acting Chair of Political Science, and Coordinator of the minor in Peace and Conflict Studies at Bowling Green University.

Harvey Starr is Dag Hammarskjöld Professor in International Affairs Emeritus at the University of South Carolina-Columbia.

Michael Stohl is Professor of Communication, Political Science, and Global Studies, and the Director of the Orfalea Center for Global and International Studies at the University of California-Santa Barbara.

Ole Magnus Theisen is Associate Professor Sociology and Political Science at the Norwegian University of Science and Technology (NTNU) in Trondheim.

Peter Wallensteen is the Dag Hammarskjöld Chair in Peace and Conflict Studies at Uppsala University and the Richard G. Star Mann Sr. Research Professor in Peace Studies at the University of Notre Dame.

Franke Wilmer is Professor of Political Science and International Relations at Montana State University-Bozeman.

ACKNOWLEDGMENTS

The idea for this project emerged over a decade ago, and we wish to express our sincere appreciation to each of our contributors for their patience and cooperation during the long gestation period.

We would especially like to acknowledge our many debts to Ted Robert Gurr, who has been a mentor and friend for more than four decades. His scholarly contributions to the study of conflict over more than a fifty-year career are exceptional in terms of both quantity and quality. The breadth and depth of his vision are reflected not only in his own work but in that of the many colleagues and former students whom he has inspired.

Daily headlines track the deadly conflict and violence that become the data compiled by the scholars of interstate and intra-state war and terrorism who continue to draw on Ted Gurr's seminal contributions. While the data indicate that violent conflict is actually less prevalent though often more intense than two decades or two centuries ago, there seems little doubt that conflict will persist and that technology will continue to expand the capacity of individuals, organizations, and states to do harm to one another. Our contributors also agree with Ted that conflict is an inevitable concomitant of social structures and social change. In the contemporary era, globalization has produced not only greater interactions but also inequality and diversity, which in turn increase the risk of conflict between states, groups, and individuals.

Fortunately, a century of total war, cold war, proxy war, asymmetric war, and hybrid war has also seen greater efforts to understand both the causes and consequences of conflict and the mechanisms that manage violence. Whatever the future may hold for the prevalence and intensity of conflict, history has shown conflict to be not only persistent but also controllable. Indeed, the fields of war studies and peace studies are the twin components of the field of conflict studies.

We hope that others in these fields will build on the insights provided by the contributors to this volume and further efforts to manage the pernicious effects of war and conflict.

A collection such as this is the work of many hands. We thank the publishers, Routledge, for their support; our editor, Jennifer Knerr for her encouragement and perseverance over many years; Ze'ev Sudry for the conflict-free production process; and Victor Faessel for his assistance with the bibliography.

Michael Stohl, Peter Nils Grabosky, and Mark I. Lichbach

Introduction

1

STATES AND PEOPLES IN CONFLICT

Pillars, Forms, and Transformations in Conflict Studies

Mark I. Lichbach, Peter Nils Grabosky, and Michael Stohl

What connects the civil war in Somalia, insurgency in Syria, counterinsurgency in Afghanistan, guerrilla war in Chechnya, 9/11 terrorism in the United States, racial riots in Baltimore, religious clashes in India, antiglobalization protests in the Battle of Seattle, strikes by west-coast longshoremen, environmentalist social movements in Latin America, extremist political parties in Western Europe, drug-related criminal gangs in Mexico, military coups in Egypt, ethnic secessionism in the Ukraine, 1989 revolutions in Eastern Europe, state collapse in Libya, foreign military interventions in Iraq, state repression in Venezuela, genocide in Rwanda, peace agreements in Bosnia, corruption in Russia, and democratic consolidation in Poland? In this volume, leading scholars from the fields of conflict studies and contentious politics study the many causes, concomitants, and consequences of actual or threatened violence involving the state. Contention within and across national boundaries are addressed.

The context for our work is that we now see a world that is globalized, interconnected, and interrelated, across many different sectors and processes, but which may also be seen as divided into zones of peace, democracy, and prosperity coexisting with zones of political turmoil, internal war, and arrested economic development. Many of the boundaries between zones of peace and zones of turmoil are often drawn much more clearly by observers, both scholars and pundits, than the closer examinations in this volume reveal. Toward this end, we have assembled a group of scholars to evaluate the state of the art in conflict studies—particularly the important theoretical and methodological questions that will guide future research. The chapters survey theoretical and empirical research on the origins, processes, patterns, and consequences of most forms and contexts of political conflict, protest, repression, rebellion, war, and terrorism

within and across state boundaries. The guiding research questions to which the
essays respond include:

How can we best conceptualize and understand the conflictive and cooperative
 interactions between rulers and the ruled?
How do the attempts to establish stable patterns of rule by those who claim
 authority interact with the efforts of conflict groups to contest power?
How and why do states, groups, and other social collectivities cooperate, given
 conflicting interests and worldviews?
How and why do they sometimes not accommodate one another's demands and
 grievances?
How do changing global and local contexts affect the processes of conflict and
 cooperation?

Throughout the volume, leading scholars of conflict studies focus on their particular areas of theoretical expertise. The chapters integrate extensions of their
personal research agendas with overviews of entire bodies of topically defined
literature examining the pillars and forms of conflict. These chapters are therefore
simultaneously original research contributions in their own right, and broader
assessments of the state of knowledge. Each chapter highlights the theoretical and
methodological controversies of research with respect to a particular aspect or
form of conflict, identifying the currently contested terrain of theory, data, and
analyses to produce conclusions about the state of knowledge. Each also offers
conclusions on the questions, problems, and data that need to be addressed if we
are to improve conflict studies in the future. The primary focus is on research that
employs systematic methods of observation and comparative, often quantitative,
analysis to develop and test explanatory propositions, with due attention directed
to conceptual and normative questions. With a very broad scope of theoretical
and topical coverage, and careful attention to the corpus of rigorous scholarship,
the volume will serve as a comprehensive handbook of systematic research on
contentious politics, political violence, and instability.

In Part One, "Pillars of Conflict," our contributors examine several issues in
the study of conflict, both of long-standing and recently arising. These include
how discrimination produces the grievances that lead to conflict; how liberalism
insulates regimes against violent dissent; how religion can be a source for mobilizing protest and rebellion; how patterns of political authority in the state are the
context within which dissent occurs; how state repression both deters and accel-
erates protest and rebellion; how internal wars are connected to their external
environment; and how climate change can play a role in dissent.

In Part Two, the focus shifts to "Forms of Conflict," in which our contributors
examine several of the most important types of conflict: terrorism, revolutions, state
failure, genocide and mass murder, transnational conflicts, and civil wars. All have been
the subject of enormous literatures, which our contributors grapple with and extend.

Part One, "Pillars of Conflict," begins with a chapter examining one of the key pillars at the base of conflict: discrimination and the grievances that arise from it. Victor Asal and Kathleen Deloughery address a long-standing debate among scholars: Is civil conflict best explained by motive, or rather by opportunities and resources for action? On the one hand, Ted Gurr and his intellectual progeny see relative deprivation grounded in discrimination as the basis for conflict, while scholars such as Tilly regard organization and resources as the primary explanatory factors. The chapter examines some of the key works in the field on both sides of the debate and some of the key methodological issues that contribute to ongoing scholarly contention. Those who challenge the empirical findings of the Gurr school claim that results are inaccurate when cases are selected on the dependent variable. However, Asal and Deloughery note that the findings reported by these critics are based on poorly specified variables that are unsatisfactory proxies for discrimination.

They argue that solutions to this apparent impasse may reside in further work on selection bias and group inclusion issues by the Minorities at Risk research group, and on a recently developed Ethnic Power Relations (EPR) dataset, which permits a more direct operationalization of grievance. They highlight recent findings that groups are more likely to engage in conflict with the state when their representatives have been excluded from power, when they have high mobilization capacity, and when they have past experiences with conflict. They then describe recent research on terrorism, based on the Global Terrorism Database (GTD). Grievance terrorism is more likely in countries with large heterogeneous populations, where the proportion of the population and the proportion of groups that are excluded from government are greater. Asal and Deloughery conclude by stating that grievance, and the discrimination in which it is grounded, certainly do matter.

The next chapter, by Mark Lichbach, examines the role of liberalism in modern conflict. He asks if conflict involving religious groups is inherently grounded in religion, as suggested by "religious determinists," or whether it should be viewed as reflecting political and economic contention, as claimed by "religious epiphenomenonalists." The question is of more than intellectual interest, since the resolution of conflict that arises from nationalist struggles or class conflict may depend on different conditions, and may be amenable to different strategies of resolution, than that of conflict that is based "purely" on religion. Specifically, Lichbach seeks to determine whether successful liberalism (a more secular culture, religious pluralism, thriving markets, and a democratic and globalized polity) serves to reduce the relative prevalence of religious conflict. To this end, he notes that success in mobilizing collective action, by attracting militants, may hamper success in collective bargaining. Power, Lichbach observes, requires compromise, which in turn can inhibit mobilization. He constructs a database of "Unarmed Civil Society Clashes" drawn from the *World Handbook of Political Indicators IV* data. These represent conflicts between non-state groups and institutions; conflicts involving state institutions or armed non-state actors such as terrorist groups are excluded. He subjects the data to both pooled and mixed effects logistic regressions, and concludes that liberalism does not mitigate contentious religious politics. After controlling for liberalism, the least violent clashes occur when secular actors target each other, while the most violent clashes entail religious actors targeting secular actors. The chapter concludes with the observation that societies can accommodate both modernity and religion. However, this can occur only when religion is recognized, respected, engaged, and negotiated, a situation best achieved by empowering religious moderates.

The relationship between religion and conflict is addressed in the chapter by Jonathan Fox. In the latter decades of the twentieth century, social scientists largely focused on modernization and therefore anticipated the demise of religion as a pillar of conflict. The events of 9/11 were a game-changer. Systematic evidence reveals that religious conflicts are becoming more common. Fox identifies five ways in which religion relates to conflict. Threats to religious belief systems and to the collective identities that form around them may elicit a hostile defense. The rules of behavior embraced by many religions may lead to holy war, or to a lesser but nonetheless hostile response directed at those who might challenge them. Religion may be invoked to legitimize authoritarian regimes or liberation movements. Religious institutions may serve as a basis for mobilization. And, finally, religious identity as group affiliation may facilitate participation in collective action. Fox's review of empirical studies of religion and conflict concluded that religion is not a basic cause of ethnic conflict. Rather, the basic cause is separatism, with religion being an exacerbating factor. Fox notes a number of other variables that may intervene between religion and conflict, including the economic, political, and cultural factors. Religious conflicts tend to invite international intervention, and states tend to intervene on behalf of groups with whom they share affinities. Muslims appear to be overrepresented in conflicts, mostly with other Muslims. Fox concludes his chapter by noting that the systematic study of religion and conflict remains in its infancy. The complexity of conflict requires that religion be integrated with general theories, and that tools be developed to specify when and to what extent a conflict involves religious issues. He identifies the Religion and State (RAS) database as a means to this end.

The state and political authority constitute the next pillar of conflict to be examined. Keith Jaggers' chapter reviews three state-centric theoretical perspectives on conflict: the *State autonomy* perspective reflects the extent to which state institutions are liberalized so as to regulate and manage domestic inequities. Essentially, this concerns the relationship between democracy and conflict. *State capacity* refers to the state's ability to organize and control people, materials, and territories—in other words, its infrastructural power. *Political opportunity* pertains to how the state provides avenues for grievance articulation and conflict resolution—what might be called regime openness. Together, the three perspectives address *why*, *how*, and *when* people rebel. Jaggers' review concludes that the state autonomy perspective has the least explanatory power. He notes the fragility of new democracies, and their vulnerability to social instability. This recalls Lichbach's reference to "thin democracies" in this volume, and also resonates with the observations of Grabosky in his chapter that rates of conventional crime tend to increase immediately after the transition from authoritarian to democratic rule. In contrast, Jaggers finds stronger support for the state capacity and political opportunity approaches. Economic development tends to inhibit conflict, as does the capacity of the state to raise taxes independent of economic development. Perhaps surprisingly, the size of a state's military apparatus is lacking in explanatory power. Jagger notes that state capacity theory suffers somewhat from problems of variable specification and operationalization. With regard to political opportunity, Jaggers observes that semi-democratic regimes are at greater risk of violent political conflict. The overall relationship is curvilinear, described by an inverted Gleditsch and Ruggeri (2010) U-shape. Jaggers concludes by inviting research that integrates the three theoretical perspectives.

The relationship between internal and external conflict, a pillar of conflict with a long social science history, is the focus of a chapter by Harvey Starr and Marc Simon. They—as does Wallensteen (chapter 14)—note that in recent years the most common form of conflict is that which occurs *within* states. Their discussion begins by outlining a number of similarities between external and internal conflict. It then moves to the authors' observations on how linkages between the two are formed. Finally, they consider how the study of conflict crosses these boundaries. Parties to conflict need to be aware of both the local and the wider implications of their intended courses of action. Dealing with a conflict at one level has implications for conflict at another level. At stake is their own legitimacy, at home and in the eyes of the international community. From this flows their capacity to mobilize support for their cause. The current term for this phenomenon is "two-level game." The authors describe their two-level simulation project, which explores how basic strategies (deterrence or co-optation of threats) and structural variables (system size, threat distributions, and alliance structures) affect the outcome of the two-level security problem. They conclude that bipolar systems were more stable, which seems entirely consistent with developments over the previous half-century. Hegemonic regimes fare best when they adopt a deterrence posture for external relations and a co-optation strategy domestically. In contrast, failing states are best able to avoid collapse by appealing to international allies for legitimacy or resources. Starr and Simon conclude with the caution that no single methodology can provide a definitive solution to the two-level game, and that conflict linkages will remain a fruitful area of research.

Environmental pillars of conflict have long been considered by conflict researchers. Climate change has been referred to as the great moral issue of our time, and as a serious threat to the national security of nations large and small. Theisen, Gleditsch, and Buhaug provide an overview of the scant literature on the subject, a literature that is certain to grow. Their chapter focuses on domestic conflict as it may be affected by short-term environmental change, including precipitation, rising sea levels, rising temperatures, and natural disasters (other than geological, which do not result from climate change). The authors conclude that the effects of climate change on violence are not direct, but rather mediated by factors such as food prices, economic development, and human population movements. In addition, they observe that the impact of climate change may be mitigated by the resilience of affected societies. They cite some support for the climate change–scarcity–conflict model. Findings relating to communal violence are inconclusive. Developing a better understanding of these links is a priority for researchers, as is attention to the differential impact or disaggregated effects of major climatic events. In addition, the authors see a need to differentiate between "new" conflicts, as opposed to those pre-existing conflicts that are prolonged by climate change. Given the absence thus far of conclusive findings, Theisen et al. note that overstating the effect of climate change on conflict may impair the credibility of climate change research in general. There are, after all, a number of other very compelling reasons to control global warming.

Grabosky's chapter explores long-term trends in crime and violence, a topic addressed initially by historians and social theorists such as Norbert Elias (1939). Since the 1970s it has become the focus of inquiry by a diverse range of scholars, including criminologists, psychologists, political scientists, and even archeologists. The chapter identifies research that has found significant effects of international conflict and civil war on rates of "conventional" criminal violence or "street crime." The decline in human violence that has been observed for over three millennia, albeit punctuated by episodic temporary increases, has been attributed to what might be termed a "civilizing process," reflecting a growing capacity for impulse control. Consistent with Lichbach's observations in this volume, long-term trends and temporary departures there from can also be explained by the trajectories of stable and effective government, and to the legitimacy that tends to accompany them. Cross-sectional variation in crime has also been explained in part by variations in legitimacy. An interesting and transitory exception has been apparent in transitions from authoritarian to democratic rule, where, in settings as diverse as South Africa, Taiwan, and the former Soviet Union, the immediate aftermath of regime change was marked by increases in crime, which Lichbach would see a reflection of Hobbes. Other cross-sectional studies have identified poverty and economic inequality to be predictors of crime, results that are consistent with the legitimacy hypothesis. Overall, findings at the aggregate level of analysis fit well with solid criminological evidence at the individual level.

Part Two, "Forms of Conflict," begins with the study of terrorism. Scott Englund and Michael Stohl summarize and explore the more significant research to date on terrorism. They note that, for an issue as prominent as terrorism, the quantum of rigorous scientific research on the topic has been astonishingly small. By way of illustration, a meta-analysis of research on counter-terrorism strategies, conducted under the auspices of the Campbell Collaboration, identified over

20,000 studies but found only seven to be of sufficient methodological rigor for inclusion (Lum et al. 2006). The chapter provides an overview of available sources of data on terrorism and notes the lament of Sageman (2014) that research opportunities are constrained by the fact that significant amounts of potentially useful data are held by government agencies and are not accessible to researchers. Englund and Stohl base their essay on three themes originally articulated by Gurr: situation, structure, and disposition. By *situation*, they refer to the relationships and relative strengths of political opponents in a conflict. They note that weak states are at risk of being both the sources and the targets of transnational terrorist attacks. So too are democracies, by virtue of their openness. *Structure* represents the root causes of a conflict: in other words, "the economic and political structures that establish and constrain regime and citizen." Englund and Stohl report that high unemployment, economic inequality, and social exclusion among heterogeneous groups increase the risk of terrorism. *Disposition* refers to individual perceptions regarding the acceptability of terrorism as a political strategy. The search for explanations based on abnormal psychology has proven to be fruitless. Rather, perceived persecution of one's in-group, moral outrage at a major injustice, resonance with personal experiences, and mobilization by an active network are the factors that dispose one to terrorism. The chapter concludes with a caution against continued reliance on untested knowledge claims and a plea for the careful collection and analysis of data.

Colin Beck's chapter on the study of revolutions reviews four generations of scholarship. The first comprised historians of revolution. The second explored aggregate social psychology, focusing on phenomena of mobilization. The third generation, in the tradition of Skocpol (1979), gave emphasis to the state and highlighted structural rather than psychological processes. More recently, scholars of revolution have begun to attend to internal economic strains on states as they are affected by international and transnational relationships. Beck's synthesis of current knowledge predicts that revolutions are more likely to succeed when strained states, governed by inflexible regimes faced with broad alliances of opponents, fail to repress initial insurgent challenges. Looking to the future, Beck invites attention to non-violent regime change, such as that which characterized the demise of the former Soviet Union and (relatively speaking) the end of the Apartheid era in South Africa. Strategies of non-violence are more conducive to legitimacy, at both domestic and international levels. His observations resonate with those of Lichbach's chapter in this volume, which speak to the instrumental value of non-violent social movements. Beck also notes the opportunities to investigate micro-mobilization, based on systematic surveys and interviews of participants in recent revolutions. Such methods allow demographic, attitudinal, and cultural insights that may have eluded previous scholars of revolution. Among the other issues identified by Beck as potentially fruitful for further inquiry are revolutionary aftermaths. When may a revolution be deemed to have ended, and with what effect, in both short- and long terms? Beck's invitation to "recapture the long tail of revolution" is exciting, if somewhat daunting. One is reminded of the response attributed to Chinese premier Zhou En-lai in 1972 when asked about the significance of the French Revolution: "It's too early to say."

The question of state failure has attracted considerable interest from both policy-makers and academicians since the end of the Cold War. In their chapter, Monty Marshall and Benjamin Cole review some of the conceptual and methodological issues that have accompanied this growing attention. They note that terms associated with state failure are often used loosely and interchangeably. Moreover, cause, correlation, and consequence are often confounded. The chapter addresses some of the criticisms that have been directed at the state failure research agenda. With some irony, they note that the very idea of a failed state is "West-centric" and that the West, overtly or covertly, has played a significant role in contributing to state fragility and failure in the first place. Failed states have concerned policy-makers because of their supposed vulnerability to exploitation as safe havens by transnational criminals and terrorist groups. However, the authors observe that states with limited infrastructure and low connectivity may be less at risk of such exploitation than are states that are weak, but still functioning. The State Failure Task Force was established by the US government in 1994 to study the correlates of state failure. One sees the influence of government in the relatively low profile this project has taken in the scholarly literature, and in the change of label to "Political Instability Task Force." Marshall and Cole observe that general forecasting models of state weakness or failure are often less useful to policy-makers, relying as they do on proxy variables such as infant mortality rather than theoretically justified causal factors. The chapter concludes by noting the growing complexity of domestic political systems and of the world system more generally. The authors suggest that, given the dramatic increase in institutions of civil society, and in the greater salience of NGOs generally, complex social systems analysis can facilitate even greater insight regarding the fragility of states.

The practice of genocide has a gruesome historical pedigree, but the term did not exist until the waning months of World War II, when the Holocaust of European Jews became publicized. Armenians were quick to remind the world of their nation's fate at the hands of Turkey during World War I, and, beginning in the 1980s, comparative genocide studies attracted increasing scholarly attention. Barbara Harff's chapter begins with an essay on conceptual and terminological clarification. Genocide is systematic and intentional action, designed to destroy a communal, political, or politicized ethnic group. It can be perpetrated by non-state actors as well as by governments. The practice of genocide did not end with the Holocaust, and Harff herself has identified nearly fifty examples occurring since World War II. The scientific study of genocide has continued apace, and Harff's chapter goes on to summarize recent research on the explanation and prediction of genocide. She observes that genocide has tended to occur in an atmosphere of exclusionary ideologies and in situations where states are habituated to the use of violence in response to challenges to state security.

Consistent with Black's (2011) general theory of social conflict, Harff also observes that genocides have tended to occur *inter alia* in the aftermath of state upheaval, including in circumstances of state failure, abrupt regime change, and defeat in international war. Harff identifies additional risk factors, including ethnic and religious cleavages, low economic development, and the lack of interdependent relations with other states. Lichbach, in his chapter, refers to such circumstances as "zones of political turmoil." Harff concludes with some observations on the development of early warning indicators, consistent with the work of Gurr and colleagues on minorities at risk. The chapter ends with a very timely, and equally ominous, observation about the prospects for Syria.

Globalization—the rapid movement across state boundaries of people, ideas, commerce, and much else—has brought about dramatic change in social movements concerning indigenous rights. Struggles that were previously confined to remote localities, limited to action and reaction between indigenous peoples and their governments, and barely visible (if at all) to the outside world, are now the subject of worldwide coverage in mass and social media, amplification by large and influential NGOs, and consideration in international governmental fora. The international system consists of networks that enhance, and those that threaten, the interests of indigenous peoples. To explore how these struggles impact indigenous peoples, and how the struggles of those people affect international and civil conflict, Pamela Martin and Franke Wilmer compare two Latin American countries. In Bolivia, the poorest country on the continent, 60 percent of the population is indigenous. Ecuador, slightly better off economically, has a slightly smaller proportion of indigenous citizens (45 percent). Both countries seek to protect indigenous rights and to honor the preference of some indigenous groups to be left alone. Problems arise, however, when these interests are threatened by pressures to develop natural resources. Tension thus exists in both countries between the fulfillment of spiritual and of material needs. Martin and Wilmer explore interesting circumstances arising in the new world system, where international human rights ideas and norms contribute to domestic political change and domestic mobilization affects international norms. Resistance to neoliberalism is not without risk, although Bolivia's nationalization of some natural resources and redistribution of wealth has proven popular with the electorate. The country's GDP has trebled during the tenure of its first indigenous president, Evo Morales, who has been elected on three occasions. The complexity of contending networks of indigenous interests and their neoliberal adversaries, globally and locally, is substantial. Whether the processes that have seen Latin American democracy born of conflict are reversible remains to be seen.

In the final form of conflict addressed in the volume, Peter Wallensteen reviews recent trends in the study of war and identifies potentially fruitful areas for research. He observes that the end of the Cold War produced a paradigm shift in conflict studies. No longer was local armed conflict viewed through the lens of great power confrontation. Rather than moves on a Cold War chessboard, such conflicts have come to be perceived as humanitarian issues. Research began to focus on the underlying importance of economics, identity, geography, and access to weaponry. Inter-state conflicts are now much less frequent, and are currently one-tenth as common as civil wars, which have become much more numerous. In seeking to explain the decline in inter-state war, Wallensteen observes a greater sensitivity to public sentiment on the part of leaders, both democratic and authoritarian. The spread of democracy and improvements in social welfare and in the status of women may be indicative, although the salience of these factors may be less in Asia than in Europe and North America. Accompanying these trends are varied and intensified efforts at preventing, containing, and resolving these conflicts. The ability of the international community to respond to conflicts, although still limited, has improved significantly. Wallensteen asks, as does Lichbach's chapter in this collection, whether such interventions may in some cases actually prolong conflict. Looking to the future, Wallensteen notes the rise in data resources and research programs relating to conflict, including the Correlates of War, Minorities at Risk, and the Uppsala Conflict Data Program, among others. He also notes the growing interest in comparative interpersonal violence, discussed in Grabosky's contribution to this volume. His concluding observations encourage attention to the influence of external debt, and financial crises more generally, on conflict. Spatial analyses may also open up new fields of research on the location and spread of conflicts, as well as tactical aspects of peacekeeping.

The concluding chapter features a look to the future of conflict research by one of the most prominent conflict researchers of the past four decades, Ted Robert Gurr. The chapter charts a course for conflict studies into the future. Gurr suggests that quantitative empirical research and comparative case studies will remain rewarding strategies, as they are eminently complementary: findings in one genre may be tested in another. An appropriate division of labor will enhance both generalizability and understanding. Among the potentially fruitful programs of research that he identifies are comparative case studies of militant Islamic groups such as Islamic State, the Taliban, the Algerian Salafist Group for Preaching and Combat (GSPC), Al-Shabaab, and Boko Haram. Among the issues that these studies might address are ideology, sustainability, and processes of mobilization. Gurr's reference to new technologies of mobilization is certainly apposite; he cites journalist Abdel Bari Atwan's very recent book on the Islamic State subtitled *The Digital Caliphate*. This observation converges with Lichbach's discussion of the expansion of dissent, attributable in significant part to the widespread availability of digital technology.

Gurr points to another interesting research direction: the role of violent jihadist groups as institutions of governance. "Chaotically ungoverned regions" are naturally attractive to groups such as Islamic State. Despite the terror employed to establish control over such locations and their populations, they may provide a modicum of stability, exercising a degree of social control, conflict resolution, and providing basic regulatory services. Lichbach might observe that the weak pretensions of democracy that characterize contemporary Afghanistan deliver less protection from fraud, crime, and corruption than do the Taliban in areas under their control.

Gurr concludes by observing that conflict scholarship will continue to evolve. New research questions, as yet unforeseen, will emerge. So too will methodologies and datasets. One notes that, a generation ago, scholars did not ponder the effects of climate change, or of digital technology, on political conflict.

One final note before proceeding: the combined bibliography for this book is quite extensive and thus has been posted as an online eResource on the book's web page.

PART I
Pillars of Conflict

2

GRIEVANCE

The Nexus Between Grievances and Conflict[1]

Victor Asal and Kathleen Deloughery

Rebels have always claimed that grievance plays a key role in why they take up arms. The Declaration of Independence promulgated in 1776 by the Continental Congress of the United States is fairly clear on this point when it states that "The history of the present King of Great Britain is a history of repeated injuries and usurpations" (Jefferson 1776) and then goes on to elucidate a laundry list of grievances against King George III. A century later and a continent away, the premier theorists of revolution, driving many of the revolutions of the twentieth century, wrote that:

> Freeman and slave, patrician and plebeian, lord and serf, guild-master and journeyman, in a word, oppressor and oppressed, stood in constant opposition to one another, carried on an uninterrupted, now hidden, now open fight, a fight that each time ended, either in a revolutionary reconstitution of society at large, or in the common ruin of the contending classes.
>
> *(Marx and Engels 1848)*

Both rebels and theorist/rebels claim in their literature that oppression and injury is a key motivator for turning to violence and the right to "levy War" (Jefferson 1776). We should note that this connection is not one that is simply a product of the Age of Enlightenment and its aftermath. Speaking of the rebellion against the Romans, Josephus identifies not only religious grievances but also unfair taxation as one of the key factors leading to the revolt (Josephus 2009). Josephus argued that sedition was increased by the behavior of procurators such as Festus, who "did not only, in his political capacity, steal and plunder every one's substance, nor did he only burden the whole nation with taxes … and nobody remained in the prisons as a malefactor but he who gave him nothing" (Josephus 2009, 748).

Political scientists, sociologists, and other social scientists look for more than the word of rebels (who have their own motivations that may be less than pure) or at only one case as evidence that grievance plays a key role in the outbreak of rebellions, ethnic conflict, or other forms of sub-state political violence. Even a consummate opportunist such as the National Union for the Total Independence of Angola (UNITA)'s Jonas Savimbi, who was at times a Marxist and anti-Marxist, a Portuguese collaborator and anti-Portuguese revolutionary, and often a killer and exploiter of his own people, argued that he was fighting against oppression (Heywood 2000; Vines 2006). More importantly, as Marx and Engels argue, oppression is omnipresent (Marx and Engels 1848). If this is the case, it is very possible that structure and opportunity may play a much more important role in determining when groups decide to use violence than do the grievances that are present. As Marx argues:

> The tradition of all dead generations weighs like a nightmare on the brains of the living. And just as they seem to be occupied with revolutionizing them-selves and things, creating something that did not exist before, precisely in such epochs of revolutionary crisis they anxiously conjure up the spirits of the past to their service, borrowing from them names, battle slogans, and cos-tumes in order to present this new scene in world history in time-honored disguise and borrowed language.
>
> *(Marx 1852)*

Grievance and discrimination intuitively appeal as root causes of civil conflict. As suggested by the historical statements of revolutionaries above, the literature on conflict has been divided on the importance of how people and groups are treated and their propensity to use political violence. Much of the disagreement revolves around the degree to which discrimination and grievance is seen as being ubiquitous. As Collier and Sambanis (2002, 4) point out, "Understanding the causes of observed conflict is not necessarily synonymous with understanding its motivation. Motive may or may not be more decisive than opportunity for action." If everyone has a grievance then the utility of grievance as a potential explanation for violence is negligible. If that is the case, then opportunity and resources are keys to explaining violence, and discrimination is simply not that important as a cause of violence. On the other hand, it is also possible that not all types of griev-ance and discrimination are created equally and thus certain kinds of grievance play a crucial role in a triangle of contention that it makes up along with political opportunity and resource mobilization. Fundamentally, the authors of this chapter believe this to be true. Everyone may carry grievances with them, ranging from the fact that their salary is too low to an inconvenient slight at the hands of a bigot, or even that they feel they are not receiving the respect they deserve.

Ted Gurr's work, from his groundbreaking book *Why Men Rebel* (2010) to his work in *People versus States* (2000), has been posited on the idea that grievance matters and that certain types of grievance are much more combustible than others. For example, a grievance that could be generated by the following communiqué may be one of a theoretically different order:

> The Corps Commander shall carry out sporadic bombardments ... In order to kill the largest number of people ... all persons captured ... shall be detained and interrogated ... and those between the ages of 15 and 70 shall be executed after any useful information has been obtained ...
>
> *(Gurr 2000, 127)*

This message comes from orders that were delivered to an Iraqi officer in June 1987. The key question about the nexus between grievance and conflict is not what we or others intuitively feel about how such discrimination may contribute to civilians taking up arms against their oppressors, but on what research has been able to affirm.

Gurr's work (1970; 1993a; 1993b) stands in sharp contrast to other scholars' arguments about the key causes of conflict. Indeed, one might argue that much of the literature on contentious politics over the last forty years is a response to the relative deprivation gauntlet that Gurr laid down. Tilly's (1978) work *From Mobilization to Revolution* pushed back against Gurr's argument by arguing for the dominance of organization and resources as explanations for outbreaks of political violence.

Indeed, McAdam et al.'s *Dynamics of Contention* (2001), Tilly's *Politics of Collective Violence* (2003), and much of the other contentious politics literature is an extension of this ongoing dialectic between the importance of grievances and the importance of resources (McAdam 2010) and opportunity structures (Tarrow 1998). Skocpol (1979) challenged the grievance model as well, with a focus on deeper levels of structure, and argued that the key to social revolutions was the confluence of international challenges and domestic disunity among elites. From a rational actor perspective, Lichbach also challenged the grievance perspective with *The Rebel's Dilemma* (1995), and argued that the key challenges that required explanation were how actors were mobilized into rebellion and how the cooperation necessary to bring about a successful revolt was achieved. For Lichbach, the key issue is to identify the key strategies that allow for the dilemma of cooperation to be overcome.

Gurr, in his work *People versus States* (2000), responds to most (although not all) of these critiques. He concedes the importance of resources and opportunity structure but argues that grievance caused by state action is a key component of ethnic conflict. Drawing on the Minorities at Risk (MAR) database (1993b), he argues that discrimination creates grievances that are a key ingredient that should not be overlooked. The current scientific literature on how grievance and discrimination affect violence is still contentious, however, and in the following pages we will examine some of the key works in this area and the reasons for this ongoing contention.[2] In some of the recent empirical literature, motive[3]—at least as far as grievance is concerned—has not done very well as an explanation for the onset of civil war. Indeed, many have found that grievance is not a significant factor in the onset of conflict.[4] This finding is particularly surprising in the case of ethnic wars, which would seem to be inherently related to some sense of group grievance. While conceding that motivation—"greed or grievance"—must have some place in explaining civil war, Collier et al. (2003, 89) go on to argue that, for the most part, grievance is not a useful tool for explaining civil wars, for even "Extreme cases of ethnic abuses of power have often failed to trigger civil war . . ."

On the other hand, others have found significant evidence supporting Gurr's (2000) argument that grievance is integrally tied to the use of political violence by ethnic groups (Regan and Norton 2005; Cederman et al. 2010; Wimmer et al. 2009). This chapter first outlines some of the research that focuses on grievance and discrimination as causal factors in explaining the outbreak of civil conflict as well as the critiques of this approach. Next, we examine recent research that lends new support to the connection between grievance and violent conflict and spend significant time examining the recent work of Cederman, Wimmer, and Min (Cederman et al. 2010; Wimmer et al. 2009), who use a new dataset that addresses many of the methodological concerns raised about previous findings and whose findings appear to lend strong support to the argument that—at least when it comes to ethnic conflict—grievance matters a great deal.

Critics of the work by Gurr and others, while correct in pointing out potential selection biases, have been flawed because they employed proxies for grievance and discrimination that simply do not capture grievance in any meaningful way (Fearon and Laitin 2003). Recent work by Cederman and others address the selection bias and use direct measures of discrimination. They find strong support for the basic argument that groups that are aggrieved are more likely to use violence (Cederman and Girardin 2007; Wimmer et al. 2009).

Why Rebel?

Given the intuitive nature of grievance as a cause it is no surprise that, in challenging grievance, Collier and Hoeffler (2004, 2) contend that "The political science literature explains conflict in terms of motive: the circumstances in which people *want* to rebel are viewed as sufficiently rare to constitute the explanation." Until recently, much of the literature has argued that this is indeed the case. While Gurr's *Why Men Rebel* (1970) is not the first formulation of the grievance argument, it is a touchstone for much of the literature and a useful starting point for this discussion. Gurr (1970) argued that people are motivated by relative deprivation and that, given the right conditions and sufficient provocation, people will rebel. Relative deprivation as defined by Gurr is:

> a perceived discrepancy between men's value expectations and their value capabilities. Value expectations are the goods and conditions of life to which people believe they are rightfully entitled. Value capabilities are the goods

and conditions they think they are capable of attaining or maintaining given the social means available to them.

(Gurr 1970, 13)

When people experience the frustration brought on by relative deprivation they will be more likely to turn to violence; the greater the intensity of the frustration, the greater the likelihood of the use of violence (Gurr 1970). The relative deprivation argument has received a number of criticisms, in part because the measures being used in the analyses were not really capturing frustration and certainly not the intensity of frustration (Aya 1990). Gurney and Tierney (1982) argued that relative deprivation could result in very different psychological constructs that would not lead to challenges to authority.

A focus on grievance that was not tied to psychological factors but directly to discrimination, inequality, and oppression was theoretically robust to this challenge and the literature that operationalized grievance in this way continued to grow. Others have also argued that exclusionary or repressive regimes are more prone to revolution (Hibbs 1973; Reynal-Querol 2002; Goodwin 2001a; Elbadawi and Sambanis 2002). Others focusing specifically on economic inequality as a cause of grievance have provided evidence that grievance caused by economic inequality leads to civil war (Muller 1985b; Seligson and Muller 1987; Muller 1988). Much of the work focusing on ethnic conflict specifically has made use of the MAR database, created by Gurr (2000), which identified the coding of discrimination as a more concrete way to examine grievance as a possible motivator for rebellion. Gurr argues that discrimination creates grievance by keeping ethnic groups out of the opportunity structure of the state because "Political discrimination means, by definition, that minorities encounter restrictions on political participation and access to decision making" (Gurr 2000, 123). The MAR database was created to test empirically the impact of this and other kinds of discrimination (as well as other variables) on the likelihood of political violence; it has information on over 300 minority groups, primarily from the 1990s but with some information going back to the 1980s and earlier:

> MAR focuses specifically on ethnopolitical groups, non-state communal groups that have "political significance" in the contemporary world because of their status and political actions. Political significance is determined by the following two criteria: The group collectively suffers, or benefits from, systematic discriminatory treatment vis-à-vis other groups in a society; and, the group is the basis for political mobilization and collective action in defense or promotion of its self-defined interests.
>
> *(MAR Project 2004)*

In the MAR datebase Gurr coded discrimination at four different levels, from no discrimination to exclusive/repressive policies. Examining the likelihood that a group will rebel, Gurr, working both alone and with others, has found that political discrimination is a significant cause of ethnic conflict, especially when it is combined in a causal explanation with resource mobilization (Gurr 1993a; Gurr 1993b; Gurr and Moore 1997; Gurr 2000). Perhaps the most advanced work using MAR to look at ethnic grievance is the work of Norton and Reagan (Regan and Norton 2005). Using the MAR group as the unit of analysis, Regan and Norton explored what factors led groups to rebel. They found that states that do not discriminate experience much less rebellion, and that repression "is one of our strongest predictors of protest, rebellion, and civil war, but that relationship displays a different directional impact depending on the outcome. Repression will tend to decrease protest but increase rebellion and civil war" (Regan and Norton 2005, 335). In addition to empirical research driven by yearly datasets collected at the group or country level, work has also been done that looks at the nexus between grievance and mobilization (if not violence) from an experimental perspective. One example is the work of Grant and Brown (1995), who found, through experimental manipulation, support for the relative deprivation argument and a relationship with ethnocentrism.

Against Grievance

Much of the work discussed above has been challenged because the unit of analysis is the group and one of the factors for choosing the group was the level of discrimination. In essence, challengers argue that the findings based on MAR are not accurate because the researcher is selecting on the dependent variable (Fearon and Laitin 1996). Based on this and other issues, the finding that grievance is a factor in civil war has been rejected (Laitin 2002). Collier and Hoeffler (2001), among others (for example, see McCarthy and Zald 1977), see grievance as being so prevalent that it is of secondary importance, if any. As Collier et al. (2003, 56) point out, "Political grievances and the political conflict they generate are universal." They go on to call it "naïve" (p. 61) to believe that ethnic grievance is a source of violent conflict in areas where natural resources are exploited to support rebellion. They believe that, owing to this, the key to understanding the onset of civil wars is opportunity. In other words, "it is the circumstances in which people *are able* to rebel that are rare" (Collier and Hoeffler 2001, 2). It is important to note, however, that nowhere does Gurr (1970; 1993a; 1993b; 2000) argue that grievance or discrimination are the only factors in the turn to political violence by nonstate actors. Gurr clearly recognizes that the ubiquity of ethnic discrimination stems from "Groups that won out in conquest, state building, and economic development established patterns of authority and various kinds of social barriers to protect their advantages, including the policies and practices for which we use the shorthand label of 'discrimination'" (Gurr 1993a, 36). Others argue, though, that this means we must put the focus on opportunity. As Fearon and Laitin argue:

> (i)f, under the right environmental conditions, just 500 to 2000 active guerrillas can make for a long-running, destructive internal war, then the

average level of grievance in a group may not matter that much. What matters is whether active rebels can hide from government forces and whether economic opportunities are so poor that the life of a rebel is attractive to 500 to 2000 young men. Grievance may favor rebellion by leading nonactive rebels to help in hiding the active rebels. But all the guerrillas really need is superior local knowledge which enables them to threaten reprisal for denunciation.

(Fearon and Laitin 2003, 88)

So, for Fearon and Laitin (2003), the key issues are factors such as mountainous regions and poverty, which facilitate insurgency. Collier et al. (2003) support this argument, saying that ethnicity matters little. For Fearon and Laitin (2003, 4) the "entrepreneurs of violence" are facilitated by economic decline, autocratic and incompetent regimes, and states "dependent on primary commodity exports."

There is, nevertheless, a problem with the findings against grievance as well. If MAR has the problem of selecting on the dependent variable then the key research that has undermined these findings is based on measures that do not really capture grievance or discrimination. We focus here on the empirical findings of two works that minimize the importance of ethnic grievance. Collier and Hoeffler (2001) do not find support for grievance in their research. While elements of ethnic dominance may increase the likelihood of civil war, grievance as a whole does not. And, with a slightly different emphasis on what they call conditions of insurgency, Fearon and Laitin (2003) come to similar conclusions in their research.

Collier and Hoeffler (2001) use four measures for grievance: fractionalization, political repression, ethnic dominance, and the Gini coefficient of land ownership. Fearon and Laitin (2003) also use two of these measures (ethnic fractionalization and democracy) in their analysis. While the critics of MAR are correct about the problems of selection bias, there is not enough attention in their own work to identifying variables that successfully capture the nature of grievance. None of the variables that Collier and Hoeffler (2001) or Fearon and Laitin (2003) use can be regarded as direct proxies for ethnic grievance or discrimination. This makes their results suspect if used as a basis for dismissing the importance of discrimination and grievance. The Gini coefficient of land ownership does capture inequality, but not in any way that is directly connected to ethnicity. Ethnic fractionalization may or may not be related to discrimination but it does not capture oppression, discrimination, or inequality itself. The same is true for the percentage of the population of the largest ethnic group. What these measures capture are differences in the demography of the country and these do not necessarily mean there is grievance or discrimination. As Cohen argues:

Men may and do certainly joke about or ridicule the strange and bizarre customs of men from other ethnic groups, because these customs are different from their own. But they do not fight over such differences alone. When men *do*, on the other hand, fight across ethnic lines it is nearly always the case that they fight over some fundamental issues concerning the distribution and exercise of power, whether economic, political, or both.

(Cohen 1974, 94)

Related to the use of democracy as a proxy for grievance and discrimination, Fearon and Laitin argue that "Other things being equal, political democracy should be associated with less discrimination and repression along cultural or other lines, since democracy endows citizens with a political power (the vote) they do not have in dictatorships" (2003, 73). Marshall et al. (2006) identify the United States as a democracy in 1809, which is a good fifty-five years before the end of slavery and 155 years before the civil rights act of 1965 that provided some basis for protections against inequality for a large minority of people living in the United States. But other things are not necessarily equal. Democracy should thus not serve as a proxy for grievance or discrimination.

Current Research

Since much of the research finding discrimination significant is flawed because of selection bias issues in the current datasets, such as MAR, and much of the work that finds that grievance is not statistically significant has been done using proxies that do not really capture grievance or discrimination (see Collier and Hoeffler 2001; Fearon and Laiton 1996), the literature until recently has not been able to move strongly ahead in terms of identifying the actual relationship between grievance and violent conflict. One effort currently underway is the project "Minorities at Risk: Addressing Selection Bias Issues and Group Inclusion Criteria for Ethnopolitical Research," which is collecting data on a sample of groups so that the selection bias problem can be controlled for in a statistically appropriate fashion (Birnir and Wilkenfeld 2007). Recent experimental research using a survey simulation applied to 2932 US adults finds that strong support for grievance played a role in participants supporting the use of violence and saying that they were actually willing to use violence themselves (Lemieux and Asal 2010). The participants read a scenario where they were told they were part of an ethnic minority. The script treatments varied the level of discrimination and the level of risk. Controlling for psychological factors as well as socio-economic factors, the study found strong evidence that the perception of grievance was a robust predictor at the individual level of a willingness to support and a desire to participate in violence (Lemieux and Asal 2010).

The most important new contribution to the study of conflict and grievance is based on a new dataset called the Ethnic Power Relations (EPR) dataset (Wimmer et al. 2009; Cederman et al. 2010). This dataset covers every country over the period 1945–2005. For each country, experts on ethnic politics coded information on each ethnic group's access to power. An ethnic group is included in the dataset only if there is at least one politician who claims to represent the interests of that group (Wimmer et al. 2009). Four variables in the dataset that have been explored in past work may allow for even more serious progress in our understanding of ethnic conflict: the percentage of groups that are excluded from the political process; the percentage of the population represented by excluded groups; the percentage of the population represented by groups that are powerless, but not discriminated against; and the percentage of the population represented by groups that are discriminated against.

This dataset is more comprehensive than other datasets examining ethnic groups since it covers all countries. This coverage allows for a non-selected examination of how the role of ethnic minorities affects armed internal conflict. In addition, the dataset directly measures exclusion from power. Past datasets have used proxies for exclusion, such as linguistic fractionalization or ethnic polarization. A direct measure will perform better than a proxy in returning unbiased estimates, especially in the case that the proxy is not a good measure of exclusion. Additionally, the sample is not restricted to mobilized ethnopolitical groups. Finally, in some countries, majorities are actually excluded from the government by a ruling minority. This dataset is one of the first to include those groups as well. One potential drawback of the dataset is that it focuses only on executive-level power. Therefore, groups that are represented at the local, regional, or national but sub-executive level may still be included in this dataset as excluded. Therefore, while other datasets may have undercounted the number of politically excluded groups, this dataset may actually be overcounting their number. When excluded groups or populations are used as an independent variable, as in all of the analysis reviewed and presented here, overcounting can lead to biased, and thus unreliable, estimates of the parameters in the model. Finally, the data was coded by consulting experts. However, experts do not exist in a vacuum; rather, they have their own belief systems and biases that will impact on how they code data (Password 2007). Additionally, experts may not be picking up on the changes that are occurring in a country over the entire time period covered. However, coding based on news-papers and history books, a potential alternate approach, runs the risk of picking up biased measures of ethnic discrimination, as only reported discrimination will be observed.

Using the EPR dataset, Cederman and his colleagues make important contributions in their two papers precisely because they do operationalize grievance and they do so for a dataset that does not select on the dependent variable in any way. Their first paper examines the question of whether ethnic diversity leads to armed conflict from the point of view of the state experiencing the conflict (Wimmer et al. 2009). Using a state year analytical model, they find that internal armed conflicts are more likely in states where large portions of the population are excluded from the political system owing to ethnicity. They argue, therefore, that capability and greed are not the driving factors determining internal armed conflicts and civil wars. They also test hypotheses related to power-sharing relationships and past levels of direct/indirect rule. Past studies have returned inconsistent results on whether or not exclusion plays a role in increasing the likelihood of armed conflicts. For example, Gurr (1970) argued that people are motivated by relative deprivation to rebel under the right conditions. Empirical results supporting Gurr's theory show that exclusionary or repressive regimes are more prone to revolution (Hibbs 1973; Reynal-Querol 2002; Goodwin 2001b; Elbadawi and Sambanis 2002) and that economic inequality leads to civil war (Muller 1985a; Seligson and Muller 1987; Muller 1988). On the other hand, for Fearon and Laitin (2003), the key issues are not relative deprivation, but factors such as mountainous regions and poverty, which facilitate insurgency. For Fearon and Laitin (2003, 4) the "entrepreneurs of violence" are facilitated by economic decline, autocratic and incompetent regimes, and resource issues. Collier et al. (2003) support this argument, saying that ethnicity matters little. This study represents the first time that ethnic exclusion is statistically significant across all specifications using a global dataset. Additionally, the dataset measures exclusion directly, rather than proxying for exclusion using a variable such as linguistic fractionalization. A one standard deviation increase in share of excluded population results in a 25 percent increase in the probability of ethnic conflict. Importantly, they find that, once the sample is restricted to ethnic internal conflicts only, the results are even more robust.

Next, Cederman et al. (2010) examine why ethnic groups choose to rebel using a group-level analysis based on EPR data. They find that competing ethnonationalist claims over a state are the main force behind internal armed conflicts. The three main conclusions are that groups are more likely to engage in conflict with the state if their representatives have been excluded from power, especially recently; if they have high mobilization capacity; and if they have past experiences with conflict. This paper also breaks from past literature in that it looks not only at state collapse but also views the role of the state as very important in determining ethnic conflicts. Additionally, this paper examines both groups that start armed conflicts and those that support armed conflicts against the state. They find that groups that are excluded or downgraded from political power are significantly more likely to participate in armed rebellion. While mobilization, and thus capacity, is also determined to be important, this article also finds an important role for grievance. Those arguing that capacity matters the most may find fault in the way that mobilization capacity is measured in the data analysis. Group size is used as a proxy for mobilization capability. We believe that other potential proxies that could be included are distance to a central city, diaspora support, and access to other resources.

The EPR also allows us to extend the research on grievance and conflict beyond the primary type of conflict usually studied by researchers interested in grievance and political violence, which is civil wars. While the data presented in Cederman et al. (2010) examines the role of grievance and capacity in internal conflicts, we have used the data to examine the role of ethnic grievance in terrorism.[5] The data used for this preliminary analysis comes from two primary sources. Terrorism is typically divided between two different typologies: institutional and grievance (Bonanate 1979; Wittebols 1991). Therefore, a careful analysis of the role of grievance in these different types of violence is necessary. Institutional terrorism, also called top-down terrorism, is usually perpetrated to protect a powerful group's interest. The most common example of institutional terrorism is state terrorism or state-sponsored terrorism. Grievance terrorism, on the other hand, is trying to promote a cause or achieve power. Using the same data as Cederman et al. (2010), we can access information on groups and populations that are currently outside the system of power in a state. Therefore, these groups may use terrorism as a way to alter the power relationship in a state.

Data on terrorism is coded from the Global Terrorism Database (GTD). The GTD is a comprehensive dataset covering both domestic and transnational terrorist events from 1970 until 2007. It is the only worldwide dataset that also contains information on domestic terror events for each year—vastly important when studying grievance as a cause of terrorism. The vast majority of the attacks in the GTD are domestic attacks. As a simple point of comparison, there are over 80,000 individual attacks listed in the GTD. Compare this number of attacks to the number of attacks in the International Terrorism: Attributes of Terrorist Events (ITERATE) dataset, which contains information only on transnational attacks from 1968 to 2004 (Mickolus et al. 2002). This dataset contains information on only around 12,000 terrorist attacks. Therefore, by using the GTD, we are able to obtain a fuller picture of the total amount of terrorism occurring in the world. Instead of supplying a single definition of terrorism, the database sets up several criteria that an event must meet in order to be considered a terrorist event. All attacks in this analysis meet the following four criteria: the incident must be intentional; entail violence or the threat thereof; be carried out by sub-national actors; and be outside the context of legitimate warfare. In addition, at least one of the following two conditions must be met for inclusion: the act must have a political, social, ideological, or religious goal; and the act must be carried out to influence a group larger than the immediate victims. However, this dataset is not without its faults. The information in the GTD was collected entirely from public sources. Therefore, bias could be introduced to the model if attacks are not reported. Attacks that are stopped in the planning stages and not reported to the media are also not included. Finally, commonly used control variables—GDP per capita, population, and democracy—were added to the regression. All of these variables were taken from the Quality of Government dataset (Teorell et al. 2008). GDP per capita (Heston et al. 2011) is a measure of state resources, which should have a dampening effect on the number of terrorist attacks a country faces, as rich countries are better able to deter attacks. These countries will also be better positioned to respond to attacks, perhaps making them less favorable targets

(Sandler and Lapan 1988). A country with a large population (Heston et al. 2011) is likely to have a more heterogeneous population, making grievance terrorism more likely. In addition, a large population may imply more potential targets, increasing the potential number of terror attacks. Finally, more attacks will occur in these countries because it is harder to police a larger population (Eyerman 1998), thus lowering the probability of being caught and increasing the probability of success for the terrorist organization. Democracy was coded from the Polity IV dataset (Marshall and Jaggers 2002). Terrorist organizations are more likely to form and go unnoticed in democratic societies because these societies allow freedom of movement and ideas (Hamilton and Hamilton 1983). Therefore, terrorist attacks may be more likely in democratic societies. On the other hand, since democracy allows for an exchange of ideas through a political process, the need to resort to terrorism may be diminished, therefore reducing the total amount of terrorism in democracies. Additionally, year fixed effects were included, as terrorism has different trends over time. Finally, standard errors were clustered over country, to account for the fact that different countries experience different levels of terrorism for reasons not included in the regression.

Using a zero-inflated negative binomial regression, we tested how the different measures pulled from the EPR dataset relate to the amount of terrorism in a country in one year. Both the proportion of the population represented by excluded groups and the proportion of groups excluded from the government are statistically significant in explaining the amount of terrorism—the higher the exclusion, the more terrorism a country experiences. For each additional 1 percent of the population that is represented by a group that is excluded from the political system, the number of terror attacks increases by 0.0163. The average country excludes groups representing 16 percent of their population from the political process. Therefore, the average country would experience 0.25 more terror attacks in a year than a country that does not exclude any of their population from politics. Remember that Wimmer et al. (2009) found that a one standard deviation increase in the share of the population excluded led to a 25 percent increase in armed conflict. Here, a one standard deviation in the share of the population excluded leads to only a 4 percent increase in the number of terror events in a country in a given year. Similarly, the average country excludes 50.5 percent of political groups from the process. Therefore, the average country experiences 0.875 more attacks in a year than a country that does not exclude any political organizations. Neither the proportion of population that is powerless nor the proportion of population that is discriminated against were statistically significant.

While the magnitude of the effect of ethnic exclusion was larger in terms of increasing the likelihood of internal armed conflict than in increasing the likelihood of terrorism, political exclusion does increase both of these violent phenomena. In the future, care can be taken to look only at acts of domestic terror, and potentially even to disaggregate grievance terrorism from institutional terrorism in this analysis. Given the precedent set in Wimmer et al. (2009), one would expect the effects to become more significant, and potentially the magnitudes of these effects to be larger as well. Additionally, Cederman et al. (2010) found a similar relationship between group exclusion and the likelihood of that group using violence against the state. Their additional information on mobilization and past conflict would be useful to add to our analysis, if possible. Our short examination of terrorism lends strong support to the previous findings using EPR: when a measure for grievance is used that is not marred by selection bias and which also meaningfully captures aspects of grievance, there is strong evidence that grievance, or discrimination against a group, does significantly increase the likelihood that representatives of that group will turn to violence.

Discrimination Against Some as an Indirect Cause of Violence in Society

When Gurr began his research, the focus of grievance was on the psychological concept of relative deprivation (Gurr 1970). Gurr was criticized for not linking relative deprivation in a clearly operational path to the outcome of political violence (Aya 1990). Gurr responded to these critiques by identifying a theoretical model that clearly tied grievance to discrimination and a measure that was eminently operationalizable and that provided significant evidence in support of the relationship between grievance and political violence (Gurr 1993a; Gurr 1993b; Gurr and Moore 1997; Gurr 2000; Regan and Norton 2005). While appropriately criticizing the MAR project for selection bias issues (Birnir and Wilkenfeld 2007), critics of the work by Gurr and others have been flawed because they employed measures that simply do not capture grievance in any meaningful way (Fearon and Laitin 2003). Recent work by Cederman and others addresses the selection bias issue and finds strong support for the basic argument that groups that are aggrieved are more likely to use violence (Cederman and Girardin 2007; Wimmer et al. 2009).

In concluding, we would like to broaden our scope and identify another direction in which grievance and discrimination ties to the likelihood of political violence in a society beyond the obvious link of aggrieved parties taking up arms against those they view as their oppressors. Specifically, new research has found that discrimination against women and inequality between men and women are both strongly correlated to political violence (Caprioli 2005).

While quantitative research into gender inequality and discrimination started by focusing on the international level of analysis (Caprioli 2000; Melander 2005b), more recent research has found that the treatment of women is correlated to levels of domestic political violence, from civil wars (Caprioli 2005) to terrorism (Robison 2010). One of the reasons why these findings are interesting within the context of our previous discussions about conflict and grievance is that, while women can organize and protest, they cannot (any more than men) in any meaningful way secede from a country. Additionally, there has been no meaningful long-term sustained effort at violent resistance staged by women against the long-standing discrimination and violence directed against them. One of the arguments that has been made for this link is that women have been excluded from power and thus from the decision-making process and when you bring them into power they are likely to restrain the use of violence because they are not as likely to be as militaristic for a variety of reasons (Enloe 2007). Another possibility is suggested by both the growing literature on gender discrimination and the previous literature on ethnic conflict and grievance. It is possible that discrimination—whether against those who can respond violently or against those who cannot—has a sustained and negative impact on society. In effect, discrimination primes society for violence. One of the key avenues is to build on Gurr's (2000) work on ethnic grievance and to extend our empirical resources to enable the investigation of a wider array of grievances and their impact on a wider array of contentious politics.

Conclusion

In conclusion, it is important to note that, while one of Gurr's most important contributions is theoretical, the enormous amount of time and resources he has put into creating data that allows the construction of various theories of ethnic conflict is equally important. The MAR database, including groups that both do and don't rebel, has allowed for the empirical testing of the impact of not only grievance but also other theories, such as opportunity structure and resource mobilization. Despite the critiques of MAR, as we have noted, a new ethnic conflict database has affirmed Gurr's finding (Cederman et al. 2010; Wimmer et al. 2009). While there have been some data collections that allow for the testing of elements of religious ideology (Fox 2004a), and others, as noted above, have looked at the impact of gender (Caprioli 2005), there is still a tremendous dearth of data that would allow us to tease out the complex of factors and their relations, which lead to different kinds of political violence outside of the level of analysis of ethnic groups. The creation of such new data will allow for an exploration of theories both old and new in new settings, helping us better understand why people rebel—or not.

Notes

1   We would like to thank our reviewers for their comments for improving our effort with this chapter.
2   For a much more extended discussion of the methodological issues raised in this chapter see Asal et al. (2010).
3   One of the other key motives discussed in the empirical literature is greed (Collier and Hoeffler 2004), which has received some support, but this chapter focuses on grievance

so we will not spend a great deal of time looking at greed except within the context of how authors cite it as a counter argument to grievance.

4   Perhaps the most important example of research that rebuts grievance is the article by James Fearon and David Laitin (Fearon and Laitin 2003), which we will discuss more fully later in the chapter.

5   The analysis presented here is part of a larger project.

3

LIBERALISM[1]

The Role of Modern Liberalism

Mark I. Lichbach

Whites against Blacks, Serbs against Croats, Christians against Jews, Russians against Chechens, Hindus against Muslims, and Sinhalese against Tamils: When will groups in civil society get along and when will clashes between such groups be violent?

More specifically, does religion cause violent clashes? Does religion directly matter to today's contentious global politics? What is the contemporary role of religion in contentious political violence? How much religious violence do we actually find nowadays among groups in civil society? In particular, are clashes involving religious groups now more violent than clashes involving secular ethnic and class groups?

The statistical literature on religiously contentious global politics has examined major wars (Austin et al. n.d.), international crises (Fox and Sandal 2011), the clash of civilizations (Fox 2004a), riots (Varshney 2002), minority religious protests and rebellions (Fox 2002; 2004b), terrorism (Toft 2012a), suicide terrorism (Pape 2005), state failure (Fox 2004b), ethnic wars, genocides, politicides, and revolutionary wars (Fox 2012), political terror and state repression (Soysa and Nordas 2007), violent religious persecution (Grim and Finke 2007; 2011; Finke 2013), civil wars (Svensson 2007; Toft 2007; 2011), armed intrastate conflicts (Ellingsen 2005; Finke and Martin 2011; 2012), interstate and intrastate territorial conflicts (Pearce 2005), large-scale political violence (Fish et al. 2010), the intensity and duration of internal conflicts (Lindberg 2008), and religiously inspired hostilities and violence (Grim 2012; Finke and Harris 2012).

With respect to the theoretical literature, many—call them religious determinists—argue that contention involving religious groups is more prone to violence than contention involving any other type of group in civil society. Others—call them religious epiphenomenalists—counter that violence involving religious groups is more apparent than real: nationalist and economic forces lie behind contentious religious politics.

The debate is particularly relevant to the contemporary era of globalization. The religious epiphenomenalists suggest that nowadays, in a time when economic inequality generates populist backlashes, antiglobalization protests over neoliberalism are paradigmatic of contemporary global struggles (DeVries and Lichbach 2007). The epiphenomenalists thus suspect that, at root, today's contentious politics is about states and markets. While globalization may create Jihad and McWorld—in other words, economic markets and religious fundamentalism (Barber 1995; Huntington 1996)—the epiphenomenalists believe that, in the last analysis, the bases of political mobilization are nationalist struggle and class conflict. Removing these factors makes contentious religious politics no more violent than contentious politics involving secular groups.

Global jihad and the Arab Spring, the religious determinists counter, are paradigmatic of today's transnational disputes having real religious roots. Religious contention over state building in the new millennium differs in terms of causes, courses, and consequences from the class and national contention over state building that occurred after World War II. The determinists contend that the most significant and most comprehensive political challenge to the contemporary liberal world order, especially to its grand strategies of development, is revolutionary religious violence. The death of religion, claim the determinists, has been greatly exaggerated.

The epiphenomenalist perspective indeed derives from ideas about class revolutions and nationalist movements that were used to explain the global struggles of the 1960s. While popular when contemporary comparative politics was born, these themes never totally dominated the field. Moore (1966) and Huntington (1968), after all, were contested by Lipset and Rokkan (1967). For another example,

> Tilly was frequently confronted by a range of arguments—many, as he recognized, extending E.P. Thompson's (1963) work in *The Making of the English Working Class* ... that began to deny the salience of class for collective action. Many of these arguments sought to show how other identities—based on race, ethnicity, nationhood, religion, gender—were equally or more salient than class for explaining social processes.
>
> *(Krinsky and Mische 2013, 14)*

The debate between religious determinists and religious epiphenomenalists in contemporary comparative politics is therefore as old as the modern study of comparative politics itself. The literature on the significance of religion in the academic study of comparative politics (Grzymala-Busse 2012) and international relations (Fox and Sandler 2004; Fox 2008; Toft et al. 2011), doubtless as large and as growing as the work on religion and violence (Juergensmeyer et al. 2013; Seiple et al. 2013), continues this debate.

The epiphenomenalists who hold that the religion–violence nexus has nothing to do with religion per se suspect that statistical facts nowadays advanced about religious clashes are, in fact, artifactual. Religious epiphenomenalists schooled in the thought of the 1960s will thus wonder whether it is really religion that is causing initiator–target clashes to be violent and hence whether the religion–violence nexus is really spurious. Why is religion so often linked to violence with their secular opponents? More generally, why is religion fueling so many of today's diverse social struggles? What is behind its contemporary collective agency and causal power? How, exactly, did religion become so politicized?

To capture how religious epiphenomenalists would explain these stylized facts we offer a liberal theory of the religion–violence nexus. Via its strategic microfoundations of collective action (CA) and coercive bargaining (CB), the theory demonstrates how liberalism can defang religious groups and thereby reduce the severity of clashes involving religion.

The theory assumes that the successes of liberalism minimize religious grievances but even more importantly that liberalism's successes influence strategizing by religious groups: under successful liberalism, attempts to mobilize a religious group brings its inclusion in bargains that empower religious moderates. Clashes involving religious groups—religious initiators and secular targets, religious initiators and religious targets, and secular initiators and religious targets—thus should be no more violent than clashes involving class and nation—secular initiators and secular targets.

The theory also assumes that under successful liberalism religious initiators's grievances against liberalism are no longer rooted in monotheistic perspectives that tend toward a rigid Manichean dualism, and therefore religious initiators have no greater capacity to generate factions than secular initiators. Clashes between religious initiators and secular targets thus should be no more violent than clashes between secular initiators and secular targets, and clashes between religious initiators and religious targets should be no more violent than clashes between secular initiators and religious targets.

Finally, the theory assumes that under successful liberalism bargaining with secular targets has no greater capacity to generate factions among religious initiators than bargaining with religious targets, and that bargaining with religious targets has no greater capacity to generate factions among secular initiators than bargaining with secular targets. Clashes between religious initiators and secular targets thus should be no more violent than clashes between religious initiators and religious targets, and clashes between secular initiators and religious targets should be no more violent than clashes between secular intitiators and secular targets.

If these two assumptions about successful liberalism turn out to be false, then the following ranking of the severity of clashes holds: secular–secular clashes will be the least violent; religious–secular clashes will be the most violent; and secular–religious clashes and religious–religious clashes will be in the middle, with the former slightly less violent than the latter.

The theory is indeed best elaborated counterfactually. The theory thus attributes the correlation between religion and violence to the failures of a liberalism that has not always been a successful strategy for building states with harmonious church–state relations. Hence, the situational context that produces the global diffusion of violent religious countermovements is the blowback from state building failures and the backlash from failed paths of development. In other words, development strategies that do not deliver the goods they promise—strategies that have performed poorly for self, group, and country—weaken regimes and leave their civil societies vulnerable to contentious religious politics. The statistical relationship between religion and violence is thus politically and socially constructed by macro contexts that produce the grievances that generate religious violence. Since anything that increases the failures of liberalism increases the chances of grievance-fueled violent contentious politics, if these factors are controlled for the religion–violence correlation is wiped out.

Since grievances against liberalism are endless, why has religion, and not some other cleavage in civil society, become a major vehicle of protest and a significant vessel of violent opposition to liberal paths of development? Religion coordinates opposition to liberalism in another important way. The micro part of the theory, rooted in rational choice theory and game theory, suggests the following: while religious communities often have the capacity to solve their CA problems, mobilizing their followers into politics is done at the cost of intensifying their CB problems, making it difficult for mobilized religious groups to negotiate peaceful agreements addressing their grievances. In other words, religious groups often lack the organizational structure to control the CA mobilization of the potential spoilers of CB agreements. While solving the CA problems of religious groups thus leads to more CA, as more religious actors are mobilized into politics radicals gain the upper hand. The extremists produce CB problems, resulting in violent contentious politics. To avoid potential CB problems, religious groups thus need organization that manages CA and CB. With such organization in place to control the mobilization of the potential spoilers of CB agreements, solving problems of religious mobilization leads to more CA with fewer CB problems.

While the theory thus states that failed liberalism enflames religious groups because it maximizes their grievances, failed liberalism, even more importantly, influences their strategizing: attempts to demobilize religious groups bring about their exclusion from bargains and hence empower radicals. Under failed liberalism, clashes involving religious groups are thus more violent than clashes involving class and nation. Moreover, anything that increases controlled religious CA (a) increases the probability that contentious religious politics takes the form of nonviolent protest, and (b) decreases the probability that contentious religious politics takes the form of violent confrontations. If the factors that produce organized religious CA are controlled for, the religion–violence correlation is wiped out.[2]

In sum, the micro answer to the question: Why have religious disputes become a core political battle of our times? is that, under failed liberalism, religion has the capacity to solve its CA problem but lacks the ability to solve its CB problem. Nevertheless, if the micro response was all there was to the question, religious violence would have been as prominent in the 1960s as it is now in the new millenium. Hence, just as macro structures require micro foundations, micro answers must be set within macro contexts. We therefore use both parts of the theory to generate hypotheses that challenge our principal result about types of clash and violence. The micro and macro aspects of the theory turn out to be complementary, and we will show how the shortcomings of one are addressed by the other.

We therefore advocate a strengthened modern liberalism—in other words, a liberalism that can empower religious moderates and produce peaceful bargaining outcomes, thereby making contentious religious politics more peaceful. Only an envigorated religious liberalism and a strengthened modern orthodoxy can allow us to have our religion without giving up our modernity and to have our modernity without giving up our religion.

A Macro Theory of Religion–Violence Clashes: Liberalism

The Big Picture

Religion causes violence because state building is inherently violent and the violence causes religion. Put otherwise, religious violence occurs within a global problem situation consisting of stronger groups aiming to defeat their weaker rivals, thereby establishing control over the state. A powerful administrative apparatus, the strong believe, will allow it to govern the weak over ever larger territorial domains. As state building generates resistance from rivals in civil and political society, the contestants for power mobilize and join ongoing political struggles about taxation, the distribution of rights and privileges, and leadership succession. As local and national counter-elites resist state rule, the state's opponents attempt to change the governing coalition. The consolidation and monopolization of state power thereby occurs via violent contention among rival claimants.

The failures and successes of state building eventually become clear, ideologies develop, and, as Moore (1966) wrote, global political struggles emerge over grand strategies of world politics, paths of development, and alternative modernities. Contentious global politics thus consists of countermovements challenging the prevailing global order. Struggles over various bases of global politics emerged from each of the French Revolution's three great themes. Liberty begot contention over democracy, equality disputes about communism, and fraternity debates about fascism. The mobilization of CA by political contenders and their consequent CB with the state occurs within, and is structured by, these relational institutions, networks, and contexts of global governance. Since the stakes are high the struggles are often violent: ongoing patterns of resistance and rule generate the institutional structures of the state that ultimately influence the outcome of national struggles over paths of development (Lichbach 2013).

State building disputes therefore provide the causal collective human agency, or the dynamic motor force, behind revolutionary global change. The historical protagonists for change support world-historical projects consisting of grand strat-egies for alternative modernities. The mobilization and countermobilization of elites and publics, played out in arenas of public discourse, ultimately determine political power. Interstate conflicts and internal wars are thus fueled by transna-tional carrier groups aiming to participate in global governance and state structures. And so, as Moore (1966) asserted, state building occurs amid contentious world politics.

Critics of liberalism adopt this perspective, and point to the contradictions of the paths of development pursued by the modernity generally found in the West, and particularly in the strategies that characterize the US. Some critics suggest that the liberal international order has proven unstable because embedded liber-alism generates the neoliberal trilemma (Ruggie 1982). Whatever its deep struc-tural causes, the problems of modernity are evident in the many failures of the secular nationalism that controls liberal state power. Secular Western models of statehood have been plagued by poor performance in many areas. Critics point to the unattractiveness of secular culture—its moral vacuousness, corruption, and decline; the emptiness of pluralist tolerance and multicultural inclusion; market failures and economic crises; democratic dysfunctions and populist movements; state breakdowns and political corruption; and global hegemonies hiding behind global governance.

Performance failures influence religion's view of the state and consequently the state's view of religion. A crisis of legitimation results. With regard to liberal modernity, many say, "I've seen the modern world, and it's not that great." As lib-eralism fails to adequately respond to citizen claims about justice and security, the success of religion in the developed world is manifested in new forms of spiritual-ity, and the success of religion in the developing world is demonstrated by the vitality of traditional religions.

Disappointed and disillusioned with the liberal order, many lose faith in Western secular paths of modernity and development. The belief that atheism and agnosticism are not working, and the sense that liberal modernity is an alienating illusion, are therefore the fundamental causes of religious violence.[3]

The failures of liberal state building strategies lead religious groups to innovate new strategies of development. As religion challenges the structures of liberalism, it contests liberalism's secular national civic culture with a vision of religious heteronomy; liberalism's pluralistic civil society of legitimate competition among groups with nationalist and transnationalist configurations of power; liberalism's capitalist market economies with state-run socialist forms; liberalism's democratic governing institutions with theocratic authoritarianisms; liberalism's neutral state bureaucracy managing an administrative welfare state with governmental rules and regulations privileging specific religions; and liberalism's cosmopolitan international order of states facilitating peace and trade with an international order where hegemonic religion rewrites state boundaries. Religious revolutions are thus attempts to address the problems accumulated over centuries of failed liberal modernity.

Over the past few decades, religion has indeed become a major challenger to the core liberal global order. Religious movements, operating as translocal, trans-state, and transregional networks, have waged global struggles against states and indeed the contemporary state system. The challenge is powerful because universal religion is an imagined international community whose claims of a higher spiritual authority threaten the mundane political order. Hence, just as at the birth of the state system in the seventeenth century, and just as at the birth of socialism in the nineteenth century, we again find two grounds for understanding ultimate collective identity, two bases of moral legitimacy, and two competing theories of international order: secular nationalism associated with the liberal nation-state and a religious worldview tied to nonstate crossborder networks. In other words, there are two rival powers: a world of states and a world of supraterritorial religious transnationalism.

State and religion therefore struggle over the organization of the global order. In terms of Polanyi's (1944) double movement, the state system is challenged by a countermovement of transnational religion. As religion and the state offer two alternative sources of social regulation and political control, they generate competing discourses about grand stategies for governing populations.

Liberalism in the West, especially in the US, offers models for state building, grand strategies of development, and paths of modernization that encompass culture, nation, market, democracy, state, and the global order. Liberalism defeated fascist and communist revolutionary violence. Will it defeat religion that also uses revolutionary violence?

Testable Hypotheses About Contentious Religious Politics

The failures of liberalism lead to popular grievances against its secular culture, religiously pluralistic society, market-induced poverty, autocratic governing regimes, religiously repressive states, and globalized hegemonic international order. Successful liberalism, on the other hand, defangs religion.

H.1. The more secular the culture, the less the probability of violence involving religious groups.

H.2. The more religiously pluralistic the society, the less the probability of violence involving religious groups.

H.3. The greater the market-induced prosperity, the less the probability of violence involving religious groups.

H.4. The more democratic the governing regime, the less the probability of violence involving religious groups.

H.5. The less religiously repressive the state, the less the probability of violence involving religious groups.

H.6. The more globalized the hegemonic international order, the less the probability of violence involving religious groups.

Clashes involving religious groups—religious initiators and secular targets, religious initiators and religious targets, and secular initiators and religious targets—thus should be no more violent than clashes involving class and nation—secular initiators and secular targets.

While they study mobilization and bargaining rather than explore grievances, micro theorists might agree that the macro failures of liberalism generate grievances, and that high levels of grievance lead to the uncontrolled CA mobilization that makes it difficult for religious groups to bargain peacefully. In other words, micro theorists could also suggest that the macro factors attributed to liberalism—its secular culture, religiouslypluralistic society, market-induced poverty, autocratic governing regimes, religiously repressive states, and globalized hegemonic international order—increase grievances and hence increase the probability that contentious religious politics will be violent rather than nonviolent.

However, the micro theorists would suggest that the macro theorists focused on liberalism only distinguish clashes involving religious actors from clashes involving secular actors. The macro theorists, who say nothing about strategic initiators, strategic targets, and strategic interactions between initiators and targets, thus leave us wondering: Are clashes involving religious initators more violent than clashes involving religious targets? And wouldn't the macro perspective lead us to believe that clashes between religious initiators and religious targets will be the most violent of all types of clashes?

We therefore use micro theories of CA and CB to fill the gaps left by macro theories of grievances. CA and CB theories probe more deeply into the strategic interactions behind the causal collective human agency responsible for religious violence. By encouraging us to refine our understandings of actors and events, they allow us to explore the micro mechanisms and processes behind religious violence. CA and CB theories also enable us to investigate micro-level factors behind religious violence, specifically focusing on how the transnational connections of actors are behind violent clashes. We therefore turn to the micro part of our theory.

A Micro Theory of Religion-Violence Clashes: Collective Action and Coercive Bargaining

Improving the Existing Literature

We pose two interrelated micro questions. Will target groups of claim-takers credibly commit to policies acceptable to initiator groups of claim-makers? Or must the initiators continue to mobilize and contest the target's allocations of desired goods? While different peace- and conflict-generating processes—the bargaining theory of war (Fearon 1995) and the collective action (CA) theory of dissent (Lichbach 1995)—have focused on these different sides of a single coin, arbitrage of the two rational-choice theories can yield a resolution.[4]

According to conventional and academic wisdom, initiator extremists can scuttle an initiator–target peace agreement (Hardin 2002; Kydd and Walter 2002; for a general review, see Lichbach 1995, 36–8). The general fear here is of populism, or what Barber (2003) calls *Strong Democracy*. Too much participation and mobilization by initiators politicizes conflicts; polarizes political parties; encourages the articulation rather than the aggregation of interests; and destabilizes policy-making. Radicalism and fanaticism, in other words, have no good end. When the claim-making of populist initiators spirals out of control the result is authoritarian solutions rather than democratic ones and revolutionary regimes rather than reformist ones.

The extant literature therefore maintains that, if initiators demobilize, and especially disarm, their radicals and fanatics, targets can commit to policies of moderation and appeasement. The demobilization of zealot initiators allows targets to make credible commitments that deter initiators from violence and eliminate the target's incentive for violence. Restraining initiator mobilization, especially of those who couple intense demands with violent strategies, thus secures initiator–target peace.

Since protest matters—initiator mobilization can produce policy success—this resolution is empirically problematic (Amenta and Caren 2004). In the US, for example, civil disobedience by Blacks led to new civil rights legislation. The resolution is also analytically puzzling: If initiators demobilize, why should a target credibly commit to their policy accommodation? Without the continuing threat of bus boycotts and labor strikes, Black political progress was unlikely.

How, then, do liberal institutions of popular participation influence credible commitments and contentious peace? No general analysis connects the logic of popular mobilization to the logic of credible commitment. We offer an argument that simultaneously solves the CA problem of the initiator and the credible commitment problem between the initiator claim-maker and the target claim-taker so that a peaceful, albeit contentious, liberal equilibrium results.

We achieve this result with a model that stresses the value of initiator power. If a target's offer demobilizes initiator moderates, the target knows that the moderate initiators will drop out of the fight; since the target will then face only radical initiators, initiators realize that their chance of victory is higher before an agreement is reached; the initiator thus fights before an agreement can be struck. Initiator mobilization—the ongoing mobilization of moderates—can therefore buttress the target's accommodation of the initiator's claims. Rather than undercutting peace, politically active initiators thus undergird peaceful contentious politics. A peaceful initiator–target equilibrium, in other words, requires the initiator to resist the target's efforts to split its coalition: moderate and extremist initiator factions must continue to cooperate. The moderates, not only the radicals, must continue to solve the initiator's CA problem. Unlike the traditional literature, which stresses keeping extremists on board for peace, we therefore focus on keeping the moderates on board for mobilization.

Targets may be able to empower moderate initiators to create organizations that will allow them to join target institutions, thereby preventing initiator extremists from trashing initiator–target agreements. In other words, the target might be able to assist moderate initiators. The paradoxical solution to the CA–CB problem is therefore for the target to mobilize the initiator such that its moderates, and not its radicals, solve the initiator's CA problem. The moderate-led initiator then remains mobilized, and the radicals remain part of the mobilized initiator.

Since the initiator no longer fears that bargaining with the target will cost it its coalition's power to affect change, and since the target no longer attempts to demobilize the initiator, the initiator has no reason to resort to violence: since internal CA issues have been defused, the initiator can credibly commit to the target. Since the target now faces a mobilized and, most importantly, a cohesive initiator, the temptation to renege on the promises it made to the initiator will not be present. The target can thus credibly commit to the initiator as well. Indeed, if the initiator's CA problems diminish over time, the target's willingness to offer the initiator credible policy commitments increases.

We now present our model, which is an arbitrage of the literatures on the bargaining theory of war in ethnic politics (Fearon 1995; 1999) and CA problems of mobilization in the contentious politics (Olson 1965; Lichbach 1995). We will show how initiator mobilization, spearheaded by moderates, is a necessary condition for a peaceful, albeit contentious, liberal equilibrium.

Fearon's Model

While Fearon's (1995; 1999) influential bargaining model of ethnic politics assumes that the parties to contentious politics—here the initiator and the target—must divide some resource, it also assumes that fighting over the distribution can impose quite large costs on the initiator (c) and the target (C). Given the potential gains from cooperation, the parties ask: Why can't we all get along? If the initiator and the target could commence negotiations, reach a settlement, and assure themselves that their agreement was self-enforcing, they could share the resource and save the c + C costs of contentious warfare, avoiding a fight and leaving both sides better off.

Fearon's model also locates a potential pitfall: once the initiator agrees to negotiate rather than to fight, the target can take advantage of it. In other words, the target cannot credibly commit to caring about a demobilized and disarmed initiator. Left to pursue their own interests, targets behave opportunistically toward initiators, callously taking advantage of them. Since the initiator cannot believe in the credibility of the target's promise to treat it well, at the beginning of the game the initiator prefers to fight rather than to negotiate.[5] Of course, most groups in most places at most times get along. The central empirical problem of the bargaining theory of contentious politics is therefore to locate the institutions and environments that induce targets to make the credible commitments to initiators that guarantee peaceful contentious equilibria.

To grasp these issues, consider the generalization of Fearon's model (Figure 3.1). At the beginning of the game, the initiator chooses whether to negotiate or to fight; in the middle of the game, the target makes an offer x to the initiator; the game concludes when the initiator chooses to accept the offer or to fight. Resources are allocated as follows: the total surplus available to both initiator and target is normalized to 1. If at the beginning of the game the initiator decides to fight, its payoff is $p_1 - c$ (if the initiator wins the fight, it receives 1 with a probability of p_1, 0 with a probability of $1 - p_1$, and, regardless of the outcome, it must pay the c costs of fighting); and the target's payoff is $1 - p_1 - C$ (if the target wins the fight, it receives 1 with a probability of $1 - p_1$, 0 with a probability of p_1, and, regardless of outcome, it must pay the C costs of fighting). If the initiator decides to negotiate, the target keeps 1—x and gives the initiator x, which are the payoffs if the initiator accepts the target's offer. If the initiator decides to reject the target's offer of x and to fight, the probability of an initiator victory is updated to p_2, and payoffs are calculated as they were at the beginning of the game.

Fearon treats the key probability (p)—the chances that the initiator wins and captures the gains from a fight—as exogenous. His model, moreover, is driven by the assumption that:

$$p_2 < p_1 \tag{1}$$

In other words, once the target makes its offer (x) and a potential initiator–target agreement is on the table, the probability of an initiator victory in a fight decreases, presumably because the target's proposal defuses initiator claims, buying off the

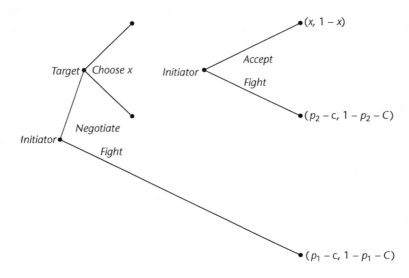

FIGURE 3.1   Initiator–target game: extensive form

moderates and thus decreasing the initiator's bargaining power. The initiator thus prefers to fight at the beginning of the game, when $p = p_1$, rather than at the end of the game, when $p = p_2$. The result of striking early, of course, is more violent contentious politics rather than more peaceful albeit still contentious politics. Moreover, the target's offer in the middle of the game to the initiator is:

$$x = p_2 - c \tag{2}$$

Since the probability of the initiator's victory (p_2) has decreased, the target's offer (x) is less than it might have been earlier. Since both its probability and its utility of victory decrease during the game, the initiator prefers to fight at the outset.

On Fearon's assumptions, the initiator therefore fears that the target's peace offer will cost it power and resources. After the target has suitably weakened it, the initiator fears that an untrustworthy adversary will then victimize it. The root problem is credible commitments: in extending its offer, the target opportunistically takes advantage of the initiator. The target, growing in relative strength, will make so meager an offer that the weakening initiator must begin a fight. A sufficient war-avoiding bargain is unavailable. Unable to make a dynamic commitment, the target leaves the initiator with no choice but to seize the advantages of striking first and of undertaking a preemptive war.

While there is already a lot of wisdom here, Fearon recognizes that he assumes unitary actors. He (1999, 116) thus suggests that,

> whereas in the model I treat the majority and minority groups as unitary actors, in reality intragroup politics matters significantly. To understand how it matters, however, I argue that one needs a prior understanding of the core commitment problem clarified by the simple model.

Fearon (1995, 382, 409, 410) had earlier begun with "rational unitary states" and asked "how war could occur." Here, Fearon (1999, 119) recognizes that "in the model I assume the two ethnic groups can be represented as 'unitary' actors, when in fact what 'the group' decides to do is the product of complicated internal political dynamics." Hence,

> this commitment problem is definitely not the only source of ethnic violence. For example, the internal dynamics of nationalist movements within groups also seem quite important. I will argue, however, that even when other factors matter they frequently interact with and are shaped by this underlying commitment problem.

He concludes that "intragroup dynamics can militate against efforts to construct credible guarantees" (Fearon 1999, 120). In effect, (1999, 121) Fearon is urging us to develop the idea that "factors affecting the severity of the commitment problem" include "the social and political organization of the minority."

We will now develop Fearon's insight. A CA interpretation of the probability of an initiator's victory, and more generally of the initiator's and the target's strategic calculi, will add further insights to Fearon's seminal work.

Adding Olson to Fearon

Modelers typically assume that it is the government that must make credible commitments to peace. Fearon thus studies the strategic calculations that underlie the target regime. Nevertheless, in adding CA elements to Fearon's model we focus on the initiator's CA problems in sustaining mobilization over time. Credible commitments to initiator–target bargains result from solutions to its two central CA problems.

The first initiator CA problem affecting target credibility is the mobilization of extremists. If an initiator is split between moderates and radicals, the radicals can bring down an initiator–target agreement. The initiator, through its violent activities, is a threat to peace. If radical initiators, as many claim, reduce the chances that targets will make credible commitments, extremists should be demobilized. A common expectation is that if initiators disarm their radicals and fanatics targets can commit to policies of moderation and appeasement. Demobilization of extremists allows targets to make credible commitments, which deters initiators from violence and, in turn, eliminates the target's incentive for violence. Restraining initiator mobilization therefore secures initiator–target peace.

As specialists in violence, however, radicals enjoy low costs and high benefits from violence. Raising the costs and lowering the benefits of initiator mobilization allows fanatic initiators to monopolize the political space. Unless moderate initiators remain mobilized, reducing extremism is unlikely to produce peace. To successfully reduce extremism, alternative avenues of mobilization must be available to the moderate initiators. The second CA problem that affects target credibility is thus the mobilization of moderate initiators.

These twin CA problems affect the willingness of the target to offer credible commitments to the initiator. From the initiator's point of view, if it remains unified then it can extract a tougher deal from the target. Empowering initiators protects initiator interests in the post-agreement world. The possibility of gaining better terms from the target make it worth the price to the initiator of laying down its arms. From the target's point of view, if initiators demobilize, why shouldn't it renege on its policy accommodations? Without the continuing threat of protests by moderate initiators, violence is likely. Aware that the threat of initiator mobilization produces the target's policy commitments that yield a mutually beneficial peace, a prescient target realizes that an initiator that can restrain its target is a useful adversary. If initiators are able to effectively tie a target's hands, the target will thus seize the opportunity and unconstrain the initiator so that the initiator can constrain it.

		Target	
		Join Fight	Abstain
Initiator	Join Fight	$p_1(2) - c, p_1(2) - c$	$p_1(1) - c, p_1(1)$
	Abstain	$p_1(1), p_1(1) - c$	$p_1(0), p_1(0)$

FIGURE 3.2   Initiator–target game: normal form

In order to show how these CA ideas affect credible commitment theory, we stay as close as possible to Fearon's model. Instead of a single initiator at the beginning of the game, assume the following: if the initiator coalition chooses to fight rather than to negotiate, a two-person game occurs between moderate and radical factions. As under Fearon, each faction receives $p_1 - c$.

Depending on how resources are allocated, the within-initiator game produces 0, 1, or 2 cooperators. To see the pure-strategy equilibria, Figure 3.2 sets out the game in normal form. If $p_1(2) - c \geq p_1(1)$, or $p_1(2) - p_1(1) \geq c$, mutual cooperation is Nash: since each initiator faction believes that it contributes more to the collective victory that its individual costs, both factions decide to join the fight against the target. If $p_1(0) \geq p_1(1) - c$, or $c \geq p_1(1) - p_1(0)$, mutual defection is Nash: since individual costs exceed the gains from an increasing likelihood of victory, both factions abstain from the fight against the target. Finally, two equilibria can arise in two ways. If $p_1(1) \geq p_1(2) - c$, or $c \geq p_1(2) - p_1(1)$, the initiator factions play a chicken game: there are two equilibria in which one faction cooperates and the other defects. If $p_1(2) - p_1(1) \geq c$ and $c \geq p_1(1) - p_1(0)$ mutual cooperation is Nash and mutual defection is Nash, and we have a coordination problem.

Now suppose that p_1, the probability of victory by the initiator at the beginning of the game, is an increasing function of the number, which can either be 0, 1, or 2, of cooperating initiator factions:

$$p_1(0) < p_1(1) < p_1(2) \tag{3}$$

For example, if both reformists and radicals cooperate in fighting the target, $p_1(2) = .5$; if the reformists defect and the radicals must fight alone, $p_1(1) = .2$; and if no one cooperates in the decision to fight, the initiator cannot win, or $p_1(0) = 0$.

By the end of the game the target has made its offer. If the initiator coalition again chooses to fight rather than to negotiate, the two-person game reoccurs between moderate and reformist factions. A similar payoff structure exists, and a similar inequality holds:

$$p_2(0) < p_2(1) < p_2(2) \tag{4}$$

The defection of the radicals still hurts the initiator's cause.

Given this set up, one likely CA mechanism behind Fearon's assumption (1) above becomes clear: the target's offer in the middle of the game induces the defection of the moderate initiators from the fight at the end of the game:

$$p_2(1) < p_1(2) \tag{5}$$

Another likely CA mechanism is that sustaining mobilization over time is difficult, the opportunity costs of participation have taken their toll on the initiator, and it is the moderate initiators who defect. Under either interpretation, we have a new understanding of the credible commitment problem in contentious initiator–target politics: if the initiator knows that the target's offer will split its coalition—in other words, if the initiator believes that time will diminish its capacity for mobilization—the initiator realizes that its CA problems will increase in the future. To avoid an even more severe rebel's dilemma, the initiator fights at the outset of the game.

Supplementing credible commitment ideas with CA thinking also tells us about initiator–target bargains. Suppose that the initiator has solved its CA problem with a strong institution. Such an organization can withstand the target's efforts to split its coalition, allowing the organization to withstand the simple test of time. Then:

$$p_1(2) < p_2(2) \tag{6}$$

and the CA problem of the initiator has not increased. If the initiator knows that it will continue to solve its CA problem, it will negotiate early on. Moreover, a high probability of a minority victory induces the target to offer the initiator larger concessions:

$$x = p_2(2) < p_2(1) - c \tag{7}$$

After the target's offer, a well-organized initiator, or one that continues to solve its CA problem, maintains its probability of victory and thereby induces a better offer from the target. Initiator mobilization has thus increased the target's offer (x), thereby expanding the bargaining space. Most importantly, the initiator has obtained the enhanced credible commitments it needs from the target, and it refrains from fighting.

And herein lies the paradox: the efficient use of target power is not to overpower the initiator in a fight but, rather, to empower the initiator to avoid a fight. Since targets benefit from the threat of losing fights to initiators, targets help initiators impose on targets the threat of such a harsh penalty.

The key insight here is that a necessary condition for the initiator and the target to credibly commit to each other is that the initiator retains its ability to fight the target in the second stage of the game. The target must assure the initiator's power by co-opting moderate initiators and assisting their efforts at uniting the initiator coalition. In the first stage the initiator can credibly commit to the target if it knows that in the second stage its bargaining position will not weaken. And then, in the second stage, when the latter remains as mobilized and thus as capable as in the first stage, the target will not be able to renege on its first-stage commitments to the initiator.

Counterfactually, demobilizing in the first stage prevents the initiator from retaining its potential fighting capacity for the second stage. As outlined above, this could happen in one of two ways: (a) if the target insists that the moderate initiators jettison the radicals as a prerequisite to an agreement, then in the second stage the moderate initiators, who are now co-opted by the target, recognize that their fighting capacity has been significantly diminished; and (b) if the target actively demobilizes the initiator by increasing the costs of mobilization compared with the benefits, it is the moderate initiators who will drop out by the second stage; since the radical initiators are specialists in violence, they will be left alone to solve the CA problem of the initiator. The outcome in both cases is the same: the initiator is better off fighting at the beginning of the game because at that point it is more powerful. Radical initiators will dominate the bargaining process and peace, albeit a contentious peace, will not be possible.

Interpretations

The arbitrage of bargaining models and CA models has thus proven valuable. CA theories are partial equilibrium theories and bargaining theories ignore internal processes. A penetrating theory of contentious initiator–target politics must involve a two-level or nested game, with between-group and within-group components, that integrates both perspectives. While CA theory without bargaining theory misses important strategic interactions, bargaining theory without CA theory misses significant mechanisms. Fearon is indeed right; credible commitments lay behind contentious politics. The reasoning, however, flows through CA thinking about the potential changes in bargaining power. Olson lurks behind Fearon.

Modeling group mobilization thus shows that initiator CA is part of the contentious politics process, that institutions empower and exclude, and that power accompanies credible commitments and creates mutual gains (Moe 1988). Recognizing that initiator–target agreements involve the exercise of power is the key to reconciling the two types of rational-choice theory and to handling conflict and cooperation in one framework. Behind mutually beneficial exchanges lies agreements; behind agreements lies credible commitments; behind credible commitments lies political power; and behind political power lies group mobilization. CA's context is a larger game of resource allocation, and the rebel's dilemmas context is the grander institutional framework of politics. Initiator–target agreements are therefore about jobs, language, policing, abortion rights, and tariffs—in other words, entire structures of cooperation. These agreements are networks of contracts, nexuses of mechanisms, and complexes of institutions with rules about how policies (the distribution of gains) and organizations (group mobilization) influence incentives and information. In a slogan:

initiator CA → target's credible commitments → contentious political peace.

Power and distributional issues affect commitment issues and thereby influence efficiency. Or, in a formula, the target co-opts the initiator and the initiator co-opts the target, facilitating initiator mobilization and target credibility. Solutions to an initiator's CA problems that empower its moderates thus turn out to be a target's commitment.

In sum, when will a target claim-maker and an initiator claim-taker get along in the game of contentious politics? Our conclusion was clear: only when the initiator maintains power. Commitment mechanisms must involve more than today's resource-allocation settlements: targets must assure initiators that the initiator will be able to influence the target's future policies. The twin keys to contentious political peace are thus target credibility and initiator power. To avoid clashes that involve target–initiator violence, initiators must remain mobilized so that they can continue to advance their interests and to further press their claims.

Initiators, no less than political scientists, know that welfare = w(policy), policy = p(institutions), institutions = i(power), and power = x(mobilization). To maintain or increase their future welfare, initiators thus attempt to maintain or increase group mobilization. The goal of initiator politics is to keep the group engaged in CA. Initiators thus seek the size and the strength required for power and influence.

Initiators who cannot remain mobilized cannot trust targets. Is that not the lesson of the nineteenth- and twentieth-century revolutionaries who were promised reforms that never materialized? As their movements dispersed, states revoked their commitments, accommodations were withdrawn, and repression was instituted. The stumbling block to initiator mobilization, of course, is that target power resists committing itself to initiator power. And absolute power absolutely refuses to commit to overcoming its power advantage. Just like the initiator, the target wants to maintain or increase its power so that it can sustain or raise its welfare. The logic of the contentious politics game, however, often leads targets to recognize the value of counter-power by initiators: targets can have too much power for their own good; initiator CA lies behind the target's credible commitments to the initiators; initiator mobilization makes initiator–target bargaining dilemmas easier to solve; and the credible limits or constraints on target opportunism include initiator mobilization.

Power, in sum, requires compromise. Target hegemony requires initiator consent, and the buy-in to target power involves initiator power. Everyone needs a little help from their friends, and in contentious politics targets need the assistance of initiators. In the end, the target shares the initiator's goal of sharing power. To be a partner with the target, however, an initiator must sustain its mobilization.

To assure peace, targets and initiators thus must have the institutional capacity to credibly commit to resource-allocation agreements. If target and initiator knew that the initiator's CA problem could be solved, both would be more willing to compromise their differences and avoid costly fighting. Since initiators must prove that they can solve their rebel's dilemma, some uncertainty will always remain. Doubt about solving the rebel's dilemma is the most important part of the uncertainty about initiator–target bargaining dilemmas.

Conclusion

If all of this sounds like liberalism and acts like liberalism—well, it is liberalism. The macro part of our theory therefore focused on the institutional capacity of liberalism to reduce the violence of contentious religious politics.

We now need deeper probes of liberalism. Is the violence that often results from religion initiators and secular targets robust to all specifications of liberalism? Or do certain contemporary liberal versions of culture, society, market, democracy, state, and globalization reduce the influence of religion on violence?

We hope so. Our theory is based on the conviction that in the competitive international environment religion should be part of the settlements, arrangements, agreements, and understandings about liberalism and state building. Religion needs to be recognized, respected, engaged, and negotiated so that the public sphere can deal peacefully with shared values of democracy, citizenship, justice, tolerance, pluralism, identity, trust, meaning, community, virtue, and order. A liberalism that involves a culture, society, market, democracy, state, and globalization that empowers religious moderates can produce peaceful bargaining outcomes in which religious actors lack the incentive to target secular actors with violence—or at least no more incentive than secular actors have to target other secular actors with violence.

Only such an invigorated religious liberalism and strengthened modern orthodoxy can allow us to have our religion without giving up our modernity and to have our modernity without giving up our religion.

Notes

1 Victor Asal, Roger Finke, Jonathan Fox, Peter Nardulli, Barbara Osband, Noam Osband, and Charles Taylor provided valuable comments on an earlier draft.
2 The reverse may also be true: CB problems produce the CA problems of global religious movements.
3 Others suggest that religion is filling the void left by the failed secular nationalist variants of communism and fascism that during the nineteenth and twentieth centuries contested liberalism (Juergensmeyer 1993; 2008).
4 For related rational-choice ideas see Iannaccone and Berman (2006), Berman and Laitin (2008), and Berman (2009), and for a review of the formal literature see Lichbach (2009).
5 In Weingast's (2002) model of reciprocal vulnerability, initiators must also credibly commit to targets.

4

RELIGION

Influences on Domestic and International Relations

Jonathan Fox

Before it is possible to discuss the role of religion in conflict it is necessary to define the word "religion." This is not a simple task, and there are many competing explanations.[1] Be that as it may, many of the definitions of religion used in the social sciences have one thing in common—they tend to define what religion does and not what it is. That is, they address the role religion plays in society and avoid a concrete definition of religion itself. This approach allows social scientists to deal directly with the question of how religion influences human behavior, and avoids a number of philosophical and existential issues that are difficult, if not impossible, to resolve. There are also some who do not try to define religion at all, but use the definition that was once employed for a notably unreligious topic: I cannot define it but I know it when I see it.

This chapter covers the following issues. First, it discusses why until recently there has been so little written on the topic of religion and conflict. Second, it proposes a set of criteria for evaluating the various impacts of religious phenomena on conflict. It then reviews the empirical studies of religion and domestic conflict that are currently available. Fourth, it explores the impact of religion on international conflict. Finally, it discusses the "state of the discipline" and suggests what needs to be done to further our understanding of the role of religion in conflict.

Theories of Religion and Conflict

For most of the twentieth century the most prominent theory on religion and conflict was that religion had no real influence. A major assumption common to all of the social sciences was that religion was a primordial phenomenon that would decline in importance in modern times and would eventually lose all relevance. That is, processes inherent in modernization were expected to cause the demise of religion. Mass education and literacy would undermine both the primitive beliefs of the populace and the hold of the clergy upon their minds. Scientific knowledge and rationalism would replace religion as the bases for social institutions, understanding the world and guiding human morality and behavior. Technology would provide freedom and opportunities not previously available. Modern communications would expose people to new ideas. Modernization would lead to democratization, which, in turn, would lead to a decline in the power of religion in the political arena. Finally, urbanization would undermine the small traditional community that was part of the enforcement mechanism for religious societies. In political science this school of thought was known as modernization theory; in sociology it was known as secularization theory.[2] While these theories were less influential among those who focused on regional studies, they were dominant among Western academics, especially among those at the cores of their disciplines, including those who developed theories on conflict.

Several events in the late twentieth century, including the Iranian revolution, the various Islamic opposition movements that followed it, and the election of Ronald Regan to the US presidency with the help of the religious right, caused a reassessment of this body of theory. However, until the 1993 clash between the Branch Davidians and the US government in Waco, Texas, most academics thought that religious violence in the West was unlikely (Kaplan 2002). Even after this incident, such events were considered marginal and deviant. Thus, the terrorist attacks of September 11, 2001 were a shock to most academics "not because of the violence involved, but because it looked like a throwback to more primitive times" (Beit-Hallahmi 2003, 23). Even after 9/11, many seem to be resisting the idea that religion may somehow be the cause of this type of violence. This type of resistance is typified by the Bush White House's arguments that "terrorism" and not Islam is the cause and, if Islam is the cause, it is attributable to only a few deviant Muslims. Others, such as Kimball (2002), have made the argument that since all authentic religions promote peace any religion that promotes violence is not a true expression of religion. Robert Jervis (2002, 37), sums up this issue succinctly when he states that "terrorism grounded in religion poses special problems for modern social science, which has paid little attention to religion, perhaps because most social scientists find this subject uninteresting if not embarrassing."

This brief history of the argument that religion is unimportant in modern times is critical to understanding the present state of knowledge and research on religion and conflict. In short, for most of the history of the social sciences the dominant paradigm was that religion was irrelevant. The few who believed that religion continues to have an influence spent much of their effort on arguing against this paradigm, which diverted further energies from the actual study of religion and conflict. As a result, until the late 1990s little effort was put into developing theories of religion and conflict and, even today, the legitimacy of efforts to study religion and conflict is repeatedly challenged. A recent study of religion in political science journals shows that, while there has been some improvement, religion is still an understudied topic (Kettell 2012).

Be that as it may, I argue that there are five ways in which religion can influence conflict. The first is through *belief systems*. All religions include belief systems. These systems, among other things, provide believers with a guide for understanding the world. Religious belief systems fulfill a human need for answers to many basic questions. How do I make sense of the world around me and the events that occur in it? What is my place in that world? Where do I belong? How do I determine the correct behavior for myself and others? Why do bad things happen in this world, especially to good people? What happens to us after we die? All of these are among the questions that religions seek to answer.

In answering these questions, religion often becomes more than just a set of beliefs. It becomes a basic and inseparable part of a believer's identity and, as a consequence, becomes an essential part of that believer's psyche or self. This is also true on the group level, where religion can contribute to a collective identity and sense of belonging. This creates a classic in-group/out-group dichotomy which in its most extreme form can define anyone who is not in the group as an enemy or a threat. In addition, because religious beliefs can become embedded in individual and group identity, any perceived threat to a religious belief system is also perceived as a challenge to that individual or group. That is, since religious belief systems can become intertwined with identities to the point where they are indistinguishable, threats to a religion are often perceived as dangers to all believers. This type of threat generally produces a defensive reaction, which is often violent. Wentz (1987) describes this as the walls of religion: people build psychological walls, and sometimes physical ones, to protect their religious communities and defend them at all costs.

The second religious influence on conflict is religious *rules and standards of behavior*. Most religions include some form of instructions to believers regarding required behavior. This generally includes acts which are required of believers as well as acts which are forbidden. This aspect of religion can lead to conflict in two ways. First, many of these rules involve violence. The concept of holy war, which is present in all three Abrahamic religions, is an excellent example of this. However, in order to cause conflict, the required actions do not need to reach the level of holy war. Second, it is often the case that actions inspired by a religion which are not in and of themselves confrontational can lead to conflict. This is because, under the correct circumstances, almost any religious action has the potential to be perceived by an adherent of another religion as a threat. For example, the simple act of non-Muslims praying in public, and in some cases even in private, is seen by many Muslim states as an affront to Islam and is banned. Saudi Arabia has the most extreme version of this policy. During the first Gulf War, when US soldiers were sent there they were warned to avoid public displays of religion in order to avoid offending their hosts. More recently members of the Islamic State in Iraq and Syria see the mere presence of non-Muslims as counter to their perception of an Islamic state and have expelled or killed most religious minorities in the territories they control.

Europe is also not immune to this type of impulse. In 2004 France passed a law banning overt religious symbols in schools that many believe was targeted at the head coverings of Muslim women. Local governments in Germany, Norway, Belgium, and Switzerland have passed bans on these head coverings, albeit usually applied only to schools or public officials. Similarly, a 2009 Swiss referendum banned the building of minarets, an essential feature of mosques. While no other national government in the West has limited the building of mosques, local governments in Austria, Australia, Denmark, Germany, Greece, Italy, Malta, Norway, and Spain have all used various tactics to limit them.

This potential for interaction between the first and second ways that religion can influence conflict demonstrates that, while the two are distinct conceptually, in practice it is difficult to separate them. That is, religious rules and standards of behavior are usually involved when religious belief systems are involved and vice versa. For example, holy war is most often invoked when there is a perceived threat to a religion. Nevertheless, it is conceptually important to make the distinction between these two processes in order to fully understand how they relate to conflict.

Unlike the previous two influences of religion on conflict, which describe ways religion can cause conflict, the following two describe ways in which religion can influence conflicts that already exist. The third way religion can influence conflict is through *legitimacy*. Religion is a classic source of legitimacy, which can legitimize or delegitimize nearly any type of action, including conflict. One interesting example of this dynamic is Juergensmeyer's (1993) argument that in the Third World the Western ideologies that have guided most governments have failed to deliver the economic prosperity and social justice promised. As a result, many of them are suffering from crises of legitimacy, thus allowing religious movements to emerge as legitimate opposition movements. In another context, Koesel (2014) argues that religion can often be a critical element in legitimizing authoritarian regimes.

The fourth religious influence on conflict is *religious institutions*. Classic mobilization theory[3] holds that any group that has an existing set of institutions which organize them, such as religious institutions, can use those institutions as a basis for mobilization. Thus, the presence of religious institutions can facilitate mobilization for conflict. However, there is also a countervailing trend in which religious institutions tend to be conservative and support the status quo. Comparative research by Fawcett (2000) and Gill (1998) suggests that when religious institutions benefit from the status quo they tend to support it. When some aspect of the status quo is a threat to these institutions or the religion they represent, they tend to support the opposition.

The final link between religion and conflict, *religious identity*, overlaps with all of the previous four. However, it needs to be discussed and analyzed separately, because it also has a distinct influence. For example, many who do not engage in religious activities enjoy following religious rules or participating in religious institutions, and sometimes even those who do not really believe may still identify with their nominal religion. That is, they may still feel part of the group. Classic identity theory posits that such identification makes people more likely to participate in conflicts involving that group (Horowitz 1985).

All of these five religious influences on conflict overlap. For example, conflicts involving religious belief systems will generally invoke religious legitimacy and identity, and will often mobilize religious institutions. This creates a reality that is far more complex than is implied by these five distinct factors. Yet in order to fully understand the impact of religion on conflict it is essential to understand each of these concepts distinctly. Only then can they be combined in order to comprehend the more complex reality.[4]

It is a common misconception that only religious fundamentalists are violent. Not all fundamentalists are violent and not all religious violence is at the hands of fundamentalists. The paths to conflict described above are potentially common to all interpretations of religions. Fundamentalism is one form of belief system that is no different from others in this respect. What distinguishes fundamentalism is that it is a reaction against modernity. Fundamentalists see modernity as a threat to traditional religion and try to establish a society that recreates what they believe to be a more authentic form of their religion that existed in the past. They tend to focus on texts as the basis for determining the proper forms of behavior and in doing so often create new and innovative interpretations of their religion. Thus, while trying to recreate an authentic past, they generally create something uniquely modern. While this general perception that aspects of modernity are a threat to their religion is an oft-traveled path to violence, this tendency does not come close to reaching the level of determinism. Some fundamentalists seek to act within the law to push their agenda. Others seek to create a closed society that is shielded from the dangers of the outside world.[5]

Empirical Studies of Religion and Conflict

This section examines the empirical findings on the impact of religion in conflict. It is based primarily on the findings presented in my book *Religion, Civilization, and Civil War* (Fox 2004a), with some updates. These finding focus on data from the Minorities at Risk (MAR) and Political Instibility Task Force (PITF)[6] projects, along with additional data on religion. The MAR project, founded by Ted Gurr, focuses on ethnic conflict from 1945 to 2000. The PITF project was also deeply influenced by Gurr. The studies discussed here look at ethnic wars, revolutionary wars, and mass killings between 1969 and 2014. This discussion is divided along the lines of the influences of religion on conflict described in the previous section of this chapter. It is also important to note the following definition: ethnoreligious conflicts are conflicts between two ethnic groups whose members belong to different religions.

Belief Systems, Rules, and Standards of Behavior

When operationalizing these concepts, one is generally forced to boil them down to the more general proposition that religious motivations influence conflict. This is the general proposition discussed here. The research shows that, while religion influences ethnic conflict, religion is not a basic cause of ethnic conflict. One of the more dramatic examples of this more general finding is that, throughout the 1990s, no ethnoreligious minority engaged in terrorism, guerilla warfare, or civil war unless it expressed some desire for self-determination.[7] That is, non-separatist ethnic conflicts that are not religious do sometimes include these types of violence but there were no examples of this type of violence by ethnoreligious minorities during the 1990s unless separatism was a factor in the conflict. This includes minorities such as the Copts in Egypt and the Bahai in Iran, who were subject to among the highest levels of religious discrimination during the 1990s.[8]

The logical conclusion based on these findings is that religion is not a cause of ethnic rebellion. If it were, there would be cases where religion alone, and not in combination with separatism, would cause rebellion. Since ethnoreligious minorities rebel only when separatism is an aspect of a conflict, the logical conclusion is that the basic cause of these conflicts is separatism, with religion being an exacerbating factor.

An important additional factor is whether religious issues are involved in the conflict. This can be measured by evaluating whether ethnoreligious minorities express religious grievances.[9] Those minorities that express religious grievances engage in higher mean levels of rebellion than those that do not. However, even those separatist ethnoreligious minorities that do not express religious grievances engage in higher mean levels of rebellion than non-ethnoreligious separatist minorities. Thus, religious identity alone can exacerbate separatist conflicts, but the involvement of religious issues in a conflict exacerbates it even more.

Interestingly, this trend is not constant over time. Before 1980 ethnoreligious separatist conflicts and other separatist conflicts had nearly identical mean levels of rebellion. Beginning in the early 1980s, ethnoreligious separatist conflicts started becoming more violent relative to other separatist conflicts. This trend increased steadily through 2000.

Another element which complicates this picture is the argument that many forms of nationalism, including separatist nationalisms, have religious origins. Anthony Smith (1999; 2000) argues that many but not all nationalisms originated at least in part from religion. Thus, it is arguable that religion directly causes conflict through its influence on nationalism. While this certainly may be the case, the fact that an ethnoreligious minority must form separatist desires before it will engage in terrorism, guerilla warfare, or civil war demonstrates that purely religious motivations do not directly lead to ethnic rebellion. Rather, at the very least, they need to be funneled through some not-fully-religious factor such as separatism before the violence occurs. Thus, religion can be an indirect cause or exacerbating factor of ethnoreligious conflict, but there is no evidence that religious motivations directly cause ethnic rebellion.

Separatism is not the only non-religious factor that influences ethnic rebellion. Other factors include the extent of international military intervention,[10] the spread of conflict across borders,[11] support by the minority for militant organizations,[12] and repression of the minority.[13] Thus, even when religion does influence a conflict, this influence is one among many. Interestingly, other factors predicted to be important influences are not significant when controlling for these variables. Those non-significant factors include economic,[14] political,[15] and cultural grievances,[16] cultural differences between the two groups, and whether the state is democratic.[17]

There is additional evidence that religious motivations influence conflict. The discussion until this point examined the influence of religion on the behavior of minority groups within a state. However, there is strong evidence that religious factors also influence the behavior of governments. Cultural,[18] political,[19] and economic[20] discrimination, as well as repression by governments against ethnic minorities, are all influenced by religious factors. For example, all of these types of discrimination and repression are more common against minorities which express religious grievances or demands for more religious rights.[21] Interestingly, while autocracies discriminate against ethnoreligious minorities more than do democracies, the type of government which discriminates against them the least is semi-democracies—those governments which fall between democracies and autocracies.[22]

International intervention is also strongly linked to religion. First, religious conflicts attract more intervention. Ethnoreligious conflicts attracted political intervention[23] by foreign governments 48 percent more often than other ethnic conflicts, and military intervention 17 percent more often. Among ethnoreligious conflicts, those groups that expressed religious grievances were 62 percent more likely to attract political intervention and 80 percent more likely to attract military intervention by foreign governments than were ethnoreligious minorities that did not express religious grievances. Second, a large majority of interveners are religiously similar to the minorities on whose behalf they intervene: 72 percent of political interventions and 73 percent of military interventions by Christian governments were on behalf of Christian minorities. Similarly, 90 percent of political interventions and 91 percent of military interventions by Muslim governments were on behalf of Muslim minorities.

This finding that states tend to intervene on behalf of groups with whom they share affinities is also true of ethnic affinities (Davis et al. 1997; Davis and Moore 1997; Saideman 2002). Ethnic affinities are also among the influences on international wars (Brecher and Wilkenfeld 1997). However, none of these findings regarding ethnicity are nearly as strong as the findings presented here regarding religion.

Another interesting finding is that religious grievances are negatively associated with ethnic protest.[24] As religious grievances increase, protest decreases. This is true when controlling for factors including other types of grievances, repression, separatism, regime type, international intervention, the spread of conflict across borders, cultural differences, religious legitimacy,[25] and political mobilization.[26] However, when minorities express demands for more religious rights unconnected with religious discrimination they tend to protest more. One possible explanation for this phenomenon is that religion is so important and primal that it is beyond protest and leads directly to violence.[27] This explanation is problematic, however, because, as noted above, while religion exacerbates ethnic violence it does not cause violence. Another potential explanation is that this represents the level of freedom in society. Religious discrimination, the basic cause of religious grievances, is more common in less-free societies where protest is more difficult. In contrast, demands for more religious rights are more common in societies where political expression, including protest, is allowed. This explanation is also problematic because the tests that produced these findings controlled for regime type and repression, but it is arguable that these variables missed some aspect of the extent of freedom of expression in society.

There is growing evidence from other studies that attacks on religious belief systems can result in violence. Muchlinski (2014) shows that violations of religious freedom result in more violence. Saiya and Scime (2014) similarly show that religious terror is correlated with the absence of religious liberty. Basedau et al. (2014) show that religious grievances are linked to conflict behavior by religious minorities in developing countries. Several studies show that conflicts that involve religious issues last longer and are more difficult to resolve (Johnstone and Svensson 2013; Svensson 2013).

Legitimacy and Institutions

Religious legitimacy has multiple influences on ethnic conflict. One of the most interesting is its influence on grievance formation. Religious legitimacy in some circumstances boosts secular grievances[28] and in other cases curtails them. When religious issues are not important in a conflict, as measured by the presence of religious grievances, religious legitimacy is associated with higher levels of secular grievances. However, when religious issues are important religious legitimacy is associated with lower levels of secular grievances. This means that religion can be co-opted to support grievance formation but the presence of religious issues in a conflict overrides secular issues and causes a focus on religious issues.

Religious institutions have a similar dual influence on conflict. Religious institutions tend to inhibit ethnic conflict under most circumstances. However, when religion is an important issue in a conflict they tend to facilitate ethnic mobilization for protest. When self-determination is an issue they tend to facilitate mobilization for rebellion.

These two findings show that there are dual and conflicting trends among religious elites who influence religious legitimacy and control religious institutions.

On one hand, they want to preserve their religion and its institutions. On the other hand, they need to remain relevant to their adherents. Thus, when the religion is itself at stake they will fully support opposition movements. When the religion is not at stake, they will support popular secular causes such as separatism and grievances over a whole range of issues even if doing so may threaten a loss of government support or even government retaliation against their institutions. However, in cases less extreme than separatism this support is low key, in that they support the legitimacy of the grievances but do not use religious institutions to mobilize against the government.

Religious legitimacy is also associated with higher levels of cultural, economic, and political discrimination as well as with higher levels of repression.

Identity

Although a gross oversimplification, most studies that include religious identity operationally boil this factor down to the propositions that groups that have different identities are more likely to fight each other, and that religious conflicts should be disproportionally common and violent. As measured by the MAR data, the percentage of politically active ethnic minorities that are also ethnoreligious minorities is very stable over time. Between 1945 and 1989 45.4 percent of ethnic minorities included in the MAR data were ethnoreligious minorities. By 2000 this percentage increased slightly, to 48.1 percent. In a subset of 105 ethnoreligious minorities for which more detailed information was collected for the period 1990–96 religion is among the primary issues in only twelve cases and was a secondary but significant issue in twenty-seven cases. Thus, religion is a significant issue in only 37 percent of ethnoreligious conflicts. In the other 63 percent it was not an issue at all, or only a marginal one. Thus, religious identity alone can paint a different picture than when evaluating whether a conflict has religious content.

As the MAR dataset focuses on politically active ethnic minorities and not just those that engage in violence, an examination of those groups which do engage in violence produces a different result. The overall trend is that, until the late 1980s, violent ethnoreligious conflicts were less common than violent non-religious ethnic conflicts. During the period 1950–79 ethnoreligious minorities constituted between 34 percent and 40 percent of ethnic minorities who engaged in rebellion, except in the 1955–59 period, when ethnoreligious minorities were 48 percent of ethnic minorities engaged in rebellion. Between 1980 and 1984 this percentage rose to 48 percent. Between 1985 and 2000, the only period for which yearly data is available,[29] ethnoreligious conflicts constituted a slight majority of 51 percent to 52 percent of violent ethnic conflicts in 1985, 1986, 1993, 1996, 1997, 1998, and 2000 and were never less than 44 percent of all violent ethnic conflicts. Thus, violent ethnoreligious conflict is becoming increasingly common relative to other violent ethnic conflict. However, ethnoreligious conflict is not significantly more common than other ethnic conflict, violent or non-violent.

The PITF data shows a similar trend. Violent religious conflict is less common than violent non-religious conflict, but the proportion of conflict that is religious rose in the 1990s.[30] As shown in Figure 4.1, until the 1990s religious conflict—which includes both inter-religious conflicts and conflicts that include religious content, such as the violent opposition movements in Egypt and Algeria—was far less common than non-religious conflict. From 1991 to 2001 between 42 percent and 49 percent of conflicts were religious ones. Beginning in 2002, religious conflicts became a majority of all conflict. Toft et al. (2011) found a similar increase in religious conflict over time.

In short, the overall trend is for religious conflicts to become increasingly common. This began in the mid-1980s in the MAR data and in the early 1990s in the PITF data. By the new millennium they began to constitute about half of all violent conflict, as compared with about 30–40 percent in earlier decades. If one focuses on conflicts which involve religious issues, however, as opposed to merely identity, they constitute a smaller proportion of conflicts. These results clearly show that the anecdotal evidence that religious conflicts are becoming more common is supported by more comprehensive and systematic evidence.

The discussion up to this point has focused on the number of groups engaged in violent conflict. A second aspect of the question of religious identity and conflict is whether religious conflicts are on average more violent than non-religious conflicts. In the MAR data there is no significant difference in the level of violence of ethnoreligious and non-ethnoreligious conflicts when not controlling for other factors. As discussed above when controlling for separatism, however, ethnoreligious separatist conflicts start becoming more violent than other separatist ethnic conflicts from the early 1980s, with this trend increasing in strength through 2000. A recent study using an updated version of this data also found that religious discrimination leads to higher levels of political violence (Akbaba and Tydas 2011). The PITF data shows that religious conflicts tend to be more violent in that they average more deaths than non-religious conflicts.

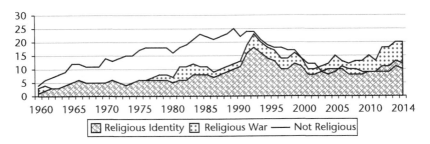

FIGURE 4.1   Religious conflict in the PITF dataset, 1960–2014

Sources: Political Instability Task Force dataset (www.systemicpeace.org/inscrdata.html) and author's own data on religion.

Other studies also produce mixed results. Rummel (1997b) found that the number of religious minorities present in a state is directly related to the extent of ethnic violence. Reynal-Querol (2002), Basedau et al. (2012), and Olzak (2011) found that religious polarization and fractionalization increases the incidence of ethnic civil war. Roeder (2003) found that sectarian differences contributed to domestic conflict. Henderson (1997; 1998) found that states with different religions are more likely to go to war with each other. Henne (2012a, 39) found that "suicide attacks by groups with a religious ideology are more violent than those with nationalist or leftist ideologies." However, Pearce (2005), using territorial conflicts in the Uppsala dataset, found no connection between religious identity and conflict. Similarly, Fearon and Laitin (2003) find that religious diversity does not influence the extent of domestic conflict.

In sum, the evidence on whether religious conflicts are more violent is mixed. While in a plurality of studies religious conflicts are shown to be more violent, there are also several studies which contradict these findings.

Specific Religious Identities

A common claim made with regard to religion and conflict is that members of some religions are more prone to conflict than others. Recently, this type of argument has focused on Islam and takes two forms. First, some, such as Huntington (1993; 1996), argue that Muslim groups or states in general are more violent. Second, some, such as Pipes (2002) and Pipes and Stillman (2002), argue that a militant branch of Islam to which some Muslims belong accounts for this violence.[31]

As is the case with the previous section, this argument contains two segments—the argument that Muslims are more often involved in conflict and the argument that conflicts involving Muslims tend to be more violent.

Both the MAR and PITF data show that Muslims are involved in more conflict proportional to their percentage of the world population than groups of other religions.[32] After Muslims, Christian groups were most likely to be involved in conflict. This relationship remains constant throughout the period 1945–2001. In the MAR data only Muslim groups have become increasingly more likely to be involved in violent conflict since 1985. These findings are consistent with a study by Ben-Dor and Pedahzur (2003) of Islamic vs. non-Islamic terrorism which shows that for most of the period 1988–2002 the majority of terrorist incidents were perpetrated by Islamic groups. Toft et al. (2011) found, similarly, that 82 percent of religious civil wars between 1940 and 2011 involved Muslims.

However, most conflicts involving Muslims are with other Muslims. This is true of 51 percent of Muslim groups involved in conflict in the MAR data for the entire period 1945–2000. In the PITF data this is true of 68.1 percent of Muslim groups involved in conflict between 1950 and 1989 and 63.6 percent of Muslim groups involved in conflict between 1990 and 2001. Between 2002 and 2014 this increased to 70.9 percent.

The evidence on whether conflicts involving Muslim groups are more violent is mixed. The MAR data shows that Christian groups are consistently the least violent when using rebellion as a measure of violence. Compared with Christian groups, Muslim groups have become increasingly violent. In the 1970s Muslim groups were 32 percent more violent than Christian groups. This increased to 59 percent in the 1980s and 71 percent in the 1990s. When looking at the violence of Muslim groups compared with groups that are neither Muslim nor Christian, the results are similar. In the 1970s Muslim groups were 6 percent less violent than these groups, but in the 1980s they were 8 percent more violent and in the 1990s 38 percent more violent.

The results from the PITF data do not consistently show any religion to be more violent but they do show that the vast majority of religious conflicts involve Muslims. However, Ben-Dor and Pedahzur (2003) show that there has been a significant increase in the proportion of yearly deaths in terrorist incidents perpetrated by Muslims. Between 1988 and 1997 the number of yearly deaths in terrorist incidents perpetrated by Islamic groups was about the same or less than the number of deaths in terrorist incidents perpetrated by non-Islamic groups. From 1998 to 2002, however, there were considerably more deaths in terrorist incidents perpetrated by Islamic groups. The study also shows that Islamic groups use suicide bombings, the most violent form of terrorism, far more often than do non-Islamic groups.

Religion and Conflict in International Relations

International relations (IR) is unique among the social sciences in that it had no theory explaining why religion was unimportant. Rather, the assumption that religion was irrelevant was taken for granted. A survey of major international relations journals between 1980 and 1999 shows that, pre-9/11, articles in these journals almost never considered religion an important influence on IR (Philpott 2002, 69).[33] Furthermore, when religion is shown to have an influence it is generally placed into some other category, such as terrorism, institutions, civil society, culture, or civilizations (Kabalkova 2000, 682–3). That is, if an IR scholar must deal with religion, at least before 9/11, she would usually avoid using the term "religion" by including it as a subset of some other phenomenon. The "clash of civilizations" debate is a classic example. Even though the central argument of Huntington's (1993; 1996) theory predicted a post-Cold War increase in clashes between his "civilizations," which are for the most part religiously homogeneous, both Huntington and his detractors generally managed to avoid the term religion.

One possible reason for this is that the Treaty of Westphalia, which established the modern state and the modern basis for relations between states, was a rejection of the religious bases of international conflict that preceded it (Philpott 2002, 67). This led to a general belief in the discipline that the era of religion causing wars was over (Laustsen and Waever 2000, 706). Another possible explanation is the

Western-centrism of the discipline of IR. That is, the argument that religion is becoming irrelevant and modern IR theory are both deeply rooted in the historical experience of the West. Modernization theory essentially argues that the processes that were believed to be causing religion's demise in the West would also occur in the non-West. Counterexamples in the non-West were considered primordial throwbacks which would eventually dissipate as the non-West modernized.

Despite its international focus, IR is perhaps the most Western of the social sciences. Those who dominate the field are Western and the discipline's origins are rooted in the West. The core of today's IR evolved from national security theories developed by NATO thinkers during the Cold War. Thus, the East–West focus of the Cold War paradigm which was based on the clash between two secular ideologies, liberalism and communism, and included radically secular theories such as realism is the foundation of modern IR. The attacks of 9/11 were the first to intrude upon the West in a way that could not be ignored. The Iranian revolution and the Islamic revolutions that followed it took place outside of the West. Those few events which did occur in the West killed relatively few people. Even after 9/11, the trend of placing religion into some other secular category persists in some circles. President Bush's "war on terrorism" is just one example of this.

Because of this, the thinking on the link between religion and conflict is less developed in the IR literature than it is in the other branches of the social sciences. It is possible, however, to provide an overview of the ways in which religion can potentially influence IR. While this discussion is intended to highlight the links between religion and conflict, it also applies more generally to the links between religion and IR.

Two of the categories of links between religion and conflict discussed earlier also apply to IR. Religious belief systems can profoundly influence IR. Everybody has some sort of belief system, though not all of those belief systems are religious ones. Thus, it is fair to say that at least some policy-makers have religious belief systems which influence their decisions. In addition, the religious beliefs held by the general populations of states can be influential. Policy-makers, even in non-democratic states, would be unwise to take an action that goes against a belief that is widely held among their constituents. This would also include failing to take an action that is widely popular. This dynamic helps to explain the finding presented above that most international interventions by states are on behalf of minorities which are religiously similar to them.

Religious legitimacy is also a potential influence in IR. It is a powerful tool of persuasion that can be used on a variety of audiences that IR policy-makers want to convince. This includes their own constituents as well as officials of foreign states and the populations of foreign states. Religious legitimacy is also a versatile tool, because most religious traditions are diverse and can be used to support a wide variety of actions. It is not difficult to find justifications for both war and peace in most religions (Appleby 2000; Gopin 2000). However, religious legitimacy is a double-edged sword. Just as policy-makers can use it to support their policies, those who oppose their policies can use it against them. Thus, religion's versatility is both an advantage and a disadvantage. Another limit on religious legitimacy is that it is less effective across religious traditions. That is, there are certainly similarities across religious traditions, but talking about Jesus is unlikely to convince a Jew. Furthermore, there are many people who are not religious who are unlikely to be persuaded by religious arguments and, in some cases, will be put off by them.

There are several indications that religious legitimacy will continue to have an impact on IR. First, there is a growing recognition that norms, including religious ones, are becoming more important in IR (Cortell and Davis 2000; Wilmer 1993). Second, instrumentalist theory posits that politicians use aspects of their culture to further their political aims. While this body of theory has rarely been applied to religion[34] and is not generally applied to IR, it is clearly applicable to both. Third, many, including Huntington (1993; 1996), argue that identity is important at the international level. Fourth, the modern international laws of war have their roots in religious thinking on the topic. For example, the Western tradition traces back to St Augustine's *City of God*.

Another important impact of religion on IR is that local religious conflicts are often international issues. Few domestic conflicts are fully local. During the Cold War few domestic conflicts avoided being influenced by the East–West struggle, and since 1990 many such conflicts have been the subject of international intervention. Furthermore, domestic conflicts often spread across borders in a number of ways. Bordering states are often inundated with refugees. Groups that in one state are oppressed minorities often have kin-groups that are politically influential in other states. Rebel groups often make use of international borders to further their cause, especially when they receive support from bordering states. Civil wars in one state often provide the training for foreigners who wish to bring the revolution to their home states or elsewhere. This certainly occurred in Afghanistan. Finally, if the rebels win, the change in government effectively creates a new foreign policy. In cases of religious revolutions such as the one in Iran, this can include efforts to export their revolution. Of course, all of these factors can be applied to both religious and non-religious conflicts. However, a study of the spread of ethnic conflict across borders using the MAR data shows that religious conflict spread more easily (Fox 2003b).

Local conflicts can also become internationalized. That is, the parties to local conflicts often use international forums to further their cause and try to rally support from foreign states. The Palestinian–Israeli conflict is a prime example of this. For decades elements of the conflict have been fought out in UN forums, including both the General Assembly and the Security Council. This also includes activities at UN forums such as the 2001 World Conference Against Racism, Racial Discrimination, Xenophobia, and Related Intolerance in Durban, South Africa. At this conference activists for both sides of the Palestinian–Israeli conflict were so prominent that they dominated the headlines.

Holy sites are also international issues. The holy sites of the three Abrahamic religions in Israel clearly fit into this category. The destruction of the colossal Buddhas by the Taliban government in Bamiyan, Afghanistan, in 2001 also attracted considerable international attention from, among others, the UN Secretary General Kofi Annan, the head of UNESCO, numerous diplomats, and several prominent museums. Even Islamic states such as Iran and Pakistan expressed opposition to the Taliban's actions.

There are a number of transnational phenomena that are at least partly religious in nature. Religious fundamentalism, especially in the form of political Islam, is perhaps the most important of them. Fundamentalism is defined in part as a reaction against modernization (Appleby 2000), which is an international process. Thus, fundamentalism is in this sense international in its origin and it is not surprising that fundamentalism is transnational in its scope, aims, and aspirations, to the extent that it can be said to have them. While most fundamentalist movements are local and generally focus on influencing their own states, they are often part of formal and informal international networks. For instance, Hamas, a Palestinian Islamic organization whose goals are mostly domestic, receives financial support from individuals in many foreign states as well as from some Muslim governments. In addition, there is abundant evidence that domestic fundamentalist groups are linked to a transnational network of such organizations. This is especially true of the militant ones.[35] Even local fundamentalist groups have long-term transnational aims and aspirations, because the truth of their religious beliefs does not recognize international borders. That is, they wish to "establish a new social order [that] in principle transcends any primordial, national or ethnic units and new socio-political collectivities" (Eisenstadt 2000). Some organizations, such as Al-Qaeda, are themselves international in their composition and goals, but such organizations are in the minority.

The character of fundamentalist movements is also transnational, or at least similar across borders and religious traditions. "Fundamentalists seem to have more in common with one another across traditions than they do with their non-fundamentalist coreligionists, at least with regard to seminal questions such as the role of revealed truth in guiding human inquiry" (Marty and Appleby 1993, 5). This is also true of their tactics. For example, a nearly universal tactic is doing local charity and welfare work in order to increase support. In the long term it is likely that the true influence of fundamentalists will be a result of their ability to influence people's minds through these activities and other forms of peaceful persuasion rather than through the portion of them who engage in violence.

In recent decades terrorism has become increasingly associated with religion and, especially, fundamentalism. Terrorism has been linked to religion for over a thousand years, with some examples being the Muslim Assassin sect and the Zealot rebellion in Israel against Rome in the first century CE (Rapoport 1984). In the past few decades the majority of terrorist acts and new terrorist groups have been religious ones (Weinberg and Eubank 1998; Weinberg et al. 2002) and have been linked in particular to Islam (Ben-Dor and Pedahzur 2003). Thus, the events of 9/11, which caused an increased awareness of the potential danger of religiously motivated terror, reflect a larger trend.

One explanation for this trend is the reaction of fundamentalists against modernity. The political, social, and economic entities that represent modernity are seen to pose a threat to the morals, belief systems, and traditional lifestyles of fundamentalists. This leaves them two options—to shield themselves from the world or to change the world to suit their ideology. While some fundamentalists choose the former option, others choose the latter. Why does this predisposition to reorder the world lead to terrorism? Because many see it as the only option available. Peaceful options have not worked sufficiently to satisfy some fundamentalists. Most terrorist groups do not have the conventional military resources to directly challenge the power of modern states. The only option left, as some see it, is asymmetrical warfare or, in other words, terrorism. Their ideologies justify it as a tactic of last resort in a world where there is a struggle of life and death between the forces of good and evil.[36]

Cross-border proselytizing is another source of international tension. Missionaries, primarily but not exclusively from Christian and Muslim sects, actively try to spread their religions across borders. Many countries feel that this is an attack on their indigenous cultures and religion. Even some Western states, such as Germany, Greece, and France, restrict these missionaries and have government bodies which monitor and sometimes harass "cults" that seem to be defined as religions which do not have a long history of presence within their state.

Human rights, including religious human rights, is becoming an increasingly international issue. A number of international and regional treaties protect these rights. This is becoming an increasing source of tension, as there are significant differences in Western and non-Western concepts of what those rights should include. This is especially true of tensions over issues such as women's rights and family planning. It is also particularly the case for tensions between the West and Muslim states.[37]

Finally, when discussing IR and religion, the "clash of civilizations" debate cannot be avoided. In 1993 Samuel Huntington published an article in *Foreign Affairs* claiming that in the post-Cold War era most conflict will be between large cultural groupings that he calls civilizations. He elaborated on this argument in a 1996 book. This theory has many critics and the debate over the theory was, with the possible exception of the democratic peace literature, the most voluminous debate in IR journals during the 1990s. This debate is also interesting because, even though Huntington's civilizations are largely homogeneous along religious lines,[38] both Huntington and his detractors largely avoided the term "religion."[39]

When using the MAR and PITF datasets, the overlap between religious identity conflicts and civilizational conflicts is between 70 percent and 96 percent, depending on the definition of religious identity used and the types of conflict examined. The empirical findings on this theory are nearly unanimous. Analyses of the

MAR and PITF datasets show that civilizational conflicts were a minority of conflicts both during and after the Cold War. In addition, they are no more violent than other conflicts (Fox 2004a). Nearly every other empirical study of the theory also falsifies it. Most of them find specifically that civilization has no impact on conflict or that civilizational conflicts are less common than non-civilizational ones (Chiozza 2002; Ellingsen 2002; Henderson and Singer 2000; Henderson and Tucker 2001; Russett et al. 2000). One finds that conflict resolution has been more successful in civilizational conflicts (Leng and Regan 2002). Another finds that, while civilizational conflicts are less common than non-civilizational ones, declining as a proportion of all conflict, and do not last longer than other conflicts, in the post-Cold War era they have been marginally more violent (Tusicisny 2004). The others found that civilizational variables did have an impact on conflict, though less than that of other factors (Henderson 2002; Roeder 2003).

These results lead to the following conclusions. Huntington's concept of civilizations is a surrogate variable for religion, and a poor one at that. Roeder's (2003) direct comparison of the impact of religion and civilization on conflict shows that religion has a stronger impact. My own analysis of the MAR dataset produced similar results (Fox 2004a). However, these findings are not out of line with the general findings presented here on religion and conflict—that religion is not generally the primary cause of a conflict but does have a significant impact on conflict. Thus, the claims made here with regard to religion are less ambitious than those of Huntington and, based on the evidence, more accurate.

Thus, the "clash of civilizations" argument is really a side-issue in IR. Civilizations can approximate religion, but looking at religion itself produces more accurate results. This is because the civilizations concept is limited to the religious identity aspect and cannot encompass other aspects of religion, including belief systems, legitimacy, and institutions. IR theory would greatly benefit from leaving the concept of civilization behind and focusing directly on religion.

The State of the Discipline

The study of religion and conflict remains in its infancy. It was rarely taken seriously before 1980 and until the late 1990s was studied seriously by only a few scholars. Much work needs to be done to further develop all aspects of the discipline. Theories of religion and conflict must themselves be further developed. In addition, religion is rarely the sole cause of conflict. For instance, both Fox (2004a) and Henne (2012b) find that, while religion rarely causes ethnic and international conflict respectively, it can increase levels of violence in those conflicts. Thus, religion is more often one among many influences on a conflict. Accordingly, these theories of religion and conflict must be integrated with general theories of conflict.[40]

It is important to develop better means to differentiate between religious identity conflict and conflicts in which religious issues are involved. That is, we need better tools to know when a conflict involves religious issues as opposed to when the two sides of a conflict just happen to belong to different religions. Clearly, this applies most often to cases of ethnic conflict and other instances where the two sides of a conflict belong to different religions rather than cases like fundamentalist opposition to a state. When everyone involved in a conflict belongs to the same religion and they are fighting about religious issues, religion is clearly an element of the conflict. However, even this type of conflict does not occur in a vacuum and other economic, social, and political factors are usually in play.

The Iranian revolution is an excellent example of this. The opposition to the Shah included a coalition of forces including economic classes and secular political opposition movements. It was only after the Shah was ousted that the fundamentalist faction emerged as the winner in the struggle between the various factions of the opposition movement. In other words, the Iranian revolution likely would not have succeeded without the support of secular elements of Iranian society, and certainly many of those who participated had motivations other than religion. Thus, even in cases many consider to be clear examples of religious conflict there is a need to develop a means to measure the religious content of a conflict.

In order to do this we need to develop better variables that measure the influence of religion on politics and conflict. Most quantitative studies of the topic focus on religious identity. This is not surprising, as these are the easiest variables to collect. Most existing non-identity variables, such as those developed by Pearce (2005), Henne (2012b), and Svensson (2013), use the presence of religious issues in a conflict to measure its non-identity religious nature. Yet this is a crude variable that measures either the presence or absence of religious issues but not the extent to which religious issues and ideologies drive a conflict. As discussed above, Fox (2002; 2004a) has also developed variables for religious grievances, legitimacy, discrimination, and institutions. However, these variables are designed specifically for the MAR dataset and are not easily used with other datasets. More recently, Basedau et al. (2014) have developed similar grievances variables for a MAR-like data collection using religious minorities.

A recent improvement is the Religion and State dataset (RAS), which contains 150 variables measuring separation of religion and state, including thirty types of religious discrimination, twenty-nine types of government regulation of the state's majority religion, fifty-one types of religious legislation, a measure for the official status of religion in the country, and a number of measures examining some specific topics such as religious education and limits on proselytizing in more detail (Fox 2015).[41] This data, which includes minority-specific codings for the religious discrimination variable for 597 religious minorities, in addition to the country-level codings, is suitable for analysis in conjunction with most conflict databases and will do much to address this religious data gap. Considerable data collection is still required, however. For instance, there is a need to develop variables that measure the impact of religion on international conflict. Certainly the RAS dataset can be helpful in this respect as a measure of the extent to which a government supports religions, but it is limited in two respects. First, the RAS dataset includes data only from 1990 to 2008, while most of the data in international conflict datasets is for pre-1990 conflict. Second, the RAS dataset does not address whether international conflicts have religious content.

This process of developing variables and collecting data also has an additional advantage. Religion is a concept that is difficult to define. Developing useful measures of religion requires us to think of ways to more concretely define and understand religion, or at least its influences on conflict. Thus, the process of developing and executing data collection efforts will, regardless of the results of the analysis of that data, improve our ability to understand religion.

Conclusion

Despite all these shortcomings, the field of religion and conflict has advanced significantly in the past decade. Before the mid-1990s no data was available and no empirical studies were published addressing the topic. Furthermore, few scholars were working in the field. By 2000 this began to change, with a small but significant number of scholars producing serious work in the field. For better or for worse, Osama Bin Laden did more to advance the study of religion and conflict than anyone else. The events of 9/11 have caused a major reassessment of the role of religion in motivating conflict. More academics are addressing the topic and, more importantly, more graduate students are interested in making it the topic of their dissertations. I expect that a chapter on this topic written a decade from now will have considerably more material to draw upon.

Notes

1 For a brief survey and discussion of some of the classic social science definitions see Turner (1991, 243–5).
2 For a survey of modernization theory see, among others, Almond (1960), Apter (1965), Deutsch (1953), and Halpern (1964). For a survey of secularization theory see, among others, Beckford (1985), Glasner (1977), Martin (1978), and Wilson (1966; 1976). For a more comprehensive discussion of the debates over modernization and secularization theory see Fox (2015). For a discussion of how this debate relates to international relations theory see Fox and Sandler (2004, 9–33).
3 See, for example, Tarrow (1989, 7) and McCarthy and Zald (1977, 1217–18).
4 For a more detailed discussion of the religious influences on conflict see Fox (2002).
5 For more, see Appleby (2000).
6 The PITF project is formerly known as the State Failure Project.
7 The information on terrorism, guerilla war, and civil war comes from a MAR rebellion variable that is measured on the following scale: 0—none; 1—political banditry, sporadic terrorism; 2—campaigns of terrorism; 3—local rebellions; 4—small-scale guerrilla activity; 5—intermediate-scale guerrilla activity; 6—large-scale guerrilla activity; 7—protracted civil war, fought by rebel military with base areas. The MAR self-determination variable measures whether the minority has expressed an active desire for some form of self-determination.

8   Religious discrimination is a composite measure which includes the following factors: restrictions on public observance of religious services, festivals, and/or holidays; restrictions on building, repairing, and/or maintaining places of worship; forced observance of religious laws of another group; restrictions on formal religious organizations; restrictions on the running of religious schools and/or religious education in general; restrictions on the observance of religious laws concerning personal status, including marriage and divorce; restrictions on the ordination of and/or access to clergy; restrictions on other types of observance of religious law.

9   This variable measures whether the minority expresses grievances over the same issues as listed in the religious discrimination variable as well as general religious grievances.

10 International military support includes any of the following actions by a foreign state: funds for military supplies or direct grants of military equipment; military training or the provision of military advisors; rescue missions, cross-border raids, or peacekeeping; and cross-border sanctuaries or in-country combat units.

11 This includes contagion—rebellion in the same region—and diffusion—rebellion by similar groups elsewhere in the world.

12 This includes how many such organizations the group supports and the exent of support for these organizations.

13 The repression variable is based on the following factors: small-scale arrests of group members; large-scale arrests of group members; the arrest of group leaders; show trials of group leaders; torture of group members; execution of group members; execution of group leaders; reprisal killings of civilians; killings by death squads; property confiscated or destroyed; restrictions on movement; forced resettlement; interdiction of food supplies; ethnic cleansing; systematic domestic spying; states of emergency; saturation of police/military; limited use of force against protestors; unrestrained use of force against protestors; military campaigns against armed rebels; targeting and destruction of rebel areas by military; military massacres of suspected rebel supporters; other government repression.

14 Economic grievances include grievances expressed over the following issues: diffuse economic grievances, explicit objectives are not clear; a greater share of public funds or services; greater economic opportunities, including better education and access to higher-status occupations or resources; improved working conditions, better wages, and protective regulations if sought specifically for group members; protection of land, jobs, or resources being used for the advantage of other groups.

15 The political grievances variable is based on grievances expressed over the following issues: freedom of expression; free movement, place of residence; rights in judicial proceedings; political organization; voting; recruitment to police and military; access to civil service; and restrictions on attainment of high office.

16 The cultural grievances variable is based on grievances expressed over the following issues: speaking and publishing in group's language or dialect; instruction in group's language; restrictions on marriage or family life; restrictions on organizations that promote the group's cultural interests. The MAR version of the variable also includes a religious element but it was removed for the purposes of this study because of covariance with the religious grievances variable.

17 This variable measures whether the state is democratic or autocratic based on the competitiveness of political participation, the competitiveness and openness of executive recruitment, and constraints on the chief executive. It was taken from the Polity dataset. For more details see Jaggers and Gurr (1995) and the Polity website at www.cidcm.umd.edu/inscr/sf.

18 Cultural discrimination includes discrimination over the same factors that are listed as bases of cultural grievances.

19 Political discrimination includes discrimination over the same factors that are listed as bases of political grievances.

20 Economic discrimination is coded on the following scale: 0—none; 1—the group is economically advantaged and public policies are designed to improve the relative economic position of other groups; 2—significant poverty and under-representation in desirable occupations owing to historical marginality, neglect, or restrictions but public policies are designed to improve the group's material well-being; 3—significant poverty and under-representation owing to historical marginality, neglect, or restrictions but there is no social practice of deliberate exclusion, few or no public policies aim at improving the group's material well-being; 4—significant poverty and under-representation owing to prevailing social practice by dominant groups, and formal public policies toward the group are neutral or, if positive, inadequate to offset active and widespread discrimination; 5—public policies substantially restrict the group's economic opportunities in contrast with other groups.

21 This variable represents demands for religious rights that are unconnected to religious discrimination.

22 For more on this finding see Fox and Sandler (2003).

23 Political intervention includes any of the following acts by a foreign government: ideological or diffuse support; nonmilitary financial support; access to external markets and communications; and peacekeeping units or instituting a blockade.

24 The MAR variable for protest is coded as follows: 0—none reported; 1—verbal opposition (public letters, petitions, posters, publications, agitation, etc.); 2—scattered acts of symbolic resistance; 3—political organizing activity on a substantial scale; 4—demonstrations, rallies, strikes, and/or riots, total participation less than 10,000; 5—demonstrations, rallies, strikes, and/or riots, total participation estimated between 10,000 and 100,000; 6—demonstrations, rallies, strikes, and/or riots, total participation over 100,000.

25 This variable is measured by whether the state supports a particular religion.

26 This variable measures the number of political groups supported by an ethnic minority and the extent of support for those groups.

27 For more detailed versions of this argument see Girard (1977), Juergensmeyer (1997), and Rapoport (1988).

28 Grievances over political, economic, and cultural issues.

29 Before 1985 the rebellion data is available only for five-year periods.

30 All conflicts in the PITF dataset are by definition violent ones.

31 Certainly, neither of these arguments is undisputed. For a more detailed discussion of this debate see Fox (2003a).

32 This result was produced by dividing the number of conflicts in which a religious group participates by their proportion of the world population.

33 Of 1600 articles in four major international relations journals (*International Organization, International Studies Quarterly, International Security,* and *World Politics*) only six articles "featured religion as an important influence."

34 One exception to this is Hasenclever and Rittberger (2000).

35 See, for example, Stern (2003).

36 For more on this topic see Drake (1998), Hoffman (1995), Juergensmeyer (2000), McTernan (2003), Rapoport (1988), and Stern (2003).

37 For more on the general topic of religion and international relations see Fox and Sandler (2004) and Philpott (2000; 2001; 2002).

38 Huntington (1993; 1996: 45–8) divides the world into eight major civilizations, all of which, except the African civilization, include religion in their definitions. The Islamic and Hindu civilizations are wholly defined by religion. The Confucian–Sinic civilization includes Confucianism, and by inference Buddhism, as a "major component" (Huntington 1996, 45). The West is, in part, defined by "the effects of the Reformation and . . . [its] combined Catholic and Protestant cultures" (Huntington 1996, 46). The Slavic–Orthodox civilization is based, in part, upon the Orthodox branch of

Christianity (Huntington 1996, 45–6). Latin American culture is distinguished from the West, in part, by the fact that it is primarily Catholic (Huntington 1996, 46). The Japanese civilization has a distinct religious tradition including Shintoism.

39 For a more thorough discussion of this debate see Fox (2004a, 155–74).
40 One example of such an effort is Fox (2002), which develops a theory of religion and conflict and integrates it with Gurr's (1993a; 2000) Minorities at Risk model of ethnic conflict.
41 See also the project website at www.religionandstate.org.

5

POLITICAL AUTHORITY

Assessing the State of the "State" in Recent Cross-National Empirical Research

Keith Jaggers

"The state," according to Kimmel (1990, 145),

> is more than an object of revolution, the prize to be won by the victorious party in revolutionary struggle. The state itself, its administrative bureaucracy, representative institutions, executive leader, is intimately involved in revolution, as cause and consequence, and as historical agent in its own right.

Accepting this line of reasoning, Goodwin (1997; 2001a) has argued that state-centered theoretical approaches to social relations comprise some of the most powerful analytic tools currently available to analysts of social revolutions. The unifying element of this approach rests on its emphasis on the state's potential ability to "shape, enable, or constrain the economic, associational, cultural and even social-psychological" conditions and forces typically associated with revolutionary activity and outcomes (Goodwin 1997, 11). In this chapter, I will attempt to critically evaluate the empirical power of the three dominant state-centric theories outlined by Goodwin—the state autonomy approach, the state capacity perspective, and the political opportunity approach—in light of the recent cross-national statistical research on violent political conflict.

More specifically, this survey will attempt to assess the manner in which state institutions and structures impact the social grievances, organizational capacity, and political opportunities associated with violent collective action. Each of the three state-centric approaches surveyed here focuses our attention on one of these core dimensions of collective political action: while the state autonomy perspective directs our attention to the generation and aggregation of social grievances that are said to motivate revolutionary activity, the state capacity and political opportunity perspectives concentrate, respectively, on the organizational capabilities and institutional conditions that impact rebel group mobilization and action. In other words, these three core state-centric approaches provide us with potential insights into the central questions of *why*, *how*, and *when* people rebel.

In this analysis, I will focus on how each of these state-centric perspectives define and employ the concept of state power. Following the lead of Mann (1986), the concept of state power can be broken down into two distinct (although not completely independent) dimensions: *infrastructural power* and *despotic power*. While despotic power refers to the autonomy of state elites to act without routine negotiations with, or institutional constraints from, other social actors, infrastructural power denotes their capacity to enforce their political authority throughout society. While the former dimension of social power defines the autonomy of state elites with regard to policy deliberations, the latter determines their autonomy with respect to policy implementation. Focusing on the concept of infrastructural power, state capacity theorists see civil unrest as the manifestation of a state's inability to penetrate society and enforce its political authority. While political opportunity theorists acknowledge the role of infrastructural power in their models of civil unrest, nevertheless, like state autonomy theorists, their central focus is on the distribution of despotic power within the polity. However, while state autonomy theorists see the institutionalization of high levels of despotic power as facilitating the social grievances that spark revolutions, political opportunity theorists posit that the political mobilization of social discontent is not likely to occur when despotic power is either highly concentrated in authoritarian political structures or widely dispersed in democratic political institutions. So, while state autonomy theorists see democratic institutions as a bulwark against insurrectionary movements, political opportunity theorists see the process of democratization as both politically perilous and socially unstable.

While each of the state-centric perspectives can find some empirical support in the literature, efforts to operationalize these approaches and test them across a wide spatial–temporal domain has proven to be a difficult task. While the state capacity and political opportunity perspectives have found more support in the empirical literature than the state autonomy perspective, the most fruitful empirical work currently being conducted does not draw strict theoretical borders between these perspectives but, instead, seeks to uncover the interrelationships between them. Additionally, recent efforts to move away from crude measures of both despotic and infrastructural power, by focusing on direct government policies and actions rather than on broad institutional, socioeconomic, and geographic conditions, has increased our understanding of how the state impacts revolutionary behavior.

"Competing" Theoretical Approaches

People rebel, according to the state autonomy perspective, when state elites are unwilling to liberalize their political institutions to effectively regulate and manage the economic inequities embedded within the capitalist social order. The state autonomy approach starts from the basic assumption that state officials have independent political identities and organizational goals from society's dominant economic actors. Instead of conceptualizing the state as structurally bound to class interests, this perspective provides state actors with a *potential autonomy* from those forces that control the dominant modes of economic production within society. By assigning state actors the tasks of maintaining social stability, promoting regime persistence, and ensuring long-term market expansion, the state autonomy perspective acknowledges the incentives afforded to state actors to establish and enforce ideologies and institutions that promote social inclusion, facilitate economic redistribution, and encourage political equality.

By incorporating dissatisfied and disenfranchised groups into the political structures and processes of society, state actors attempt to neutralize threats posed by aggrieved class actors by providing them with an ideological stake in the social and political order. "The ballot box," according to Goodwin and Skocpol (1989, 495), "has proven to be the coffin of revolutionary movements" because under a system of democratic governance the state is viewed as "an instrument to be pressured and influenced, not as something to be seized or smashed" (Goodwin 2001b, 278). As succinctly elaborated by Mann (2001), the *raison d'etre* of modern democracy is found not in the promotion of individual rights and freedoms but in the preservation of state power through the reduction of class exploitation and conflict.

While the state autonomy perspective sees the establishment of democratic institutions of governance as providing a barrier against social instability, the state capacity perspective posits that it is the degree of governance, not the type of government, that provides us with the greatest insights into the dynamics of violent collective action. Choosing to sidestep the issue of what motivates people to rebel, the state capacity approach, instead, directs its analytic focus on the state's ability to organize and control people, materials, and territories. The core proposition of the state capacity approach is that states achieve domestic peace not through the functional integration of societal values or the eradication of social grievances but through the acquisition and monopolization of societal power. As argued by Mann (1986, 7),

> There is, thus, a simple answer to the question of why the masses do not revolt . . . . The masses comply because they lack collective organization to do otherwise, because they are embedded within collective and distributive power organizations controlled by others. [That is,] they are *organizationally outflanked* . . .

Further elaborating on this point, Mann argues that states can possess two distinct types of organizational power: despotic power and infrastructural power. While despotic power refers to the range of action that state elites can take without routine negotiation with civil society, infrastructural power denotes the institutional capacity of a central state, despotic or not, to penetrate its territories and implement decisions (Mann 1993, 59). By understanding these two dimensions of state power, we can talk about state strength in terms of either its authoritarian control *over* society or its ability to implement its agenda *through* society. While the former dimension of power gives us significant insight into the ability of the state to make policy decisions autonomously from other social actors, it tells us relatively little about the state's actual ability to execute and achieve its political agenda or its capacity to quell social unrest.

While it is common for state actors to seek to consolidate their rule through the establishment of despotic power arrangements, unless the state's infrastructural power is also significant the concentration of despotic power in the pursuit of this end may actually exacerbate revolutionary activity within society (Dix 1984; Farhi 1990; Goodwin and Foran 1992; Wickham-Crowley 1992). As pointed out by Goodwin (1997, 19), "Unless state violence is simply overwhelming, indiscriminate coercion tends to backfire, producing an ever-growing popular mobilization by armed movements and an even larger body of sympathizers." Additionally, state capacity theorists argue that efforts to liberalize the political order without concurrent increases in a state's infrastructural power will also provide the conditions for social unrest as the political mechanisms for grievance articulation and social mobilization outpace the state's institutional capacity for grievance reduction and conflict management (Huntington 1968). Thus, if we want to understand the dynamics underlying the decision to rebel, state capacity theorists suggest that we should focus our theoretical attention on the degree of infrastructural power wielded by state elites rather than on whether despotic power is institutionalized in an authoritarian or democratic manner.

Political opportunity theorists, while sensitive to the role of infrastructural power, nonetheless argue that state capacity theorists are too quick to abandon the independent role that the distribution of despotic power plays in our understanding of the dynamics of social movements and political instability. Contrary to the expectations of state capacity theorists, political opportunity theorists argue that the decision to rebel often has more to do with the manner in which a state organizes and wields its political authority—how it structures the channels for grievance articulation and conflict resolution—rather than with how much infrastructural power it has under its control (Meyer 1999, 82). From this perspective, it is not the level of grievance harbored by political challengers or the balance of resources between these challengers and state forces that determines the prospects for rebellion but the permissiveness of the political environment— that is, the amount of political space, or opportunity, afforded to challenger groups to mobilize in collective action by the institutional structure of the polity (McAdam 1983; Jenkins 1985; Tarrow 1994; Jenkins and Klandermans 1995; Meyer 2004).

According to Koopmans (1999, 95), the political opportunity model of collective action revolves around three core propositions:

1. Variations in opportunity are the most important determinants of variations in collective action;
2. Relevant variations in opportunity results primarily from the interaction of social movements with political actors and institutions; [and]
3. Variations in such opportunities are not random or a mere product of strategic intervention, but are to an important extent structurally shaped.

While Goodwin and Jasper (1999, 30) contend that this perspective borders on the tautological and Gamson and Meyer (1996, 275) worry that the concept of political opportunity is "in danger of becoming a sponge that soaks up every aspect of the social movement environment," these criticisms tend to identify problems of method rather than of theory (Meyer 1999, 87). According to Meyer and Minkoff (2004, 1458), in order to rectify these problems "we need to pay much more systematic attention to questions of operationalization of the concept and specification of political opportunity models . . . ." More specifically, in order to avoid these methodological pitfalls one must be careful to (1) isolate the structural opportunities for collective action from the actual mobilization of the movement itself; and (2) specify, *a priori*, the core structures that are predicted to impact political opportunities for collective action.

In an effort to add some conceptual and empirical clarity to the political opportunity perspective, McAdam (1996, 27) proposed a "highly consensual list of dimensions of political opportunity," which can be used to predict collective political action across a wide spatial–temporal domain. Included in this list are the following: (1) the relative openness of institutionalized political systems; (2) the stability of that broad set of elite alignments that typically undergird a polity; and (3) the state's capacity and propensity for repression. While the third opportunity structure posited by McAdam is theoretically problematic because it conflates the idea of political opportunity (which is defined by the degree of despotic power wielded by state agents) with the concept of state capacity (which is defined by the degree of infrastructural power held by these agents), nevertheless, this list does provide us with a useful starting point from which to explore the relationship between institutional opportunities and violent collective action.

Following the logic of political opportunity theorists, the level of political conflict in society is dependent on the organizational permeability, political permissiveness, and institutional durability of a state's political regime. Regime attributes are deemed to be important because they directly impact the incentive structures associated with collective action. More specifically, the level of despotic power represented by the political regime influences the prospects for collective action by (1) structuring the probability of successful mobilization; (2) determining the direct costs associated with mobilizing collectively; and (3) establishing the opportunity costs associated with the decision to rebel.

As detailed extensively in the social movement literature, the incentives for collective action increase as the probability of successful mobilization rises and the threat of state sanction falls. While social grievances may permeate society, so long as the political opportunities for successful mobilization remain low and the prospects for state sanction remain high the incentive structure confronting potential rebels will continue to favor free-riding over collective action. In contrast, political regimes that establish institutional avenues for collective mobilization at a relatively low cost to those who join provide incentives for the establishment of regime-challenging social movement organizations.

However, while the incentives for collective action are enhanced when the prospects for successful mobilization are high and the threats of regime sanction are low, these should not be seen as sufficient conditions for the advent of insurrectionary activity. Regime structures also influence the decision to rebel by determining the availability of non-violent avenues for grievance articulation. So long as alternative channels for grievance articulation exist, the opportunity costs of armed insurrection are expected to remain high, thereby decreasing the incentives for rebellion (Reynal-Querol 2002, 35). It is important to note that political opportunity theorists do not conceptualize opportunity costs in the same manner as do state capacity theorists. While state capacity theorists tend to conceptualize opportunity costs as the income rebels forego when deciding to engage in one form of *economic activity* (rebellion) over another form of economic activity (farming, shoemaking, computer programing, etc.), political opportunity theorists, in contrast, view opportunity costs as the income political challengers forego when choosing to engage in one form of *political activity* (rebellion) over another form of political activity (lobbying, party activism, voting, etc.). Since more institutionalized channels for political participation tend to require less time, energy, and commitment than is typically incurred by those joining a rebel movement, political opportunity theorists conclude that the opportunity costs associated with joining such an organization, if other avenues for political advocacy and influence peddling exist, will be high. However, if there are no alternative political avenues available to citizens, the opportunity costs of joining a rebel organization are theorized to fall.

For political opportunity theorists, rebellious activity is predicted to occur only when political structures are aligned in such a way as to convince individuals that the prospects for successful collective mobilization are reasonably high, the risks of regime sanction are relatively low, and the availability of alternative avenues for grievance articulation and advocacy are rather limited. While democratic regimes are expected to increase the prospects for successful mobilization and reduce the threat of regime sanction, both of which increase the incentives for collective action, the high opportunity costs associated with violent collective activity in democratic political systems undercut the emergence of widespread rebel movements.

Moreover, while autocratic regimes are expected to lower the opportunity costs of rebel activity, the limited prospects for successful mobilization combined with the high threat of regime sanction are predicted to weaken the incentives for political insurgency. Thus, while regime types that embody both high (autocracies) and low (democracies) levels of despotic power provide some incentives for collective political action, the political opportunity for mass insurrection in both is actually quite limited. In contrast, states that employ only moderate levels of despotic power are posited to produce the greatest opportunity for violent collective action (Meyer 1999).

Caught between the pressures for political liberalization and the desire for political control, semi-democratic regimes provide a political environment that encourages political efficacy without actually establishing effective institutions of political representation and accountability. Unable to channel their political efficacy into institutionalized modes of political voice, citizens of semi-democratic regimes often turn to street protests and demonstrations as a way of influencing government. Reluctant to either establish effective institutions of democratic governance or return to full-scale authoritarian control, political elites in semi-democratic regimes often come to grudgingly accept the collective organization of civil society as a necessary, albeit unfortunate, part of political liberalization. Under this type of political order, the new-found political tolerance of political elites increases the prospects for successful collective mobilization and, in the process, encourages moderate levels of unconventional political activity. This tolerance for collective action, however, is far from complete.

While state agents in semi-democratic regimes are often willing to tolerate some demonstration of collective power by civil society they are usually unwilling to forfeit their ability to employ state coercion as a means for limiting the physical size, political scope, and timing of these collective demonstrations of power. Despite the continued reliance on state repression as a mechanism of political control and conflict regulation, the application of coercive power by this type of regime tends to be highly erratic and ineffective. So long as state repression remains both limited in scope and highly sporadic in use, the incentives for collective action will remain moderately high. At best, the sporadic and limited use of state repression associated with semi-democratic regimes tends to increase the grievances of political challengers without significantly undermining their capacity and willingness to act collectively against the state (Mason and Krane 1989; Mason 1990).

Moreover, semi-democratic regimes decrease the opportunity costs associated with violent collective action. While fully democratic regimes provide significant opportunities for grievance articulation and advocacy through institutionalized (and less costly) political channels, semi-democratic regimes do not provide as many political alternatives. Lacking significant institutional alternatives to collective mobilization, citizens of semi-democratic regimes are not confronted by the high opportunity costs associated with selecting to engage the state in potentially violent collective action found in more open societies (Reynal-Querol 2002, 35).

By increasing the prospects for successful collective mobilization while simultaneously lowering both the threat of state sanction and the opportunity costs associated with joining a rebel movement, states that provide mid-levels of political openness—and exert intermediate levels of despotic power—provide significant incentives for violent collective action organizations to emerge.

The State Autonomy Perspective: An Empirical Assessment

While the salutary power of democratic institutions to ameliorate social conflict has long been theorized, its empirical power has only recently been tested across a wide spatial–temporal domain. While initial empirical investigations into the democracy–internal peace hypothesis provided significant support for the state autonomy perspective (Krain and Edson Myers 1997; Rummel 1997a), these positive findings tended to disappear as more statistically sophisticated and theoretically nuanced analyses were conducted. For example, democracy levels have consistently been shown to have no impact on either the onset of civil war (Fearon and Laitin 2003; Collier and Hoeffler 2004; Fearon 2010; Thies 2010) or the occurrence of low-intensity civil conflict (Miguel et al. 2004). Further undermining the democracy–domestic peace hypothesis, both Collier et al. (2004) and Fearon (2004) found that higher levels of political freedom had no statistically discernible impact on civil war duration. Moreover, DeRouen and Sobek (2004) concluded that the level of democracy within society had no impact on civil war outcomes. Finally, while Walter (2004) found that while "clear democracies" were better equipped to prevent the recurrence of civil war than weaker democracies, she was unable to find support for the general proposition that increases in political freedom inhibits the recurrence of revolutionary conflict in war-prone societies. At best, the most recent wave of empirical studies of civil conflict tend to see democracy as a permissive, rather than a proximate, factor in the inhibition of civil war. As argued by Elbadawi and Sambanis (2002), although democracy is not a robust variable, nevertheless, it may still provide a small measure of explanatory power not captured by other social and political indicators.

While recent statistical studies provide only limited support for the state autonomy hypothesis that democracies are better equipped to resolve social tensions peacefully than are other regime types, before prematurely abandoning this perspective a closer examination of these studies seems warranted. Two central questions must be explored: (1) is the dearth of support for this relationship a product of the weakness of the state autonomy theory or simply the result of inappropriate sample selection; and (2) does this lack of empirical support prove that democratic institutions are ineffective at inhibiting domestic political conflict or does it merely demonstrate a failure to theoretically specify the conditions under which democracy can, and cannot, be expected to regulate conflict?

First, one potential explanation for the generally weak empirical support for the inverse relationship between democracy and domestic political violence may be found in the common methodological practice of aggregating both ethnic and non-ethnic conflict into a single indicator of "civil war." Could it be that the inclusion of ethnic-based conflicts in the samples under investigation has prevented us from observing the power of democratic institutions to inhibit class-based violence? Sambanis (2001, 259), for example, has argued that not all civil wars are the same and that "as we undertake further study of the causes of civil war, it is important to know if our conclusions apply equally well to wars of different types." Mann (2001) expands on this argument by positing that there is little theoretical reason to expect that our traditional class-based models of civil war will provide us with a powerful explanation of political violence in the contemporary world. This is because our class-based models have very little to say about the dominant form of civil violence in the post-Cold War era—namely, ethnonational war. In contrast to the expectations of the state autonomy perspective, much of the literature on ethnic conflict tends to see democracy not as a mechanism for social integration and pacification but as a trigger for political instability and violence (Rabushka and Shepsle 1972; Rothschild 1981; Horowitz 1985).

Given the possibility that ethnic and non-ethnic conflict are triggered by distinct social and institutional processes, should we expect increased support for the hypothesis that democracy inhibits class-based political violence once we remove episodes of ethnic conflict from our samples? Fortunately, Sambanis (2001) provides us with some insight into this question. However, his findings provide *less*, not more, support for the state autonomy perspective. Analyzing the onset of non-ethnic civil war in the post-colonial era, Sambanis was unable to find any empirical support for the hypothesized negative relationship between the level of democracy and the onset of non-ethnic civil war.

While the recent wave of empirical studies has not provided much support for the hypothesis that democracy can serve as an effective counterweight to the mobilization of insurrectionary groups, surprisingly, the conflict-inhibiting power of democracy is more clearly observable in societies where ethnicity, rather than class, represents the dominant social cleavage. In particular, Gurr (1993a; 2000) has amassed a significant body of evidence showing that democratic regimes experience fewer ethnic wars and have lower magnitudes of ethnic rebellion when compared to other regime types. However, this result has not gone unchallenged in the literature, with other researchers showing that democracy exacerbates ethnic divisions and produces greater violence between "at-risk minorities" and the state (Saideman et al. 2002). Moreover, even if we discount Saideman's findings, Gurr's conclusion that democracy inhibits ethnic violence may be challenged on methodological grounds. As pointed out by Gurr himself in an earlier study, we need to be careful not to draw hasty conclusions regarding the explanatory power of democracy with regard to the occurrence of ethnic conflict (Gurr and Moore 1997). According to these authors, the negative relationship between democracy and ethnopolitical rebellion may be spurious—that is, democracy may simply be a proxy measure for repressive state behavior and may not be significant once this repressive behavior is accounted for in the statistical models (Gurr and Moore 1997).

While democratic states are generally less likely to employ state-sanctioned repression than their more autocratic brethren (Poe and Tate 1994; Davenport 1995), it is important not to conflate these concepts for it is not the regime type of a state that makes it more or less repressive but the level of threat it faces. As both Regan and Henderson (2002) and Davenport (2004) have empirically demonstrated, while democracy generally inhibits state repression, this relationship continues to be highly sensitive to levels of domestic and international threat. As such, it makes sense to separate these two concepts in future research. Providing some evidence in support of this conclusion, Gurr and Moore (1997) were unable to find any support for the hypothesized negative relationship between democracy and ethnic violence once they controlled for the level of state repression.

A second potential explanation for the lack of empirical support for the hypothesized relationship between democracy and domestic political violence stems from the theoretical decision to treat democracy as a universal antidote to violent collective action. Given the fact that the capacity of democratic regimes to regulate political conflict is based, at least in part, on their ability to redress socioeconomic grievances, does it make sense to theorize about the conflict-inhibiting power of democratic institutions independent from the larger socioeconomic and political environments in which these regimes are situated?

First, is it reasonable to expect democratic leaders that operate in environments of economic scarcity to be as effective at redressing societal grievances as those that operate in advanced industrial societies? Democratic rulers in poor societies are often placed in the untenable political position of presiding over government institutions that facilitate grievance articulation but lack the resources necessary for effective grievance reduction. Frustrated by the inability of democratic leaders to provide the resources they demand, opposition groups often mobilize their followers in street demonstrations, political protests, and insurrectionary movements (Huntington 1968). Empirical results provided by Hegre (2004) confirm the proposition that the relationship between democracy and domestic political violence is contingent upon the level of economic development. Using an interactive variable that combines the impact of democracy and development, Hegre's results identify two interrelated relationships: (1) that democracy inhibits violence only at middle and high levels of economic development; and (2) that increases in economic development reduce the risks of domestic political violence only in democratic regimes. Hegre concludes that, while autocratic regimes are more effective at regulating societal conflict than democratic regimes in poor societies, the conflict-inhibiting power of autocratic regimes diminishes with development while the regulatory capacity of democratic regimes increases. Given these findings, state autonomy theorists need to be more explicit about the economic conditions under which democracy can, and cannot, be expected to be forwarded by state actors as an antidote to class grievances and violence.

Second, state autonomy theorists may also want to be more explicit about the characteristics associated with democratic governance that contribute to conflict resolution. If democracies are indeed less likely to experience insurgencies, we need to spend more time identifying the causal mechanism behind this process. Keefer (2008), for example, posits that not all democracies are either interested in, or capable of, addressing the social grievances that underlie political conflict. What determines the success of state elites in regulating social conflict is not the mere presence of democratic institutions of horizontal and vertical accountability but, instead, the ability of these democratic elites to make credible promises to large segments of their citizenry by providing them with public goods. As pointed out by Keefer (2008, 59), "political credibility—proxied by the age of the ruling party, whether the ruling party is programmatic, or by the years of continuing competitive elections—significantly reduces the probability of civil war." This is the case because a history of competitive elections, under which programmatic (rather than personalist or factional) political parties emerge, weakens the incentives for rebellion by increasing the size and scope of public goods distribution within society. By contrast, young electoral democracies, which are typically dominated by factional interests and personality-based parties, often rely on clientelism and patronage networks that are ineffective at delivering public goods to large swaths of society and, as a result, continue to stoke the grievance-fomenting insurrectionary movements. While Hegre (2004) argues that democracies are equipped to address the social grievances of society only at higher levels of development, Keefer's work indicates that, even at low levels of economic development, the institutionalization of a competitive electoral system, when coupled with the establishment of programmatic political parties, can provide a sufficient level of credibility to the political order to derail efforts aimed at mobilizing the populace in violent political action.

The State Capacity Perspective: An Empirical Assessment

State capacity theorists posit that the onset, duration, and intensity of violent political action can best be explained by variations in the infrastructural power of the state. Unfortunately, there is no universally accepted measure of this concept that would allow us to systematically assess its empirical power. A review of the recent empirical literature indicates that infrastructural power tends to be operationalized in one of three distinct ways: (1) measures that address the structural barriers to state penetration; (2) measures that evaluate the past political performance of states; and (3) measures of a regime's current administrative and coercive strength. While each of these provides us with some insight into the capacity of states to penetrate society, all have significant weaknesses that make them problematic measures of the concept at hand.

The first approach tries to capture the concept of infrastructural power through an inventory of the geographic and demographic barriers to state penetration.

The logic behind this approach posits that states that are unable to easily penetrate large tracts of land within their territorial borders (owing to dense forests, mountainous topography, territorial fragmentation, etc.) will likely find themselves at a distinct organizational disadvantage to those rebel groups who occupy these "isolated" regions. While the amount of mountainous terrain within societies has been identified as significantly related to the onset of civil war (Fearon and Laitin 2003; Hegre 2004; Fearon 2010; Thies 2010), other studies have shown it to be irrelevant to the onset of ethnic war (Fearon and Laitin 2003) and low-level political conflict (Hegre 2004). Moreover, Elbadawi and Sambanis (2002) conclude that the amount of territory covered in forest has no significant impact on the prevalence of civil war. This result is supported by the work of Collier and Hoeffler (2004), who do not find mountainous terrain *or* forest cover to be strong predictors of civil war initiation. Further contributing to this empirical confusion, while Collier et al. (2004) find that civil war duration was unrelated to these geographic variables, DeRouen and Sobek (2004) concluded that higher levels of forest cover increase the likelihood of prolonged conflict while higher levels of mountainous terrain reduce civil war duration. Finally, states with non-contiguous territorial borders have been shown to be no more likely to either experience a conflict (Fearon and Laitin 2003; Thies 2010) or fight longer ones if they should occur (Fearon 2004) than states with contiguous borders. In summary, if these geographic measures accurately capture the concept of state capacity, then the empirical power of this concept reveals itself to be quite limited.

While very few definitive empirical statements can be made about the impact of geographic measures of infrastructural power on revolutionary behavior, what can we say about the empirical effects of demographic barriers on state penetration? As argued by Fearon and Laitin (2003, 81), a large population base makes the prospects for state monitoring and enforcement more difficult, as it requires "the center to multiply layers of agents to keep tabs on who is doing what at the local level . . . ." From this perspective, increases in population not only expand the pool of potential rebels in society to be monitored by state agents but also make the decision to join the ranks of the rebels less risky. However, if this population is geographically concentrated, in either large urban centers or in a few regional enclaves, the barriers to entry for the state are predicted to fall and, in turn, the potential for collective action is expected to decline (Collier and Hoeffler 2004).

Providing some support for the state capacity perspective, the explanatory power of these demographic variables has been repeatedly demonstrated in recent studies of domestic political violence. For example, the onset of low-level armed conflict (Hegre 2004), civil war (Sambanis 2001; Elbadawi and Sambanis 2002; Fearon and Laitin 2003; Collier and Hoeffler 2004; Hegre 2004; Fearon 2010; Thies 2010), and ethnic war (Fearon and Laitin 2003) have all been shown to be associated with increases in population, as have longer civil wars (Collier et al. 2004) and conflicts in which government forces fail to achieve an outright victory and must simply agree to live in "truce" with rebel groups (DeRouen and Sobek 2004). Moreover, Collier and Hoeffler (2004) conclude that increases in the geographic concentration of a state's population have a powerful negative effect on the onset of revolutionary activity. Despite the relative strength and consistency of these results, Fearon (2004) could not find any support for the claim that higher levels of population produced longer civil wars, while DeSoysa (2002) concluded that the "population density" of a state (i.e., the number of people per square kilometer) *increases* the prospects for domestic political conflict. However, given DeSoysa's lower threshold for civil war inclusion—twenty-five battle deaths versus the standard criteria of 1000—it may be that demographic concentration contributes to sporadic outbursts of low-intensity conflict but not mass-based civil insurrection. Despite some contradictory findings, the recent wave of empirical studies of civil violence seems to suggest that, while state regulation of violent conflict is only weakly influenced by geographic barriers to state penetration, it is strongly impacted by demographic barriers to the exertion of state power. From this we can conclude that, while the state capacity approach may be a potentially powerful predictor of the dynamics of civil violence, what determines the infrastructural power of the state is still poorly understood.

A second approach to measuring the infrastructural power of states is to look at their past political performance in regulating violent collective action. If we argue that "strong" states are less likely to experience episodes of civil war than "weak" states, it seems reasonable to conclude that those states that have experienced less historical political violence are, by definition, "stronger" than those with a more bellicose past. This reasoning gives us some theoretical basis to understanding why "societies that have experienced one civil war are significantly more likely to experience a second or third war than are societies with no prior history of violence" (Walter 2004, 371). While this approach does not give us any additional insight into what determines the infrastructural power of states, it does allow us greater insight into what states will be most vulnerable to civil violence.

In an influential study of civil war onset, Hegre et al. (2001) concluded that an increase in temporal proximity to a previous episode of civil war significantly increases the probability that a state will experience renewed conflict. Providing more evidence to this point, Collier and his associates found that a "typical country reaching the end of a civil war faces around a 44% risk of returning to conflict within five years" (Collier et al. 2003, 83). While other empirical studies have shown past political violence to be a strong predictor of future political instability (Auvinen 1997; Ellingsen 2000; Sambanis 2001; Elbadawi and Sambanis 2002; Collier and Hoeffler 2004), Fearon and Laitin (2003) found that the presence of a distinct civil war within the last year *reduces* the probability of the onset of both civil and ethnic war the following year. While this finding is important, it is probably insufficient, however, to overturn the general body of evidence that indicates that strong states in the past will continue to be strong (and peaceful), while weak states will continue to be weak (and violent).

While the empirical relationship between the temporal proximity of past domestic conflict to future rebellious activity is statistically robust, Walter (2004) points out that not all civil wars are the same. How a previous conflict was conducted and, ultimately, resolved provides us with some significant insight into the prospects for the recurrence of civil war. More specifically, Walter's (2004) analysis indicates that the longer the duration of a previous civil war episode, regardless of whether the government won a "decisive victory" or resolved the underlying grievances of the rebels, the lower the probability that civil war would return to these societies. Moreover, confirming Sambanis's (2000) earlier finding, if governments agree to partition their countries in an effort to resolve these initial conflicts they are significantly more likely to face additional civil violence in the future (Walter 2004). Importantly, while Walter's study indicates that the decision to partition state territory will increase the prospects for new civil wars, it does not seem to contribute to the rekindling of the wars that produced these partitions in the first place. While territorial partition seems to have no impact on the decision of politically autonomous former rebel groups to engage in future acts of violence against their respective states, it has a strong impact on the decision of other "non-autonomous" groups to do so. Walter (2004, 379) explains this phenomenon to be the result of copycat movements who see government concessions over territory as a sign of state weakness. So, while territorial partition may provide state agents with an effective strategy for resolving current political conflicts, this strategy highlights the weakness of the state's capacity to penetrate society and erodes the prospects for long-term political stability and state viability.

A third approach to assessing the infrastructural power of states is to construct measures of bureaucratic strength and coercive reach. One common approach to measuring these dimensions of infrastructural power is to simply factor in the variable of time. The logic behind this decision rests on the assumption that the longer a state has been in existence the greater the odds that it will have higher levels of infrastructural power than younger states. This relationship, which posits state longevity to be negatively related to civil unrest, has been shown to hold across time (Hegre et al. 2001) and when tested against both civil and ethnic war (Fearon and Laitin 2003), with the odds of civil war onset being the highest during a state's first two years of independence (Fearon and Laitin 2003; Fearon 2010).

While the empirical record attests to the vulnerability of young states to political disorder, time should not be seen as a sufficient condition for the expansion of state capacity. Many developing states, for example, continue to persist in strictly juridical terms even though they lack the infrastructural power to extend their writ much beyond the capital city. Supported by both an international legal system based on the concept of juridical sovereignty and a pipeline of resources from powerful international benefactors pursuing both humanitarian and geostrategic agendas, weak states continue to survive in the modern international system even though they often fail to meet the basic standards of empirical statehood posited by state capacity theorists (Jackson and Rosberg 1982). Given this fact, we should not conflate the concept of state persistence with state capacity but, instead, pursue more direct measures of infrastructural power.

Efforts to more directly measure the infrastructural power of states typically take one of two forms: (1) those that inventory the size of a state's coercive capabilities; and (2) those that proxy coercive effectiveness through measures of economic development. While both efforts seek to evaluate the financial, organizational, and political strength of state actors, both approaches have significant problems. First, efforts to measure the infrastructural power of states through indicators of military capacity start from the questionable assumption that large militaries signal state strength. Recent empirical studies on civil war onset and outcome suggest that indicators of military size are, at best, inconsistent predictors of political stability.

In general, there is little empirical evidence to suggest that the size of the state's military apparatus will weaken the prospects for civil war. In fact, the limited evidence found in the literature tends to suggest that higher levels of military expenditures have no significant deterrent effect on the prospects for civil war (Auvinen 1997; Henderson and Singer 2000; Collier et al. 2003). One potential explanation for this unexpected result can be found in the fact that military spending is strongly correlated with rising levels of political insecurity, as less effective governments commonly attempt to prevent rebellion by substantially raising conventional military expenditures (Collier et al. 2003, 71). High military spending, then, is often a sign of state weakness rather than state strength.

Since the size of the military apparatus seems to be a poor measure of state strength, most analysts have chosen to use economic development data as a proxy for state capacity. As argued by Fearon and Laitin (2003, 80),

> a *higher per capita income* should be associated with a lower risk of civil war onset because (a) it is a proxy for a state's overall financial, administrative, police, and military capabilities, and (b) it will mark more developed countries with terrain more "disciplined" by roads and rural society more penetrated by central administration.

In general, the empirical literature confirms the negative relationship between measures of economic development and the onset of both civil (Ellingsen 2000; Henderson and Singer 2000; Sambinis 2001; Elbadawi and Sambanis 2002; Fearon and Laitin 2003; Collier and Hoeffler 2004; Fearon 2010; Thies 2010) and ethnic (Saideman et al. 2002; Fearon and Laitin 2003) war. Collier and his associates (2004) also found that higher levels of economic development are correlated with shorter civil wars, although this result could not be replicated by Fearon's (2004) research. Despite some contradictory findings, there exists a persuasive body of evidence that suggests that states at higher levels of economic development confront fewer, but not necessarily less protracted, civil and ethnic wars.

Despite the overall strength of this relationship, the conflict-inhibiting nature of economic progress confronts an apparent paradox: while economic progress has been noted virtually everywhere in the developing world in the second half of the twentieth century the number of armed conflicts, surprisingly, increased steadily throughout most of this period. As pointed out by Mack (2002, 521), "Should we not have expected the reverse to be the case, given the importance that both Collier and Hoeffler and Fearon and Laitin attach to rising incomes as an antidote to war?" In order to make sense of this paradox, Hegre and his associates (2001) posit that the relationship between economic development and the onset of domestic political violence is parabolic, rather than linear, in structure, with the highest probability for civil war expected to occur at mid-levels of economic development. The hypothesized curvilinear nature of this relationship flows from Huntington's (1968) argument that the process of economic development increases the prospects for civil unrest owing to the intersection of rising societal expectations with the persistent institutional weakness of the state apparatus. That is, improvements in economic development typically increase societal grievances *without* creating equivalent, and immediate, increases in state capacity. While Hegre and his associates (2001) found empirical support for the inverted U hypothesis, other researchers have failed to substantiate the claim that middle-income countries have a greater propensity for protracted civil unrest (Fearon and Laitin 2003; Collier et al. 2004). While no definitive statements regarding the development–instability nexus can be derived from the empirical record at this juncture, the persistence of this debate should, at a minimum, call into question the central empirical assertion of state capacity researchers that increases in economic development proxies concomitant increases in state power.

While the conflict-inhibiting power of economic development—either in its monotonic or parabolic form—has been shown to have some empirical support, the real problem with employing this indicator rests in trying to explain why this is the case. As suggested earlier, state capacity theorists, such as Fearon and Laitin (2003), view economic development as a proxy for a state's infrastructural power. While this is a reasonable inference, this is only one of many possible reasonable inferences that can be drawn from the finding that economic development serves as an effective prophylactic against insurgency. A cursory review of the recent empirical literature reveals that economic development is associated with (1) an increase in state capacity (Fearon and Laitin 2003); (2) an increase in the opportunity costs of joining a rebel movement owing to rising economic prospects (Collier and Hoeffler 2004; Collier et al. 2004); (3) an increase in *both* state capacity and the opportunity costs to potential rebels (Sambanis 2001; Elbadawi and Sambanis 2002); and (4) a decrease in economic grievances (Auvinen 1997; Henderson and Singer 2000; Hegre et al. 2001). All of these explanations are equally plausible and all demonstrate the general lack of fit between the empirical proxy—economic development—and the theoretical construct that it seeks to capture. Lacking any definitive mechanism for untangling the causal forces contained within the concept of economic development, we would be well advised to be cautious when making any claims that the violence-inhibiting power of this variable stems from one specific theoretical perspective. While states operating in environments of economic prosperity can safely be said to hold, on average, higher levels of state power than those operating in environments of economic scarcity, for state capacity theories to be empirically persuasive they will have to find more direct, and empirically less ambiguous, measures of infrastructural power to test their theoretical arguments.

Political Opportunity Perspective: An Empirical Assessment

While there exists significant empirical support for the state capacity hypothesis that lower levels of infrastructural power produce higher levels of social unrest, the political opportunity hypothesis—that states wielding mid-levels of despotic power are the most prone to violent insurrection—has also found significant statistical support. Building on the positive results of earlier studies (Muller and Seligson 1987; Boswell and Dixon 1990; Muller and Weede 1990), recent studies have shown that the prospects for both civil unrest (Ellingsen and Gleditsch 1997; Ellingsen 2000; Henderson and Singer 2000; Hegre et al. 2001; DeSoysa 2002; Fearon and Laitin 2003) and ethnic conflict (Sambanis 2001; Reynal-Querol 2002) are related to regime openness in an inverted U pattern. Representative of this work, Goldstone and his associates found that weak democracies confront a hazard of ethnic war over 800 times greater than that experienced by either strong democracies or any autocratic regime (Goldstone et al. 2004, 27). Moreover, both Schock (1996) and Auvinen (1997) found that semi-democratic regimes experienced higher magnitudes of political violence than other regime types.

Despite the strong initial support for the inverted U hypothesis, some recent empirical analyses have failed to demonstrate this relationship, finding semi-democratic regimes to be no more likely to fall prey to civil war than other regime types (Sambanis 2001; Elbadawi and Sambanis 2002; Collier and Hoeffler 2004). Moreover, in her study of civil war reoccurrence, Walter (2004) found that while semi-democratic regimes are no more likely to experience a renewed civil war than autocratic regimes, they are significantly more likely to experience a return of violent instability than fully democratic regimes. While the body of evidence still strongly favors the claim that semi-democratic regimes are more prone to violence than either democratic or authoritarian regimes, these non-findings should give us pause. How can we explain the lack of support for the political opportunity hypothesis in these studies?

Recall that political opportunity theorists make three core arguments regarding regime structures and political violence: (1) that more open regimes increase the prospects for successful collective organization; (2) that more open regimes reduce the risks associated with collective action; and (3) that less open regimes lower the opportunity costs of violent collective action. While each of these arguments posit a linear relationship with collective political violence, the fact that the first two pull in the opposite direction to the third provides the theoretical rationale behind the proposition that regimes at mid-levels of political openness are the most prone to instability. While the linear structures of the first and third arguments seem empirically well grounded, the second argument, that collective action is a relatively safe, low-cost endeavor in semi-democratic systems (compared with authoritarian systems), has proven itself to be more problematic. In fact, the research conducted by Regan and Henderson (2002) discussed earlier should, at a minimum, make us question the proposition that increases in regime openness produce concomitant decreases in state repression. If we find that regime openness and respect for human rights are not associated with one another in a linear manner, then one of the undergirding propositions of the political opportunity perspective becomes severely compromised.

Failure to find support for the inverted U hypothesis may stem from the fact that state repression may also be related to regime openness in an inverted U pattern (Fein 1995). In contrast to the argument put forward by political opportunity theorists, regimes that exert mid-levels of despotic power may not actually lower the risks associated with violent collective action. Adding empirical support for this position, both Regan and Henderson (2002) and Fearon (2010) found that semi-democratic and weak authoritarian regimes in the developing world were, in fact, *more likely* to utilize the tools of state coercion than were either fully auto-cratic or consolidated democratic regimes. This finding can be explained by the higher levels of threat perceived by state actors in these types of regime. While consolidated democratic regimes channel political opposition into highly institu-tionalized and regulated avenues of political participation, fully autocratic regimes can shut down the institutions of public debate before grievances escalate into demands for political reform. In both cases, the demands from civil society are perceived to be of limited direct threat to the continued rule of state elites. However, the institutional weakness associated with semi-democratic regimes encourages their leaders to respond harshly to opposition threats out of fear of political usurpation; "because leaders of semi-democratic regimes view their regimes as more vulnerable to threats, they respond more harshly to threats" (Regan and Henderson 2002, 124).

If the relationship between regime openness and state repression is indeed parabolic in structure, then the political opportunity hypothesis that political liberalization is related to civil unrest in a curvilinear manner is severely weak-ened. Under these conditions, the threat of violent collective action would be most likely to occur in regimes where there is a high probability of successful collective organization (e.g., democracies), low opportunity costs associated with violent collective action (e.g., autocracies) *and* a low threat of direct regime sanc-tion (e.g., democracies *or* autocracies). In this scenario, semi-democratic regimes would seem to offer little advantage over the other regime types when it comes to mobilizing for violent collective action.

While it may be true that highly autocratic states (that is, those states with high degrees of despotic power) *may* be able to limit the avenues for political expression so completely that widespread acts of state repression become unnecessary, this level of control over society has more to do with the ability of states to penetrate society (that is, with their level of infrastructural power) than with the institutional design of the regime itself. In other words, when it comes to the decision to join a rebellion, potential recruits will likely be more influenced by the *de facto* capacity of the state to regulate and sanction their behavior rather than by the *de jure* design of the regimes that govern them. While regime structure (or the distribution of despotic power) may tell us something about the institutional ability of rulers to isolate themselves from the demands of civil society when developing policy initiatives, it tells us relatively little about their actual capacity to prevent civil society from responding to these initiatives through non-conventional means. In short, the potential for regime sanction should not be derived from the institutional design of the regime itself, but instead should be measured independently from the allocation of despotic power in society. It is a mistake to assume that closed states (those with high levels of despotic power) can actually penetrate society and sanction political challengers.

While the vulnerability of semi-democratic regimes to civil unrest has shown itself to have some support in the empirical literature, the theoretical explanation for this relationship remains underdeveloped. As suggested by Hegre et al. (2001, 34), "Compared to well-established democracies or autocracies, intermediate regimes have a higher hazard of civil war, as do regimes just emerging from a political transition. Are these two findings one and the same?" In other words, are semi-democratic regimes associated with higher levels of domestic political violence because the institutional incoherence of these regimes provides ample political opportunities and incentives for collective action (a political opportunity argument) or because they are more unstable and, hence, less likely to be able to effectively penetrate and control society (a state capacity argument)? Or, perhaps, is it the interaction of these two factors—institutional incoherence and institutional instability—that provides the fertile ground for civil unrest and political chaos found in semi-democratic regimes?

A number of recent empirical studies have tested the relationship between regime instability and the propensity for domestic political violence. By regime instability I am referring to the stability of authority relations within the polity. Polities with little observable change in their levels of despotic power are regarded as having stable authority patterns, while those in which the allocation and distribution of despotic power is in constant flux are said to exhibit unstable patterns of authority. Using a two-point shift in the 21-point Polity index as a measure of regime instability, Hegre and his associates (2001) found civil war onset to be strongly associated with temporal proximity to changes in authority patterns. While Hegre was unable to substantiate this finding in a subsequent study (2004), the relationship has nevertheless been documented in other analyses (Ellingsen 2000; Fearon and Laitin 2003; Fearon 2010). In addition, it has been shown that regime change has an impact on the prospects for civil war onset irrespective of the direction or magnitude of the changes in political structure (Hegre et al. 2001). Whether the state is shedding or accumulating despotic power seems to have little discernable impact on the occurrence of civil war, although Fearon (2010) did find a slightly stronger tendency for civil war to follow regime shifts in the direction of authoritarian rather than democratic rule. Despite the relatively strong support for the proposition that regime instability promotes the onset of civil war, Fearon and Laitin (2003) found regime instability to be unrelated to ethnic war onset, while Saideman and his associates (2002) concluded that regime instability *decreased* the magnitude of ethnic mobilization and rebellion.

The finding that regime instability increases the hazards of civil war onset confirms the political opportunity argument posited by McAdam (1996, 27) that institutional instability provides fertile ground for opposition movements to take root. By upsetting the broad set of elite alignments that undergird the polity, regime transitions send powerful signals to potential challenger groups that the political regime may be beset by internal power struggles and, hence, vulnerable to social mobilization (Tarrow 1994). Regime instability, in other words, provides a rare opportunity for political challengers to forge temporary alliances with disgruntled elite factions necessary for the effective organization of rebellion. While this is a compelling theoretical narrative, once again, this argument, which emphasizes the "internal power struggles" within the state coalition and its "vulnerability to social mobilization," seems to better reflect the power distribution logic of state capacity theory rather than institutional design arguments favored by political opportunity theorists. While these two state-centric approaches typically try to establish strong theoretical boundaries to separate themselves from one another, these borders are actually quite permeable and, ultimately, may prove to be counter productive.

The political opportunity perspective, then, provides us with two empirically supported explanations for the onset of violent collective action. First, regimes that exert mid-levels of despotic power tend to be more vulnerable to the onset of civil war than do those regimes which exert only limited or extreme amounts of despotic power. Second, states that are plagued by regime instability (and, hence, low infrastructural power) also tend to be beset by societal violence. At this juncture it is now necessary to ask whether these two explanations are theoretically and empirically related to one another. Could it be that semi-democratic regimes experience higher hazards for political conflict because they are the most vulnerable to regime instability?

As first pointed out by Gurr (1974), polities with mixed authority patterns (e.g., "semi-democracies," "anocracies," "weak authoritarian regimes," "partial democracies," "illiberal democracies," and "institutionally incoherent polities") tend to experience much lower rates of political persistence, or regime durability, than those regimes with more coherent authority patterns. Providing additional support for this finding, Hegre and his associates (2001) documented the median life span of semi-democratic regimes during the period 1800–1992 at 5.8 years, while full autocracies and democracies persisted 7.9 and 10 years, respectively.

From the body of empirical evidence discussed above we can make three statistical statements and draw one empirical inference. First, semi-democratic regimes experience higher hazards of violent political conflict than either fully democratic or fully autocratic regimes. Second, semi-democratic regimes experience higher hazards of regime instability than either fully democratic or fully autocratic regimes. Third, unstable political regimes experience higher hazards of civil war than stable political regimes. From these three findings we can infer that a significant portion of the political violence experienced by semi-democratic regimes can reasonably be attributed to the propensity for regime instability associated with this regime type.

Despite the relatively strong empirical support for the political opportunity theory, a recent study by Gleditsch and Ruggeri (2010) has reconsidered the central premise of this perspective, which identifies the institutional arrangement of despotic power as the driving force behind the opportunity for collective action. From their perspective, higher incidents of civil unrest are not caused by the political opportunities created by the "incoherent" structure of the regime itself but, instead, by the manner in which state rulers enter and exit their positions of authority. In particular, they hypothesize that "irregular leadership changes"— those in which executive recruitment is defined by non-constitutional and often coercive transfers of power, better signal windows of opportunity for violent collective action than the semi-democratic nature of the regime itself. These abrupt and unpredicted transfers of power vividly demonstrate the weakness of the state and, as such, alter the decision-making calculus of potential rebels in favor of collective action over free-riding. This study is particularly important because of both its empirical results and theoretical implications.

While the inverted U hypothesis was confirmed by Gleditsch and Ruggeri (2010) in their initial model of civil war onset, once they introduced the influence of "irregular leadership transitions" into their models the violence-inducing nature of semi-democratic regimes began to weaken as the positive (although time-dependent) influence of irregular leadership transfers was empirically captured. In fact, their models tend to show that, contrary to the general expectation of political opportunity theorists, the relationship between democracy and civil unrest is both *monotonic and negative in structure*. That is, as predicted by state autonomy theorists, higher levels of democracy weaken the prospects for civil unrest. According to Gleditsch and Ruggeri (2010, 306),

It is unlikely that something about the institutions of a partial democracy per se increases the risk of conflict, but rather something about the ways in which a country comes to be a partial democracy that may be associated with a higher risk of conflict.

While civil violence will likely occur in societies with incoherent authority patterns, nonetheless, this is not the primary cause of political violence. Instead, these semi-democratic structures, in which state elites employ a mix of accommodative and repressive political strategies, simply reflect the weakness of the infrastructural power of these elites to penetrate and control their societies. By failing to consolidate and centralize their infrastructural power, these elites remain vulnerable to challenges to their authority and are constantly beset by the threat of irregular transfers of power. It is the unstable and unregulated nature of elite recruitment, not the anocratic structure of the regime itself, that signals state weakness and provides the opportunity for potential political challengers to mobilize mass political action against the state. While the empirical results presented by Gleditsch and Ruggeri (2010) still affirm democratic liberalization as an effective tool for ameliorating social unrest (a state autonomy argument), the ability of liberal reforms to quell political violence is ultimately dependent on the capacity of the state to increase its infrastructural power (a state capacity argument) and limit the prospects for irregular leadership transfers that can signal state weakness and encourage civil unrest (a political opportunity argument). In this way, this study combines, and affirms, insights from all three of the state-centric perspectives outlined by Goodwin and offers us the best course for further inquiries into the relationship between political authority and civil violence.

Conclusion

In addition to outlining the three dominant state-centric theoretical approaches to violent collective action, this analysis has sought to evaluate the explanatory power of these theories against the recent cross-national statistical research. In summary, the state autonomy perspective has fared the least well. Its central hypothesis, that higher levels of democracy produce lower levels of violent collective action, has received only limited support in the empirical literature (e.g., Hegre 2004; Keefer 2008; Gleditsch and Ruggeri 2010). In contrast to the relatively weak performance of the state autonomy perspective, both the state capacity approach and the political opportunity perspective have garnered stronger empirical support. While low levels of infrastructural power have been shown to increase the prospects for domestic political violence, mid-levels of despotic power have also been consistently correlated with escalating levels of bellicosity. Despite these positive results, persistent methodological issues have been observed in these empirical studies.

While the state-centric approach has provided scholars of domestic political conflict with a number of testable propositions and a handful of tantalizing results, the field nonetheless remains plagued by theoretical debates, methodological controversies, and contradictory findings. Moreover, the intellectual balkanization surrounding these approaches, in which they are viewed as competing perspectives to the study of civil unrest, has further hindered our progress. Instead of seeking to stake out intellectual ground at the expense of alternative state-centric approaches, efforts such as that of Gleditsch and Ruggeri (2010), which seek to empirically identify the interrelationships between democratic reform, state capacity and political opportunity, should be actively encouraged.

6

DYNAMICS AND PROCESSES

Linkages Between Internal and External Conflict

Harvey Starr and Marc V. Simon

This chapter provides an overview of major approaches and directions to the study of conflict primarily by international relations scholars in recent years. Several major trends in the study of world conflict over the past two decades may be discerned. First, many scholars have explicitly looked at conflict *processes*—whether in the origination, escalation, duration, or termination of conflict. Secondly, such studies have self-consciously identified the *contexts* in which such processes have taken place, and the conditions under which these processes are most likely to take place. Thus, what had been formerly considered to be subfield focused on "international conflict"—with a heavy reliance on a Realist view that the only conflict of consequence occurred between "states"—became a subfield much more fully placed within the broader study of *social conflict* (for an overview, see Pruitt and Kim 2004). As such, the study of conflict processes returned to a group of trends that first emerged in the 1940s and 1950s, which relied on the multidisciplinary study of conflict (e.g., Wright 1942; 1968).

With these two basic trends as a foundation, several other distinctive features of recent scholarship may also be noted. As part of a broad-based critique of Realism, and a major movement away from its core assumptions, the study of conflict came to include a variety of international and domestic actors, not only states. Along with the study of transnational relations, interdependence, and the amorphous idea of "globalization," various transnational actors (particularly terrorist groups), and domestic actors (particularly ethnic groups and minorities within states), have been studied as conflict groups (highlighted by the work of Gurr, e.g., 2000). Owing to a variety of factors, over the course of the post-World War II period the dominant form of conflict has clearly moved from inter-state conflict to *intra*-state conflict.[1] Thus, over the past fifteen to twenty years many students of "international conflict" also moved into the study of civil wars and other forms of domestic conflict (e.g., Midlarsky 2009). At the same time, scholars were devoting far more time to studies in which the dependent conflict variable was not "war" but "militarized disputes," employing the Correlates of War Militarized Interstate Disputes (COW MIDs) datasets.[2]

In addition to focusing more explicitly on the domestic aspects of conflict, another of the more important variations in focus has been adding the *political* domestic environment to the more usual focus on economics. This is best illustrated by the significant attention devoted to the democratic peace (and its multiple variants and spin-offs) over the past twenty-five to thirty years.[3] Yet another trend that adds to the complexity already mentioned has been the inclusion of *spatial* dimensions to the more usual and ubiquitous temporal setting (e.g., Starr 2005; 2013). The spatial dimension is best illustrated by works involving the study of diffusion processes and the now omnipresent use of contiguity in both inter-state and intra-state conflict.

In order to deal with the broad issue of contexts in all of its forms and combinations, an essential starting point is to review the nature of conflict. Beginning with broad characterizations of social conflict, we first outline a number of commonalities that exist across both internal/domestic and external/international conflict. This discussion employs an agent–structure perspective whereby decision-making and action-taking agents sit within multiple and overlapping environments which affect both decisions and actions (e.g., Friedman and Starr 1997). Thus, one goal of our discussion is the demonstration that such commonalities can be addressed using the opportunity and willingness framework (Most and Starr 1989), which was developed as an extension of the interests of Harold and Margaret Sprout (1956; 1969) in understanding non-deterministic "environments."

Our second goal is to investigate further *how* internal and external linkages are created. This brings in the spatial dimension, and will be done through a discussion of boundaries/borders. This discussion will begin with a basic overview of space and spatiality, how location affects conflict, and how borders delineate both the internal and external domains of conflict. Several broad models connecting the internal and external will be noted, because they demonstrate how the application of opportunity and willingness, substitutability, and spatiality can help us understand conflict processes. We will tie together the various strands of literature discussed in this chapter by describing a computer simulation developed by the authors as part of their Two-Level Security Management Project (e.g., Simon and Starr 1997). We will discuss why simulation may be a useful way to deal with the complexity of studying conflict processes and indicate a number of implications from the findings generated by our particular simulation.

Finally, we will consider how the study of conflict crosses boundaries. In this respect, the study of conflict reflects themes in the field of international relations and the political science discipline in general. These themes reflect debates over both the way scholars approach their research and the substance of that study. Crossing boundaries entails crossing levels of analysis, something that is facilitated by the use of agent–structure models. The study of conflict processes does so by looking at the ways in which processes might work differently under different conditions which reflect a range of levels of analysis. Crossing boundaries also entails crossing sub-disciplinary boundaries. The study of international conflict reflects a more general trend regarding International Relations and Comparative Politics, whereby the lines between these subfields are increasingly blurred (see Werner et al. 2003, 1).

Starting with Thucydides and Aristotle, Russett (2003) notes that the great writers on politics understood how what "we call international relations and comparative politics informed each other" (2003, 9). While Starr (2006, 3) has argued that this trend toward "reintegration" was initiated by the introduction of transnational politics over forty years ago, he also notes that "it gathered force in the work of James Rosenau (e.g. 1990) on 'turbulent systems' during the 1980s and 1990s . . . ."[4] Crossing boundaries thus entails merging various aspects of IR and Comparative Politics—domestic and external processes and factors (Stohl 1980). This is best captured in the study of internal and external conflict as two-level games, the democratic peace, and political economy. The single most prominent example may be found in the path-breaking project on the logic of political survival (Bueno de Mesquita et al. 2003). Their model of political survival has been applied not only to the democratic peace but to some of the most central questions raised by Comparative Politics and International Relations. Following from the above, scholars must also cross boundaries in terms of methods and approaches, requiring scholars to more clearly specify the differences (and similarities!) between "qualitative" and "quantitative" research and the relationship of basic research to applied research.

Theoretical Frameworks: Models of Internal–External Relationships

Starr (1994) attempted to explain the lack of cumulation and progress in work written primarily in the 1960s that studied the relationships between internal and external conflict. A number of deficiencies of theory, logic, and research design were identified. By identifying a number of analogies between civil conflict and inter-state war, a "common logic" of conflict was developed which focused on the calculations of governmental decision-makers who were required simultaneously to deal with domestic and foreign threats to state/governmental security. The common logic rested on analogies that reflected similarities in the forms, components, and sources of conflict and similar processes of choice. These analogies focus on the *choices* made by government leaders and the leaders of either external or internal challengers. They include analyses based on "power," in the sense of resources that were required to deal with internal or external challengers, and the consequences for extracting such resources domestically or internationally. Returning to a basic definition of conflict—that social conflict derives from *incompatibilities* between social units—it is clear that there is a common core of sources of internal and external conflict.[5] Governments face incompatibilities with other governments and with internal opposition over "who gets what when and how." Many students of revolution and war base their analyses not only on the cost–benefit calculations of governments but also on those that challengers make before taking on a government—calculations that include the probability of winning. For example, Tilly's (1985b) approach to collective violence strongly parallels Gilpin's (1981) view of hegemon–challenger relations at the level of the international system. The literature on social movements and political protest is more explicitly concerned with the collective action problem (Olson 1965), and has evolved into theoretical debates which divide neatly into those focusing on willingness and those which emphasize opportunity (see Opp 2009).[6]

Analogies exist in the similarity of typologies of conflict based on the extent/size/intensity of the violence (whether internal or external). Both types of conflict may be characterized along other lines in addition to sheer size—the consequences for change and order. Midlarsky (1990, 174) notes: "Revolutions and systemic wars share one final overarching similarity. At bottom, they are concerned with the choice of a societal order, at both the domestic and international levels." Goldstone's work on revolution (1991) presents a typology of relationships that broadly reflects Midlarsky's view on small wars, wars among some large powers, and systemic-change hegemonic wars. Goldstone (1989, 224) notes simply: "In sum, revolution, like war, is in Clausewitz's famous dictum, 'politics by other means'." A foundational synthesizing thread is the survival of governments or leaders from either external or internal challenges.

Both types of conflict require at least two parties, and the emergence of violent conflict is the result of the *interdependent choices* of the two parties. As Most and Starr (1989) make clear, both parties *must* possess *both* the opportunity and willingness to pursue the conflict. Thus, such interdependent-outcome phenomena cannot, logically, be explained by linear, additive, cross-sectionally analyzed combinations of single-actor attributes (Most and Starr 1989).

In regard to conflict processes, both forms of conflict are concerned with "mobilization, organization, and collective action" (Oberschall 1978, 305) to support a unit's efforts against some opponent. Conflict at either level can escalate to violence or to higher (or broader) levels of violence, or de-escalate to stalemate or resolution (on escalation, see Pruitt and Kim 2004). Escalation may involve the expansion of the conflict to new areas, or the addition of new parties/combatants. Internal coalitions may grow around the government and its primary opposition in the same way that alliances form in the international arena. That is, *diffusion* processes are inherent in social conflict. Thus, the interaction opportunity model of diffusion (Most and Starr 1980) can be used to deal with the growth of violent conflicts at both levels.

Theoretically, the common logic based on opportunity, willingness, and the choices of leaders compels the analyst to theorize explicitly the nature of the linkages between internal and external conflict. For example: *Under what conditions* will internal conflict-to-external conflict relationships be found? *Under what conditions* will external conflict-to-internal conflict relationships be found? Did internal conflict increase the probability that a government would attack another state, or be the target of an external opponent? Did a war situation lead a government to crack down on internal opposition or weaken a government to the point that an internal opponent was willing to initiate violence?

Internal–External Conflict and Multiple Games[7]

The framework set out above highlights the strategic choices made by leaders whose government or internal opposition group is in conflict with another party. These leaders must consider the goals of the external opponent as well as the views of members of their own group or constituencies (or, in Bueno de Mesquita's terms, the "selectorate"). This problem has a long history in sociology, as in the work of Simmel (1950), Coser (1956), and their predecessors. Since the publication of Putnam (1988), this phenomenon has been broadly termed "two-level games."

Putnam (1988, 427) addressed the complexity that decision-makers face—dealing with external actors (in his work, other states) as one game, but needing internal support or ratification for the agreements made with external parties (a second game):

> Neither of the two games can be ignored by central decision-makers ... Each national leader appears at both game boards ... *The unusual complexity of this two-level game is that moves that are rational for a player at one board (such as raising energy prices, conceding territory, or limiting auto imports) may be impolitic for that same player at the other board* [emphasis added].

Because of the complexity of the games, decision-makers might get caught in a series of remedial moves from one arena to another as the feedback from an action in one arena worsens the game in the other. In a related discussion of how preferences aggregate, Kuran (1988, 24) notes that the use of "multiple models ... means that surprise is inevitable. . . . The surprises are likely to be diagnosed incorrectly."[8]

A related version of what is "rational" when leaders face multiple games is provided by Tsebelis (1990) as "nested games." Tsebelis is concerned with the *appearance* of irrationality in the choices of decision-makers, when observers perceive people making what seem to be suboptimal choices. He argues that this occurs because decision-makers play multiple games in multiple arenas, "[where] any of the actor's moves has consequences in all arenas; an optimal alternative in one arena (or game) will not necessarily be optimal with respect to the entire network of arenas in which the actor is involved" (1990, 7–8). Putnam highlights another dimension which needs to be stressed: the individuals involved in decision-making may not fully understand how decisions made in respect to one arena will affect another. Individuals acting under some form of bounded rationality can easily find themselves making a series of remedial moves in one arena and then the other, reacting to the negative consequences of their actions. Thus, the whole set of possible relationships between internal and external conflict may be seen as some form of a nested or two-level game. As such, our logic must expand to take into account opportunity, willingness, and substitutability.

Opportunity, Willingness, and Substitutability

Friedman and Starr (1997) consider the work of Harold and Margaret Sprout and Starr's opportunity and willingness framework as the "first generation" of international politics agent–structure theorists. The Sprouts' (1956, 17–19) notion of the "ecological triad"—i.e., entity, environment, and entity–environment relationships—addressed the relationship between agency and structure, the internal and the external. The Sprouts provided three useful ways to address the ecological triad: (1) environmental possibilism refers to structure and is defined as "a number of factors which limit human opportunities, which constrain the type of action that can be taken as well as the consequences of that action" (Most and Starr 1989, 27); (2) cognitive behaviorism represents "the simple and familiar principle that a person reacts to his milieu as he apperceives it—that is, as he perceives and interprets it in light of past experience" (Sprout and Sprout 1969, 45); (3) environmental probabilism represents both the core concept of uncertainty in political behavior (Cioffi-Revilla and Starr 1995, 451) and what may be viewed as a synthesis of these first two relationships. It refers to "explanation or prediction by means of a generalized model, of the average or typical person's reaction to a given milieu" (Sprout and Sprout 1956, 50). In other words, the attributes of an agent's environment "provide cues as to the probability of certain outcomes" (Most and Starr 1989, 27).

These three Sproutian views on the relationship between entity and environment were developed "as alternatives to environmental determinism, where, by definition, decision-makers are incapable of choice given the characteristics of the environment, or 'milieu'" (Sprout and Sprout 1969, 44). Most and Starr's (1989, 27–9) discussion of the virtues of the ecological triad can itself be viewed as a statement of the agent–structure problem, in that the ecological triad is applicable across levels of analysis and forces analysts to look within *both* the unit of analysis/ entity and its environment. The ultimate entities, single decision-makers "make choices within a complex set of *incentive structures*. This can be captured only by looking at all three parts of the ecological triad" (Most and Starr 1989, 29).

Most and Starr demonstrate that the two pre-theoretic concepts of opportunity and willingness can serve as organizing concepts for the international relations literature and that all independent variables explaining social phenomena can be characterized as either agent or structural variables. The inter-relationship between agency and structure is presented in the terms of Russett's menu metaphor (1972).

The menu "provides a number of behavioral/choice possibilities, not determining the diner's choice, but limiting it" (Most and Starr 1989, 28). The agent must be able to "read" the menu (cognitive behaviorism), reflecting the Sprouts' insistence that agents must be aware of the possibilities made available by the environment. Factors based in both the agent (values, preferences, resources, etc.) and the structure (prices, size of portion, etc.) will make certain choices more or less likely (environmental probabilism).

The menu metaphor is also useful for thinking about the relationships between opportunity and willingness. Most and Starr (1989) and Cioffi-Revilla and Starr (1995) demonstrate how opportunities (the menu) create the incentive structures for willingness (the food orders actually chosen). Indeed, a common theme in such works is how opportunity can generate greater levels and forms of willingness. But willingness can also lead to different levels of opportunity, as an agent can ask for something that is *not* on the menu. By so doing, the agent may also change the menu itself. Technological innovation, for example, changes both the meaning of the geopolitical context and the available set of environmental possibilities (e.g., Siverson and Starr 1991; Goertz 1994). Similarly, all human innovation, including the creation of new ideas, ideologies, and modes of organization or production, change the "menu."

As noted, a fundamental premise of the opportunity and willingness framework is that *both* the environment/structural level and the decision-making/choice level are required for behavior, as well as for a full description and explanation of behavior. In addition, opportunity and willingness must have crossed some minimal levels or thresholds before behavior occurs. This jointly necessary view of opportunity and willingness as a statement of the agent–structure problem represents a central prescription for theories of foreign policy analysis and the common logic used in this chapter.

The Spatial Dimension: Interaction Opportunity and Identity

One key component of the menu items that face the decision-makers of any conflict group is spatial, involving location and territory. Spatiality has an impact on both opportunity and willingness because of its impact on the physical and psychological environment (see especially Starr 2003; 2005). In particular, Starr (2003; 2013) reviewed geographers' thinking about space and spatiality to help political scientists understand why the spatial or locational settings of behaviors need to be included along with the temporal dimensions. Spatiality confronts scholars with the question of "distance"—how close or far units are within some concept of space, a classic question raised by many students of conflict, including Boulding's (1962) seminal notion of the loss-of-strength gradient (LSG) (see Gleditsch and Ward (2001) and Henrikson (2002) for discussions of distance).

Territory serves at least two distinct purposes in the study of conflict. First, by defining territorial political units, territory creates spatial arrangements of the units indicating the physical distance between those units. This "distance" is dynamic, in that the *time–distance* between those units changes with changing technologies of transportation and communication, or with changes of the arrangements of the units through alliances or the merging of units through conquest or voluntary integration. As noted in Starr and Siverson (1990), alliances can act as *political technology* by changing the *absolute* distance between units. State A, which does not have a contiguous border with State B, is now able to border State B through an alliance with State C, which is contiguous to B. This exact issue arose regarding NATO, Turkey, and Iraq prior to and immediately after the onset of the 2003 Iraq War, given the desire of the US to reduce the LSG of bringing military force to bear on Iraq. The conquest of territory can create new borders (as in the expansion of Russia or the US across their respective continents, or the Napoleonic expansion across Europe). The breakup of states or empires can create new borders (as in the post-USSR or post-Yugoslavian situations, or the redrawing of the world map after World War I, with the dissolution of the Ottoman, Russian, and Austro-Hungarian empires). Borders were also altered with the reunification of Germany after the fall of the Berlin Wall and dissolution of the Warsaw Pact.

These spatial arrangements are important aspects of opportunity. States that are in close proximity to each other are better able to interact. This is the "interaction opportunity" argument or approach, deriving from the Sprouts as well as geographers such as Zipf (1949, 6) and his "principle of least effort." Proximity also makes states (or other social units) that are close to one another "relevant" to one another—they are both easier to get to and more important (Gleditsch's 2002 (p. 68) "connectivity matrix" analysis extends the concept of actors which are "relevant" to each other through spatial or behavioral proximity).

Secondly, the spatial concept of boundaries affects willingness. As the place where peoples live, territory provides an important component of group identity (e.g., Coser 1956) and becomes endowed with extraordinary symbolic importance to people. In addition, territory also provides real resource value to people (e.g., arable land, potable water, minerals, access to seas or rivers, and other topographic features of military value). Territory, and territorial proximity, takes on value across many dimensions: *territory is important to humans* across all levels of social aggregation. It both becomes a source of conflict and raises the stakes of any conflict. Thus, the spatial proximity of states increases the probability of conflict both through interaction opportunities as well as creating the stakes or causes of conflict. The results of the many studies of spatiality, territory, borders, and conflict have been summed up in a number of excellent reviews (see, e.g., Vasquez and Senese 2003; Diehl 1999; Hensel 2000; Starr 2005). Findings include that conflict over territory is exceptionally difficult to resolve; that proximity, especially as measured by contiguous borders, increases the probability of conflict; and that proximity increases the probability that conflict will diffuse to other areas.[9] However, it is only recently that such factors have been explicitly added and addressed in the study of civil war (see the work of various scholars associated with Peach Research Institute Oslo (PRIO), especially Buhaug and colleagues: Buhaug and Gates 2002; Buhaug and Lujala 2005; Raleigh et al. 2010).

Substitutability

Even if we can establish the opportunity and willingness for some goal-oriented action, we must account for the problem that actors may choose from many different, substitutable actions to achieve the goal. Combining opportunity and willingness with Most and Starr's concept of "substitutability" makes it extremely difficult to explain international political and foreign policy outcomes. Drawing on the menu analogy, Most and Starr (1989, chapter 5) note that opportunity or willingness can operationally occur or be made available in any number of alternative, non-unique ways. Alternative possibilities or bases for choice produce "substitutability," which Most and Starr see as theoretically crucial for understanding the logic of causality (see also Palmer 2000).

This problem is especially apparent when we try to explain the frequency of particular outcomes. For example, when we can identify factors that create the opportunity and willingness for a state to attempt to improve its security, we must recognize that there may be dozens of alternative, substitutable policies that can achieve that goal (e.g., war, sanctions, negotiation, arms buildup, alliances, aid, trade, etc.). Therefore, the observed frequency of these outcomes can vary widely from the frequency of the conditions that cause them. This problem makes it very hard to develop general theory to account for changes in frequency of particular outcomes. Two areas of research offer some useful insights for addressing this problem. It may be that policy choice is affected by cultural norms, which is the focus of constructivists. Policy choice may also be affected by the size of existing "repertoires" (as part of the structure of opportunities; see Tilly's (2008) work on repertoires of protest). The choice of policy may also be heavily dependent upon the decision-making model used, and the growing body of work in this area is quite helpful (see Mintz and DeRouen 2010).

A substitutability approach is thus crucial for our examination of the relationships between internal and external conflict. States and non-state actors use many different means to influence their adversaries and friends. This covers all foreign policy decision-making, as well as specific models of political survival or strategic viability. Cioffi-Revilla and Starr (1995) explain the crucial place of substitutability in our understanding of behavioral phenomena. If the necessary conditions for any behavior to take place are opportunity and willingness (first-order factors of causality connected by the Boolean AND), it must be understood that either opportunity or willingness can be provided through any number of alternative, substitutable modes (second-order factors of causality connected by the Boolean OR). While opportunity and willingness make the occurrence of behaviors more difficult, substitutability makes them *easier*.

Research and the Substitutability Problem

This view of opportunity/willingness and substitutability fits naturally into the notions of two-level or nested games. Dealing with conflict at one level has consequences for conflict at other level(s). Following Tsebelis, outside observers might have trouble understanding how decision-makers could have arrived at and followed a certain policy because of its consequences at one level, in that they do not understand how external security/survival/viability might be "nested" within internal security/survival/viability, or vice versa. In trying to understand the causes of violent conflict, scholars have often tried to explain one or more particular types of violent responses to conflict (war, militarized disputes, arms races, threats of force). Often this is compared with a choice of less violent or nonviolent strategies (economic sanctions, diplomatic sanctions, negotiation, etc.). Yet, rather than focusing on particular strategies, and thereby becoming vulnerable to the classic substitutability problems, some scholars have used the natural dichotomy between violence and nonviolence, or repression and accommodation, as a way to address the issues raised by substitutability.

This method has been applied frequently in the literature on domestic conflict, particularly that which focuses on the responses of governments and rebels to different influence tactics. A good example from the rationalist perspective is Mark Lichbach's work (1984; 1987) on dissident responses to state repression versus accommodation. Lichbach builds on work modeling domestic conflict which uses this conceptualization, or a more simple scale of "hostility" or "conflict," to describe the range of possible tactics (e.g., Tsebelis and Sprague 1989; Wintrobe 1990). Work by Moore (e.g., 2000) makes the focus on substitutability explicit. Solving the substitutability problem is also implicit in the competing framework of "contentious politics" (McAdam et al. 2001; Tilly and Tarrow 2006), which employs "levels of contention" and also accounts well for spatiality and other contextual factors.

For international conflicts, a focus on particular types of conflict or policy response has been more dominant, though additional attempts to deal with substitutability have emerged in recent years (see Morgan and Palmer 2000). The human rights literature has also been concerned with the causes of repression (Poe et al. 1999; Davenport and Armstrong 2004) as well as the effects of repression and human rights violations on foreign aid decisions (Carey 2007; Demirel-Pegg and Moskowitz 2009). General Realist arguments about state response to changes in power or threat (e.g., Walt 1987) have long argued that balancing and bandwagoning behavior (which are analogous to coercion and accommodation) are the two most important general strategies states use.

The difficulty with using such general concepts in the study of state behavior shows itself when we address specific foreign policy issues. In particular, literature on the use of force and diversionary theories of war (e.g., DeRouen 1995) in its attempt to identify the alternative triggers of force sometimes neglects the alternative policy responses available (this problem has been very usefully addressed more recently by Oakes 2012). Another approach attempting to deal with this problem in the case of US intervention in internal conflicts is Regan (2000b), in which military, diplomatic, and mixed options are considered along with the crucial "do nothing" response.

Thus, substitutability presents a formidable obstacle to the analysis of conflict. The problem of including all alternative triggers of policy and considering the range of policy responses compounds itself if we attempt to take a two-level approach. Conflicts and threats at the international or domestic level can trigger policy responses of either repression or accommodation in either or both arenas. These triggers and responses also have effects in both arenas. Trying to sort out this tangle of causes and effects has led us to make some rather grand simplifications and to use some unconventional methods of analysis in the simulations we have developed to deal with internal–external security and substitutability.

Methods to Address the Substitutability Problem

The problems raised by substitutability can be addressed with several methodologies. The first step is to build a model that captures the essential conflict processes for the dependent variable of interest. Simple regression models can be a useful starting point for examining most questions. For instance, Poe and Tate (1994) examine states' human rights performances using cross-national data and find a variety of relevant factors. The liberal/democratic peace puzzle has been addressed by a series of studies using sophisticated logistic regression models that have identified factors which contribute to war (and peace) between pairs of states (Russett and Oneal 2001). But these models cannot tell us much about the *process* which produces the outcomes involved.

Regression models help to identify the key causal factors (usually opportunity variables) that are the foundation of our theories. Research on decision-making (e.g., Mintz and DeRouen 2010) can make an important contribution, being essential for understanding willingness as well as the process by which substitutable options are evaluated. Experimental methods (e.g., Mintz and Geva 1997) are extremely useful for understanding the limits of rationality and the sets of conditions that affect the models that leaders apply in their decision-making.

Yet, if we want to understand broader, systemic implications of particular choices, dynamic models are necessary. These allow us to specify particular processes and determine the long-term implications of particular types of condition (opportunities) and decision trigger (willingness). Dynamic models are very useful for identifying political dynamics and strategic interactions that are not easily captured as variables in regression models. The problem with these models, especially ones which try to represent so much complexity, is that they are very difficult to operationalize and test empirically. Purely mathematical analysis may produce some insights, but without some empirical validation these are not likely to be taken seriously and, as Lichbach (1992) notes, have not resulted in cumulation. Some of this may be provided by carefully designed comparative case analyses.

One useful method for examining complex dynamic models is computer simulation.[10] Simulations can be constructed to include many variables and multiple, complex causal paths, all grounded in the current state of empirical knowledge and theory. A variety of baseline conditions can be input into the simulation, and their long-term implications (given various, theoretically grounded processes) are output. While simulations in our discipline do not approach the complexity of climate models in the hard sciences, the problems addressed and the methodologies are similar. Simulations allow us to model and analyze causal chains so that we can begin to understand which factors are most important in driving them. They are especially useful when we are studying phenomena such as the relationship between internal and external conflict, where many conflicting influences are present and where the choices of decision-makers at particular times during the process may be crucial in producing different outcomes.

Two-Level Security Simulation Project

The Model

We developed an agent-based model that seeks to capture the essence of the two-level security game and represents internal–external relationships (see Figure 6.1). Governments are the agent in the model. Their decision-makers evaluate the threats that they face in each arena and then compare threat levels to their state's capacity for addressing those threats. They have a choice of two broad policies.

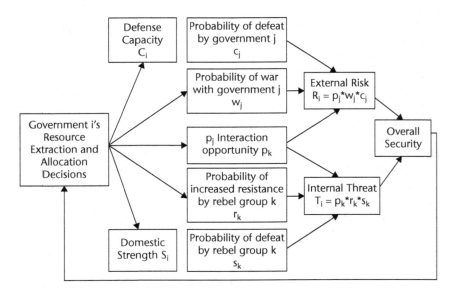

FIGURE 6.1 Summary of functional relationships in the model

They can either extract resources (from society or allies) to build capacity and deter threats, or allocate resources from state capacity in order to buy off or co-opt threats. The model assumes bounded rationality, and its core decision rule is derived from a Realist perspective: at any given time, a state seeks to reduce its most pressing threat, either international or internal.

States in this model possess some baseline level of capabilities for addressing threat, which we designate as C_i = state i's defense Capacity against external threats; S_i = state i's domestic defense capacity, the Strength of the government against internal opposition; and SOC, a set of societal (economic, population, etc.) resources from which states can extract. Below are formulas used to calculate Risk and Threat for state i from state j and rebel group(s) k:

$$R_i = \sum p_{ij}w_{ij}c_{ij} \tag{1}$$

$$T_i = \sum p_{ik}r_{ik}s_{ik} \tag{2}$$

where

R_i = the external (international) Risks faced by state i

T_i = i's internal (domestic) risk (Threat)

c_{ij}, s_{ik} = i's perceived probability of defeat in war with state j or rebellion with group k

w_{ij}, r_{ik} = i's perceived probability of war with state j or revolt from rebel group k

p_{ij}, p_{ik} = interaction opportunity between state i and state j or rebel group k

This model assumes that decision-makers act based upon a rational, expected utility calculation, but without much foresight. The decision trigger occurs when levels of threat outweigh capability in either arena. When that trigger indicates action, a state either extracts or allocates resources to reduce its most pressing threat.

The Simulation

The simulation allows us to examine how different contexts (system size, threat distributions, alliance structures) and different strategies (extraction versus allocation) affect the outcome of the two-level security problem. We first created a baseline system with ten states (two major and eight minor powers) from which changes can be measured. We assigned each state a low level of internal threat from its rebel groups and a baseline tendency for choosing extraction versus allocation, based on arguments in the literature about the prevalence of hawkish and dovish factions within governments and the tendency for bureaucratic norms of behavior or operational codes to develop (e.g., Ikle 1971; Barnet 1972). Threat ratios (c and s) are calculated based on ratios of capability among actors:

Capabilities ratio—external security $c = 1-[C_i/(C_i + C_j)]$
Capabilities ratio—internal security $s = 1-[S_i/(S_i + S_j)]$

An array of interaction probabilities (p) is assigned on the assumption that most states in this system interact frequently. Values w and r are assigned based on findings in the literature about the frequency of war and revolts. States are also assigned high levels of legitimacy and moderate economic growth rates.

After a system of states is created we specify the short-term effects of extraction and allocation decisions. Allocation reduces the willingness of the actor receiving the allocation to attack or rebel. The extraction of resources (from society, an ally, or by switching resources between internal and external capabilities) increases state capacity but can also strengthen rebel groups, depending on the level of government legitimacy and the level of threat. Literature on social movements and the diversionary theory of war suggests that the more legitimate the government and the higher the threat the more likely the public is to rally around the flag (modeled as an increase to societal resources) and the less likely rebels are to gain resources. If legitimacy is low the effect is reversed. States can also extract from their most friendly ally. However, because alliances enmesh states in the geopolitical web and can also act as conduits for the spread and amplification of conflict (e.g., Siverson and Starr 1991), extraction from allies increases interaction opportunities (p) with that ally and with the rest of the system.

The simulation thus creates short-term benefits and costs for state action but, owing to the two-level game, the longer-term consequences are unspecified. This is illustrated in Figure 6.2.

To run the simulation, each state acts once in each round. Then the effect of all the extraction and allocation decisions is calculated simultaneously before moving to the next "round." We run the simulation for 500 rounds, which could be conceived as months of time. The decision process is randomized, so that a state might have a 60 percent chance of extraction and a 40 percent chance of allocation in any given round. Because of randomization, we average results from 100 iterations of the simulation (of 500 rounds each). After we generate results from a baseline system we vary parameters in the model and observe the longer-term consequences for security (both internal and external) and for economic growth.

The major benefit of this simulation is that it allows us to examine standard findings in the literature in the context of an explicit two-level game. This lets us determine the extent to which the domestic security game and internal–external

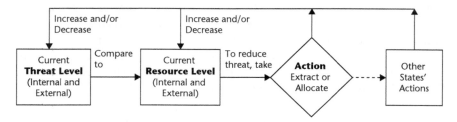

FIGURE 6.2 The simulation model: conflicting effects of extraction and allocation

conflict linkages, which are usually neglected, affect these findings. We have investigated issues including hegemonic decline, democracy, and state failure. Some results are outlined in the next section.

Results

Simon and Starr (1996) focused on system-level factors and the rise and decline of major powers. We verified the conventional wisdom on polarity: bipolar systems were most stable, producing the fewest changes in major/minor power status. States in bipolar systems also improved domestic security. Multipolar systems were more volatile: states had a more difficult time maintaining international security levels in systems with four or more major powers. Increasing the system size reduced international security but increased domestic security (because states more easily obtain resources from allies in a larger system). With regard to hegemonic decline, we found that the choice of strategy (extraction versus allocation) in each arena (international versus domestic) was a key factor. The hawkish strategy of extraction worked, but only if employed in one arena, *not both*. Too great a reliance on extraction accelerated the depletion of societal resources and caused decline. We found that a hegemon that relied on extraction to deal with international threats and allocation for domestic ones was best able to thrive and avoided decline. This insight into strategy adds to our understanding of the imperial overstretch argument (Kennedy 1988).

Next, we examined issues in the democratic/liberal peace literature: specifically, the survival of weak, "endangered" democratic states (Simon and Starr 2000). We modeled the theorized consequences of democracy: greater legitimacy, a tendency to solve domestic disputes without violence (our allocation strategy), and more favorable treatment from democratic allies (reduced willingness for war between democracies). Then we used the simulation to compare the conditions which allowed a weak, endangered democracy to regain favorable international and domestic security as well as economic growth.

We found a systemic threshold effect: democracies did better as long as there were at least two democracies in the system, but gains diminished as the system became more democratic. In systems without democratic allies, endangered democracies performed no better than the non-democracies. However, ally support was not itself sufficient to save the weak democracy. While ally support provided greater gains in security and resources than the factors of legitimacy and the dovish allocation strategy, it was clear that *both* were necessary for the endangered democracy to consistently perform better than an endangered non-democracy.

In Simon and Starr (2002) we allowed states to adapt their strategy based on the outcome of recent rounds of the simulation. We also tested the effect of non-compensatory decision models (Mintz 1993) and prospect theory's emphasis on loss aversion (Levy 1992) on performance.

We assumed that allowing states to learn would lead states to choose what we had found to be the optimal strategy (international hawk/domestic dove). Yet this did not occur. Democracies tended to move away from the dovish domestic strategy toward a more hawkish one, despite the fact that this hurt their long-term performance. This tells us that the short-term security incentives faced by states are *not* responsible for democracies' choice to pursue a dovish strategy against domestic opponents. Indeed, short-term security incentives in our model push states toward a more hawkish strategy. But since we found that states do better in the long run with the dovish domestic strategy we conclude that democracies choose a dovish strategy owing to societal or bureaucratic norms, not short-term security incentives.[11]

Finally, Englehart and Simon (2009) adapted the simulation to model Englehart's (2007) argument that leaders of failing states often fund militia groups outside the state apparatus to suppress domestic threats. While this further weakens state capacity, Englehart argues that this is preferable for leaders who fear coups or loss of power from a stronger state apparatus; militias also help to redirect rebel hostility toward militias and away from the state. We modified the simulation to examine whether this short-term strategy by leaders of failing states would indeed be effective. We found that failing states were best able to avoid absolute collapse by improving legitimacy *or* by extracting resources from international allies. The militia strategy did help in the short term, but led to failure in the long run. Also, failing states in smaller or less threatening regional systems of states tended to do better. Finally, we found a timing threshold for the extraction strategy—it was effective only if employed early. Once societal resources had depleted beyond a certain level, extraction accelerated state failure. This explains why failing states with access to mineral resources or allies can maintain themselves for quite a long time, despite low legitimacy, strong rebel groups, and a growing influence of militias (see Iqbal and Starr 2016, chapter 5).

Conclusion

As noted at the beginning of this chapter, the study of conflict demands the use of sophisticated theory and methods to deal with phenomena that can be characterized by "complex causation." If we conceive of conflict as a process or series of processes that involve agents working within structures (that is, different environments or levels of analysis, and requiring decision-makers to contend with multiple, simultaneous games), then investigators, singly and as a scholarly community, must cross several boundaries. In this chapter we have briefly outlined a number of the environments that must be taken into account, as well as presenting the ways in which an agent–structure framework such as opportunity and willingness can be useful for scholars who wish to make meaningful connections across boundaries. We have argued that the two key environments in the nexus of civil and international conflict (Stohl 1980), domestic and external factors, can be jointly accounted for using the frameworks of two-level/nested games and foreign policy substitutability. We have also presented a simulation model that brings together the various theoretical strands discussed, and whose findings support the plausibility and utility of these various theoretical approaches.

Yet we emphasize that no single methodology provides a clear solution to the problems inherent in conflict research, and no grand or synthetic theory appears on the horizon to establish a new paradigm. The agent–structure problem is indeed a problem. Our understanding of the effect of structures on conflict, from anarchy and alliances to bureaucracy and elections, is strong and improving. But substitutability reminds us that we must take care not to examine the effects of structures in isolation from each other. Nor can we examine the effects of structures in only one arena of conflict. Our simulation showed that sometimes a two-level game model predicts outcomes different from conclusions drawn by theories that account for only one level. So the international/domestic boundary must be crossed. But even when we do this well we are not certain of how agents will respond to structure. We have made much progress, but have still not captured the "essence of decision" (Allison 1971) that might connect decision-making models to the conditions or contexts which trigger decision. Thus, the connections between internal and external conflict will remain a fruitful area of research for scholars of conflict.

Notes

1 For example, data on the number of active international and internal conflicts shows that the percentage of international conflicts declined from about 40 percent during the 1950s to only 4 percent during the period from 1975 to 2008 (Gleditsch et al. 2002).

2 See Ghosn et al. (2004) on the Uppsala Conflict Data Program (UCDP); www.pcr.uu.se/research/ucdp/datasets/.

3 This literature is now so vast that extensive citation would be impossible. For two useful book ends, however, see Russett (1993) and Russett and Oneal (2001).

4 Indeed, this "reintegration" may have started as early as the 1950s, with the social communication/transaction model of integration developed by Karl Deutsch (e.g., Deutsch 1954; Deutsch et al. 1957).

5 The commonality also applies in structural conflicts (Galtung 1985; 1990), where incompatibility is expressed in social, economic, or political rules (or "structures") that provide advantages to some social units (groups or states) and disadvantages to others.

6 Theories of social movements and protest which emphasize willingness include relative deprivation (e.g., Gurr 1970), identity (Melucci 1988; Touraine 1981), and framing (Snow et al. 1986; Tarrow 1992). Those which emphasize opportunity include resource-mobilization (e.g., McCarthy and Zald 1977) and political opportunity structures (McAdam 1983).

7 The material in this section draws from Starr (1994).

8 This last point is crucial to the whole two-level game concept. If decision-makers do not use multiple models, then the two-level game becomes just a complex one-level game.

9 The interaction opportunity model holds only that closer units will interact more. Most of our assumptions and thus studies have applied this idea to conflict rather than

cooperative behavior. However, G. K. Zipf's (1949, 6) "law of least effort" applies to interactions in general, *positive* as well as negative. Studies by Starr and Thomas (2002; 2005) indicate that high levels of ease of interaction across borders—high interaction opportunities—are also related to positive Deutschian interdependence/integration effects. They argue that simply categorizing two states as being contiguous may not adequately reflect the expected underlying behavior.

10 Simulation is part of the developing area of computational social science (see Cioffi-Revilla 2010).

11 This finding complements the cultural or value components of theories behind the democratic peace, as well as liberal explanations for inter-state cooperation in regimes based on a combination of Axelrod's "shadow of the future" and metanorm concepts (1984; 1997).

7

CLIMATE CHANGE AND ARMED CONFLICT[1]

Reviewing the Evidence

Ole Magnus Theisen, Nils Petter Gleditsch, and Halvard Buhaug

A liberal peace seems to be in the making (Gleditsch 2008), with a decreased number of armed conflicts since the end of the Cold War (Gleditsch et al. 2002) and a lower severity of war as measured by battle-related deaths (Lacina et al. 2006; Human Security Report Project 2010), despite an uptick in recent years (Pettersson and Wallensteen 2015). There is a long-term decline in violence, within as well as between states (Goldstein 2011; Pinker 2011). Figure 7.1 illustrates the trends in the frequency and severity of armed conflict in the period 1946–2014. During the same period there has been a strong increase in democracy, trade, international economic integration, and membership in international organizations, as well as in international peacekeeping and mediation efforts, which jointly contribute to explaining the decline.

Financial crises, globalization, population growth, and fundamentalist ideology are widely seen as severe obstacles on the continuing road towards a less violent world. But the greatest challenge to the global liberal peace, according to an increasingly widespread view, is the threat of climate change. Fears on this score have been expressed by, for example, the Norwegian Nobel Committee (Mjøs 2007), the United Nations Security Council (UN 2007), and US president Barack Obama (2009), and more recently linked to the Syrian conflict (Kelley et al. 2015). Despite this rhetoric, there is no consensus to date that short-term climate variability, such as prolonged droughts or unusually warm weather, has any observable effect on the general pattern of conflict in modern times.

The Intergovernmental Panel on Climate Change (IPCC) is the main source of scientific information on the causes and consequences of climate change and has had a strong influence on the agenda of the public debate. The Third and Fourth Assessment Reports (IPCC 2001; 2007) made scattered comments on violent conflict in the reports from Working Group II on "Impacts, Adaptation,

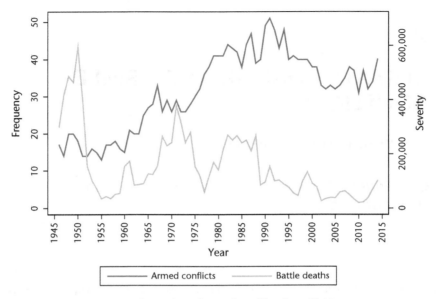

FIGURE 7.1   Frequency and severity of armed conflict since 1946

Source: Data from UCDP/PRIO Armed Conflict Dataset, v. 5–2015 (Gleditsch et al. 2002; Pettersson and Wallensteen 2015) and PRIO Battle Deaths Dataset, v. 3.0 (Lacina and Gleditsch 2005). Data, precise definitions, and sources can be found at www.prio.org/data and www.pcr.uu.se. The figure includes all state-based conflicts with at least twenty-five battle deaths in a calendar year.

and Vulnerability" (notably in the Africa chapter of AR4), but these comments were weakly founded in peer-reviewed research. Since then, a more directly relevant literature has emerged. The Fifth Assessment Report (AR5, IPCC 2014) has a more extended discussion. The Human Security chapter (chapter 12) concludes that there is no robust evidence for a link between climate change and armed conflict, but that factors known to be associated with conflict (such as poverty and economic decline) are likely to be influenced by climate change. However, no probability assessment is provided and, since correlations are not transitive, one cannot assume that a change in a variable associated with conflict will necessarily produce conflict. The Africa chapter (chapter 22) and a chapter on emergent risk (chapter 19) go further in asserting the probability that climate change will increase conflict, while a methods chapter assessing the robustness of findings in the other chapters (chapter 18) completely rejects the climate change–conflict nexus (Gleditsch and Nordås 2014).

Linking Climate Change to Conflict

Three physical effects of climate change (natural disasters, sea-level rise, and increasing resource scarcity) are frequently assumed to lead to loss of livelihood, economic decline, and increased insecurity, either directly or through forced migration. Interacting with poor governance, societal inequalities, and a bad neighborhood, these factors in turn may promote political and economic instability, social fragmentation, migration, and inappropriate responses from governments. Eventually this produces increased motivation for instigating violence as well as improved opportunities for mass mobilization.[2]

In the following we review the evidence for some of these links via four contexts frequently invoked in writings on climate change and security: changes in precipitation, rising temperature, rising sea level, and natural disasters. We leave out the question of whether climate change could lead to more interstate conflict. The literature on resource scarcities and violence generally sees interstate conflict over these issues as a more remote possibility (Homer-Dixon 1999, 5). We have also left out studies that look at climate and conflict in a very long-term perspective (up to a millennium). The rise of the modern state, large-scale international trade, and industrialization has taken place during the last two centuries, a period with little change in climate averages. With the exception of studies that directly investigate the effect of weather on local prices and the subsequent effect on conflict, we leave out the burgeoning literature on food prices and conflict. International food prices are predominantly driven by the price of oil and fertilizers, hoarding and market speculation, and, recently, biofuel production (Tadesse et al. 2014).

The focus on short-term variation in rain and temperature is partially due to data constraints, as there are few other environmental indicators that are exogenous to human behavior. Besides, short-term changes do not facilitate adaptation and external intervention, so any observed correlation is more likely to reflect a genuine causal relationship. Long-term effects of climate change on conflict necessarily imply a complex causal chain, the elements of which are hard to isolate and detect in a systematic, quantitative manner. One of the main projected effects of global warming, meanwhile, is greater variability in precipitation and temperature patterns, which may lead to an increase in extreme weather events and disaster rates (Kirtman et al. 2013; van Aalst 2006).

Evidence

Changes in Precipitation and Temperature

The simple scarcity (or neo-Malthusian) model of conflict assumes that if climate change results in a reduction in essential resources for livelihood, such as food or water, those affected by the increasing scarcity may start fighting over the remaining resources. Alternatively, people may be forced to leave the area and create new scarcities when they encroach on the territory of others, who may also be resource-constrained. Barnett and Adger (2007) review a broad range of studies of both of these effects, focusing particularly on countries where a large majority of the population is still dependent on employment in the primary sector. If climate change results in reduced rainfall and higher temperature that jointly cause droughts and reduced access to the natural capital that sustains livelihoods, poverty will be more widespread and the potential for conflict greater.

A long line of research links hot temperatures to individual aggression, including violent crime and riots. Anderson (2001) suggests, therefore, that global warming may increase violence. But the causal mechanism proposed in these studies—personal discomfort—is different from the scarcity thesis that is at the core of the relationship proposed in the literature on climate change and armed conflict (Reuveny 2007; Burke et al. 2009), and the kind of violence is also different. Other studies that focus on individual-level behavior, drawing on relative deprivation or opportunity cost arguments, find scarcity to be associated with more violence or crime. Mehlum et al. (2006) report that, in nineteenth-century Bavaria, excessive rainfall ruined harvests, raising rye prices and in turn leading to higher rates of property crime.[3] Likewise, Miguel (2005) concludes that both positive and negative extremes in rainfall increased the frequency of witch killings in a rural Tanzanian district. Using a field experiment from semi-arid Tanzania, Lecoutere et al. (2010) find that water scarcity drives conflictive behavior, particularly for poor and marginalized households. Hidalgo et al. (2010) find that rainfall deviations as an instrument for agricultural economic shocks lead the rural poor to invade large landholdings in Brazil, and particularly so in municipalities with a highly unequal land distribution. Thus, if we were to make an inference from unorganized events with low levels of violence to organized armed conflict, we would expect worsening climatic conditions to bring about more armed conflict.

Table 7.1 provides an overview of quantitative studies of the relationship between various climatic factors and different forms of organized violence. Each column represents a specific conflict type under study, whereas each row corresponds to a proposed climate–conflict connection. The table reveals a lack of empirical consensus for most suggested linkages. The discrepancy is partly a consequence of the diversity of indicators applied, although it is also in part a consequence of differences in samples, time periods, and estimation techniques. For a limited number of cells, findings seem to be more coherent. For the most severe form of violence—civil war onset and incidence—we cannot make any inferences about robust linkages. However, for the category that covers conflict events, unrest, and political violence, temperature spikes appears more systematically related to higher frequency, and there is some support also for the scarcity perspective for droughts and natural disasters. The link between communal violence and natural disasters also receives some support. In addition, there is some support for less intense forms of violence being linked to food production and prices, which in turn are affected by the weather. However, the low number of studies— in particular for studies testing indirect mechanisms—and the non-random selection of cases demand caution about drawing strong general conclusions.[4]

TABLE 7.1 Climate factors and organized conflict—quantitative studies

Hypothesis	Civil conflict onset/incidence	Civil conflict/levels of unrest/political violence	Communal violence	Riots/urban unrest
Short-term rainfall deficiency increases risk/wetness decreases	Support for 2, none 12, support against 3 = *no support* (17)	Support for 5, mixed 1, none 2, some support against 1 = *some support* (10)	Support for 2, mixed 1, none 3, some support against 1, support against 2 = *inconclusive* (9)	Support for 1, none 1, some support against 1 = *inconclusive* (3)†
Short-term warming increases risk	Support for 2, none 7 = *no support* (9)	Support for 4, some support for 1, none 1 = *support* (6)	None 1, mixed 1 = *inconclusive* (2)	Support for 1, some support for 1 = *some support* (2)†€
Natural disasters increase risk	Support for 2, some support for 1, none 2, support against 1 = *inconclusive* (6)*	Support for 3, none 1 = *some support* (4)	Support for 2, some support for 1, none 1 = *some support* (4)€	NA
Economic growth instrumented by shock in precipitation/temperature/disasters	Support for 3, none 5 = *inconclusive* (8)*	Support for 1 = *inconclusive* (1)	Support for 1 = *inconclusive* (1)€	Support for 1 = *inconclusive* (1)
Water scarcity (stable)	Support for 2, none 2, opposite 1 = *inconclusive* (5)*	NA	NA	NA
Land degradation (stable levels) increase risk	Support for 2, none 2 = *inconclusive* (4)§*	NA	NA	NA
Less vegetation increases violence	Support against 1 = *inconclusive* (1)*	None 1 = *inconclusive* (1)†€	Support against 1 = *inconclusive* (1)€†	NA
Food prices instrumented by precipitation/temperature/disasters	NA	Support for 1, some support for 1 = *some support* (2)†€	NA	Support for 2 = *some support* (2)

(Continued)

Table 7.1 (continued)

Hypothesis	Civil conflict onset/incidence	Civil conflict/levels of unrest/political violence	Communal violence	Riots/urban unrest
Population size instrumented by rainfall	Support for 1= inconclusive (1)*	NA	NA	NA
Rainfall and higher temperature shocks jointly increase risk	Some support for 1, 1 mixed = inconclusive (2)*	None 1, some support against 1 = inconclusive (2)	NA	Support for 1= inconclusive (1)†€
ENSO episodes increase risk	Support for 1, none 2 = inconclusive (3)	None 1 = inconclusive (1)†	None 1 = inconclusive (1)†	NA
Flood through displacement instrumented by rainfall	Some support for 1 = inconclusive (1)*	NA	NA	NA
Food production, including instrumented by rain	NA	Some support for 1, none 1 = inconclusive (2)€	NA	NA

*All studies at annual level; †All studies at monthly level; €All studies at sub-national level; §Measure questionable.

Note: Civil conflict is an armed conflict between government and organized rebel forces; civil conflict/levels of unrest/political violence encompasses diverse forms of violence, typically event-based studies, where the organizational form is unclear, or where the three other categories do not fit; communal violence is an armed conflict between two organized non-state groups; and a riot is spontaneous protests by (mostly) unorganized actors. Figures denote the number of studies that support, give some support, do not support, or contradict the hypothesis at the left; total number of studies per outcome is given in parenthesis. All relationships based on a single study are characterized as inconclusive. A detailed description is available online at www.prio.org/data/replication-data/.

Riots and small-scale clashes are other suggested social consequences of climate change related to armed conflict. Inspired by the psychological hypothesis that heat creates aggression, Yeeles (2015, 166) finds city temperature to be correlated with the rate of urban riots, and a similar, if less robust, pattern is reported for drier periods and warmer months within each city as well. Analyzing food-related unrest specifically, Bellemare (2015) reports that the number of natural disasters globally leads to an increase in global food prices, which in turn increases risk, whereas increasing volatility decreases risk. Smith (2014) finds rainfall deficiency to affect spikes in domestic food prices, which in turn increases the monthly risk of urban unrest. Both Maystadt and Ecker (2014) (on Somalia) and Raleigh et al. (2015) (on sub-Saharan Africa) conclude that deterioration in weather patterns exerts a direct effect on violence as well as an indirect effect through the food-price mechanism. Wischnath and Buhaug (2014a) find that a growth in food production decreases the intensity of state-based conflicts in Indian states. Kim (2014, 15), using deviations in temperature and precipitation as instruments for economic growth, notes that lower economic growth increases the risk of anti-government protests. All in all, there is some evidence that weather-driven spikes in food prices increase the risk of various forms of organized violence. There is some debate, however, on the relevance of global food prices at the local level in certain developing regions (see Smith 2014; Raleigh et al. 2015 for skepticism towards relying on global prices) and whether labeling food riots as such is appropriate (Sneyd et al. 2013).

Some statistical studies of conflict in Africa suggest that communal conflicts are more prevalent during or following wet periods (Raleigh and Kniveton 2012; Theisen 2012). The first study also notes an increased risk following particularly dry periods, in line with Fjelde and von Uexkull (2012), who find drier years to be less safe. Thus, the support for the scarcity scenario is mixed. Anthropological research on cattle raids in Africa returns contradictory results. A study of the Marsabit district in Kenya for the period 1919–2005 reveals that death rates tend to be higher in years with abundant rainfall than in dry years (Witsenburg and Adano 2009; Adano et al. 2012). Another study from the same region reports a higher frequency of raids in seasons with less vegetation, but no effect of precipitation (Meier et al. 2007). The causal argument is that dry periods are associated with cooperative behavior, whereas wet periods increase the opportunities for raiding (Eaton 2008). Using a contest success function model Butler and Gates (2012) deduce theoretically that the presence of biased property rights institutions in periods of relative rainfall abundance is crucial in determining whether eastern African pastoralists engage in inter-ethnic violence or focus on production. Inspired by the Marsabit study described above, Ember et al. (2012) analyze violence for the neighboring Turkana district for the period 1998–2009. Contrary to studies that find wet periods to be more violent, they find both drier months and drier years to be significantly more deadly than wetter months or years.[5] They attribute the divergent findings to different time periods and mobility patterns in Turkanaland. Other possible explanations for differing results may be that the study by Witsenburg and Adano uses archival and locally gathered information, whereas the Turkana study is based on media reports, or that Turkanas simply raid more out of hunger and drought than do neighboring groups—a view supported by a recent in-depth study (Schilling et al. 2012). In a follow-up study of Marsabit, Ember et al. (2014) find that different ethnic groups have different livestock raiding patterns: most attacks occur during dry periods whereas two groups mostly attack during wet periods. They argue that this reflects differences in subsistence patterns. Similarly, Detges' (2014) study of pastoralist violence in northern Kenya reveals that the spatial attributes of resources are crucial in explaining pastoralist violence, as violence takes place in areas that have higher mean rainfall and are closer to well sites. A survey of three Kenyan counties finds the perception that an increase in droughts decreased the support for violence (Linke et al. 2015, 42). A study of the Mopti region of Mali finds no relationship between climatic conditions and land-use disputes (Benjaminsen et al. 2012). Rather than natural resource scarcity restricting mobility for pastoralists, political negligence, rent seeking, and corruption appear to be at the heart of the conflicts.

Overall, there is little sign of convergence in the relationship between precipitation, drought, and communal conflict in Africa. Much of this research is on pastoralist societies in drylands and it is reasonable to assume that the mechanisms at play are different from those driving civil wars. Indeed, Raleigh and Kniveton (2012) find that communal violence takes place in less-populated areas, in contrast to the findings for civil war (Theisen et al. 2011/12). They also observe that communal violence events increase in frequency following wet periods, whereas the opposite holds true for events in civil conflicts. Owing to a lack of reliable data there are few studies on climate factors and small-scale violent conflicts outside East Africa. One exception analyzes Hindu–Muslim riots in India and finds negative rainfall growth decreases economic growth, which in turn increases the risk of riots (Bohlken and Sergenti 2010). Given economic and organizational constraints and—not least—the fact that rebels are fighting a government, armed civil conflicts are quite different from individual crimes and low-level violence. Statistical studies of civil conflicts globally (Esty et al. 1998; Raleigh and Urdal 2007) or in Africa (Hendrix and Glaser 2007) provide only limited support for neo-Malthusian hypotheses. For instance, Raleigh and Urdal (2007, 674) conclude on the basis of local-level data that the effects of land degradation and water scarcity were "weak, negligible, or insignificant." Moreover, for the "favorite case" of Darfur, Kevane and Gray (2008) find precipitation levels to increase from the early 1980s until 2003, when the conflict escalated. Brown (2010) corroborates this result, showing that for the same period the vegetation cover of the area increased. Likewise, Rowhani et al. (2011) discovered a positive association between ecosystem productivity and civil conflict areas in eastern Africa. One study of conflicts in dryland areas finds that, although conflict incidence does not generally increase with resource scarcity or overuse, there are nonlinear interactions between the explanatory variables that show an effect of resource scarcity. However, it differs between contexts: the level of natural resource endowment decides how the level of human well-being (IMR and GDP per capita) or overuse (soil degradation) affects conflict proneness (Sterzel et al. 2014).

Many studies of weather patterns and conflict have been inspired by Miguel et al. (2004), who presented the first systematic analysis of rainfall variability and civil war in Africa. Although their article used negative rainfall growth as an instrument for economic shocks, its conclusion that loss of rainfall increases conflict risk has immediate implications for the climate–security debate. This study has come under some fire, partly relating to how conflicts are coded (Jensen and Gleditsch 2009) and partly because of the way climate anomalies are measured (Ciccone 2011; see also response by Miguel and Satyanath 2011). Other recent studies fail to discern a robust link between rainfall as an instrument for growth, on the one hand, and civil conflict, on the other (Brückner 2010; van Weezel 2014).[6] One study finds droughts in sub-Saharan Africa to significantly reduce population size, which in turn decreases conflict risk (Brückner 2010).

Koubi et al. (2012) apply both temperature and precipitation deviations as instruments for economic growth to see if this variation in growth predicts the onset of civil conflict. Unlike Miguel et al. (2004), they fail to observe any relationship between worsening climate and economic performance and find only weak support for the notion that climate-driven economic shocks increase conflict risk in non-democratic settings. In work somewhat more supportive of the scarcity–conflict hypothesis, Gizelis and Wooden (2010) conclude that countries with poor institutions and high but stable levels of water stress are more prone to civil conflict.

A study of temperature and conflict (Burke et al. 2009) finds civil war in sub-Saharan Africa in the period 1981–2002 to be significantly more widespread during warmer years, concluding that civil war incidence would increase by about 50 percent by 2030 on current climate emission trajectories. This result is questioned by Buhaug (2010a; 2010b), who argues that it is sensitive to three analytical decisions: estimation technique, sample period, and choice of conflict data. While the jury is still out on the methodological divide, Burke et al. (2010) concede that temperature is unrelated to African civil war in more recent years. Burke and co-authors have not responded to the third issue raised by Buhaug. Other recent studies on climate factors and civil conflict onset or incidence, most on sub-Saharan Africa, fail to uncover robust effects of precipitation (Burke et al. 2009; Buhaug and Theisen 2012; Brückner 2010; van Weezel 2014) or both precipitation and temperature (Couttenier and Soubeyran 2013; Dell et al. 2012; Klomp and Bulte 2013; for Asia, see Wischnath and Buhaug 2014b).[7] However, Hendrix and Salehyan (2012) find civil conflict onset in Africa to be more likely in wet years. Moreover, in a global study Salehyan and Hendrix (2014) find more political violence (conflict incidence and violent attacks) in wetter years, in particular in less-developed, more agriculturally dependent societies. They find less robust effects of temperature, although some effects for persons killed in anti-state attacks. Partly in contrast to this, Landis (2014) finds little support for the argument that temperature and precipitation shocks affect civil and less intense conflicts, but that warmer regions are more at risk, in particular if they have a distinctly seasonal climate. Finally, Hsiang et al. (2011) report that civil war risk in the tropics and subtropics is significantly higher during El Niño periods than during La Niña. The analysis reveals that the El Niño effect does not work through local variations in temperature and precipitation. A more recent study on sub-Saharan Africa (Klomp and Bulte 2013) does not find any linkage between the El Niño–Southern Oscillation (ENSO) episodes and civil conflict.[8]

All of the above studies of weather patterns and civil conflict are conducted at the national level. But rainfall patterns do not follow national boundaries and conflicts, too, are often spatially detached from the outline of states. In the first spatially disaggregated study of rainfall variability and armed conflict, Theisen et al. (2011/12) find no support for a localized, short-term impact of drought on conflict for Africa. Wischnath and Buhaug (2014b) replicate this non-finding between rainfall and conflict for Asia, and also report no significant temperature effect. The lack of robust findings linking climate factors and civil conflict outbreak or occurrence need not mean that there is no linkage. Indeed, using a geographically disaggregated design, von Uexkull (2014) finds that prolonged droughts are associated with an increase in the number of civil conflict events. Partly in contrast to this, Bollfrass and Shaver (2015) find higher temperature and more precipitation to significantly increase the incidence of civil conflict at the local level.

Several recent studies break with the conventional country–year format and analyze conflict events[9] at the sub-national level at the monthly intervals for East Africa (O'Loughlin et al. 2012; Raleigh and Kniveton 2012), Somalia (Maystadt and Ecker 2014), or Sudan (Maystadt et al. 2015). All of these studies report that drier or warmer periods—or both—see more civil conflict events.[10] In the most comprehensive disaggregated study to date with regards to forms of violence O'Loughlin et al. (2014) find abnormally warm periods to be more at risk, whereas moderately dry months decrease the risk in the aggregate model. The findings are contingent on the form of violence studied, however. The discrepancy between studies of conflict events, which quite often find a linkage in the expected direction between climate factors and conflict, and studies analyzing the onset of civil conflicts, which generally fail to uncover such an association, could be due to different dynamics being measured. Thus far, there is more evidence of the individual battles in an ongoing conflict to be affected by weather variables than its outbreak. In this instance, it is relevant to note that daily weather and seasons have also been found to systematically affect the timing of attacks in specific conflicts (Carter and Veale 2013; 2015).

Natural Disasters

Global warming is predicted to increase the frequency and intensity of extreme weather events, and thereby natural disasters. There has been a sharp increase in the number of hydro-meteorological and climatic disasters over the last half-century (Figure 7.2),[11] although it is unclear how much of this can be accounted for by improved reporting, population growth, and shifting patterns of settlement (Guha-Sapir et al. 2011, 1). Asia is the region most heavily affected. Geological disasters such as volcanic eruptions, earthquakes, and tsunamis do not concern us here, since they are unlikely to be influenced by climate change.

The severity of disasters, measured as the number of casualties, shows no evident time trend, presumably because of increasing coping capacity in many countries, which compensates for the increase in the absolute number of disaster events. Future economic development is likely to further increase the ability of many societies to absorb natural disasters without great loss of human life, so an increase in extreme weather events need not be accompanied by higher casualty figures.

Natural disasters are expected to exacerbate conflict risk primarily through economic loss and a weakening of government authority. One statistical study does indeed find the risk of civil conflict onset to be higher following natural disasters (Nel and Righarts 2008). However, this result is challenged by Slettebak (2012),

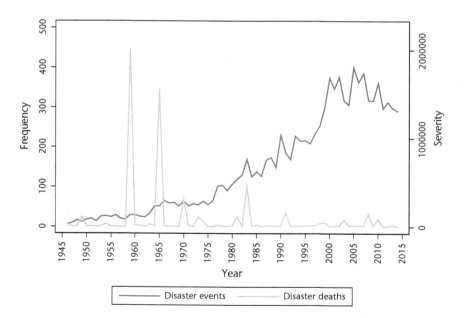

FIGURE 7.2   Hydro-meteorological disasters since 1946

Source: Data from EM-DAT, Centre for Research on the Epidemiology of Disasters (CRED). Data available from www.emdat.be.

who reports the opposite effect and attributes it to a tendency to unite in adversity.[12] Omelicheva (2011) finds that when state fragility is taken into account the risk of state failure in the aftermath of a disaster is minimal or disappears. Besley and Persson (2011) show that climatic disasters do not affect growth, but increase the risk of civil war, but only in fragile states. Another recent study, Bergholt and Lujala (2012), reaches the opposite conclusion: climatic natural disasters have a negative impact on economic growth but have no effect on the onset of conflict, neither directly nor as an instrument for economic shocks. The discrepancy between these two studies is arguably due to the former studying the incidence of civil war, which could introduce endogeneity problems. The only analysis of natural disasters and terrorism to date (Berrebi and Ostwald 2013) reports that the number of deaths in natural disasters per year increases the risk of both domestic and transnational terrorist attacks. Whereas private targets in domestic and transnational terrorist strikes are equally affected by disasters, transnational attacks against government targets are affected only by disasters in the current year. In contrast, the effects of natural disasters on domestic attacks targeting the government grow over time.

Two studies that compare the pre- and post-disaster levels of civil unrest find post-disaster periods to have significantly higher levels of unrest (Drury and Olson 1998; Nardulli et al. 2014), although the latter report that the results are driven by only one in six disasters. Moreover, for the majority of operationalizations the destabilizing effects were greater outside 500 miles of the disasters' epicenter—contrary to what one would expect from theories on the behavior of disaster victims. Analyzing climatic disasters' effects on political violence and riots in Indian states over time, Slettebak (2013) finds that disasters are not correlated with riots alone, but at increasing levels of literacy disasters increase riot levels. The number of events of another form of violence, political violence, increases in province-years with more disasters and lower levels of literacy. However, the substantive effects of these partly contradictory interaction effects are not very strong.

Studies analyzing natural disasters and local and communal violence at the subnational level are supportive of a link, although the synchronic research design of some of these studies limits causal inference. One study, using survey material on Indonesia, concludes that villages that had suffered a natural disaster during the previous three years were more likely to experience violent conflict (Barron et al. 2009). Likewise, in a synchronic analysis of 186 pre-state and early-state societies Ember and Ember (1992) find that societies with natural disasters experienced a higher frequency of warfare. In a follow-up study focusing on East Africa, Ember et al. (2013) report a greater prevalence of intergroup warfare in non-state societies with a higher incidence of natural disasters. But in state societies the tendency is the opposite—here more frequent disasters reduce intergroup warfare, although only at the 10 percent level of significance. They conclude, in line with Ember and Ember (1992), that fear of loss of resources is more important than actual loss in motivating people to fight. These studies find warfare to be more likely to be caused by disasters than the opposite, but the synchronic design makes it harder to draw inferences. To sum up, less-organized forms of violence appear to be more affected by natural disasters than civil conflicts, but the effects are not always in the expected direction, as shown by Ember et al. (2013) for state societies and by Slettebak (2013) for riots in India.

Sea-level Change and Migration

Working Group I of the IPCC's Fifth Assessment Report (2014, chapter 13) forecasts a global mean sea-level rise of between 0.26 and 0.98 m within this century, depending on the scenario chosen. Sea-level rise will threaten the livelihood of the populations of small island states in the Indian Ocean, the Caribbean, and the Pacific. However, a much larger number of people in low-lying areas, both rural and urban, and particularly along the coasts in South Asia and West Africa, may become more exposed to soil erosion, seasonal flooding, and extreme weather. Depending on the degree of protection that can be offered, this in turn may generate "climate-induced migration."

The nature and extent of migration in response to climate change are unknown, and whether such displacement will cause severe host–newcomer tensions is also open to debate (e.g., Nicholls and Tol 2006). Owing to conceptual problems (what is an environmental migrant, and is it a useful concept?) and, consequently, a lack of systematic data, the impact of environmental change on migration has not been subject to much rigorous comparative analysis (Gleditsch et al. 2007). Studies that look at a non-random set of cases with out-migration in areas with severe environmental degradation (e.g., Reuveny 2007) provide suggestive evidence that climate change could trigger more human mobility. Ghimire et al. (2014), representing a rare quantitative exception, find that flood-induced displacement increases the propensity for civil conflict incidence, whereas the risk of new conflicts breaking out is unaffected. Perch-Nielsen et al. (2008, 390) modify the view that disasters will induce conflicts, as natural disasters such as floods "will not likely be a major mechanism" driving migration, but rather temporary displacement; sea-level rise, however, will have a stronger effect. Moreover, although climate change may increase the motivation for migration, it may at the same time reduce the mobility capacity (Foresight 2011). Thus, the net impact remains unknown, and the main effect of climate change on migration is likely to be indirect, affecting economic and social variables that already drive migration. Yet, the state of research in this area is too patchy to draw general conclusions about the likely future implications of climate change on migration and conflict. Accordingly, we see this as one of the most important (but also challenging) priorities for future research on the security implications of climate change. The recent Foresight (2011) report on migration is an important step in the right direction.

Uncertainty, Assumptions, and Research Priorities

Despite recent progress in forecasting (e.g., Goldstone et al. 2010; Hegre et al. 2013), social scientists are still poorly equipped to predict rare events such as violent conflict outbreak. Climate change is just one of many areas where policy prescriptions are dependent on more successful efforts at prediction (Schneider et al. 2010). In order to improve our understanding of where, when, and how climate change may generate instability and conflict, several challenges should be addressed. Here, we will briefly discuss three research priorities that relate mostly to the quantitative empirical literature, though we acknowledge that a number of important challenges remain also within case-based research and more theoretical work, including scenario building and other non-statistical forecasting techniques.

First, we need to develop a better understanding—and empirical modeling—of plausible indirect links between environmental variability and change and armed conflict (Buhaug 2015). To date, most research on the security effects of climate change is limited to investigating direct associations, despite the fact that the literature on resource scarcity and violence (Homer-Dixon 1999), as well as that on climate change and conflict (Buhaug et al. 2010), points to the importance of mediating factors. One of the most frequently mentioned yet critically understudied topics is the effect on migration and its social consequences, including conflict. The comprehensive Foresight report (2011) concludes that climate change will likely trigger out-migration from vulnerable regions and amplify current urbanization trends. With regards to the effect migration may have on violent conflict, its conclusions are very modest and focus far more on how conflicts make populations vulnerable to environmental adversity, concluding that "Overt conflict between migrants and established residents remains the exception rather than the rule" (Foresight 2011, 114). Long-term economic development is arguably another important mechanism. While the discussion above has shown that there is mixed evidence regarding the effect of climatic shocks via economic growth on civil conflict, rainfall variability is found to decrease growth in sub-Saharan Africa (see, e.g., Barrios et al. 2010) and higher temperatures are found to harm exports from poor countries (Jones and Ohlken 2010). However, much less is known about longer-term growth and development, partly because over the longer term it is harder to single out the unique effect of climate factors. Nevertheless, we know that low economic development is highly correlated with conflict (Hegre and Sambanis 2006) and the potential indirect effects of climate change on conflict through development should therefore be high on the agenda for future research. In order to gain more insight into possible processes connecting climatic factors and violent conflict, such as migration and economic development, high-quality case studies are still much in need for future theory development.

Second, the study of the disaggregated effects of climate change remains crucial. Along the same lines, identifying the most vulnerable groups of societies and evaluating their potential for armed mobilization is an inherent challenge. Actors and agency tend to be vaguely portrayed, or outright ignored, in the relevant empirical literature, although important steps forward have been taken by recent survey studies (e.g. Barron et al. 2009; Schilling et al. 2012; Linke et al. 2015). Similarly, abnormal timing and intensity of precipitation (and temperature) can be just as devastating for subsistence-based livelihoods as annual aberrations from the norm (see Mortimore 1998). The IPCC scenarios point to a 90 percent likely increase in short-term variability, and a few conflict studies have taken this insight into account (Carter and Veale 2013; Fjelde and von Uexkull 2012; Hidalgo et al. 2010; Maystadt and Ecker 2014; Nardulli et al. 2014; O'Loughlin et al. 2012; Raleigh and Kniveton 2012; Theisen 2012; Theisen et al. 2011/12; Wischnath and Buhaug 2014a; 2014b; Witsenburg and Adano 2009). However, it is much more challenging to determine the proper spatial and temporal scale for indirect effects than for direct effects. For instance, to assess whether national aggregates or sub-national indicators are the most appropriate in studying the effect of drought on food prices requires assessing the degree of integration of local food production in the national and international market (among a host of other factors). Regarding the temporal scope, studies at the monthly level report more findings, but it remains to be singled out what are caused by tactical concerns and what might be affecting the motivation for fighting.

Third, we need to even more critically distinguish between mechanisms that trigger new unrest and mechanisms that serve as catalysts for the continuation of violence. We also need to scrutinize the full range of social outcomes potentially relevant for the impacts of climate change-related phenomena. Thus, non-violent protest, regime changes, and coups also deserve systematic scientific scrutiny. The spatial and temporal coverage of these types of conflict data are still limited, so improved data collection is a priority. Moreover, future research should consider possible positive effects of climate change and associated societal adaptation for human and national security, including their role in triggering more cooperation over common-pool resources (Böhmelt et al. 2014; Ostrom 1990).

Conclusion

Given the potential range and scope of the consequences of climate change, it is not surprising that there is widespread concern about its security implications. In part, this concern has been directed at raising awareness about "environmental security" in a broad sense. Unless managed properly, climate change will have many serious effects on peoples and societies worldwide. The hardships of climate change are particularly likely to add to the burden of poverty and human insecurity in already vulnerable societies with weak governments. However, the use of such wider concepts of security must not stand in the way of a focused effort to analyze empirically the possible link between environmental change and violent conflict.

Given the general lack of consensus for a historical climate–conflict link,[13] simply assuming that such a link will materialize in the future may lead peacemaking astray. This can eventually also undermine the credibility of the IPCC and the efforts to reach a consensus of knowledge about human-made climate change and a concerted global effort at mitigation and adaptation. The climate–conflict discourse can also be exploited by actors who want to escape responsibility (Salehyan 2008). Indeed, the expressed view of the Khartoum government is that the Darfur conflict has its roots in environmental factors exogenous to the regime.

Finally, what if the academic community were to conclude that climate change has a trivial impact on armed conflict risk? Does it matter? It matters a great deal for the credibility of climate change research. It is an abuse of the precautionary principle to promote low-probability, low-impact hazards to major threats. For adaptation to climate change, clarifying the conflict effects may also be important. Preventing armed conflict is likely to require countermeasures that are different than preventing biodiversity loss. For the need to mitigate the effects of climate change, however, the effects of climate change on conflict probably matter very little. There are many other reasons to reduce the human impact on the climate and to prevent global warming from getting out of hand.

Notes

1 This is a revised and updated version of Theisen et al. (2013), with permission from the editor and publisher. The academic literature on this topic is currently undergoing a major expansion. Our cut-off date for inclusion is mid-2015, with apologies to any authors that we might have missed. Our work on this issue has been supported by the Research Council of Norway, grant no. 240315/F10.
2 Buhaug et al. (2010) provide a more comprehensive exposition of possible causal linkages between climate change and violent conflict.
3 Conversely, the study suggests that rates of violent crime dropped owing to a rise in beer prices.
4 A summary table obscures the fact that not all analyses are of the same scope and rigor and have equal potential for generalization. However, the lack of consensus on specification issues precludes us from ranking studies according to such (yet to be established) objective criteria.
5 This is also partly at odds with the findings of Meier et al. (2007), who study Turkana and some adjoining areas and find that months with more vegetation see more frequent raids.
6 Brückner (2010) finds an effect at the 10 percent level of significance.
7 Couttenier and Soubeyran (2013) find a non-robust link between drought severity and full-blown civil wars in Africa.
8 That said, there is no consensus on the extent to which global climate change will impact the incidence and severity of El Niño and La Niña episodes (IPCC 2007, 780).
9 These studies use events that cover different forms of violence, such as rebel–government interaction, militia operations, and communal conflicts.
10 As noted above, Raleigh and Kniveton (2012) find more communal violence in the wake of wetter periods, whereas the converse is true for civil violence events.
11 Guha-Sapir et al. (2011, 7) define a disaster as "a situation or event which overwhelms local capacity, necessitating a request to a national or international level for external

assistance; an unforeseen and often sudden event that causes great damage, destruction and human suffering."

12 Nel and Righarts (2008) find stronger results for geological than for climatic disasters. Studying earthquakes, Brancati (2007) observes a conflict-inducing effect.

13 Several earlier summaries of the extant literature (Adger et al. 2014; Bernauer et al. 2012; Gleditsch 2012; Klomp and Bulte 2013; Meierding 2013; Scheffran et al. 2012) point in the same direction. Hsiang et al. (2013) represent a dissenting voice, though see also the response by Buhaug et al. (2014).

8

COMPARATIVE AND HISTORICAL STUDIES OF CRIME[1]

Trends, Patterns, Contexts

Peter Nils Grabosky

Long-term trends in crime and violence have attracted the attention of social scientists for many years. As with much of social science, the geographical focus of inquiry has tended to rest on Europe and North America. There, scholars identified a remarkable downward trend in criminal violence over the past millennium. But human violence long predates the written record. Examinations of prehistoric archaeological sites have suggested that the prevalence of interpersonal violence was nearly 100 times greater some 5000 or more years earlier (Pinker 2011, 49).

Most "conventional"[2] crime, especially violent crime, can be regarded as a microcosmic form of conflict. As many of the studies cited herein will illustrate, it is often a byproduct of political conflict as we know it. This essay will review empirical research to explain variations in crime over time and across nations, with particular attention to non-Western settings and to large-scale cross-national analysis. It will note the difficulties faced by those who undertake statistical analyses of crime, as well as the abundant opportunities to explore territories yet uncharted.

Crime trends, like most trends in human behavior, rarely appear smooth and uninterrupted. So it is that scholarly attention has also been drawn to fluctuation around the long-term decline in interpersonal violence. The end of World War II saw a reversal of this trend and commensurate increases in property crime as well. Then, beginning in the 1990s, a sudden decline in crime rates was visible in most Western nations, persisting even through the economic crisis of 2008. These exceptional developments stimulated a great deal of research across the social sciences, primarily by criminologists and economists. With the accumulation of knowledge about crime trends in Western societies, the relative ignorance about patterns of violence in developing nations and in non-state societies provided new research opportunities. In addition, places as diverse as the former Soviet Union, South Africa, and Taiwan experienced transitions from authoritarian to democratic rule and were soon confronted by significant increases in crime, at least in the short term. Such similarities too are remarkable, especially given the wide variation in political, social, and economic circumstances experienced in these transitional states.

In 1977 Gurr and his colleagues published a 790-page book entitled *The Politics of Crime and Conflict: A Comparative History of Four Cities* (Gurr et al. 1977). The work was funded by what was then the Centre for the Study of Crime and Delinquency of the National Institute of Mental Health (NIMH).

The project was vast and ambitious, the main objective being to identify and explain crises of public order in four cities (London, Stockholm, Sydney, and Calcutta) over the previous two centuries. The concept of public order crises was viewed expansively, to include whatever forms of individual deviance or collective action were regarded as offensive by authorities in power at the time. The project also sought to identify state responses (in law and policy) elicited by these crises and, in turn, the impact that these responses had on subsequent patterns of disorder.

Gurr and his colleagues (1977) reported a long-term decline in crime in London, Stockholm, and Sydney over the course of their recorded histories. The declines were particularly pronounced with regard to crimes of violence, and somewhat less so with regard to property crime. These declines "bottomed out" around the time of World War II and rose steeply thereafter. The long-term decline was attributed to the historical evolution of humanitarianism in industrial societies, which reflected increasing civility on the part of both rulers and the ruled. By contrast, patterns of crime in Calcutta followed a different path. Violent crime peaked on four occasions, at roughly twenty-five-year intervals, between 1870 and 1970. Cycles of property crime were similar until the time of independence in 1947, when they declined. Political, cultural, demographic, and economic circumstances set Calcutta apart.

The observed trends were not unique to the three "Western" cities, and have been observed in various other locations (almost all of them also Western industrial jurisdictions) by a number of scholars. Subsequent reviews reported similar findings of a long-term decline followed by a recent temporary increase (Eisner 2003; Spierenburg 2008; LaFree et al. 2015).

Gurr (1981) complemented the four-city study with additional evidence from the United States and England, reaffirming the long-term decline reported earlier. He did observe, however, three episodic surges in US crime (beginning around 1850, 1900, and 1960), that led him to refine his explanation of (declining) crime as a product of long-term cultural change. Among the sources of deviation from the long-term trend that he proposed were war, urbanization, and fluctuating economic conditions. Gurr added to the complexity of his explanation by noting subcultures of violence in the United States (specifically the southern states) and by observing the differential impact of economic conditions on racial groups.

Gurr drew further on the burgeoning criminological literature by suggesting that the significant increases in post-World War II property crime observed in most Western societies could be attributed to unprecedented material abundance: there was simply more to steal than at any time in the past, and crime follows opportunity (see Cohen and Felson 1979; Felson and Clarke 1998).

Few subsequent attempts at long-term comparative historical analysis were made until Eisner's (2003) comprehensive study of European homicide rates. Eisner compiled a *History of Homicide Database* comprising quantitative data on homicide in European jurisdictions over several centuries. The data were based on national statistics (which became available in most countries beginning in the nineteenth century) as well as data compiled by individual historians for specific jurisdictions for earlier periods. Eisner reported a long-term decline across Europe similar to that observed in London, Stockholm, and Sydney by Gurr et al. (1977). The magnitude of the decline reported by Eisner varies from 90 to 98 percent, depending on the location. The onset of the decline observed by Eisner, however, was not uniform across Europe, and tended to vary across regions. It originated in north-west Europe, then appeared sequentially as it progressed across the continent, reaching south-west Europe last. Consistent with the findings of Gurr et al. (1977), Eisner noted that European homicide rates, after "bottoming out," began to increase in the aftermath of World War II.

While very long-term trends, because of the questionable quality and fragmentary nature of their underlying data, may not lend themselves to the most sophisticated statistical analysis, they are amenable to a degree of rigorous interpretation. Eisner's impressive attempt at contextual explanation is exemplary. He suggested that the decline in European homicide rates tended to correspond with the diffusion of urbanization and industrialization across the continent. As modernization spread southward across Europe, homicide rates declined in parallel. He observed this pattern within countries such as Italy and France, as well as cross-nationally. In addition, he observed that the overall decline in European homicide tended to coincide with the proportion of homicides that were committed by a male offender against a male victim. Correlatively, the proportion of homicides involving females and family members as victims of homicide was seen to increase. Eisner further noted that the declining proportion of elites involved in interpersonal violence also corresponded with this decrease in male-on-male killing. In another study, Eisner (2011) observed a long-term decline in the homicide rate of European monarchs between AD 600 and the end of the eighteenth century.

It is perhaps not surprising that the involvement of females as homicide offenders has tended to be infrequent and relatively invariant. By contrast, Feeley (1994) observed a very high involvement of women in property crime, which declined with the advent of industrialization as factories replaced families as the locus of production. Eisner noted that the typical age of violent offenders also seems to have been exceptionally stable over five centuries, with most aged in their twenties, and with the risk of engaging in violent behavior thereafter declining with age.

The social status of violent offenders has changed significantly over time, however. As noted above, elites became less violent. Eisner attempted to theorize from the above findings by suggesting that the decline in interpersonal violence reflects the civilizing process of Western industrial society over the past 500 years. Inspired by the work of Norbert Elias [1939] (1994), he suggested that, over time, Europeans have developed higher levels of self-control and decreasing impulsivity, characteristics that contemporary criminologists have identified as significantly reducing the risk of offending (Farrington 1989).

Eisner linked these psychological variables to larger social and political changes, including the rise of the state and its monopoly on violence, and the degree of interdependency accompanying the rise of the market economy. Eisner attributed the long-term decline in violence in part to a cultural trend set by elites. Cultural change that saw the defense of one's personal honor become less important was a significant contributor to the decrease. As states began to monopolize the legitimate exercise of violence, punishment imposed in the name of the state replaced private vengeance. Governments created court systems and elites embraced alternative, less violent means of conflict resolution. Over time, duels gave way to lawsuits. With fewer violent role models, common people followed in due course (Eisner 2001). The increased availability of legal means of handling conflict, and a corresponding reduction in elite violence, is also noted by Cooney (1997).

Steven Pinker's magisterial book *The Better Angels of Our Nature* was an unprecedented integration of existing knowledge about human violence (Pinker 2011). Its goal was the description and explanation of trends in human violence from prehistoric times to the present. Originally attracted to the subject of long-term trends in violence by the work of Gurr (1989) and Keeley (1996), Pinker carefully documented the decline of violence in all of its forms over thousands of years. Over the long haul, the decrease has been dramatic. His synthesis of findings of various disciplines, from archaeology to zoology, confirmed the conclusions of scholars such as Elias, Gurr, and Eisner, not to mention Thomas Hobbes. Pinker provided an abundance of supporting evidence at multiple levels of analysis, including, *inter alia*, family, tribe, and nation-state. Despite current impressions, the "good old days" were horrific by comparison. Pinker attributed this decrease to the centralization of authority and the emergence of government, the growth of trade and commerce, the development of a humanitarian ethic, the emerging respect for women's rights, and the growing concern for human rights in general.

As far as criminal violence is concerned, the end of World War II was followed by an apparent reversal of this long-term trend. Crime rates increased in most Western societies until the last decade of the twentieth century. Varied interpretations suggest that long-term trends themselves, not to mention variations around these trends, may have multiple explanations. The inverse relationship between crime and economic well-being during the nineteenth century gave way to a positive relationship during the period after World War II. The individualism that

Eisner (2003, 131) suggests may have contributed to the long-term decline in crime has also been identified as contributing to its reversal (Eisner 2008).

An insightful discussion of the reversal of crime trends has been advanced by Savelsberg (2002). He notes the limits of unidirectional theories such as those of Elias, suggesting that the growth of organizations beyond a certain size contributes to alienation, and the physical mobility of urban dwellers to the weakening of neighborhood social networks. The combined effect of these has been a diminution of social control. In addition, Savelsberg observed that fundamental changes in the labor markets of Western industrial societies contributed to a massive loss of employment, especially for young, unskilled males. Thus, modernization has decreased crime in the long run, while contributing to its rise in the recent past. Defenders of Elias would suggest that his theory is not perfectly linear, and that temporary episodes of decivilization have resulted from crises of state legitimacy, social dislocation, and desensitization to violence.

Crime and Civil Conflict

The relationship between crime and civil disorder has been subject to considerable impressionistic discussion, but considerably less in the way of systematic analysis. Both crime and civil disorder elicit a great deal of rhetorical and ideological posturing, on the part of perpetrators as well as of authorities who seek to suppress them. Thus, one sees insurgents or protestors occasionally labeled as "common criminals" in order to justify a harsh response on the part of the state. Conversely, ordinary offenders may identify themselves as "freedom fighters" in order to acquire a degree of legitimacy or to rationalize their activity to themselves and others. Empirically, one sees a degree of convergence in the two forms of behavior. Collective political action, whether in the form of protest, strikes, or insurgency, may entail breaches of criminal law. It is quite common for political insurgents to engage in criminal activity to support their movement or activities, and many practitioners of political violence may retire to a life of crime "after the revolution." The term "fighters turned felons" represents just such a career transition. Some achieve positions of relative respectability. Mincheva and Gurr (2013) refer to fighters turned felons turned public officials," and "fighters turned felons turned entrepreneurs.

Not surprisingly, the conventional wisdom held that crime and conflict were positively related, with each reflecting the prevailing environment of social cohesion, or lack thereof. This can reflect a lack of consensus regarding behavioral norms or the extent of collective or individual discontent with the prevailing distribution of valued objects or conditions. Other plausible explanations for co-variation in the two phenomena include a Hobbesian-based hypothesis that would see all forms of disorder vary inversely with state coercive capacity.

Lodhi and Tilly (1973) sought to explore the relationship between urbanization, crime, and collective violence in nineteenth-century France. Long-term trends in property crime declined significantly during the period, while crimes against persons fluctuated within a narrow range, with no discernible trend. They observed collective violence to vary significantly over the century, independently of crimes against persons and property. Based on this comparison, complemented by cross-sectional analyses of variation across eighty-six Departments in 1841, 1846, and 1851, they concluded that crime and collective violence were essentially unrelated, the latter being driven by episodic power struggles at the national level.

In order to investigate the relationship between crime and civil disorder, Gurr et al. (1977) identified discrete "crime waves" during the history of each of the four cities they studied. These were operationally defined as periods in which the crime rate, as measured by official statistics, increased in three successive years at an average rate of 10 percent or more. They ascertained twenty-nine separate periods of significant increase in the rate of *violent* crime, of which nineteen, or 66 percent, were also characterized by significant episodes of civil disorder. Of twenty-five periods marked by significant increases in *property* crime, thirteen coincided with civil strife.

LaFree and Drass (1997) studied the relationship between crime and disorder in the United States from 1955 to 1991. Statistics of crime were extracted from Uniform Crime Reports and from revised estimates provided by the FBI. They included arrest rates by race. Measures of collective action were coded from the New York Times Index. They found a close relationship between crime rates and collective action until the mid-1970s. After that, however, the relationship was negative or nonexistent.

These inconsistent findings suggest the possibility of more than one causal process at work. LaFree and Drass suggest that the co-variation of crime and collective action prior to 1970 reflected social disorganization, while the decline in civil disorder since 1970 suggested a decline in the capacity to mobilize resources of protest, combined with a strengthened state-repressive capacity which was more capable of inhibiting collective disorder than it was of restraining individual criminal activity.

The Impact of Civil War

Ghobarah et al. (2003) sought to explain the effects of civil war on adverse health experiences, among them homicide. Their cross-sectional least-squares regression analysis of data from 177 countries found that the rate of death in civil wars during the period 1991–97 produced an increase in the number of life-years lost as a result of homicide in 1999, particularly among males between the ages of fifteen and forty-four. The estimated loss of disability-adjusted life-years was 0.14 per 100 of that cohort. The destructive aftermath of civil wars was also found in contiguous countries. By contrast, Fearon's (2011) analysis of homicide data from 165 independent countries between 1960 and 2009 reported a strong contemporaneous association between civil war and homicide, but not a lagged relationship.

At a very different level of analysis, Miguel et al. (2011) report that penalties for violent conduct on the field are more common among European soccer players who had been previously exposed to civil war in their country of origin.

The Impact of International Conflict

The relationship of war between nations to civilian criminality is varied and complex. In times of war a significant proportion of a nation's young male population may be mobilized, concentrated in domestic military installations, or sent off to fight in foreign lands. Wars may entail unique circumstances that often constrain certain forms of commercial exchange, population movement, and political expression. Curfews and censorship may be more common during wartime.

Whether the experience of war contributes to post-war criminal violence is a question that has served as the basis for speculation for centuries. Archer and Gartner (1976) proffered seven theoretical models that might explain the effects of war on violent crime. These included a *social solidarity* model, which predicted a return to pre-war levels after the cessation of hostilities; a *social disorganization* model, which predicted an increase in homicide in defeated nations; an *economic factors* model, which anticipated higher homicide rates in countries whose economies had been damaged by war; a *catharsis* model, which predicted post-war decreases in homicide for those countries whose wartime experience had been the most violent; a *violent veteran* model, which foresaw a post-war increase in homicide attributable to offending by returning veterans; an *artifacts* model, which would see post-war rates decline because of the wartime losses of young men— the most common perpetrators of civilian homicide; and, finally, a *legitimation of violence* model, in which officially approved killing in wartime would inspire post-war violence.

Archer and Gartner compiled a Comparative Crime Data File for 110 nations beginning in 1900 (Archer and Gartner 1984), and analyzed pre- and post-war homicide rates for fifty "nation-wars," comparing them with changes occurring over the same period in thirty control nations. The authors found that most of the "nation-wars" were followed by substantial increases in homicide. Their findings are conservative, since one would assume that if the artifacts model were valid the demographic changes arising from the disproportionate loss of young males in combat would lessen the population of potential post-war offenders.

Archer and Gartner (1976) observed that the increases in post-war homicide tended to be largest in those nations that had experienced the highest numbers of combat deaths. Further analysis revealed that homicide rates tended to increase for victorious as well as for defeated nations, for nations with improved economic conditions as well as worsened economies, for both male and female offenders, and for a variety of age cohorts. These findings led the authors to reject all but the legitimation of violence model to explain the effect of war on subsequent homicide.

Explaining Cross-sectional Variation in Crime Rates

Economic Inequality

Krohn (1976) conducted a stepwise multiple regression analysis of data on twenty-four nations (c.1970) from Interpol's International Crime Statistics and from the *World Handbook of Political and Social Indicators* (Taylor and Hudson 1972). He found that the Gini Index of income inequality explained 28 percent of the variance in homicide. However, the best predictor of property crime was a measure of relative affluence (GNP per capita), with 47 percent of the variance explained. Inequality added only an additional 5 percent.

Krahn et al. (1986) analyzed Interpol homicide data for sixty-five nations over four time points (1960; 1965; 1970; 1975). They found that inequality explained between 7 and 23 percent of the variance in homicide depending on the year. The relationship was more pronounced in nations that were relatively wealthy and democratic. Population growth, interpreted as representing the proportional size of the young male population, also had a net positive effect on homicide rates.

Messner's (1980) regression analysis on a sample of thirty-nine nations during the 1950s and 1960s found that 35 percent of the variance in logged national murder rates could be explained by income inequality.

Braithwaite and Braithwaite (1980) sought to explain cross-national variations in average rates of homicide derived from Interpol data over a twenty-year period (1955–74) for thirty-one countries. Preliminary correlations revealed a variety of measures of inequality, each to be positively correlated with homicide rates. Subsequent stepwise regressions, however, revealed that, controlling for aggregate economic well-being,[3] intersectoral income inequality explained little additional variance.

Pridemore (2008) maintains that the relationship between economic inequality and homicide may not be as robust as previous studies suggest. He notes that poverty, the main confounder of inequality and the most consistent predictor of US homicide rates, has been omitted from most cross-national studies. In his cross-sectional study of forty-two nations in the year 2000, the inequality–homicide association disappeared and his chosen measure of poverty (infant mortality) remained significant. Subsequently, Pridemore (2011a) replicated two previous studies of inequality and homicide but included a measure of poverty (the natural logarithm of the infant mortality rate) in each. Again, the poverty variable was significant and the inequality–homicide association disappeared.[4]

Age Structure

If, in the words of Auguste Comte, "demography is destiny," one would predict that rates of crime will vary directly with the proportion of the general population comprised of males between the ages of fifteen and thirty-four. This age/sex cohort tends to be at highest risk of offending for most offense categories, at least in the United States. Indeed, the increase in crime in the United States beginning in the 1960s has been attributed in part to the "coming of age" of the post–World War II baby boom. In contrast to the findings of Krahn et al. (1986), Gartner (1990) pooled time series and cross-sectional observations from a sample of eighteen Western industrial nations at five-year intervals over the period 1950–80 and found no age effect. Gartner and Parker (1990) analyzed homicide data from each of five countries[5] over the first six decades of the twentieth century and found inconsistent results: there was evidence of an age effect in the United States and Italy, but not in Scotland and Japan. Recent reviews of the cross-national literature by Pridemore and Trent (2010) and Trent and Pridemore (2012) also show no consistent effect of age structure. It has also been noted that homicide victims and offenders in Russia are much older (about a decade) on average than in the United States (Pridemore 2003b; Pridemore 2011b).

Trends Post-1990

The U-shaped curve that described long-term trends in crime in Western countries was marked by considerable short-term variation in the decades that followed. The post–1990 decline in the United States was particularly dramatic and attracted considerable criminological interest. Rates of crime continued the increase that began in the aftermath of World War II, and rose significantly from the mid-1980s. This increase was followed by a dramatic drop beginning in the early 1990s. By 2004 the number of homicides reported in New York City had declined to the lowest total since 1963. Assaults reported to the National Crime Victim Survey declined by 50 percent between 1994 and 2000 (Wallman and Blumstein 2006, 320). Zimring (2006) observed that the US crime drop occurred across the nation at large, including almost all demographic groups and regions, as well as crime types. US crime rates have remained relatively stable since 2000, largely withstanding the impact of the financial crisis of 2008 and the economic stagnation that followed.

The crime drop in the United States was the subject of detailed analysis by Blumstein and colleagues (Blumstein and Wallman 2006), by Zimring (2006), and, more recently, by Roeder et al. (2015). They concluded that a number of factors were influencing crime trends in a manner that defied precise attribution of relative influence. Rather than an omnibus time series regression analysis, the Blumstein/Wallman project was a compilation and painstaking analysis of specific components of late twentieth-century US crime trends. The decade of the 1990s was a period of economic prosperity. As much as one-third of the crime drop was attributed to improved economic conditions (Wallman and Blumstein 2006). The advent of crack cocaine in the 1980s was accompanied by intense rivalry among dealers, and the competition for market share was often violent. The maturation of the market was accompanied by a degree of stability, with a concomitant decrease in fatal competitive behavior.

Of debatable significance was the use of imprisonment. Rates of imprisonment in the United States began to increase during the 1970s and rose sharply for the following three decades, quadrupling during the period. By the turn of the century the United States had the highest rates of imprisonment of any Western nation. This appears to have made some contribution to the crime drop, although Wallman and Blumstein (2006, 328) noted that rates of crime did not begin to decline in the United States until 1990, two decades after the onset of the imprisonment boom. Zimring (2006) has suggested that the US crime decline was a gradual and cumulative process, affected by conditions that themselves were gradual and continuous, such as the rise in rates of imprisonment. Some estimates suggest that about 25 percent of the US crime drop was attributable to the increase of imprisonment.[6]

By contrast, the more recent contribution of Roeder et al. (2015), which combined meta-analysis and original empirical research, reported a much weaker impact of imprisonment. Their regression analysis, based on pooled time series and cross-sectional observations from fifty states and the District of Columbia for the period 1980–2013, concluded that increased incarceration had little effect on violent crime, producing a modest reduction of no more than 6 percent in property crime during the 1990s. They found that decreased alcohol consumption, growth in income, and the introduction of intelligence-led policing innovations based on the CompStat model each made a significant contribution to the crime decline.[7]

A widely publicized article by Donohue and Levitt (2001) found that the legalization of abortion by the US Supreme Court in 1973 was followed twenty years later by a significant reduction in crime. They observed that states with high rates of abortion during the 1970s experienced greater decreases in murder, other property crime, and violent crime during the 1990s than did states with low abortion rates. The authors concluded that legalized abortion accounted for as much as 50 percent of the reduction in crime that occurred during the 1990s. The Donohue and Levitt findings were the subject of subsequent theoretical and methodological debate; critics point to a failure to account for the rates of abortion prior to legalization (for an overview, see Joyce 2009). At the very least, the size of the effect attributed by Donohue and Levitt appears to be somewhat overstated.

Dramatic as it was, the decline in US crime rates was not unique. Zimring (2006) notes that a decline in crime comparable to that occurring in the United States was also evident in Canada. However, Canada did not experience a crack epidemic (and its aftermath), an increase in the rate of imprisonment, or a prolonged economic boom. What Canada did share was a decline in the proportion of the population aged fifteen to twenty-nine.

Nor was the decline in crime observed during the last decade of the twentieth century limited to North America; it was also evident in a number of other Western nations. Tonry and Farrington (2005) coordinated a comparative study of crime in eight Western countries[8] over the period 1980–99. They reported that by the end of the twentieth century homicide, burglary, and motor vehicle theft rates had fallen, and robbery showed no clear trend. Recent decreases in crime have been evident even further afield; Broadhurst et al. (2015) observed a steep decline in violence in Cambodia since 1999.

Cross-national comparability of crime data has been enhanced considerably with the development of the International Crime Victims Survey (ICVS) (Van Dijk et al. 2008). Tseloni et al. (2010) examined crime trends from 1998 to 2004 for twenty-six countries and five crime types based on data from the ICVS. They too observed a general decline in crime, and found that it was not limited to Western democracies.

Rosenfeld and Messner (2009) observed that falling crime rates in Western Europe during the 1990s occurred in tandem with those in the United States. They conducted a pooled cross-sectional and time series analysis of burglary rates in nine European countries and the United States between 1993 and 2006. They concluded that burglary rates varied inversely with prevailing economic conditions, specifically with consumer confidence, and also varied inversely with rates of imprisonment. The overall effect of imprisonment may have been influenced by an Italian decarceration initiative which saw the prison population of that country decline by over a third in 2006, a year that saw a 17 percent increase in Italy's burglary rate.

The idea that the legitimacy of political institutions may affect rates of crime was the focus of research by LaFree (1998). The period 1960–75 in the United States was marked by significant stresses on US political institutions arising from the civil rights movement, the Vietnam war, and the abuses of executive power culminating in the Watergate affair. These years were also accompanied by significant increases in crime. Based on bivariate comparisons of time series, LaFree concluded that the erosion of political legitimacy (along with economic stress and family disintegration) contributed to the observed increase in crime.

LaFree's conclusions left open the question of whether his findings were historically and situationally unique. Subsequent research suggests that they were not. Nivette and Eisner (2013) tested the legitimacy hypothesis with a cross-sectional regression analysis of data from sixty-five nations at the beginning of the new millennium. Their measure of legitimacy was based on the indicators developed by Gilley (2009). Nivette and Eisner found a significant inverse relationship between political legitimacy and the homicide rate. An even stronger predictor of the homicide rate was income inequality.

While no single variable has adequately explained both the rise of crime during the last half of the twentieth century and the decline of crime since the early 1990s, interesting findings have begun to emerge from research at various levels of analysis suggesting that the crime increase beginning in the 1960s, *and* the decline that began in the early 1990s, may be explained by variations in exposure to environmental lead. Although not all studies were characterized by unimpeachable methodological rigor, and effect sizes differed substantially, the convergence of findings across geographic locations, levels of analysis, and historical periods is noteworthy.

In addition to its use as a base for paint, lead was used as an additive to gasoline from early in the automotive age until its replacement by unleaded fuel beginning in the mid-1970s. The adverse effects of lead on cognitive development have long been known. So too have the effects of low IQ—impulsivity, attention deficit, and hyperactivity issues—on criminal and other anti-social behavior. A causal pathway from lead exposure to cognitive impairment to criminal behavior is certainly plausible.

Nevin (2000) observed a striking association between temporal trends in violent crime in the United States during the twentieth century and changes in leaded gasoline exposure, blood lead level, and IQ. Crime rose with the increased use of leaded gas after World War II and began to fall (after an appropriate lag) with the phasing out of leaded gas and its replacement with unleaded fuel.[9] In a subsequent article, he reported strong associations between preschool blood lead levels and subsequent crime rate trends in nine different countries (Nevin 2007). Wright et al. (2008) reported that individual prenatal and childhood blood lead levels were associated with later arrests for criminal offenses. Fergusson et al. (2008) found an association between individual dentin lead levels in childhood and subsequent criminality, as measured by arrest records and self-reported offending. Mielke and Zahran (2012) regressed rates of serious assault against vehicle lead emissions in each of six US cities. They found that, in each city, every metric ton of lead released produced an increase (after a twenty-two-year lag) in the assault rate of between 1.36 and 1.83 per 100,000 population. Feigenbaum and Muller (2016) found that city-level homicide rates during the early twentieth century were higher in those US municipalities that used lead pipes in their water systems.

Latin American and Japanese Exceptions

A significant deviation from the recent global downward trend in homicide was observed by Fearon (2011), who reports a marked *increase* since 1992 in most Latin American and Caribbean nations. This is consistent with the results of Nivette's (2011) meta-analysis of fifty-four separate studies; she found that the best predictor of homicide was a Latin American dummy variable. These findings appear consistent with a cultural explanation based on values of *machismo* and an economic historical explanation relating to conflict between gangs involved in the production and distribution of illicit drugs.

Of all non-Western countries, the one which has attracted the most sophisticated criminological analysis is Japan. Crime trends in post-World War II Japan were the opposite of those in Western countries. In contrast to the increasing rates of crime in Europe and North America during the second half of the twentieth century, the rate of crime in Japan declined noticeably until the early 1990s and rose thereafter.[10] The apparent Japanese increase occurred at a time when Western industrial societies were experiencing a decline in crime rates.

One of the most rigorous studies of Japanese crime trends is found in the work of Park (1992; 2006). His time series analyses of Japanese crime rates over the period 1954–88 sought to explain variation in each of five distinct crime types (larceny; bodily injury; rape; robbery; homicide). Park found that all but one of the five crime types (rape being the exception) varied inversely with material standards of living (as measured by new housing starts, and rates of automobile ownership and telephone subscriptions). The ratio of social security expenditure to national income was negatively related to the three violent crime types, while the proportion of the population aged fifteen to twenty-four was positively related to the two forms of theft. The clearance rate (percentage of reported crimes cleared) or the conviction rate (proportion of crimes cleared resulting in conviction) explained three of the crime types. Thus, crime in Japan was seen to vary inversely with aggregate economic well-being; the strength of the "social safety net," rates of arrest and conviction, and the relative size of the crime-prone age cohort.

The time series analyzed by Park concluded just prior to the bursting of the bubble economy and the end of the "Japanese miracle." Nevertheless, subsequent research embracing the post-bubble years has been generally consistent with Park's findings. Roberts and LaFree (2004) conducted a time series analysis of annual national data on violent crime for the period 1951–2000 and a pooled cross-sectional time series analysis of data on violent crime from forty-seven prefectures at five-year intervals from 1955 to 2000. These studies included the initial years of Japanese economic stagnation post-1990. The authors found that unemployment and the size of the young male population were the best predictors of violent crime, and the clearance rate, as one might expect, was inversely related.

The Effects of Transition from Authoritarian Rule

The past half-century has seen the demise of many authoritarian states and their evolution to relatively democratic political systems. The transition from an authoritarian regime to a less repressive one appears impressionistically to have been accompanied by an increase in crime. This has been evident in settings as diverse as post-Franco Spain, Eastern Europe, Korea, Taiwan, Egypt,[11] and South Africa. The People's Republic of China, while still relatively authoritarian, has seen an increase in crime in the aftermath of economic reform. The simple explanation for these similar patterns in such diverse settings is that when the surveillance and control capacities of the state become to a degree relaxed, crime will increase.

One may look to history to see that these patterns may operate in reverse. Based on a time series analysis of French crime statistics covering the period 1865–1913, Gillis (1989) concluded that the growth of the French nation-state and the accompanying expansion of surveillance produced a decline in serious violent and property crime. Gillis attributed the decrease to the deterrent effect produced by the increasing coercive capacity of the state. He found no influence of crime rates on the growth of national policing, concluding that crime control was a secondary motive: surveillance and repression of popular collective action by the "dangerous classes" was of foremost concern. In support of this proposition, Gillis observed that the five periods characterized by the largest increases in policing expenditure followed revolutions, coups, or major threats to the regime of Louis Napoleon (Gillis 1989, 333).

Problems of validity and reliability seriously complicate statistical analysis of crime in transitional states. Authoritarian governments may conceal crime statistics, making comparisons with subsequent regimes difficult. Karstedt (2006) notes that crime statistics published by authoritarian regimes have been "notoriously unreliable" and are quite likely to ignore violence committed by the state and its agents. Pridemore (2003a, 1344) observed that crime statistics in the Soviet era were often falsified (see also Chervyakov et al. 2002, 1721). To complicate matters further, statistics of crime in transitional states may suffer from the same shortcomings as crime statistics experienced in democratic jurisdictions where there is greater continuity of governance (Seidman and Couzens 1974; Van Dijk 2008).

Assessing the impact on crime rates of transition from an authoritarian to a relatively democratic regime is fraught with difficulty, since such transitions may be accompanied by a range of diverse circumstances. These can include, *inter alia*, communal or separatist violence, economic disruptions, a prevailing mood of anomie, the desire for revenge on the past of those who may have been disadvantaged under the previous regime, and the incapacity or unwillingess of the new authorities to exercise coercive social control. Moreover, these diverse circumstances can occur in sequence or in contemporaneous combination. Many of these variables are difficult if not impossible to quantify at the aggregate level, thereby inhibiting sophisticated quantitative analysis.

Law enforcement in the immediate aftermath of a transition from authoritarian rule may be less than ideal. The core business of authoritarian policing is the protection of the state; the core business of democratic policing is the protection of the citizenry. The shift in roles from suppression of dissent to crime management may be easier said than done. Tanner (2000) observed that most police are ill-equipped for the transition, and may be dangerously inept at such tasks as crime prevention and basic criminal investigation. An instinctive distrust of police may linger among citizens of post-authoritarian states, further straining relations between police and public. Transitional regimes may themselves experience low levels of public trust.

Despite these difficulties, a number of scholars have sought to describe and explain crime trends in transitional states. LaFree and Tseloni (2006) analyzed trends in homicide in forty-four countries over the second half of the twentieth century. They tested three rival explanatory models. The first of these, derived from the work of Elias, hypothesized that the civilizing effects of democratization would be accompanied by declining homicide rates. A contending model was based on the premise that the free market economies which accompany democratization will produce inequality and selfishness, with brutalizing effects.[12] These in turn will lead to increases in homicide. A third model, based on the trajectory of modernization, predicted an initial increase during the period of rapid societal transformation, and then a decrease as democracies mature.

LaFree and Tseloni's operational definition of democratization was derived from the Polity datasets developed by Gurr and his colleagues at the University of Maryland.[13] The authors calculated an aggregate measure which combined quantitative estimates of political competitiveness and exclusion for each nation-case. As such, it did not purport to directly measure regime repressive capacity.

LaFree and Tseloni's multilevel analysis found that homicide rates in transitional democratic regimes were 54 percent higher than in authoritarian states, but that those in "full democracies" were not significantly different from those in authoritarian regimes. The findings were thus consistent with their modernization hypothesis. They were also consistent with the work of Stamatel (2008), who found a curvilinear trajectory in Central and Eastern European countries. Significant increases in homicide rates were apparent during the initial post-communist transition, but declined subsequently.

Karstedt (2003; 2008) analyzed crime rates in post-communist countries, combining the inspection of time series with a cross-sectional analysis of democracies, authoritarian regimes, and transition countries. The work was not a statistical analysis but, rather, used as diagnostic tools comparisons and time series plots of annual homicide rates over the period 1956–98 in Bulgaria, Czechoslovakia, Hungary, and Poland. As these countries had experienced considerable waves of violence before and at the beginning of the transition, Karstedt interpreted increases in crime in post-authoritarian settings partially as the legacy of past experience. In a subsequent study focusing on prevailing value patterns rather than political structures, Karstedt (2006) analyzed a sample of eighteen democracies and eight authoritarian regimes over the period 1968–72. The democracies were primarily European; the authoritarian states were primarily Latin American and Asian. Using Hofstede's (1980/1984; 1997) value dimensions as independent variables, she reported that lethal violent crime was a function of low levels of egalitarian values and low individualism; in other words, hierarchical and collectivistic value orientations were related to higher levels of lethal violence, and democracies have a comparative advantage in terms of their more egalitarian and individualistic value patterns. In this paper she notes the relative lack of social control as a comparative disadvantage of democracies. By contrast, autocracies have to rely on a strong state apparatus and sweeping social controls to keep violent crime at low levels; their comparative disadvantage is a high level of violent social control.

One of the more interesting analyses of crime rate trends in a transitional society was originally published in the People's Republic of China by the Ministry of Public Security's Research Unit Number Five. Although not intended for widespread dissemination, it was translated and published in 1997 (People's Republic of China

1997). The article, based on descriptive interpretation rather than on statistical analysis, referred to four periods of "high tide" criminality following the 1949 revolution. First was the immediate post-liberation period, where residual counter-revolutionary elements engaged in sabotage, banditry, and espionage. The second high tide occurred during the late 1950s and early 1960s, where poor economic planning (the "Great Leap Forward") and natural disasters resulted in considerable economic hardship. The third high tide occurred during the Cultural Revolution (1966–76), a period of economic stagnation and the disruption of normal patterns of authority. Although crime statistics were not compiled during that period, robbery, looting, and mass fighting were said to have increased significantly. Durkheim would certainly have recognized circumstances prevailing at the time as anomic. When the compilation of crime statistics resumed in 1973, crime rates were 2.4 times greater than those recorded before the hiatus that began in 1965.

The fourth period of high tide coincides with the economic reforms beginning in 1978. The past three decades in China have seen dramatic changes in economy and society. State-owned enterprises were shut down or sold off. The "Iron Rice Bowl" of guaranteed employment is no more. As restrictions on population movement were relaxed, or at least enforced less rigorously, literally millions of peasants have left the land to seek a better life in cities. The message "to get rich is glorious" has made a significant impression on many. The desire for material well-being has eclipsed traditional social values, and not all of the aspirations can be fulfilled by legitimate means. The dramatic growth of the Chinese economy has produced unprecedented abundance—more things to steal. Not only have the informal social controls traditionally situated in family and workplace become significantly eroded, the coercive capacity of the state has become strained (Messner et al. 2008). Liu (2005) reports that, since 1978, economically motivated crimes (such as robbery, fraud, and larceny) have increased more rapidly than non-economically motivated crimes (such as homicide and assault).

In their history of violence in Cambodia over the past two centuries, Broadhurst et al. (2015) observed a long-term decline punctuated by occasional upward fluctuations, the most dramatic of which occurred during the Khmer Rouge regime of the 1970s. Their explanation for the long-term decline is consistent with the conclusions of Elias, Gurr, Eisner, and Pinker—the civilizing process that accompanies modernization and the strengthening of state legitimacy. They attribute the occasional episodes of increased violence to stresses occasioned in whole or in part by external intervention, including the struggle against French colonialism and the dislocations arising from World War II and the Second Indochina War. Correlatively, the periodic resumptions of the general decline in violence were explained by the gradual enhancement of state legitimacy. The assuagement by colonial authorities of peasant unrest during the 1920s, the early reign of King Sihanouk, and the era of reconstruction following the demise of the Khmer Rouge regime were the most prominent of these circumstances.

With the collapse of the Berlin Wall, the former Soviet Union and its traditional allies in Eastern Europe have also experienced significant increases in crime

(Pridemore 2003a; 2003b; Karstedt 2008). Pridemore (2003a) observes that Russian homicide appears to have been under-reported in police statistics, noting that vital statistics (cause of death data) reveal a higher incidence. A number of scholars have sought to reconstruct Russian homicide statistics based on these and previously classified data. Homicide in Russia increased between 1970 and 1985, declining slightly in the face of an anti-alcohol campaign during the Gorbachev years. With the end of the Soviet era, the homicide rate more than tripled between 1988 and 1994 (Chervyakov et al. 2002). An interrupted time series analysis concluded that these increases (as well as increases in rates of suicide and alcohol-related mortality) were associated with the breakup of the Soviet Union (Pridemore et al. 2007).

Pridemore (2003b; Pridemore et al. 2007) attributes the post-Soviet increase to a constellation of factors indicative of a decline in social and economic well-being. These include increases in unemployment, divorce, and the social disorganization resulting from rapid social change.[14] These interpretations were intuitively based, rather than derived from multivariate statistical analysis. In another study, based on time series analysis, Pridemore and Chamlin (2006) found that heavy drinking (as measured by deaths resulting from cirrhosis, alcohol poisoning, alcoholic psychosis, and chronic alcoholism) was contemporaneously related to both homicide and suicide (see also Leon et al. 1997).

Pridemore and Kim (2006) conducted a cross-sectional analysis of seventy-eight regions of Russia, and found that those regions with the greater increases in post-Soviet homicide rates exhibited less electoral support for the Communist party in the year 2000. The model controlled for the effects of negative socio-economic change, such as unemployment and poverty. They interpreted their findings as consistent with Durkheim's ideas regarding threats to collective sentiments: regions characterized by the most rapid political change (in this case, and consistent with Durkheim, change away from the collective ideals and welfare policies of communism) would be expected to have higher levels of crime. Only in passing do the authors refer to a possible diminution in the capacity of police, judicial, and correctional systems. Chervyakov et al. (2002, 1714) suggested that "over the course of the 1990s the Russian police were becoming increasingly overloaded by an explosive growth of serious crimes demanding criminal investigation."[15]

In his discussion of juvenile delinquency in post-Soviet Russia, Pridemore (2002, 194) observes that young people's participation in military service, previously "a valuable mechanism of social control," became much less common. Pridemore (2002, 195) also noted that "rigid Soviet control limited the demand and supply of illegal drugs."

Stamatel (2009) analyzed pooled data from nine countries in Eastern and Central Europe over the period 1990–2003. She found that homicide rates varied inversely with GDP per capita, and were positively related to ethnic diversity and population density. There was no significant relationship with income inequality or with divorce rates.

Other Post-authoritarian Systems

Shaw (2002) observed that crime in South Africa was high during the apartheid regime, but tended to be concentrated in black townships and was accorded less attention by authorities. Official priorities emphasized the enforcement of apartheid laws, such as those relating to the movement and control of the African population (Shaw 2002, 3). The post-apartheid era was characterized by greater freedom of movement, chronic high unemployment, and limited police resources (Super 2010). Larger cities toward the north of the country, such as Johannesburg, attracted many people from Zimbabwe and other African nations in search of a better life. Unfortunately, this placed pressure on limited services and aggravated xenophobic sentiments on the part of native South Africans, often with violent consequences.

A time series analysis of Chilean crime rates over the period 1977–93, incorporating a dummy variable for the post-Pinochet period (1990–93), reported an increase in property crime but a decrease in "all crime" during the post-authoritarian years. However, the estimated coefficients for the post-Pinochet dummy were both insignificant (Hojman 2004). Hojman (2011) subsequently noted that "neither the police nor the judicial system changed very much in Chile, at least in relation to common (as opposed to political) crime."[16] The real-wage growth rate was negatively related to theft and to crime in general. Counter-intuitively, the unemployment rate was *negatively* related to both crime measures.

On July 14, 1987, Taiwan ended thirty-eight years of martial law. A time series analysis by Denq et al. (1994) for the period 1964–90 found that the strongest correlate of crime was the rate of unemployment. Crime rates in Taiwan were high during the early years covered in the analysis, then declined irregularly until the mid-1970s. They remained relatively stable until increasing sharply from 1986. Unfortunately, for purposes of understanding the effects of transition, the time series included only four years of democratic rule. The authors did observe that the transition to democracy was accompanied by a significant increase in police strength, which grew by 25 percent from 1988 to 1990. The ratio of police to population was significantly and positively related to total crime, but *not* to burglary/larceny. This apparent anomaly may reflect an increasing police capacity to identify and record minor violent crime.

Among the few attempts to operationalize authoritarian criminal justice are those found in the work of Yoon and Joo (2005; see also Joo and Yoon 2008). Their time series analysis of Korean crime rates over the period 1964–2000 included dummy variables for years in which martial laws and extraordinary decrees were in force, as well as dummy variables for five distinct political regimes. They also included annual statistics on the number of political prisoners (offenders tried under the National Security Law). Their findings were inconsistent: crime rates were *higher* in those years when extraordinary laws were in force, but varied inversely with the number of political prisoners. Crime was also lower during the authoritarian regime of Park Chung Hee. Overall, the unemployment rate was a much better predictor of crime than were the political variables.

Despite the common experience of crime surge during periods of transition, it may be difficult to generalize across post-authoritarian experiences. Authoritarian regimes are hardly cut from the same cloth; they differ widely (Geddes 1999), and it is not surprising that the outcomes of regime change may also differ. Stamatel (2008) noted that homicide rates in post-communist states of Eastern and Central Europe varied considerably in terms of magnitude, duration, and timing. Some regime changes (such as those occurring in a number of Eastern European locations) were accompanied by significant economic dislocation. Others, such as those that took place in Taiwan, Chile, and South Korea, saw business as usual. Transitions elsewhere were characterized by greater freedom of movement on the part of the population (China and South Africa) or by political instability and ethnic conflict (Albania and Macedonia).

Conclusion

Contemporary media reporting of terrorist beheadings, torture by states that portray themselves as paragons of human rights (and by those that don't), mass shootings, and epidemics of violence against women may well give rise to the impression that humankind has never been more violent. Ironically, evidence suggests the precise opposite. It now appears beyond dispute that the human species is much less violent than in previous centuries, indeed in previous millennia. Over the long run, violence in general, and criminal violence no less, has declined as a result of modernization, the centralization of state power, and the growth of commerce. These factors have been accompanied at the individual level by the enhancement of self-control, conscience, and empathy.

This downward trend in violence has not been perfectly smooth, nor has it occurred with precise simultaneity across societies and jurisdictions. Explaining variations around this trend has provided further support for Elias's general explanation. The long-term civilizing process has been punctuated by temporary episodes of decivilization. Indeed, as Eisner has shown, contemporaneous variations in modernization have predicted the behavior of criminal violence.

Generalization about the behavior of complex phenomena across time and space is a daunting prospect. Findings to date suggest that war, economic disadvantage, and a relatively youthful population are likely to produce increased criminal violence; incarceration may contribute to a slight reduction in crime, but may be less cost-effective. Transition to democratic rule is likely to be followed by short-term increases in crime, especially when accompanied by economic hardship. Beyond this, causal mechanisms may be location-specific, as reports on Latin America may suggest.

Notes

1 The author would like to thank Rosemary Barberet, John Braithwaite, Roderic Broad-hurst, Janine Chandler, Lennon Chang, Manuel Eisner, David Hojman, Gary LaFree, Susanne Karstedt, Nadia McLaren, Won-Kyu Park, Lepa Petrovic, William Pridemore, Louise Shelley, and Michael Stohl for their advice and guidance in the preparation of this essay.
2 This essay will focus on what is generally termed "street crime," as distinct from crimes with an explicit political motivation.
3 Protein grams per capita, or GDP per capita (the latter regarded by the Braithwaites as a less ambiguous indicator of aggregate wealth).
4 Fearon (2011), however, finds that inequality still predicts homicide, controlling for GDP. He notes that the relationship between poverty and homicide is curvilinear, with the highest homicide rates found in lower-middle-income countries, rather than in the poorest.
5 England and Wales, Italy, Japan, Scotland, and the United States.
6 Harcourt's (2011) analysis of pooled data from US state jurisdictions (over 3200 obser-vations over the period 1934–2001) reported a strong inverse relationship between homicide and the total number of persons confined in prisons *and mental hospitals.*
7 CompStat, introduced in New York City in 1994, is a system of police resource allocation based on timely intelligence, where resources are allocated strategically and supervisors are held accountable for crime control outcomes in their defined area of responsibility.
8 Australia, Canada, England and Wales, The Netherlands, Switzerland, Scotland, Sweden, and the United States.
9 McCall and Land (2004) challenged the methodology of Nevin's (2000) findings.
10 Johnson (2007) disputes the magnitude of this increase, suggesting that it reflects changes in recording practices. Elsewhere (Johnson 2008), he notes that the Japanese homicide rate fell by 70 percent between 1953 and 2003.
11 David Kirkpatrick (2012) "On Eve of Egyptian Vote, Crime Wave Is the Main Topic" *The New York Times*, (May 22) www.nytimes.com/2012/05/23/world/middleeast/on-eve-of-historic-egyptian-vote-crime-wave-is-the-main-topic.html?pagewanted=2&_r=1&hpw (accessed June 6, 2016).
12 Conditions attached to IMF loans may produce further, often dramatic, recession, worse economic conditions, and increasing inequality. The contemporary Greek expe-rience is illustrative.
13 www.systemicpeace.org/polity/polity4.htm (accessed December 17, 2016).
14 These were obviously compounded by the loss of a variety of welfare benefits, includ-ing health care, social security, and free education.
15 Solomon (2005) refers to the recent proliferation of private security services and the advent of fee for service public policing in Russia, indicating a reduced capacity of police to meet demands for their services.
16 Johnson (2011) reports that the criminal justice system of the Third Reich was remark-ably lenient in its treatment of ordinary Germans, but exceptionally brutal toward those such as Jews and Communists, who were defined as enemies of the regime.

PART II
Forms of Conflict

9

TERRORISM

Situations, Structure, and Dispositions as an Analytical Framework for Studying Terrorism

Scott Englund and Michael Stohl

In his analysis of the political origins of state violence and terrorism, Ted Gurr (1986a, 62–7) identified three sets of conditions that affect the decision-making calculus of threatened elites, the situational, structural, and dispositional. This approach was also embedded in *Why Men Rebel* (1970). Situational conditions include the political traits of challenges (the status and strategies of challengers) and the elites' own political resources for countering those challenges (regime strength and police apparatus). Structural conditions are those that define elites' relations with their opponents and determine or constrain their response options. These include the state's position in the international system and the nature of social stratification and the elite's position within it. Dispositional conditions are those that can be expected to influence how elites regard the acceptability of strategies of violence and terrorism. Norms supporting the use of violence are shaped by elites' direct or mediated experience with violent means of power and are inhibited by democratic values. What is most useful about using these three sets of conditions is that it firmly places the study of terrorism in the domain of contentious politics and directs our attention to the reciprocal relationship between challengers and authorities in their competition, not only for the levers of power but also for the populations they seek to both command and represent. Sadly, this is not an approach that characterizes the vast majority of studies of terrorism since the early 1970s.

It has frequently been noted that the vast majority of the articles on terrorism as well as the vast majority of the scholarly literature on terrorism has not been approached theoretically, nor has the bulk of the research sought to develop theoretically grounded empirical studies. This has been a consistent finding of reviews of the "state of the art" for more than three decades. Writing in 1988, Schmid and Jongman argued that: "Perhaps as much as eighty percent of the literature is not research-based in any rigorous sense" (1988, 219). As a result, they concluded that: "Much of the writing in the crucial areas of terrorism research ... is impressionistic, superficial, and at the same time also pretentious, venturing far reaching generalizations on the basis of episodal evidence" (1988, 177). Ariel Merari concurred: "By and large, terrorism literature is composed mainly of studies which rely on relatively weak research methods" (cited in Schmid and Jongman 1988, 179). Gurr (1988, 2) agreed, arguing that: "With a few clusters of exceptions there is, in fact, a disturbing lack of good empirically-grounded research on terrorism." The consequence, as Merari wrote in 1991, is that terrorism research: "resembles hearsay rather than twentieth century science"—and, further, that: "This may well be an understatement" (Merari 1991, 95, 220).

In 2001 Andrew Silke compared this dearth of quantitative analysis in terrorism research at the end of the 1990s with other social sciences, specifically forensic psychology and criminology. By analyzing articles published from 1995 to 2000, Silke found 86 percent of forensic psychology and 60 percent of criminology scholarly articles used statistics. In contrast, only 20 percent of the scholarly articles on terrorism attempted a quantitative analysis. He concluded that:

> Ultimately, terrorism research is not in a healthy state. It exists on a diet of fast food research: quick, cheap, ready-to-hand, and nutritionally dubious . . . . It was found that the problems identified in 1988 [by Schmid and Jongman] remain as serious as ever.
>
> *(Silke 2001, 221)*

Writing in 2014, Marc Sageman brought the lamentations about the lack of progress in terrorism research once again to the fore. Discussing the surge of money and the resultant research on terrorism during the decade after 9/11, he commented:

> Yet, after all this funding and this flurry of publications, with each new terrorist incident we realize that we are no closer to answering our original question about what leads people to turn to political violence. The same worn-out questions are raised over and over again, and we still have no compelling answers. It seems that terrorism research is in a state of stagnation on the main issues. How did this state of affairs arise?
>
> *(Sageman 2014, 569)*

Sageman argues that the roots of the lack of progress lay both in the questions being asked and the lack of data to pursue them. As he indicated, one set of questions centered on the psychological: Why do they hate us? What is the terrorist personality? This eventually gave way to a process approach to becoming a terrorist, and to a search for recruitment devices both in the new media and in personal charismatic figures. In addition to the shortcoming in these approaches, Sageman also bemoans the lack of appropriate data for academics studying these questions, much of which is in the hands of government intelligence analysts, who do not exploit it because they lack the concepts, time, and training to do so. A serious impediment to scholars, whether fully dedicated to terrorism studies or only occasionally participating in such research, is the lack of the availability of comprehensive and reliable data (Sageman 2014, 569). And thus Sageman concludes quite harshly: "To draw my point to its extreme: we have a system of terrorism research in which intelligence analysts know everything but understand nothing, while academics understand everything but know nothing" (Sageman 2014, 576). This critique is but the last of a long jeremiad going back almost forty years about the poor quality of the research in the field.

Sources of Data for Terrorism Research

The data upon which much of the empirical study of terrorism have been based consists of three fundamental forms. First there are the aggregate datasets of incidents which generally provide the who, what, where, and when of events and, when possible, the suspected or confirmed perpetrators. These tend to be characterized by organization or at least the type of organization (e.g., Islamist, Chechen, nationalist, right wing, left wing, etc.) and the amount of damage and number of victims. These datasets may be transnational/international in scope or may focus on both domestic and international events, but almost all experts agree that they do not capture all of the purely domestic terrorism that occurs globally.

While ITERATE[1] was the source of most quantitative studies of terrorism from the 1970s until around 2005, today the most widely used source is the GTD (Global Terrorism Database). This database, which began in 1970 in the Pinkerton Agency, has over 88,000 incidents and covers both international and domestic attacks. The database operational inclusion coding rules ignore the conceptual definition that underlies the data collection and the database thus includes most non-state violence. This criticism has been noted before (Grabosky and Stohl 2010, 43). Sánchez-Cuenca (2014, 596) writes: "In fact, if you select the ten most active armed groups in the GTD, at least eight of them have featured civil wars and are groups with territorial control (De la Calle and Sánchez-Cuenca 2011, Table 3)." Thus, many non-terrorism events are included in analyses of terrorism without the analysts recognizing that the data that they are analyzing are actually not the data they are conceptualizing. In addition, at its best, as Sageman (2014, 571) notes: "From such data, one can make statements about the frequency and distribution of terrorist attacks, but little about how people turn to political violence, which requires far more detailed, comprehensive, and reliable data."

Second, there are forensic datasets that reconstruct the characteristics of captured or dead perpetrators of terrorism (including suicide terror) as well as the names and characteristics that might be gleaned from the testimony of the captured. It is from these sources that we obtain descriptive information about the basic demographics of terrorists. Russell and Bowman (1977, 17) provided one of the first demographic sets:

> Statistics compiled on over 350 known terrorists from eighteen Middle
> Eastern, Latin American, West European and Japanese groups revealed the

composite terrorist as a single male, aged 22 to 24, with at least a partial university education, most often in the humanities. Terrorists who have practiced vocations have generally been in law, medicine, journalism, teaching, and—in only Turkish and Iranian groups—engineering and technical occupations. Today's terrorist comes from an affluent middle- or upper-class family that enjoys some social prestige.

Obviously, these data do not purport to provide a reliable profile of who within each of these demographic categories might become a terrorist. Likewise, Merari (2010) provides data on suicide bombings: 2622 suicide attacks (2937 bombers) from 1981 to 2008 by year and country. He provides demographic information that indicates that 95 percent were male; 89 percent were under the age of thirty, 69 percent were under the age of twenty-five; 82 percent were single; and 91 percent were Muslim. He also provides additional demographic data by country on economic and educational status. But Merari (and others) conclude that no profile emerges.

The third form of data we have on terrorism come from more extensive analyses of the paths and pathways that individuals have taken to violent revolutionary or terrorist behavior. There are numerous biographies of revolutionary and terrorist leaders that provide insights into their paths. Juergensmeyer (2000) examines a set of radicals turned violent through religious beliefs. McCauley and Moskalenko (2011) provide perhaps the most comprehensive approach examining individual, group, and mass pathways to radicalization. What these examinations provide is the detail to understand (or speculate) as to how the individual was spurred at key decision points to move first toward radicalization and then toward the use of violence. What each of these three forms of data are not able, and indeed are not intended, to provide is the data that explain why the vast majority of the population in every demographic and under all circumstances does not become part of the long tail[2] of the distribution of terrorists within the general population.

Situations, Structures, and Dispositions

This chapter adopts the framework proposed by Gurr to organize our review of the current state of terrorism scholarship. We will consider in turn those studies that emphasize situational, then structural, then dispositional variables. Situational variables include the traits, capacities, and means of opponents in a political conflict; in this chapter we include access to "safe havens" in a failed or failing state and a state's use of violence to repress dissent. Structural variables describe the constraints on opponents in a political conflict and will include here a discussion of studies that focus on the so-called "root causes" of terror, such as economic inequality, poverty, highly stratified and unequal societies, and the relationship between democracy and incidences of terrorism. Dispositional variables consider the conditions that can be expected to influence how actors regard the acceptability of strategies of violence and terrorism.

Situations

Situational variables are those that describe the relationships and relative strengths between political opponents in a conflict. As Gurr was thinking about the state use of terror, these focused on the relative legitimacy of the state regime and of the challengers, the existence of a state apparatus for terrorizing its people and political opponents, and the tactics employed by those challenging the regime's *status quo* (Gurr 1986a). "From the rational choice perspective, these should be the most important determinants of decisions to use state violence" (Gurr 1986a, 62). Taking these and applying them to the study of non-state terror groups requires only minor adjustments. For our present purposes we will consider the following as situational variables: (1) the existence of a "safe haven" or ungoverned territory and its potential utility for terror groups; and (2) the state's use of violence and repression to effectively discourage or eliminate political challenges.

T. E. Lawrence, the British Army officer charged with leading an Arab insurgency against the Turks in World War I, identified several elements necessary for the survival of a group engaged in irregular warfare against regular formations, which included: ease of movement, a "safe haven" from attack, and secrecy. The 2002 US National Security Strategy noted among its goals to "secure porous borders," to restore and build up legal institutions and the rule of law, and to "strengthen fragile states," in places as diverse as Africa, South Asia, and the Middle East. Continuing this theme, President Obama's 2010 National Security Strategy identified multiple threats from "nations, nonstate actors, and failed states." The US Department of State has defined safe havens as "an area of relative security exploited by terrorists to indoctrinate, recruit, coalesce, train, and regroup, as well as prepare and support their operations. Physical safe havens are often found in under-governed territory or crossing international boundaries." They further conclude: "Corruption, poverty, a lack of civic institutions and social services, and the perception that law enforcement and legal systems are biased or brutal are conditions that terrorists exploit to create allies or to generate a permissive operating environment."[3] The practical connection between failed or failing states and terror is a consistent theme in counter-terror policy statements. This policy conclusion has been echoed in recent research.

Max Weber's definition of a modern nation-state is frequently employed as a theoretical starting point when studying state failure. According to Weber (1921), a state is defined as the sole entity capable of deploying the legitimate use of violence (or threat of force) within a given territory. A failed state, therefore, is one where the government's monopoly on the legitimate use of force is challenged or cannot be effectively exercised. Emanating from this inability to apply coercive power throughout its territory, failed states are also described as being incapable of providing basic services typically expected of contemporary governments. Finally, just as sovereign states have a responsibility to protect their own citizens, they also have a duty to protect the security interests of other states, to the extent that they can do so by controlling the activities of individuals and groups within their own territory (Reinhold 2011). The theoretical linkage between failed or failing states and terrorism is fairly straightforward: states that lack the ability to govern effectively or police their population will provide fertile ground for illicit activity and encourage its citizens to find alternative sources of "order" or other basic services (Piazza 2008, 471). This relationship has been challenged, however. Since failed states can no longer exercise effective domestic sovereignty, they are vulnerable to intervention by outside states. These more powerful states are presumably more effective at policing, making it more difficult for terror groups to operate.

The conclusion that the political vacuum found in failed or failing states can serve as an incubator for terrorism is therefore not fully settled, but has been subject to empirical research. Using two indices of state failure[4] and the Rand-Memorial Institute for the Prevention of Terrorism (RAND-MIPT) Terrorism Incident Database, James Piazza found a direct and significant relationship between state failure and the incidence of both domestic and transnational terrorist violence (2008). Piazza finds that: "states experiencing high degrees of state failure are indeed more susceptible to transnational terrorist attacks and disproportionately contribute to transnational terrorism that targets other countries." He further concludes: "addressing the problem of failed and failing states should be the key strategy in the war on terror" (2008, 483). Piazza's findings are robust and account for domestic acts of terror—that is, acts originating and completed in one state, by the residents of that state—and transnational terrorism—a violent act originating in one state and being carried out in another.

Clearly terrorism can exist in a state that can effectively extend its administrative and peacekeeping writ throughout its territory; terrorism occurs in failed and functioning states. Under what situations would people choose to employ violence to express their political will; which contentious political relationships are more likely to result in terrorist violence? The security literature has long tried to link state repression with the application of political violence by groups in opposition to the state. Two studies in the late 1980s and early 1990s tied state repression and deprivation in Northern Ireland to violent political dissent (Thompson 1989; White and White 1995). Others have connected state repression, the resilience of democratic values, economic inequality, and violence (Henderson 1991). But these studies blur the distinction between situational and structural conditions that contribute to terrorist violence. The aim of drawing a distinction between situation and structure is to delineate the difference between established institutional features of any given state and the choices made by the political opponents in any given structure that can either contribute to or dampen terrorist violence. Lichbach makes such a distinction clear when he applies game theory to conclude that state repression of non-violent dissent decreases a group's total dissent activity, but increases violent activity. The more consistently a regime acts to repress political dissent, the lower the level of dissent overall (Lichbach 1987).

Situational variables describe the moves political forces make within a given structure. Sometimes these choices are explicit and implemented with authority, but sometimes—as in failed or failing states—these actions are the result of an inadequate capacity to govern effectively. The consequent relationships between political actors can be more or less contentious, with adversaries more or less free to act independently. The situations in which people find themselves can be differentiated from the structures that can constrain their behavior. We now turn our attention to these structural variables.

Structures

Structural causal explanations for terrorism are those features of a society that constrain the behavior of the people living within it; they establish roles and define the allowable range of choices people have in how they can interact and delimit their power to change the environment in which they find themselves. "The structural variables in our theory include the nature of social stratification and the elite's position in it ... and the state's position in the international system" (Gurr 1986a, 65). Modifying Gurr's theory of state terrorism to apply it here, we focus on economic and political structures that establish and constrain regime and citizen. These are the fundamental "root causes" behind the decision to employ political violence. Looking for a "root cause" of terrorism suggests there is a causal relationship between underlying social, economic, political, and demographic conditions and terrorist activity. According to this proposition, certain underlying conditions and grievances help explain how, where, and why terrorism occurs. As a corollary, failing to understand the linkages between these underlying conditions and terrorist violence may result in an inadequate counter-terror strategy. Furthermore, according to this argument, an approach to counter-terrorism that ignores this relationship may even exacerbate those conditions that gave rise to terrorism and could then intensify, or substantively change, the threat of terrorist violence.

According to Newman (2006), a consensus has developed around a cluster of "root causes" that can either create permissive environments for terrorist violence or directly contribute to the radicalization of a segment of a population. These are, generally: high unemployment, economic inequality, and social exclusion among heterogeneous groups; rapid population growth (with a "bulge" of young people) accompanied by rapid urbanization; and a clash of values. No single factor can be identified as "causing" terrorism and the mix of contributing factors can vary in different circumstances. However, sufficient evidence exists to recommend studying "root causes" in conjunction with other contributing factors, such as political stability. Political stability and the ability of a government to actually govern and resolve political crises are cited as belonging to its own category of attending causes (Piazza 2009).

In spite of the possible benefits of this line of research, one might infer that suggesting that there could be a "root cause" for terrorism might also mean that there could be a "justification" for terrorist violence, as if to condone the practice itself:

> Some people are clearly uncomfortable with the idea of root causes because it disturbs the "moral clarity" that they believe is necessary to confront terrorism (Bennett 2002, 67–69). They wish to deny that any form of terrorism could be associated with a legitimate political cause, because they wish to deny that terrorist groups have any legitimacy whatsoever.
>
> *(Newman 2006, 751)*

These "root cause" studies divide into two main categories: economic structures with economic development, and political structures.

Burgoon (2006) attempted to empirically establish that generous social welfare programs reduced incidents of terrorism. By mitigating the effects of economic insecurity, inequality, and poverty, thereby reducing political instability, social welfare spending offsets preferences for violent political expression. Aside from purely economic factors, social welfare spending can also increase education levels, improve the effectiveness of legitimate, peaceful political expression, and reduce the influence of religious organizations that often supplant government sources of social welfare. Significantly, Burgoon draws from three terror datasets, encompassing three different definitions of terrorism, to include domestic and transnational incidents. He concludes: "although this evidence suggests that the substantive effects are modest, it is stable, robust, and insensitive to a broad range of alternative estimations—justifying the judgment that social policy may reduce the risk of a rare but menacing security threat" (2006, 197).

Burgoon's work drew some criticism for his inclusion of transnational threats. The connection between social spending in either the target state or by the state from where terrorists originate is not clearly explained. Krieger and Meierrieks (2010) build on Burgoon's work, but focus on domestic incidents of terrorism in Europe. They find that higher social spending in certain fields (health, unemployment benefits, and active labor market programs) was associated with a significant reduction in homegrown terrorism, while spending in other fields (e.g., public housing) is not. The findings suggest that higher social spending and more generous welfare regimes may also reduce the threat of homegrown terrorism in Western Europe. Like Burgoon, Krieger and Meierrieks do not connect domestic fiscal policy with transnational terrorism.

Although poverty is often identified as a factor that leads individuals to join terrorist organizations, some researchers have pointed out that terrorists are often drawn from higher socio-economic strata (Krueger and Malečková 2003). In fact, these researchers conclude that individuals who engage in terrorism are "at least as likely to come from economically advantaged families and have a relatively high level of education as to come from the ranks of the economically disadvantaged and uneducated" (Krueger and Malečková 2003, 141). Krueger and Malečková use individual biographical details of Hezbollah militants and Palestinian suicide bombers, comparing them with their relevant population, and find little direct connection between poverty, low educational attainment, and terrorism. Taking these data and changing the analysis slightly, Kavanagh (2011) comes to a similar conclusion: poverty is only a determining factor in a decision to join a terrorist organization among those with at least a high-school education. These studies suggest that terrorism is a political, rather than an economic, phenomenon. If terrorism is in effect a kind of political speech, then it might not differ much from other forms of political participation. Since engaging in politics requires a certain level of education, commitment, and interest, then we should expect to see individuals with higher levels of socio-economic status participating in terrorism, especially in states or regions where civil liberties are curtailed (Krueger and Malečková 2003). If this conclusion holds up, then it is sensible to study political structures as potential causal explanations for terrorism.

A democratic government—one in which people have a reasonable expectation that they can effectively participate in the political decisions that affect their lives—has been both blamed for encouraging terrorist acts and credited with dampening the likelihood that people will resort to violence to express their political will. On the one hand, the people who are targeted for violence and threats of violence can theoretically influence political decisions in democratic states; therefore, terror groups view democracies as inherently "soft" targets. Transnational terror groups thus conclude that the populations of democratic states are more sensible targets of violence and intimidation than are the citizens of undemocratic states. Secondly, since democracies tend to limit the ability of the state to monitor the activities of its citizens it is easier for terror groups to organize clandestinely (Savun and Phillips 2009). On the other hand, since democracies are inherently more open to political participation, resorting to violence to express one's political will is unnecessary (Gurr 1970). These mixed conclusions may be partially due to confusion about operationalizing the dependent variable: the terrorist act itself. Domestic acts of terror are those that originate and conclude in one state, and are perpetrated by the residents of the state in which the act is carried out. Transnational terrorism occurs across state frontiers and by people of more than one nation-state. It is difficult to theoretically link regime type with incidences of transnational terrorism.

Pape (2005) argued that democracies are particularly vulnerable to transnational terrorism because the people who are the targets of violence and the threats of violence can directly influence government policies. Savun and Phillips (2009) conclude that democracies are more likely to be targeted by transnational terror groups not because of their regime type but "because of the foreign policy they tend to pursue." Democracies, they claim, are more likely to be active internationally and to promote democratic forms of government abroad through a variety of means, thus generating resentment. So, while both of these studies see a positive relationship between democracy and the incidences of transnational terrorism, they do so for different reasons. Despite their differences, both studies conclude that the structural effects of a democratic form of government encourage transnational terrorism.

Wishing to settle the democracy debate through alternative means, Choi (2010) takes a slightly different tack, emphasizing the "rule of law" and focusing on two "fundamental components" that should be found in democratic government: (1) "fair, impartial and effective judicial systems"; and (2) "a nonarbitrary basis according to which laws and the legal system as a whole can be viewed as legitimate" (Choi 2010, 944). Limiting himself to these components of a democratic government, Choi untangled his analysis from other, possibly confounding, explanatory variables such as the openness of democratic societies that invite outsiders or the civil–legal rights that could provide cover for terrorist operatives. ITERATE and GTD data are used for the dependent variable; these two databases account for both domestic and transnational terrorist incidents. The International Country Risk Guide (ICRG), compiled by the Political Risk Services (PRS) Group, is used to measure "rule of law" along a seven-point scale. Choi concludes that: "legitimate nonarbitrary law discourages ordinary citizens from resorting to politically motivated violence over peaceful resolution of conflict . . . a strong rule of law tradition produces a dampening effect on political violence, regardless of the type of terrorism" (Choi 2010, 957).

Structural features constrain behavior in a political system. They open up certain options, while closing off others. Economic status, inequality, and education can pre-determine which choices are available to political actors before they have the opportunity to respond to the situations in which they find themselves. Political systems can invite greater or lesser participation, provide greater or lesser protections for citizens from the state, and establish more or less consistency in how laws are enforced. Structure is different from the interactions that are constrained by it, and it is different from the dispositions people have toward particular choices in how they interact. These dispositions are based on perceptions of what constitutes an acceptable set of options available in response to a situation, given certain structural constraints. We now turn to this final category: dispositional variables of individual psychology and aggregate public opinion and how they can contribute to a decision to employ terrorism as a political strategy.

Dispositions

Dispositional conditions influence how individuals regard the acceptability of strategies of violence and terrorism. As Sageman indicates, much of the approach to this question has focused on what psychological traits are related to terrorism. Summarizing the results of studies that explored these questions a decade ago,

Victoroff (2005, 33) remains the single best source of information on the lack of useful profiles or personality types arising from individual psychological approaches to the causes of terrorism. His conclusion is stark:

> The leading psychological theories of terrorism include a broad spectrum of sociological, psychological, and psychiatric approaches. Strikingly, virtually none of them has been tested in a systematic way. They are overwhelmingly subjective, speculative, and, in many cases, derived from 1920s-era psychoanalytic hypotheses that are not amenable to testing. Students of terrorism might justifiably conclude from the peer reviewed literature that the total number of published theories exceeds the number of empirical studies—an imbalance that may be of more than academic import. Even the small amount of psychological research is largely flawed, rarely having been based on scientific methods using normed and validated measures of psychological status, comparing direct examination of individuals with appropriate controls, and testing hypotheses with accepted statistical methods.

Gupta (2012, 3–4), writing almost a decade later, concurs:

> The argument that the terrorists suffer from psychological problems or some personality disorder has been put to rest by trained psychiatrists and psychologists from diverse parts of the world for nearly three decades (McCauley, 2007; Horgan, 2005a, 2005b; Merari, 2005; Merari and Friedlander, 1985; Post, 1984, 1990; Post, Sprinzak and Denny, 2003; Silke, 2003; Taylor, 1988; Taylor and Quayle, 1994).

Likewise, recent analyses of suicide terrorists and the literature about them lead to similar conclusions. Merari (2010, 5) argues:

> the prevailing view is that suicide terrorists are normal, and have no distinctive personality traits. By and large this view is influenced by the considerable diversity in suicide bombers' demographic characteristics ... the available evidence suggests that the great majority of suicide bombers had no record of mental illness.

Merari (2010, 253) raises a cautionary note by echoing one of Donald Rumsfeld's aphorisms: the absence of evidence is not evidence of absence:

> By and large, the opinion that terrorists do not have a common psychological profile (Merari, 1994; Hudson, 1999; Kruglanski, 2002; Atran, 2003; McCauley, 2004, Horgan, 2005; Richardson, 2006; Kruglanski and Fishman, 2006) rests on the absence of research rather than on direct findings.

Merari (2010, 4), recognizing the limitations of the focus on the psychological profile in building knowledge of suicide bombers, suggests an approach that should be more useful, through the recognition that there are:

> three main elements in the production of suicide bombers: the community from which the suicide bombers emerge, the group that decides to use suicide attacks as a tactic, and the individuals who are willing to sacrifice themselves in the attacks.

This approach is echoed in the recent examinations of the many different paths to radicalism (McCauley and Moskalenko 2011). Lindekilde (2014) suggests that we also know "from the extant literature on radicalization that small group dynamics alone rarely leads to radicalisation (Schmid 2013; Horgan 2008) and thus the paths are not easily modeled." We also know that there are both many more people who approve of radical movements than participate in them, and that both within radical movements and those that support them many fewer still who participate in violent acts.

Sageman (2014, 568), citing his previous work (Sageman 2008, 71–88, 125–46), suggests that there are "four elements to the process of joining a terrorist network: a perceived war on one's in-group; moral outrage at some salient major injustice; resonance with personal experiences; and mobilization by an already politically active network." When examining Sageman's network data, we find that 66 percent joined the *jihad* with their friends or had childhood friends in the *jihad*, 20 percent had close relationships in the *jihad*, and 78 percent were cut off from their cultural origins when they joined.

Sageman's thesis was savaged by a review of his work in *Foreign Affairs* by Bruce Hoffman, who argued that al-Qaeda central was not only vertical and horizontal but also still core to the terrorist threat. Fortunately, the subsequent colloquy in *Foreign Affairs*, removed from the personal animosities which caused it to be as much personal as intellectual, was illuminating (Hoffman 2008; Sageman 2008; see the discussion in Sciolino and Schmitt 2008). The debate concerned whether the data indicate that the al-Qaeda organization was still vertical and hierarchical (and effectively recruiting, as a hierarchical organization model would suggest) or whether it was horizontal and "leaderless," and thus recruits found "it." It was thus embedded in an argument about the nature of al-Qaeda itself, an organization which more often than not turned out to be a group labeled al Qaeda by journalists and governments seeking simplicity of description or to aid a political agenda wherein it was important for al Qaeda to remain the focal point (Stohl and Stohl 2007; Stohl 2012). As in much of terrorism analysis, choices about which questions to pursue were driven by political rather than intellectual considerations.

In studies of terrorists, as in the study of revolutions and social movements in general, there are great differences among leaders and followers in organizations that resort to terrorism. Whether we examine social movements in general, radical movements, or violent extremist movements (revolutionary or terrorist), the preponderance of leaders are middle or upper class, well educated, socially capable, and objectively not marginalized citizens. However, while the majority of the foot soldiers of organizations that employ violence and terrorism are not well educated or middle class, they share with their leaders the disaffection and alienation associated with marginalization. When coming from diaspora communities they perceive themselves removed from the certainties provided by being embedded in their homeland, real or imagined, contemporary or historical.

Thus, given that we know that there are no psychological or sociological profiles that "produce" radicals or extremists, and that much of the data we have do not allow us to ask what appear to be productive questions from within it,[5] how might we pursue a more productive approach? Colin Wight (2009) suggests that what he calls a "structural approach" will be more helpful than the "psychological approaches that currently dominate," and we need "a more historically grounded understanding of terrorism as opposed to the presentism that dominates post-9/11." Wight goes on to paraphrase realist Kenneth Waltz:

> a theory of terrorism will explain why it recurs and it will indicate some of the conditions that make terrorism more or less likely, but it will not predict the occurrence of particular terrorist acts. What a theory of terrorism hopes to explain is why there is such a phenomenon, not why individual acts of terrorism are committed.
>
> *(Wight 2009, 100)*

It seems reasonable that we can reconcile what Wight calls a "structural" and "historical" research agenda with the dispositional variables we advance here. Can we study with any precision certain dispositions that make terrorism more permissible or at least tolerated? While still inherently dealing with perceptions and values, these variables would need to focus less on the individual level of analysis and more on an aggregation of opinions, impressions, and preferences.

In a recent study by LaFree and Morris (2012), in which they surveyed 2557 participants in Egypt, Morocco, and Indonesia, they found that negative impressions of the United States and less favorable perceptions of their own government's legitimacy was associated with higher levels of support for Muslim-based terror attacks targeting Americans. "Our results show that respondents who viewed their own institutions more favorably were also less supportive of anti-American attitudes and attacks on the United States—especially those by al Qaeda" (LaFree and Morris 2012, 712). Their findings confirm an earlier study by Tessler and Robbins (2007), who found that in Algeria and Jordan approval of terrorism against the United States is more likely among men and women with negative judgments about their own government and about US foreign policy.

Taken together, these findings suggest that approval of terrorism is fostered by negative attitudes toward actors considered responsible for the political and economic status quo. Approving of terrorism done by others is quite different from the decision an individual makes to join in committing terrorist violence. However, the approval of terror by a significant portion of a population creates a permissive disposition for terrorist violence.

Conclusion

Which are the most useful questions to ask with respect to terrorism? Why do particular individuals, groups, organizations, or states, in specific circumstances, choose to use terrorism as a tactic, or what is the root of terrorist behavior more generally, whether within human psychology or in the world in which we live? The answer is to begin by thinking Gurr. That is, we need to concentrate primarily on the political choices, the development of contentious groups, and the interactions among contentious groups and regimes, rather than the particular individuals that engage in the behavior. We also need to separate leaders and followers. Thinking Gurr also implies the need to look for patterns and explanations across classes of events, persons, and organizations. This our statistical analyses may provide, but we also need to embed these analyses with knowledge of the particular cultures, organizations, history, and other characteristics that provide context.

What is clear is that just as there are many pathways to radicalism there are many different political goals that drive the creation of radical groups: from the return to a real or mythical past to the dream of a more benevolent future. We are aware of no studies which suggest that particular group-based motivations are more or less likely to create violent movements, although, for the obvious reasons of potential scale, appeals to nationhood have been more likely to draw adherents during the past two centuries. In the past few decades this has also been combined with religious-based appeals to nationhood, with particularly deadly results. While there is much agreement across terrorism studies that revenge, renown, and reaction might drive particular acts of terrorism, there is also much agreement that the political goals of an imagined community are most likely to underlie the movements in which they are embedded.

To better understand terrorism, we need to take thinking Gurr seriously, building knowledge on the basis of carefully collected and carefully analyzed data, providing conjectures that can be refuted, and accumulating theoretically based knowledge by expanding the range of events, processes, and settings in which hypotheses are subjected to test. As long as we continue to rely primarily on the repetition of untested knowledge claims that we all "know" are true, our "wisdom" will continue to be untested and our understanding of terrorism will not be increased.

Notes

1   ITERATE: International Terrorism: Attributes of Terrorist Events Database.
2   In "long-tailed" distributions a high-frequency or high-amplitude population is followed by a low-frequency or low-amplitude population which gradually "tails off" asymptotically. The events at the far end of the tail have a very low probability of occurrence.
3   US Department of State, Office of the Coordinator for Counterterrorism, April 23, 2015. www.state.gov/j/ct/rls/crt/2005/64333.htm (accessed December 17, 2016).
4   The databases used in their study were provided by the *Foreign Affairs* Fund for Peace and the State Failure Taskforce at the University of Maryland Center for International Development and Conflict Management.
5   Even if Sageman (2014) suggests that the material that US government intelligence agencies have might in fact provide us with more useful information were they to make it available.

10

REVOLUTIONS

Robust Findings, Persistent Problems, and Promising Frontiers

Colin J. Beck

The latest cohort of revolution studies has failed. Not because of a lack of systematic research or recurrent findings, but because the promise of a new generation of scholarship that would solve persistent problems and unify the field has not been upheld (Lawson n.d.). Over a decade ago, Goldstone (2001) noted increasing fragmentation in the social science of revolution among types, causes, processes, outcomes, and levels of analysis. The solution would be in a new approach that "may unify the results of case studies, rational choice models, and quantitative data analyses, and provide extensions and generalization to cases and events not even conceived of in earlier generations of revolutionary theories" (Goldstone 2001, 175–6). Yet this approach has not emerged. Theories of causes and mechanisms of revolution have proliferated. Even as methodological advances have been made, in both quantitative and comparative analysis, little advantage has been taken. Persistent problems still bedevil the field, such as the repression–protest paradox, outcomes of revolution, the legitimacy–stability problematic, and the role of global factors.

But, nonetheless, research has continued to produce robust findings and extend its analysis to new events, such as the Color Revolutions and the Arab Spring. Accordingly, the social science of revolution is a vibrant but disjointed field. This chapter reviews what consistent findings can be drawn out of studies of revolution. I begin by providing a brief intellectual history of the study of revolution, and identify three sets of consistent findings—the role of external strains on states, brittle regimes, and revolutionary coalitions. Next, I discuss how two recent areas of interest—nonviolent revolution and the diffusion of contention across international borders—validate earlier findings yet pose a risk of further fragmentation. I then highlight promising approaches to old problems and sketch methodological advances that could contribute to the field. I conclude by briefly considering persistent problems in the field and how they might be overcome.

The Study of Revolutions

Over the last century, scholarship on revolutions has developed across four primary generations (Goldstone 1982; 2001). With each generational turn, the subject, theory, and method has shifted to take account of new events and to address the perceived deficiencies of the prior cohort. Knowledge accumulation, while present (Goldstone 2003), has accordingly been slow; revolution presents a moving target. This section briefly reviews these generations of revolution.

The first generation of revolution in the early twentieth century primarily sought to establish revolution as a distinct phenomenon that could be compared across seemingly disparate events (Merriman 1938; Pettee 1938; Sorokin 1925). The "natural historians" of revolution (Brinton 1938; Edwards 1927) sketched commonalities in the lifecycle of revolutions, emphasizing the role of different social groups in different stages of the revolutionary process. The object of inquiry at this time was quite tightly bounded—revolutions were the "great revolutions" in which elites, armies, intellectuals, and the masses joined together to overthrow absolutist *ancien regimes*. In the absence of formalized comparative methods, scholars employed a mix of narrative contrast, process tracing, and ideal–typical configurations to understand the occurrence of revolution.

As social science moved towards more explicit study of cause and effect, a second generation of revolution studies emerged that emphasized the linkage between social processes and aggregate social psychology. In contrast to the stage theories of the first generation, mobilization was seen as the product of disruption to social equilibrium, often caused by modernization pressures (Huntington 1968; Johnson 1966; Smelser 1962). Revolution thus had its roots in mass grievances, relative deprivation, and individual decisions to participate in contention (Davies 1962; Gurr 1970; Olson 1965). Revolutionary events were defined in a larger manner—no longer just transitions away from monarchy in core states, but also modernizing events of the decolonizing periphery. While quantitative studies of revolution (Gurr 1968; Snyder and Tilly 1972) and structuralist comparative case studies (e.g., Moore 1966; Wolf 1969) began to emerge, the primary method of the second generation was illustrating theoretical claims with exemplar cases of revolution.

By the 1970s a third generation of scholarship developed, in which revolutions were seen as products of structural, not psychological, processes and mobilization was analyzed vis-à-vis organizational and tactical dilemmas (Moore 1966; Tilly 1964; 1978). A key tenet was the functional and analytical autonomy of the state both as an actor and an arena for revolutionary action (Moore 1966; Skocpol 1979). State-centered theory would dominate revolution studies for almost the next two decades, yielding the highpoint of the social science of revolution. The impact of Skocpol's approach was as much definitional as theoretical. In the late 1970s and early 1980s a common strategy of analysis was to critique prior works for not considering all types of revolution and to propose a new variant with its own causal and mechanistic pattern, such as modernizing revolutions (Dunn 1972; Walton 1984), semi-peripheral and agrarian revolutions (Dix 1983; Paige 1975), revolutions from above (Trimberger 1978), and so on. Skocpol's (1979, 4) clear elucidation of social revolution—"rapid, basic transformations of a society's state and class structures . . . in part carried through by class-based revolts from below"—suggested a parsimonious object of study (see Goodwin 2001a). Accordingly, scholarship moved quite quickly, bringing old and new events into the study of revolution. Methodologically, the third generation was accompanied by (and, in no small part, the instigator of) more rigorous comparative methodologies. Quantitative techniques were mostly left aside, as innovative strategies for examining causality and conjunctural conditions were developed (see Mahoney 2004).

But with the cultural turn more broadly in social science, the unity of the third generation approach began to disintegrate. Structural theories of revolution were considered too deterministic and poorly equipped to deal with the current frontiers. The center of revolution studies thus became issues related to the structure–culture/agency problematic (Sewell 1985; 1992), leadership and ideology (Foran and Goodwin 1993; Parsa 2000; Selbin 1993), and the role of identity and solidarity, particularly among marginalized groups (Moghadam 1995; Reed and Foran 2002; Selbin 2010; Viterna 2006). The phenomenon of interest also shifted again, focusing more on revolutionary processes rather than revolutionary onsets, incorporating episodes of dual power in revolutionary situations (Tilly 1993), electoral and pacted transitions (Lawson 2005), and failed or negative cases of revolution (Foran 2005; Goodwin 2001a). Accordingly, Tilly (1995), in his second intervention in the field, argued that general theories of revolution were doomed to fail and that the goal should be identifying combinations of mechanisms rather than invariant law-like propositions: "Revolutions are not A Single Thing . . . structure, culture, and strategic calculation are not outside of the mechanisms of contention but the raw material for their action and interaction" (McAdam et al. 2001, 226). The methods of the fourth generation, while increasingly sophisticated, retained the comparative strategies of the third.

As should be clear from even this brief review, the social science of revolution has undergone notable generational shifts in theory and the phenomenon of study, with more limited methodological evolution. With a constantly shifting dependent variable, replication and refutation have rarely been undertaken systematically. Rather, new cases are tested for congruence to old ones, and where prior theories are found lacking further explanatory factors tend to be added somewhat piecemeal (Kurzman 2004a). As a result, there has been a proliferation of causal conditions and mechanisms. Fragmented and multiplying theories of revolution are thus just as much a product of the field's evolution as of the underlying empirical reality of revolution.

Tilly was correct, perhaps, to reject single variable explanations with linear relationships to the onset or outcome of revolution. But this does not require rejecting all generalization. As Roger Gould (2003, 13) reminds us: "It is quite possible that the principal flaw of general statements is not that they are general but on the contrary that they are not general enough." We can thus identify larger sets of causal conditions that have been consistently found to matter in revolutionary episodes (see also Goldstone 2003; Mann 2013). While specific, measurable factors may differ from case to case, the abstract pattern is clear.

Consistent Findings: External Strain, Brittle Regimes, and Revolutionary Coalitions

Under what conditions do revolutions occur? Which regimes are most susceptible? How does contention transform into successful revolution? Complete answers to these key questions still elude the field. Yet, for each, there are robust sets of factors that consistently occur across the universe of revolutionary cases. These conditions are not law-like, as the exact mechanisms may differ across events, and they operate in a conjunctural and contextual fashion. Yet, even so, the social science of revolution has demonstrated that revolutions occur when state structures are under increasing strain, that particular types of regime are most brittle and at risk of revolution, and that successful revolutions involve large coalitions of social groups and elites as challengers.

States Under External Strain

That revolutions occur, at least partially, as a product of administrative strain on a state is perhaps the key finding of the field (Collins 1999). While administrative breakdown can come from intrinsic pressures, as detailed below, the instigating process is often extrinsic to the state itself. Two sets of conditions seem to yield the most pressure: economic factors and relations with other states.

Insurmountable economic pressures on states are a foremost condition for revolution. Skocpol's (1979) original state breakdown theory argued that social revolutions occurred when states faced fiscal strain, and this has been replicated in a variety of cases (e.g., Farhi 1990; Foran 2005; Goldstone 1991; Paige 1975; Skocpol 1982; Walton 1984). The exact mechanism can differ from case to case—for example, states can overextend themselves through spending (Skocpol 1979; 1982), states dependent on a single commodity or resource can lose revenue as prices change (Skocpol 1982; Farhi 1990; Foran 2005), or population growth can outstrip state capacities (Goldstone 1991). Many strains are directly connected to world economic relationships, whether dependent development, international or domestic market downturns, or legacies of colonialism (Boswell and Dixon 1993; Foran 2005; Goodwin 2001a; Paige 1975; Walton 1984). Notably, some first generation approaches to understanding revolution also emphasized economic conditions as a causal factor (e.g., Merriman 1938). On the face of it, this set of findings is not dissimilar from the social strain approaches of the second generation

(Davies 1962; Gurr 1970; Johnson 1966). But the grievances of individuals need not be the causal mechanism for a correlation between stressors and revolution. States are, after all, autonomous actors and not just aggregates of popular will (Evans et al. 1985).

A state's relation to other states and the larger international environment can also create pressures that lead to revolution. Skocpol's (1979) original theory emphasized war and military competition as an ultimate cause behind state breakdown, but later work has found little correlation and suggested that war and competition are best seen as products of the uncertainty that revolution brings (see Beck 2011; Halliday 1999; Kestnbaum 2002; cf. Mann 2013; Walt 1996). Thus, states in a "bad" neighborhood of revolutions and political instability face increasing pressure, particularly when a revolutionary regime seeks to export its revolution (Halliday 1999; Katz 1997; Walt 1996). More centrally, revolutions tend to occur when political opportunity exists at the international level, for instance, during periods of hegemonic decline or when great powers do not intervene to uphold the status quo (Foran 2005; Goldfrank 1979; Goodwin 2001a; Kowalewski 1991; Kurzman 2008). And, as detailed previously, economic and material strains are often structured by sets of international and transnational relationships.

In sum, external strains on states make revolution more likely through a combination of domestic and international processes. Crucially, it is not these conditions alone that predict the occurrence of revolution—they are just one important factor in conjunctural causation. While the exact mechanisms can and do differ from case to case, revolutions do not appear to occur at the heights of peace and prosperity.

Brittle Regimes

Not all states perform the same under pressure. Some regimes are more brittle and less able to accommodate or co-opt contention, meaning that revolution is the only way out of political dilemmas (Goodwin 2001a). The social science of revolution has emphasized the particular brittleness of patrimonial and personalist regimes, particularly in early modern states, as systems that co-opt potential rivals through political appointments are more easily strained by changing fortunes (Barkey and Rossem 1997; Bearman 1993; Goldstone 1991). Modern rentier states, highly dependent on the revenue from extraction to assure loyalty, are also more likely to crumble when resources diminish (Skocpol 1982).

In broader terms, the primary cause of brittleness is political exclusion (Foran 2005; Goodwin and Skocpol 1989). Regimes that exclude rather than co-opt their potential opponents and other legitimate social groups have a limited capacity to deal with challengers, and must rely on repression alone (Wickham-Crowley 1992). More inclusive regimes, even if only inclusive to the extent of bringing key elites into the power structure, are better able to block the formation of large oppositional blocs (Slater 2010; Walton 1984).

But other regime structures are also susceptible to revolution. States can use various methods of legitimation and inadvertently create the resource basis and constituency for opposition. For example, Islamist revolts may stem from the use of religion in the public sphere (Beck 2009; Moaddel 2002). And empires face another dilemma, as the necessity of extending imperial control through autonomous subunits creates loosely controlled peripheries (Barkey and Rossem 1997; Mann 1986). In broad strokes, the imagery of first generation scholars—absolutist monarchies facing revolution—identified these mechanisms. But, ironically, in the contemporary world the few remaining monarchies have proved to be more stable than secular authoritarian and partially democratic states.

Each of these factors is a state-intrinsic mechanism, dependent on the construction of political authority and state administrative structure. While no one type leads to revolution, it is clear that revolutions are nurtured by regimes that are unable to respond to political crises effectively owing to their underlying nature, and that thus allow broad oppositional blocs to form.

Revolutionary Coalitions

If external conditions determine a bit about when, and state structures a bit about where, then the formation of large challenging coalitions tells how mobilization can turn to revolution. Originally theorized as a primary mechanism of revolutionary success in the third generation (Dix 1984; Goodwin and Skocpol 1989; see also Tilly 1964), coalitions have been found to be an essential ingredient of the revolutionary process.

Successful coalitions can take various forms and involve different sorts of actor, as long as they are sufficiently broad and cross-cutting of social cleavages (Foran 2005). Broad coalitions make it difficult for the state to repress challenges completely (Chang 2008; Slater 2010), as targeted contenders can seek safe haven, either practically or symbolically, with other social groups (Osa 2003). Large coalitions also have the advantage of providing multiple methods of mobilization and the very real ability to bring participants out for a diverse set of reasons (Beissinger 2011; 2013). Thus, sufficiently broad coalitions sustain mobilization.

Successful coalitions also tend to incorporate elites who are uniquely well positioned to overcome state power (Barkey 1991; Goldstone 1991; Markoff 1988; Slater 2010). In fact, exclusionary states are so brittle precisely because they tend to promote elite defections and schisms. For example, one path to the successful overthrow of a regime is when its coercive forces refuse to repress challengers, as Egypt and Tunisia in 2011 so vividly demonstrated. Upon occasion, elites have even become authors of their own demise—whether as the intellectual backbones of republican movements (Kurzman 2008; Markoff 1996) or as moderates in negotiated transfers of power (Lawson 2005).

In short, the social science of revolution has moved beyond Marxist imageries of vanguards and discovered that successful challenges come when large and well-placed segments of society begin to oppose a regime. This finding is, again, not that dissimilar from the early natural histories of revolutions, that saw the entrance of new social groups into the revolutionary process as a key factor (e.g., Brinton 1938).

Overall, these three sets of factors tell us much about why and how revolutions occur. When strained states with inflexible regimes are faced with broad alliances of opponents, revolutionary contention and success are both more likely. The details, of course, do matter, but in broad strokes this imagery of revolution is both empirically substantiated and theoretically quite coherent. Yet this set of findings has not risen to the sort of consensual, synthetic paradigm that characterizes other fields of social science. As suggested above, revolution studies has grown in fits and starts and, accordingly, new events are often explored as their own subtopics rather than as further instantiations of the broader field. This can be clearly seen in recent studies of nonviolent revolution and its international diffusion.

New Topics: Nonviolence and Diffusion

In recent years, the Color Revolutions swept the partially democratic and auto-cratic post-communist states, and the Arab Spring spread across the authoritarian Middle East and North Africa. Even before the return of revolution to the twenty-first century, there was growing attention to relatively peaceable movements and contentious waves. Yet, as I describe below, most of these debates have been rela-tively self-referential, rather than seen as steps in advancing the more general social science of revolution.

With the experience of negotiated transfers of power, such as in Chile in 1990 and South Africa in 1993, the bloodless post-communist transitions in Czechoslovakia, Hungary, and Poland, and popular uprisings such as those of the Philippines in 1986, Burma in 1988, and Tiananmen in 1989, scholars began to move away from viewing revolutions as being only violent and forced transfers of power (Foran 2005; Lawson 2005; Sharp 2005; Zunes 1994). This "new" type of revolution based on nonviolent resistance has generated its own cottage industry of research (e.g., Ackerman and Kruegler 1994; Chenoweth and Stephan 2011; Nepstad 2011; Schock 2005). Scholars have argued that nonviolent strategies are a distinct phenomenon, requiring new lines of inquiry (Nepstad 2011; Zunes 1994). For instance, Stephan and Chenoweth (2008; see also Chenoweth and Stephan 2011) found, in their influential study, that nonviolent movements are more likely to succeed as the strategy enhances the international legitimacy of the contenders and diminishes the negative effect of repression on protest. Interestingly, the nonviolent resistance subfield has done little so far to synthesize its findings with the broader social science of revolution. Yet the parallels are clear.

As scholars have previously found, the global context matters for revolution (Beck 2011; Foran 2005; Goldfrank 1979; Kurzman 2008)—the international legitimacy of nonviolence is as much a product of global democratic norms as of a particular strategy of mobilization (Goldstone 2004). Second, all revolutionary movements must overcome repression to be successful, and nonviolent tactics are only one mechanism for this. Others include developing resource bases for sustained insurgencies (Fearon and Laitin 2003; Wickham-Crowley 1992), creating resilient organizational networks and forms (Chang 2008; Osa 2003), and forcing elite defections from the regime (Markoff 1988). It is also very possible that this effect is actually a moderator of a consistent prior finding in revolution—nonviolent campaigns require high degrees of solidarity and are most effective with mass support, both of which are building blocks of coalition formation. And, just as with all revolutionary situations, true social revolutions are a rare occurrence no matter the strategies employed (Tilly 1993; Goodwin 2001a). Further, nonviolent revolutions do fail in a large plurality of cases, can devolve into violent civil wars and insurgencies in others, and have in only a handful of cases delivered seemingly permanent transformations of states and society, suggesting that research on the type by itself may be relatively narrow in its contribution.

The events of 1989, the Color Revolutions, and the Arab Spring have also brought more attention to revolutionary waves and regime change cascades (see Beck 2014; Hale 2013), intimately connected with imageries of waves of democratization (Huntington 1968; Markoff 1996). A primary focus of research has been on the diffusion of contention across societies, owing to cross-national linkages among activists and the development of modular tactical strategies that can be used beyond the site of their innovation (Beissinger 2007; Bunce and Wolchik 2006; Kuzio 2006). On the other hand, others have stressed a more structural account (Hale 2005; Levitsky and Way 2006; McFaul 2007; Way 2008), which places causality in features of political structures and foreign influence. The debate here has been centered on regionally bounded contemporary events with little reference to prior cases, even though revolutionary waves are not a new or geographically limited phenomenon (see Beck 2011; Goldstone 1991; Kurzman 2008; Sohrabi 2002; Weyland 2014).

Again, the findings of this recent subfield accord well with broader revolution studies. While much of the literature on the Arab Spring is yet to be written, initial reactions by social scientists noted their agreement with prior research (Goodwin 2011; Goldstone 2011; Mann 2013). Tactical innovation and portability has long been seen as a determinant of protest cycles (McAdam et al. 2001), and revolutionary waves have long been known to have a diffusive quality (Brinton 1938). Even so, structural conditions are important in the development of contentious waves (Beck 2011; Goldstone 1991), for without political opportunity from strained states and regimes weakened by their own internal contradictions mobilization is less likely to amount to revolutionary challenge.

In short, the recent sub-literatures in revolution studies—nonviolent resistance and diffusive contentious waves—look much like the prior findings in the social science of revolution. The danger here lies in the development of research agendas limited to distinct sub-types of revolutions—a situation that characterized a stagnant field of study until Skocpol's (1979) breakthrough. Thus, the most promising research incorporates both violent and nonviolent strategies and global and local events into unified and systematic research designs, as Stephan and Chenoweth (2008) and Foran (2005) do.

Promising Frontiers: Micro-mobilization, Cultural Milieus, and Methodological Advances

In contrast to scholarly debates centered on a few instances or singular type of revolution, other research on revolution has begun to push old questions into promising lines of inquiry. Two areas stand out for their potential: new accounts and investigations of micro-mobilization, and an emergent understanding of how cultural milieus affect revolution. Research in both is characterized by theoretical synthesis and innovation that has analytical utility vis-à-vis cases of revolution from diverse times and places. Further, social science has undergone a number of methodological innovations in recent years that could allow for synthetic empirical examinations of revolution in the future.

Micro-mobilization

In the latter part of the third generation, research began to emerge on micro-mobilization in revolutionary episodes. In contrast to the presumed irrationality of participation in the second generation and the non-voluntarist, structural models of the third, scholars began to emphasize the individual rationality of revolution (Kimmel 1990; Kuran 1995; Taylor 1989). This research, rooted in rational choice models of human behavior, has been superseded in recent years by promising developments both empirical and theoretical.

First, the advent of nonviolent revolutions has allowed scholars to engage in field research, both quantitative and qualitative, of participation in revolution more easily. For instance, recent surveys and interviews of participants in Ukraine's Orange Revolution (Beissinger 2011; 2013) and Egypt's 2011 revolution (Austin Holmes 2012) provide systematic data on the demographic and attitudinal bases of mobilization. Notably, these studies find that mass participation is a social and emergent process, which resists attempts at repression and forms durable coalitions, rather than the mere product of individual calculation. Innovation in social network analysis has also allowed new ways of understanding individual activism, both contemporary and historical. Gould (1995) established the utility of historical networks for understanding how neighborhood demography and physical structure affected mobilization in France in 1848 and the Paris Commune. And Bearman (1993) and Hillmann's (2008) work on networks of nobles in early modern England has shown how coalitions form. Examining a more recent event, Viterna (2006) uses interviews and network analysis to chart paths of recruitment for women into the Salvadoran Farabundo Martí National Liberation Front (FMLN). These efforts stand in contrast to the broadly comparative methods of twentieth-century studies of revolution and have pushed accounts of micro-mobilization out of the realm of the theoretical into the empirical.

Conceptually, there have also been useful advances. In addition to the recognition that individual participation is always a social process, recent work has recognized the limits of rationality, emphasizing strategic miscalculation by actors. Weyland (2009; 2014) has argued that revolutionary waves such as 1848 in Europe result from "bounded rationality," where actors misestimate the utility of a modular repertoire for their own situation. The failure of revolutionary attempts in a wave may thus occur owing to strategic mistakes as much as elite learning and countering (cf. Beissinger 2007; Hale 2013; McAdam 1983). Miscalculation can also lead to a revolutionary outcome when a large enough segment of the population simultaneously perceives there to be a likelihood of success no matter the actual conditions, as Kurzman (2004b) argues for the Iranian Revolution of 1979. Rationality has also been paired with external, structural conditions fruitfully. For instance, Pfaff (2006) shows how the interplay between protest and the availability of exodus from an oppressive regime led to the collapse of East Germany in 1989. Perhaps most intriguing is Ermakoff's (2009; 2015; see also Sewell 1996) argument that revolutionary episodes are times when uncertainty about the future predominates to such an extent that contingent and random events can influence decision-making and affect revolutionary outcomes. For example, Salan's unplanned and spontaneous cry "Vive de Gaulle!" led to the collapse of the 1958 army coup in France. These formulations may suggest new ways of analyzing revolutionary outcomes and how seemingly small sparks, such as a Tunisian fruit seller's self-immolation, can set off widespread contention.

In short, micro-mobilization accounts of revolution have moved past debates over voluntarism versus structure and irrationality versus rationality, demonstrating the essential social and collective processes that guide participants. New methods of analysis and techniques of data collection show great promise for further development in this line of inquiry.

Cultural Milieus

After Skocpol's (1979; 1985; see also Sewell 1985) almost partisan advocacy of structural factors in revolution, the field became caught up in the larger structure–agency debate in 1980s social science. Culture—conceived in broad terms—seemed to hold a promising key for the future of the field (Foran 1993; Goodwin 1994). Initial attempts saw ideology as a factor that shaped the outcome of revolutionary situations once regimes had fallen (Goldstone 1991; Parsa 2000; Selbin 1993). Others invoked culture as an explanatory factor as challengers drew on histories of resistance as a mobilizing resource (Foran 2005; Reed and Foran 2002; Wickham-Crowley 1992). In both instances, cultural factors were important additions to otherwise structural accounts of revolution.

More recent work has pushed beyond the culture–structure dichotomy to consider the autonomous power of cultural milieus (see Stinchcombe 1986). Drawing on Sewell (1992), Sharman (2003) argues that cultural practices and norms affect state elites as much as challengers and thus have independent causal power on the occurrence of revolution. Similarly, Kittikhoun (2009) and Kandil (2011) have shown that cultural memories and discourses have direct effects on the capacities and actions of states. Systematic research has also invoked (and attempted to measure) the role of culture in contention. Hung's (2011) research on protest cycles in early modern China shows that the changing legitimacy of the imperial government affected both the rate and orientation of contentious politics, and Beck (2011) found a positive association between the growth of transnational cultural constructs and the rate of revolutionary waves in Europe since 1500.

The social science of revolution has long awaited a resolution to the culture–structure tension of third and fourth generation approaches. It appears that the field is at its advent. Norms, discourses, and memories have direct effects on who participates and how they mobilize. States and elites are both constrained and enabled by culturally structured processes. And broad cultural milieus seemingly affect the onset of revolution itself, independent of other structural features.

Empirical and Methodological Advances

Over the past three decades, methodological innovation and explication has transformed the landscape of available analytical tools. While not yet fully incorporated into the study of revolution, these advances have the potential to reshape the field, settle old debates, and open new frontiers. Advancement has occurred on three fronts: ontological; in comparative–historical methods; and in quantitative data and statistical tools.

Where second and early third generation approaches drew a relatively straight line from causal factors of revolution to the end of regimes, later third generation research began to re-emphasize the view of the first that different stages of revolutions may have different underlying processes (see Goldstone 1991; Sohrabi 1995). In the last fifteen years the emphasis among fourth generation scholars on the revolutionary process and its dynamic and emergent character is an implicit recognition of the need to separate the onset of contention and its outcome (see Tilly 1993; McAdam et al. 2001). The ontological advantage is that the field can move past selection on the dependent variable of a successful, revolutionary transfer of power. This is a helpful development but one that needs to continue to be made explicitly and adopted wholeheartedly in systematic research.

Comparative historical analysis has also come a long way since early attempts at its formalization (e.g., Skocpol 1984; Skocpol and Somers 1980). Methods for identifying and isolating causal mechanisms are much more formalized, whether through the inclusion of negative, deviant, and counterfactual cases (Fearon 1991; Mahoney and Goertz 2004), careful controlled comparisons (Slater and Ziblatt 2013), or congruence testing and Bayesian inference (Mahoney and Rueschemeyer 2003). Essential to these advances is the recognition of the role that case selection plays in comparative analysis (George and Bennett 2005). Cases can be selected through radial designs of comparison to crucial cases (Collier and Mahon 1993), representatives of typological categories (George and Bennett 2005; Ragin 2008), or mixed-methods approaches of nested case selection (Lieberman 2005; Rohlfing 2007). Analytically, Ragin's (2008) innovation of Qualitative Comparative Analysis, in which Boolean, fuzzy-set logic is used to identify conjoint causation in small- and medium-N samples, shows great promise for a field where conjunctural mechanisms are at play. Some, but not all, of these innovations have been adopted in the social science of revolution: see, for instance, Goodwin (2001a, 7) on negative cases and Wickham-Crowley's (1992) and Foran's (2005) typological QCA analysis. Given the continued pace of innovation and formalization of these methods, there is a promising future for systematic comparison in the study of revolution.

While early quantitative studies (e.g., Snyder and Tilly 1972; Gurr 1968) were generally found lacking owing to limited results and limitations in methods, tools of analysis and available data have changed dramatically. The adoption of event history and path-dependent modeling to account for temporal sequences, Bayesian statistics for inference, instrumental variables for identifying causality, and rare events logistic regression for uncommon phenomena all have direct application in providing statistical tests of revolutionary theory. Further, new sources of event data, such as the Political Instability Task Force, Nonviolent Actions and Outcomes Database, the Global Terrorism Database, and Beissinger's (in preparation) future catalog of revolutionary events, could be used for quantitative or mixed-methods analysis. Yet, so far, the social science of revolution has not widely adopted these tools.

In all areas, methodological and empirical tools have changed substantially in social science. There is now a great opportunity for revolution studies, long a bastion of historical and comparative analysis, to become less parochial in its methodology and move towards rapid knowledge accumulation.

Overall, these are promising frontiers in the social science of revolution. The two hallmark debates of the last twenty years in revolution studies, rationality and culture, seem to be on the cusp of fruitful settlement. Between research on the onset and processes of revolution that take into account micro-mobilization dynamics and the broad historical and social context of states, a new paradigm for understanding revolution could emerge. With new tools of analysis at hand, knowledge could begin to accumulate rather than just proliferate. Even so, future research on revolution will need to address a number of persistent problems.

Persistent Problems: Repression–Protest, Outcomes, Legitimacy–Stability, and Global Dimensions

Even as the social science of revolution has incorporated new events and types of contention and pushed past some of the older debates, there remain a number of unresolved questions. Some of these problems, such as the repression–protest paradox or the long-term outcomes of revolutions, are well known and have their own sub-literatures. Others, such as the legitimacy–stability problem and global dimensions of revolution, have received only implicit attention. Finally, rethinking what, exactly, the object of study should be could forge new directions. Each of these is discussed briefly below.

Repression–Protest Paradox

Sometimes repression is found to be a barrier to revolution and sometimes it is found to be a spur (Goldstone 2001; Lichbach 1987). Research on this paradox is intimately connected to the social movements literature on protest, but little consensus has resulted (Earl 2011). Repression is one of the foremost barriers to sustained mobilization, and no movement is successful without overcoming it. Yet research has also consistently found that repressive acts by a state can stimulate more protest in revolutionary situations (e.g., Khawaja 1994; Rasler 1996). Thus, the dynamic has been argued to take a U-shape (Lichbach and Gurr 1981), where repression seems to be like Goldilocks' porridge—the level needs to be just right for it to succeed (Beck 2015). Another view is that repression is a determinant of protest cycles, affecting mobilization differentially at different times (Brockett 1993; Tarrow 1989). Others have posited that repression should be embedded in the larger structure of political opportunities available to movements (e.g., Davenport 2007; McAdam 1983), further muddying an already unclear concept. As noted above, repression can be both a barrier and a spur to coalition formation, and coalitions in turn often succeed as they undermine repression's effectiveness and encourage defection by elites and repressive forces.

In short, there is as yet no clear answer to the problem of how best to conceptualize, measure, and test repression's role in revolution. It is clear that it is an important, and perhaps among the most important, determinant of not only sustained contention against a state but its success. Untangling how repression operates, and fails to operate, is a major task for the social science of revolution.

Revolutionary Aftermaths

Another well-known problem is the long-term impacts and outcomes of revolutionary situations. If revolution is deserving of attention precisely because of its potential to transform societies (Skocpol 1979) and alter global power relations (Halliday 1999; Mann 2013), then it is somewhat surprising that outcomes have received less attention. Some third generation scholars did try to assess the immediate aftermath of revolution and its connection to the ideological programs of leaderships (Foran and Goodwin 1993; Selbin 1993). But little systematic work has been done on longer-term outcomes (with the notable exception of Eckstein's (1975; 1982; 1985) assessment of revolutionary impacts on Latin American societies).

This is due, in part, to a lack of scholarly consensus on when it is possible to say a revolution ended. If it is when revolutionary challenges are no longer active, "the French Revolution ended in Thermidor in 1799 when Napoleon took power," or if it is when institutions take on a sustainable and stable form, then "the French revolution ended only with the start of the French Third Republic in 1871" (Goldstone 2001, 167). Or we might even extend the consistent turmoil of French politics through to the founding of the Fifth Republic in 1958 or de Gaulle's resignation in 1969. The lack of systematic research may also be due to fragmentation of the outcomes question into the extensive democratization literature in comparative politics, on the one hand, and dissections of post-revolutionary authoritarian states (e.g., Chirot 1994), on the other. As the history of revolution studies has shown, such fragmentation is often a barrier to knowledge accumulation.

As the comparative–historical tradition in revolution studies often begins with typologies, a good place to start might be with Stinchcombe's (1999) discussion of possible settlements of uncertainty about the distribution of power in the future. Such a framework is possibly quite helpful for understanding the current reversals and limitations of the Color Revolutions and the immediate impacts of the Arab Spring. Beck (2015) sketches such an application in his recent book. In short, a third generation account of causality and onset and a fourth generation investigation of process are not sufficient to understand revolutionary outcomes. It is time to recapture the long tail of revolution—no matter when they can be said to have ended, revolutionary situations reverberate across time and scholars need to pay attention to this.

Legitimacy–Stability Problem

Other problems are less well recognized in the field. One of these is the tension between the legitimacy of regimes and their political stability. Ever since Weber, social scientists have long recognized that legitimate authority is a basis for stable political orders. Yet history is full of numerous examples of regimes that were believed to be popularly illegitimate but persisted, such as Hussein's Iraq or the Islamic Republic of Iran since 1979, or regimes that most had thought were legitimate but whose stability collapsed quickly, such as the USSR. The basic view of legitimacy across 2000 years of political theory and social science is that it is the social psychological product of individual beliefs and collective processes (Zelditch 2001). Thus, many micro-mobilization theories of revolution implicitly try to solve the paradox (e.g., Kuran 1995; Kurzman 2004b), but explicit research on the issue in the social science of revolution has been lacking.

It is perhaps more useful to think of the legitimacy–stability problem as calling up questions about the timing of revolution, rather than using a vaguely defined (or undefined) "legitimacy" as a catch-all for surprising revolutions. Different revolutions may have different causal time horizons (Pierson 2003), whether occurring as a result of the accumulation of underlying strains and contradictions, the spark of seemingly random events setting off a cascade of contention, or some mixture of the two. Careful and systematic study should problematize this question, making a dependent variable out of the timing of revolution as much as the occurrence of revolution. As charted above, new methods of analysis could be helpful for this endeavor.

Global Dimensions

Many studies of revolutionary cases have tried to place events in their international context (e.g., Goldfrank 1979; Goldstone 1991; Skocpol 1979; Paige 1975). Yet, even so, due perhaps to the comparative method, the field has mostly been caught in a trap of "methodological nationalism," where singular societies are the focus rather than societies in interaction or transnational processes themselves (Lawson n.d.). In comparative–historical sociology there is a growing awareness of the need to take the global seriously as an autonomous object and level of analysis (Go 2014; Lawson 2015). Some recent work on revolution has tried to do this, as well (Beck 2011; 2014; Foran 2005; Kurzman 2008; Mann 2013). But there is much yet to be done. Progress might be made through synthesis with existing research traditions on the transnational system, such as world-systems analysis, world society neo-institutionalism, and constructivism in international relations, or through pioneering new accounts of the international system and revolution. Few states are islands, and the theories and methods of revolution studies need to take the global and transnational seriously.

Reframing the Question

Given the proliferation of findings about the causes of revolution, reframing the question and object of study is one possible strategy for knowledge accumulation. Goldstone (2001; 2003) has proposed that the field should problematize state stability rather than revolutionary unrest. If the paths to revolution are numerous, perhaps stable regimes display fewer configurations. Based on data collected by the Political Instability Task Force, Goldstone et al. (2010) find that regime type is more predictive of instability than economy, demography, or other factors. While more common in political science studies of regimes, research from the revolution perspective on this issue has been limited to date. It is possible that future efforts may validate the approach.

Another tack could be to formalize the implicit thread in the literature that different types of revolution may have different types of cause that are generalizable to their subset. As noted previously, this strategy was common to pre-Skocpolian theoretical debates and is implicit in more recent studies. Systematic research that identifies and disentangles these types could be a fruitful path not yet taken and a solution to fragmentation.

While progress in revolution studies has been accomplished, persistent problems still bedevil the field. Some are quite old, some are quite implicit, and some are quite new. While solutions here will not be easy, they could help to provide the basis of a new synthesis in the social science of revolution and meet the promise of earlier periods of knowledge accumulation.

Conclusion

The intellectual history of the social science revolution yields a picture of a subfield that has grown in fits and starts with a grand synthesis that is still elusive. Even so, consistent sets of findings have emerged: revolutions are more likely when states face external pressures, when regimes cannot deal with their own contradictions, and when contention is sustained by broad coalitions often involving segments of the elite. Recent studies of the nonviolent revolutions such as the Color Revolutions and the Arab Spring have validated this basic framework, even as attention has shifted from the social science of revolution more broadly to area- and type-specific studies. While the field has not resolved a number of issues, either theoretically or empirically—such as the repression–protest paradox, aftermaths of revolutionary situations, the tension between legitimacy and stability, and the global dimensions of revolution—progress has been made in fruitful directions, moving past old debates about the rationality of revolution and the culture–structure dialectic.

Running throughout this review has been the question of what revolutions are and what sort of theoretical stances can best account for them. The current wisdom is that revolutions have few to no generalizable features and that the task of research is to identify how different causal mechanisms combine in different cases. This is at its heart an ontological stance. To verify the imagery would require systematic studies designed to determine whether it is a product of careful testing and retesting of theories and cases or an artifact of the field's intellectual development. As such, generalizability or the lack thereof remains an open question.

It also appears that the social science of revolution has made the most progress when there is broad agreement about the object of study. While the early twentieth-century view of revolutions has been mostly abandoned today, the natural historians knew what types of event they were studying and created the basis for later progress. State-centered approaches of the third generation yielded a number of findings because what counted as a revolution—a social revolution— was quite clear. On the other hand, second generation accounts of revolution made little progress once trapped in conceptual debates about the various types and sub-types of event that could be considered revolutionary. And the fourth generation of revolution has fragmented into studies of sub-types and partial processes. For knowledge accumulation to again move forward, scholars of revolution will have to take this dynamic seriously and incorporate new methods of analysis that can account for complex and diverse events and causal pathways.

11

STATE FAILURE

The Problem of Complex Societal-Systems

Monty G. Marshall and Benjamin R. Cole

The end of the "super-statist" Cold War wrought significant changes to the dominant "statist" understanding of international relations, among them a new interest in the causes and international effects of fragile, failing, and failed states. In a global system where the state remains the primary organizing structure, the instability and collapse of developing states, particularly those in strategically valuable regions, caught the interest of policymakers and academics trying to understand the dynamics of the emerging globalization era in world politics. This chapter summarizes state failure research, responds to critics of the research agenda, and synthesizes both the work and its criticisms to propose an alternative methodology for analyzing state fragility: complex societal-systems analysis (Marshall 1999; 2014; 2016). We begin by examining the research agenda's key terms by reviewing both conceptual definitions and their accompanying debates. Next, we summarize recent innovations in the measurement of state fragility and failure, and review studies of state failure as both a cause and effect of other cross-national phenomena, such as organized crime, trafficking, and terrorism. We then respond to the key criticisms of the state failure research agenda before concluding with a discussion of the utility of complex societal-systems analysis to address those criticisms and as a way forward with research into the relationships among internal and external sources of governance, political conflict, and system development. We argue that a systems methodology is best suited to move the state failure research agenda beyond the behavioralist social-scientific paradigm. This paradigm depends on often inappropriate and always simplistic statistical assumptions, steeped in a presumed independence of observations drawn from an increasingly complex and interdependent social system that spans and networks the entire globalizing world.

Conceptualizing "State Failure"

Although the term "state failure" did not enter the mainstream academic vernacular until the early 1990s, recognition of the unique problems faced by societies with ineffectual states began during the Cold War. Most of these early efforts focused on development economics or were responses to problems in development studies. Huntington (1968) wrote one of the earliest tracts concerned with the domestic impediments to political order in changing societies, but his policy prescription of ensuring stability by fostering a *national security state* was claimed by his many critics to have only exacerbated the problem. In addition to developing a comprehensive model of state–society relations, Migdal (1988) provided one of the first comparative analyses of fragile states, juxtaposing Sierra Leone's post-colonial weakness with Israel's strength, and identified the importance of neighborhood effects, and conflict in particular, in determining state efficacy. Jackson (1987) provided another early analysis of state fragility, investigating the roles of the international community and international law in forcing Western jurisprudential norms of sovereignty and statehood onto African societies, generating "quasi-states" or "juridical statehood." These early studies identified the problems posed by fragile states and began analyzing the causes behind their inefficacy, articulating the concepts of state fragility and failure that would be picked up later by academics, journalists, and policymakers in the face of high-profile failures.

The use of the "failed and failing" states terminology in policy discourse is usually traced to a 1992 article by Helman and Ratner that appeared in the magazine *Foreign Policy*, titled "Saving Failed States"; they referred to

> three groups of states whose survival is threatened: First, there are the failed states like Bosnia, Cambodia, Liberia, and Somalia, a small group whose governmental structures have been overwhelmed by circumstances. Second, there are failing states like Ethiopia, Georgia, and Zaire [DRC], where collapse is not imminent but could occur within several years. And third, there are some newly independent states in the territories formerly known as Yugoslavia and the Soviet Union, whose viability is difficult to assess. All three groups merit close attention, and all three will require innovative policies.
> *(Helman and Ratner 1992, 2)*

According to Paris (2011) and Call (2011), Helman and Ratner's article was responsible for the term's circulation into the academic and policy vernaculars, but the term was quickly applied to a wider array of developing countries whose survival or viability was less clearly threatened, extending the meaning of the concept to include lesser forms of "failure." Instead of indicating the complete or impending collapse of central authority, the term came to replace more innocuous references to levels of economic development to encompass a deeper sense of political anomie synonymous with the "weak," "quasi-," or "juridical" states addressed by Migdal and Jackson, indicating an inherent inadequacy of "third-world" states to perform their fundamental policymaking function(s).

It was this expanded meaning of the term that Kaplan used in his 1994 article in *The Atlantic*, titled "The Coming Anarchy," which brought the term, and the significance of the problem, into popular discourse. Since that time, the policy communities of the leading states of the globalization era, reacting perhaps from a feeling of being overwhelmed themselves by circumstances, uncertainty regarding the apparent devolution of the state system, and a growing sense of "donor fatigue," have taken the lead in promoting and pursuing research on the problem of "state failure." At the same time, we cannot discount the disturbing perceptual effects brought about by the relatively sudden spilling out of a raft of heretofore closed societies amid the dawning of a media-driven information age. The world went from knowing very little about the internal affairs of states, and particularly states in the developing world, to having the most intimate details of everyday life across the globe reported and scrutinized on a daily basis; and this opening occurred during the peak level of armed conflicts in the world (Gurr et al. 2000, chapter 3, "Global Trends in Violent Conflict"). The so-called "CNN effect" was met with a "do something" imperative driven by an over-stimulated public and policy community in a "triumphant" West.

The concept of state failure has thus been epistemologically challenged nearly since its invention, affecting its use and analysis in both academic and policy circles and perhaps, as many critics have argued, affecting the way we understand the nature of and prospects for resolving the problem. At its core, however, the concept of state failure combines two research streams that had previously remained largely separate in Western thinking: state-building and economic development. What remained largely missing were the external, "systemic" influences emphasized by the *dependencia* critics of the Western developmental approach, who argued that non-Western countries face unique hurdles to development stemming from both the historical legacies of colonialism and the uneven development of states comprising the "world system" (Wallerstein 1974). Western approaches tend to presume that the "legacy of the past" is simply a *quid pro quo*: that is, that the uneven development of states is the natural result of political decisions and trade-offs made in the past that can be remedied in the future. What is perhaps the most pertinent "take-away" from the world-systems approach is Wallerstein's idea of the politically relevant "world" as defining one's preferred approach to understanding how that "world" works. For the world's weaker states, their "world" may not extend much beyond their own borders; for stronger states, their "world" may include neighboring states or even extend across a geographic or cultural region; for more advanced states, their "world" may extend to include both a regional focus and a number of trading partners and strategic rivals in other regions; and, for the strongest states, their "world" may extend across the globe and even beyond. States with global interests have strong incentives to better understand how the whole world works. Proactive leaders of the "globalization dynamic" can be expected to take the lead in promoting a global research agenda and to be the most concerned about the problem of "unit failures" in a globalizing world system. As a result, we can reasonably expect an (inherent) "clash of worldviews" in the globalization era and that knowledge gained through applied research can inform us of how to avoid a (contingent) "clash of civilizations." To date, state failure research has been centered mainly in the Western states: the United States, Canada, the United Kingdom, and the European Union.

As the world leader in promoting globalization and advocating a global market economy, especially since the end of the Cold War, the United States had strong incentives to examine the problem of state failure in the context of global politics. The US government's State Failure Task Force was created in October 1994

> in response to a 1994 request from senior policymakers to design and carry out a study on the correlates of state failure. The ultimate goal was to develop a methodology that would identify key factors and critical thresholds signaling a high risk of crisis in countries some two years in advance.
>
> *(Esty et al. 1995, iii)*

In the US policy community, security and intelligence agencies have tended to treat state failure strictly as a problem of central government effectiveness. The State Failure Task Force, renamed the Political Instability Task Force in 2003 (subsequently referred to here as PITF), represented the first effort to operationalize the concept of "state failure" and to use that concept to frame a "comprehensive empirical effort to identify the correlates of state failure" (Esty et al. 1995, iii).[1] The PITF "narrowly" defined state failures as "instances in which central state authority collapses for several years"; however, they identified fewer than twenty such episodes since 1955

> too few for meaningful statistical analysis. For this reason, as well as for the reason that events that fell beneath such as threshold nonetheless posed challenges to US foreign policy, the task force broadened the concept of state failure to include a wider range of civil conflicts, political crises, and massive human rights violations that are typically associated with state breakdown.
>
> *(Esty et al. 1995, 1)*

This wider range of "state breakdown" led the Task Force to operationalize a "problem set" on the basis of observed failures of regime legitimacy ("autocratic backsliding"), failures of governing capability ("collapse of central authority"), and failures to manage political conflicts without resort to armed conflict (revolutionary wars, ethnic wars, politicides, and genocides).[2] What is particularly unique and innovative in the PITF use of the term "state failure" is its recognition of the crucial relationship between the stability of state authority and the state's use of force against constituent groups. The PITF definition explicitly preferences democratic authority (in line with official US policy) such that changes in regime authority toward more democratic authority are viewed as politically stabilizing and substantial shifts away from democratic authority are considered destabilizing. The US National Intelligence and National Security Councils have adopted similar, security-oriented definitions, treating state failure as discrete events characterized by a state's partial or total loss of central government control over its sovereign territory. These perspectives have operationalized state failure as a binary variable: a state is either failed or not-failed (later modified to stable or not stable).[3]

In contrast, policy actors and academics concerned with foreign policy issues other than traditional or conventional security threats, or with broader national security conceptualizations, have adopted more nuanced definitions of state fragility and failure. These conceptualizations tend to view the state as a complex entity with multiple critical functions, including but not limited to maintenance of territorial sovereignty, and consider the state failure problem as systemic in nature. These broader policy perspectives have also tended to treat state failure as the end point of a spectrum and/or sequence of state weakness and vulnerability. The US Agency for International Development (USAID) (2005b), for example, defines "fragile" and "crisis" states as those where government does not control its territory, fails to provide "vital services" to large parts of its territory, and holds "weak or non-existent legitimacy among its citizens"; crisis states represent the most extreme cases of state fragility. Other US policy actors, such as the US Government Accountability Office, the Commission on Weak States, and the Interagency Working Group on International Crime, have adopted similar definitions, focusing on legitimacy and service provision in addition to territorial control. This broader conceptualization of state fragility and failure has also been adopted by most of the international policy community, including actors such as the World Bank's Fragile States Initiative, the Organization for Economic Cooperation and Development (OECD) Development Assistance Committee's Fragile States Group, and the British government's Department for International Development's (DfID) Crisis States Programme. These more nuanced definitions are, of course, more difficult to operationalize and problematic to analyze. Table 11.1 compares the conceptual and operational definitions of these various policy actors.

While actors in the policy community have adopted more practical definitions pursuant to their particular concerns, the academic community has been more theoretical in attempting to define and categorize the state failure problem, albeit with even less agreement on the definitions reached. Gros (1996) made one of the first attempts to categorize failed and failing states, but a systematic classification scheme did not appear until the publication of Robert I. Rotberg's edited volumes on the topic, *State Failure and State Weakness in a Time of Terror* (2003) and *When States Fail* (2004), in which Rotberg classifies and characterizes states as strong, weak, failing, failed, or collapsed. These works combined one of the first systemic theories of state failure with a series of case studies by a panel of leading

TABLE 11.1 Conceptions of state fragility and failure in the policy community

Organization	Terminology	Definition	Type	Key Factors
US Political Instability Task Force	Political instability event / State failure	Total or near-total collapse of central authority, reversion to autocratic rule, or the onset of ethnic or revolutionary war	Nominal	Armed conflict / Adverse regime change
US National Intelligence Council	Failed state	State with "expanses of territory and populations devoid of effective government control"	Binary	Territorial sovereignty
US Agency for International Development (USAID)	Fragile state / Crisis state	Government does not control its territory, fails to provide "vital services" to significant parts of its territory, and holds "weak or non-existent legitimacy among its citizens"	Ordinal	Service provision / Legitimacy
US National Security Council	Weak state	State fails to "fulfill…sovereign responsibilities"	Binary	Territorial sovereignty / Service provision
US Interagency Working Group on International Crime	Failed state	State fails to meet "standards and responsibilities of sovereign control over its territory"	Binary	Territorial sovereignty / Service provision / Legitimacy (implicit)
US Government Accountability Office	Failing state / Fragile state	States that "do not control their territory," and whose citizens "do not perceive the government as legitimate" and "do not have basic public services or domestic security"	Ordinal	Territorial sovereignty / Service provision / Legitimacy
US Commission on Weak States	Weak state / Failed state	States that fail to "control their territories," or "meet the basic needs of their citizens" or "provide legitimacy that flows from effective, transparent governance"	Ordinal	Territorial sovereignty / Service provision / Legitimacy

(Continued)

TABLE 11.1 (continued)

Organization	Terminology	Definition	Type	Key Factors
OECD Development Assistance Committee's Fragile States Group	Fragile state	States lacking "either the will or capacity to engage productively with their citizens to ensure security, safeguard human rights, and provide the basic function for development," characterized by "weak governance, limited administrative capacity, chronic humanitarian crisis, persistent social tensions, violence or the legacy of civil war"	Binary	Armed conflict Human rights Service provision
World Bank Fragile States Initiative	Fragile state	States with low income, "poor governance, internal conflicts, tenuous post-conflict transitions, weak security, fractured societal relations, corruption, breakdowns in the rule of law, and insufficient mechanisms for generating legitimate power and authority" (Wyler 2008, 26–7).	Binary	Armed conflict Rule of law Corruption Legitimacy
UK Department for International Development (DfID) Crisis States Programme	Fragile state Crisis state Failed state	Fragile states: "significantly susceptible to crisis in one or more … subsystems … particularly vulnerable to internal and external shocks and … conflicts." Crisis state: "reigning institutions face serious contestation and are potentially unable to manage conflict and shocks." Failed state: "can no longer perform its basic security, and development functions," and has "no effective control over its territory and borders."	Nominal	Territorial sovereignty Service provision Crisis management

scholars on the topic, including Michael T. Klare, Susan Rose-Ackerman, Nicolas van de Walle, and Jennifer Widner. In addition to an earlier piece in the *Washington Quarterly* (Rotberg 2002), these books build on, most notably, Zartman's (1995a) volume *Collapsed States: The Disintegration and Restoration of Legitimate Authority*, but add categories of "weak" and "failing" states in addition to Zartman's study of "collapse." Unlike Zartman, Rotberg conceives of state functions broadly, including healthcare and education provision, the maintenance of infrastructure and political institutions, economic development, and the control of corruption, among other factors. Sung (2004) offers a similarly broad definition in her analysis of state failure effects on organized crime.

As a further refinement of the "peace-building capacity" approach and in response to a USAID initiative to better understand and delineate the complexities of "state fragility" and differentiate the "risks" (or potential) for state failure from the condition (or outcome) of state failure, Marshall designed a new measure of state fragility based on a two-tiered "PESS-EL" framework developed for USAID. That framework looks at state capacity as a four-dimensional continuum of "state-society relations": political, economic, social, and security (the "PESS" dimensions), and proposes that "state failure occurs through some combination of loss of *effectiveness* and *legitimacy* (*EL*) of the institutions of each of the PESS dimensions" (Goldstone et al. 2003b, 8–9). The "State Fragility Index and Matrix" was first reported in the initial issue of the *Global Report* series (Marshall and Goldstone 2007) and was refined in subsequent editions (Marshall and Cole 2008a; 2009; 2010; 2014). By examining the principal qualities of "state–society relations" across both the applied aspects of effectiveness and legitimacy, the state fragility measure widens the scope of concern from the classic statist or "whole of government" approaches to include non-state actors in a "whole of society" perspective in which the concepts of state sovereignty and popular sovereignty are coterminous. This more comprehensive (systemic) approach is more consistent with the precepts of democratic authority and, as it includes observations of state, civil society, and public behaviors that are directly informed by the analysis of the risks of "state failure," may be considered the first societal-systems approach to the study of state fragility and failure. By providing annual, standardized, empirical assessments of the many countries comprising the globalizing world system in terms of qualities of public relations and changes in its core dimensions, the "State Fragility Index" (SFI) can be seen as a response to demands by Rotberg (2004) for such a measurement scheme and to reflect the arguments of scholars that the problem of state failure reflects both an effectiveness shortcoming and a legitimacy shortfall in governance (Ghani et al. 2006; Cliffe and Manning 2008; Goldstone 2008; Lemay-Herbert 2009; Paris 2011).[4]

Susan Rice and Stewart Patrick have also contributed significantly to the definition and categorization of state fragility and failure, and have also provided a comprehensive (one-time) measure of state fragility, the "Index of State Weakness." Rice (2003) defines state failure in terms of both security and service provision, and differentiates between "weak," "failing," and "failed" states, with the last category the most extreme. This categorization is evident in Rice and Patrick's report on the topic, *Index of State Weakness in the Developing World*, which defines "weak states" as those that

> lack the essential capacity and/or will to fulfill four sets of critical government responsibilities: fostering ... economic growth; establishing and maintaining legitimate, transparent and accountable institutions; securing their populations ... and controlling their territory; and meeting the basic human needs of their population.
>
> *(Rice and Patrick 2008, 3)*

Although not reflected in the Rice and Patrick index, Patrick (2006) has also argued for differentiating between states that are *unable* to perform their core functions and states that are *unwilling* to perform these functions. While the former are truly vulnerable to internal or external shocks, the latter may not be. Indeed, Patrick (2007; 2011) has done substantial work refining definitions of failing and fragile states, identifying important analytical weaknesses in the existing concept, particularly the failure to separate willingness from capacity to fulfill state commitments to society. As he notes, it makes little sense to group North Korea, which maintains an effective police state and boasts one of the largest militaries in the world, with Liberia, which has struggled to maintain central authority and maintain order since its independence. Taken together, these broader views of the conditions and characteristics of fragile, failing, and failed states may be seen to represent a "whole of government" approach to the general problem, and potentially the amelioration, of state failure.[5]

Since 2005 the Fund for Peace, a "non-profit research and educational organization" in Washington DC, has produced the "Failed States Index," which defines state failure as including attributes of

> loss of physical control of its territory or a monopoly on the legitimate use of force ... erosion of legitimate authority to make collective decisions, an inability to provide reasonable public services, and the inability to interact with other states as a full member of the international community.
>
> *(Fund for Peace 2012)*

Whereas the State Fragility Index (discussed above) uses only public data sources based on observable behaviors to populate its data matrix, the Fund for Peace Failed States Index utilizes a combination of (1) automated content analysis of news reports (using its CAST software); (2) quantitative data from public data sources; and (3) qualitative "expert" review and analysis to assign scores for each country on twelve component indicators.[6] In operationalizing its concept of "failure," the organization examines twelve "baskets" of social, economic, and political/military indicators, each "split into an average of [fourteen] sub-indicators" (Fund for Peace 2016); these baskets include demographic pressures, group grievances, human flight and brain drain, refugees and internally displaced persons (IDPs) (social indicators); uneven economic development, poverty, and decline (economic indicators); and external intervention, factionalized elites, human rights and rule of law, public services, security apparatus, and state legitimacy (political/military indicators). In many ways, the Failed States Index both encompasses and reflects the complexity of modern societal-systems, with its process dynamics similarly convoluted and the outcomes of its efforts similarly opaque and confounded. The Country Indicators for Foreign Policy (CIFP) project at Carleton University in Canada presents a similarly complicated assessment scheme for ranking "fragile and failed states," using as many as seventy-five "structural indicators" drawn from public data resources (Carment et al. 2010). The CIFP perspective adds environmental factors and a gender discrimination component to their holistic conceptualization of fragile and failed states and a broader systemic component by proposing that external intervention may precipitate the onset of a state failure condition.[7]

As commonly noted by state failure researchers and their critics, the total collapse of (central) state authority and the rupture of state–society relations must be considered an extreme and rare phenomenon, as the identification of very few cases, such as Somalia in 1991 or Bosnia in 1993, may reach consensus. The proposition that there is a single continuum, pathway, or trajectory connecting fragile states with failing and failed states may be overstated or overly simplistic; multiple pathways are more likely. Indeed, many of the statist approaches to state failure are based on the proposition that state politics are more or less prone to experience discreet "phase shifts" from a stable or non-crisis condition to an unstable or crisis condition and that these shifts, or onsets, may be foreshadowed by observable changes in "risk" conditions or behaviors and triggered by internal or external "shocks." This latter approach is conducive to risk assessment and early warning modeling efforts (forecasting) such as that pursued by the PITF. Marshall and Cole (2009, 21–2) provide evidence to support a systemic resiliency argument that, while no state is "immune" to experiencing failure events, the more fragile states are more susceptible to the risks of failure and vulnerable to systemic shocks; thus, the probability of failure co-varies with the degree of fragility.

Framing the Problem of State Failure as an International Security Concern

The classic conception of "state sovereignty" that forms the basis for the "anarchic" Westphalian state system is embodied in the contemporary United Nations (UN) system through the charter principle of non-interference in the internal affairs of member states.[8] Interference in the internal affairs of states in the UN system can be authorized only through a Chapter VII enforcement resolution by the UN Security Council on the basis of a recognized "threat to the peace, breach of the peace, or act of aggression" (United Nations 1945) and only after all other diplomatic remedies have been exhausted. Precepts of "popular sovereignty" are inscribed in the Charter through its inclusion of the principle to "achieve international cooperation in solving international problems of an economic, social, cultural, or humanitarian character, and in promoting and encouraging respect for human rights and fundamental freedoms" (chap. I, art. 1, par. 3). The achievement of international cooperation in the provision of developmental assistance has been actively promoted under the UN system, while direct intervention in the internal affairs of states has been strongly discouraged, even if not entirely prevented. The continuing global emphasis on development cooperation and assistance among states goes a long way in explaining why research on the problem of state failure has been promoted proactively by developmental agencies and humanitarian organizations, remains largely circumstantial, descriptive, and remedial in nature, and assumes an ever more complex, holistic, and systemic perspective. Perhaps the only exception to this developmental perspective on the problem of state failure, which tended to situate both the source and effect of the problem solely within the domestic politics of the affected state, was the political perspective of the PITF, which encompassed US globalization interests and recognized that the domestic problem of state failure can disrupt or alter the foreign relations of the affected state and increase its needs for humanitarian aid and demands for development assistance.[9]

In support of the economic development, political state-building, post-conflict recovery, and general foreign policy perspectives promoted by policymakers and agencies of the United States and other Western "donor" countries, scholars interested in the issues of fragile, failing, failed, and recovering states have produced a plethora of case studies on the domestic causes and effects of state failure. Most of the early case studies were in Africa, and included Somalia (Menkhaus 2007a; Clarke and Gosende 2003; Kreijen 2004; Gros 1996; Adam 1995; Lyons and Samatar 1995), Angola (Fituni 1995), the Democratic Republic of Congo (Weiss 1995; Lemarchand 2003; Kreijen 2004), Sierra Leone (Reno 2003; Kreijen 2004), Sudan (Prunier and Gisselquist 2003), Rwanda (Gros 1996), Guinea (Docking 2002), Chad (Widner 1995; Foltz 1995), Togo (Widner 1995), Congo (Widner 1995), Uganda (Khadiagala 1995), Liberia (Lowenkopf 1995; Gros 1996; Kreijen 2004), Mozambique (Schutz 1995), and Ethiopia (Keller 1995; Pausewang 2004). Somalia and the Democratic Republic of Congo were of particular interest to researchers because they are among the few states to experience complete collapse of central authority and institutions. The prevalence of African case studies also reflects the critically low levels of institutional capacity and inclusive governance endemic to newly independent and less-developed states in general. This early research focus on African countries has itself conditioned our early understandings of the problem of state failure. Outside of Africa, case studies have included Afghanistan (Rubin 2002), Tajikistan (Dadmehr 2003), Haiti (Gros 1996; Stotzky 1997), and Fiji (Lawson 2003), and regional studies in the Caucasus (Freitag-Wirminghaus 2002; Darchiashvili 2002) and Latin America (Kurtenbach 2002; de Leon 2002).

Following the foreign-based terrorist attacks of September 11, 2001 on targets in the United States perpetrated by agents of a non-state militant organization operating out of Afghanistan, a country widely perceived to be a failing or failed state, US policy shifted toward dealing more directly with failed states as posing a direct threat to US national security and foreign interests.[10] Up to that time, international acts of terrorism had been viewed mainly as either criminal acts by isolated extremists or small-scale attacks directed surreptitiously by "rogue" states, so-called "state-sponsored terrorism." The sudden, dramatic emergence of al Qaeda as an international non-state actor and serious security threat, coupled with the fact that al Qaeda operatives were openly training at bases in Afghanistan and were being protected by that country's Taliban regime, triggered a more intense interest in the problem of failed states as providing havens for anti-system militants and conduits for all manner of unlawful activities, such as kidnapping, piracy, and trafficking in humans and contraband. The adverse circumstances in failing and failed states were also seen as providing fertile ground for the recruitment of anti-system agents and terrorists. Chester A. Crocker (2003) argued that failing and failed states harbor transnational terrorist organizations, offering limited law enforcement, easily (and cheaply) corrupted government officials, access to weapons, and a potential recruit population with few economic opportunities and many grievances. His arguments were echoed by Rice (2003), who was also concerned with possible spillover effects that could lead to wider regional conflicts with neighboring countries. Similar arguments have been made by Fukuyama (2004), Krasner and Pascual (2005), and Carment (2007), among others; Hastings (2009) examined the role of state collapse in driving, or at least enabling, the rise of piracy along the coast of Somalia. Howard (2014) takes this relationship to the extreme in arguing that state failure is a root cause of terrorism and political violence.

The proposed linkage between failed states and anti-system behaviors and enterprises such as organized crime and international terrorism has proved tenuous at best. While these groups may have reason to seek refuge in poor, poorly governed, and failed states, the scope of their transnational activities appears to be critically limited under such logistically constrained conditions and in such remote locations. As Hastings (2009) argued, piracy and terrorism may flourish in places such as Somalia, but the pirates and terrorists must necessarily have limited international ambitions and lack operational sophistication to base their operations in a failed state, which by definition suffers severe shortages of resources and skills and lacks communication and transportation infrastructure. He raises the concern that with progressive development and state-building these "primitive" criminal groups may increase the sophistication of their operations and attacks, becoming more rather than less problematic as conditions within the state improve and the country recovers from the state failure condition. Indeed, Patrick (2007) notes, "terrorists are likely to find *weak but functioning* states like Pakistan or Kenya more congenial." A failed state, such as Somalia, with its limited infrastructure and its general lack of connectivity to the dense resource flows that characterize the globalizing economy, has far less to offer an organization with regional and global pretensions and a tactical preference for dramatic and disruptive activities, such as the al Qaeda *jihadist* network, compared with a weak but functioning and strategically located state like Afghanistan (pre-2001) or Yemen (Hehir 2007). Security analysts and policymakers have responded, turning increased attention from failed states toward the problem of "safe havens" in what they termed "ungoverned areas" in "weak but functioning" states (Lamb 2007).

The notion of "ungoverned space" is fairly straightforward. Central authorities are charged with the responsibility of enforcing the "rule of law" and, thereby, dampening and controlling criminal activities within their territory; however, some governments are either unable or unwilling to establish and enforce an effective social order across their entire territory, whether owing to lack of infrastructure and resources, inaccessible terrain, or hostile inhabitants. Menkhaus (2007b, 2) describes "ungoverned space" as a term used

> to connote a general condition of weak to nonexistent state authority in a defined geographic area. It is a relatively recent addition to the lexicon of the study of failed states, and like other terms used in that field of research it is imprecise and value-laden. The fact that it is an expression preferred by the US Department of Defense adds to the baggage the term carries; some critics of US foreign policy see it as an attempt to justify unilateral counterterrorist actions in weak or failed states.

Moreover, it is far from clear that international terrorist organizations require ungoverned spaces in which to operate or that transnational terrorism poses a significant threat to international peace and security. Many terrorist cells and organized criminal networks have been found to operate in urban locations well within a country's "governed spaces" and even within the "governed spaces" of the world's most powerful states. The hiding place of Osama bin Laden, for example, was within blocks of Pakistan's most prestigious military academy, in a densely populated city. Furthermore, Marshall and Cole (2009; 2010; 2014) have shown that the bulk of "high casualty terrorist bombings," the principal *modus operandi* of extremist groups in the recent "global war on terror," are not international events but, rather, domestic in both their direct, lethal effects and psychological impact (although the intended "audience" may be the international community).[11] The overwhelming majority of these attacks has been concentrated in three countries, Iraq, Pakistan, and Afghanistan, with limited concentrations in Israel, Russia, India, and Sri Lanka. It appears that these attacks may be fueled by political and economic grievances specific to the local context (Patrick 2007; Newman 2007; Laqueur 2003). Menkhaus (2007b), and Clunnan and Trinkunas (2010) reject the notion that "ungoverned" spaces exist at all, posing the counter-argument that some form of governance exists in all social spaces, regardless of the current attitude of central authorities. Clearly, fragile, failing, failed, and recovering states are havens for the mavens of many of the global system's most vexing ills, but this fundamental observation is more tautology than conspiracy.

The Way Forward: From State-Centric to Complex Societal-Systems Analysis

The "problem of state failure" encompasses far more than a concept, a condition, a body of literature, or a research agenda; it is emblematic of the need for an entirely new analytic approach in the social sciences: one that can account for and accommodate complexity, interdependence, the integration of theoretical and applied research methodologies—that is, complex societal-systems analysis (Marshall 1999; 2014; 2016). As noted above, the primary method for examining the problem of state failure has been the historical case study. This is a necessary first step in systematic inquiry, as it accumulates information on select cases that appear to fit the definitional criteria of the topic of interest. The identification of cases and the accumulation of information on those cases, then, inform a comparative case study approach that considers possible explanatory factors and constructs a historiographical (sequential or process) narrative based on informed and reasoned understandings drawn from a biased selection of cases (proto-theory). Once a substantial body of information is collected and explanatory propositions are articulated, then systematic coding and data collection of key explanatory variables can proceed and statistical methods can be used to test the veracity of extant propositions and suggest alternative explanations, along with the need for further information. The privatization of independent research necessarily fosters partial and disconnected explanations of complex social phenomena. The synthesis of partial accounts leads to the elucidation of grand historiographical narratives organized to highlight a foundational explanation for seemingly related social phenomena (meta-theory). Jared Diamond's *Collapse* (2005) and Acemoglu and Robinson's *Why Nations Fail* (2012) present grand systemic explanatory narratives that stand at the "outer bounds" of the private, independent inquiry into the problem of state failure. This is about as far as independent scholarly research can push systematic inquiry. The advent of personal computers has provided a platform for scientific methods and propelled private research well beyond its prior limitations but, still, far short of where we need to go in order to reasonably comprehend and effectively manage complex societal-systems. The human–engineered world is changing at an incredible pace and academic and policy research is struggling to keep pace with expanding globalization dynamics and intensifying systemic complexity.

The "behavioral revolution" in American political science, and particularly as it has progressed in regard to comparative politics and international relations, has paralleled the continuing evolution of electronic computers since the advent of that technology toward the end of World War II. The computer's capabilities for systematically storing and processing ever-expanding volumes of data points were naturally suited for application in the social sciences and public policy analysis. The confluence of computational, statistical, and empirical techniques may even be viewed as having finally disciplined the study of politics and elevated it to a "hard" science or, at least, a proto-science. Social sciences, unlike the physical sciences, have to contend with the idiosyncratic and strategic variability brought about through human agency and, unlike the biological sciences, complications resulting from strategic interaction. In essence, our acquired knowledge of physical and biological laws provides the parameters within which laws governing human behavior must operate in order to promote and perpetuate the societal-systems that sustain human life. Political science, then, must study the relationships linking individual and collective action as those actions affect and are affected by their environment. The human command of her circumstances is conditioned and, ultimately, arbitrated by the nature of his interactions with the environment: human societal-systems can only be fully understood and sustained as an integral component of the greater ecosystem. How humans behave within the global context is the subject of globalization and the object of comparative and international political science.

The behavioralist approach could thus juxtapose democratic notions of popular sovereignty with autocratic notions of state sovereignty and, in doing so, shift the focal point of political conflict studies away from the Machiavellian perspective of state security imposed through mechanisms of effective social control toward the Lockean perspective of effective conflict management and good governance maintained through deliberation and negotiation between governance prerogatives and the diverse interests and aspirations of civil society. While the state retains primacy among societal actors in the pluralist–behavioralist scheme, it loses much of its privilege and discretion: it can no longer act as necessary to ensure the stability of the state but is expected to act within the law in doing so: that is, to do what is just. While the state remains primarily responsible for ensuring system stability, the agency of the state must be viewed as only the first among many societal actors whose dynamic interactions define the qualities of the societal-system and in which both stability and change are systemic outcomes. From this point of view, the state can be understood to have "failed" in its systemic responsibilities if system change is improperly managed, by either commission or omission, such that system stability is disrupted, impaired, or lost. Such "failure" has consequences for both the societal-system that a state manages directly and the greater societal-system within which that societal-system and its state are embedded as integral parts. This sense of "state failure" stems from the circumstantial, subsidiary nature of increasing globalization and interconnectedness. Thus, the progressive development of system mechanics and an understanding of the basis for nodal dysfunction or malfunction within a complex societal-system network of global scope will require a holistic, integrated methodological approach that brings together academic, scientific, practical, organizational, and policy perspectives and spans group, state, interstate, and global levels of analysis.

The classical statist approach in the blossoming field of international relations in 1946 had to contend with just seventy-three sovereign state "actors" in the world, interacting mainly in pairs in accordance with "power laws" based on "relative capabilities" in an anarchic "billiard ball" analogy of world politics. The number of independent state actors doubled during the process of "decolonization" and infused the state system with a raft of new, underdeveloped "third-world" states, complicating the simple bipolar world order that had emerged after World War II, essentially by tossing "rubble" all over the "billiard table" with the effect that the several "billiard balls" began to react seemingly erratically. Since that time, the number of non-state, state, and interstate political actors in the world that may interact to substantially affect political outcomes at any level within the global system expands toward infinity. In mid-2011 there were nearly 200 sovereign states in the world and, according to the Union of International Associations, there are tens of thousands of international organizations (nearly 60,000 in 2004, up from fewer than 1000 in 1951).[12] National and local "civil society" organizations, economic enterprises, and social networks continue to proliferate. In the United States, for example, there were nearly 1.6 million not-for-profit (civil) organizations in 2009, over 6 million business firms in 2007, and around 140,000 "advocacy, grantmaking, and civic organizations" in 2010.[13] For comparison, there were more than 3.3 million not-for-profit organizations in 2009 in India, a relatively poor and underdeveloped country with a population about three times the size of the United States.[14] Clearly, state-centric and simplistic "causal" approaches to analysis have been critically challenged, and overwhelmed, by exponential increases in the numbers of political actors and densities of interactive dynamics. Recent analytic innovations in response to these challenges have emphasized strategic or processual sequencing rather than causal rhetoric in constructing prevention, early warning, risk assessment, predictive, simulation, projection, and formal complexity models of global and regional societal-system (dys)function, (de)generation, and (dis)integration.

As a result of our collective failure to advance our comprehension of the complexity of societal-system dynamics we continue to be surprised by major global and regional events such as the collapse of the Socialist Bloc, the dissolution of the Soviet Union, the "third wave" of democratization, the "global war on terrorism," and the so-called "Arab Spring." Part of this analytic failure is probably due to an inherent preference for or expectation of system continuity and stability. State failure is known to be a rare event; profound or cascading systemic changes are the rarest of rare events. In the absence of foreknowledge of discontinuity, the rational expectation of actors overwhelmingly favors continuity. Even with foreknowledge of precursive factors, the time and place for the onset of a disruptive or discontinuous event within a complex societal-system cannot be accurately predicted. The prediction of anomalies is not only improbable but unnecessary to the effective management of complex systems; building system resilience, reducing or remedying risk conditions, dampening systemic shocks, and preparing for timely ameliorative responses to the onset of systemic anomalies provide a superior, decentralized management strategy. Effective system management is the foundational narrative in both the Diamond (2005) and Acemoglu and Robinson (2012) treatments; system failure and, particularly, catastrophic system failure is brought about through system mismanagement and systematic neglect that result in the accumulation of limited and unresolved failures that further degrade the system and lead to unmanageable, partial or complete, system breakdown.

The goal of complex societal-systems analysis, then, is to progressively monitor and record social behaviors and circumstances (i.e., dynamics and structures), identify systemic patterns and relationships, diminish knowledge deficits through increased comprehension of processual trajectories and linkages, and apply these understandings to improve system performance, management, and response. By way of conclusion, it will be helpful to discuss the operation, approach, and principle findings of the Political Instability Task Force, which has been actively engaged in evidence-based complex societal-systems analysis for the past twenty-two years; its ongoing efforts provide the most innovative and comprehensive investigation and treatment of the problem of state failure the world has yet known. The first author of this essay has been directly involved with the PITF for the past eighteen of those twenty-two years, primarily because the Task Force commands the resources, attracts the expertise, encourages the intellectual and practical collaboration, inspires the creativity, and embodies the current and future imperative to continuously push the leading edge of complex societal-systems analysis. This assessment may seem a bit grandiose and self-indulgent, given that the PITF maintains a profile nearly invisible to the public and has published only a single professional article (Goldstone et al. 2010; although Task Force reports are produced regularly: Esty et al. 1995; Esty et al. 1998; Goldstone et al. 2000; Bates et al. 2003; Goldstone et al. 2005; Gurr et al. 2005; and Ulfelder and Lustik 2005, and the production of spinoff publications by Task Force members have been quite prolific). This low profile is partly due to the "intelligence culture" of its sponsoring agency, which is best portrayed as cautious and diligent about the information it shares with the public that may be associated with the US government, even though the evidence used is entirely open source information and openly identified in the PITF "data dictionary," its reports are unclassified and available on the Internet, and the data resources it generates are widely and promptly distributed (again, via the Internet) and made available to other researchers.[15] The PITF's low profile is also partly due to its collaborative structure, which is a "collective action" issue in which individual members of the Task Force are hesitant to promote the work of the group, and partly due to the complex and innovative nature of the work itself: the expansive and expanding body of PITF research is difficult to articulate succinctly and convey convincingly to people who are engaged in more limited and focused research, who are uncomfortable with the collaboration of policymakers and scholars in applied research, and who are not familiar with the approach of the PITF or its development over its relatively long duration.[16] From the complex societal-systems research point of view, the value of the PITF to systematic empirical research at the global (systemic) level of inquiry can be viewed as an "iceberg": the reported (visible) Task Force findings represent only the tip of the full body of its effort and contributions; the bulk of its contributions are submerged in the extensiveness and intensiveness of its foundational research efforts.

The PITF's identification, compilation, and collection of mainly state-level global data resources is one of its most important functions and, perhaps, its most valuable contribution to complex societal-systems analysis and to scholarly research more generally. The data collection effort contains state-level variables and indicators principally because most data is aggregated at the state level; very little data with global coverage is presently available with sub-state aggregation or non-state actor focus, although this dearth of systematic information is slowly beginning to change.[17] The PITF has continually reviewed public data sources to identify new, updated, and upgraded data resources and has selectively compiled relevant variables with substantial, global scope and temporal coverage for quantitative analysis.[18] The Task Force's ongoing research efforts also provide critical information regarding variables of particular interest and quantitative research "gaps," leading, on the one hand, to efforts to update, revise, and refine extant data resources and, on the other hand, efforts to collect and compile original data resources on topics and issues of particular research interest. The PITF "global merge" database allows it to investigate statistical relationships among variables of interest at the state level of analysis, for which data with substantial country scope and temporal coverage exists. As it compiles data from multiple independent sources, many of which are proprietary, the PITF database is subject to copyright and other intellectual property restrictions and, so, may not be publicly distributed. However, in recognition of the importance and value of its global data collection effort, the PITF maintains and distributes a "public data dictionary" listing all the open source variables compiled in its "global merge," along with key information regarding original source, variable definition, and coverage for each variable.[19] The PITF also distributes "replication datasets" for each of its reports and publications; these contain specific variables used in the reported models (with select variables not reported in the models), for which the PITF has obtained explicit copyright permission from the original data source.

The composition of the PITF is interdisciplinary and has been about evenly split between theoretical scholars and methodological researchers, all of whom are grounded in empirical "large-n" approaches to systematic inquiry. The Task Force is augmented with representatives from foreign policy departments and agencies within the US government and intelligence analysts who bring a practical perspective to the work of the PITF and an informed scrutiny of the more academic viewpoints of the core of scholars. The scholar members of the PITF number between ten and fifteen at any point in time and are drawn from the more senior ranks of US academia.[20] Membership has changed over time owing to natural attrition and in response to changes in policy interests and tasks; a small group of long-term members provide continuity and help maintain an intellectual coherence and historical memory for the effort, while new members are recruited to replace members who have left the group and to inform special topics of current interest. The variation in membership and focus of study stimulates creativity and expands the breadth and depth of inquiry, while its core mission, which has remained unchanged since its inception, organizes and disciplines that inquiry. The unique combination of expertise and perspective not only informs and guides the core mission to develop "a methodology that would identify key factors and critical thresholds signaling a high risk of crisis in countries some two years in advance" (Esty et al. 1995, iii) but also informs and guides the application of a broad range of methodologies to its tasks to better inform the modeling effort and increase the confidence in and robustness of its findings. Topical investigations always begin with a review of the scholarly literature and special sessions that include discussions with a range of experts in those topics. While a large part of the work of the PITF emphasizes statistical approaches, other methods are used at various times and for various purposes and include approaches as diverse as narrative case study and comparative case study, game theoretical, decision-making, process tracing, expert polling, formal modeling, neural network analysis, and data mining. Alternative sources of both independent and dependent variables are used, when these are available, and related or substitutable variables comprising "baskets" of indicators are interchanged in statistical modeling to better "map the landscape" of complex interconnectedness among system variables. Both structural and dynamical elements are examined, as are both internal (societal) and external (systemic) dimensions.[21] The result is a "living" and "learning" research effort that utilizes intensive and extensive methods to accumulate knowledge and better understand not only societal-systemic complexity, diversity, and interconnectedness but also the existential, logistical, and applied commonalities that make collective behaviors in chaotic systems comprehensible and manageable

> The Task Force has tested literally hundreds of variables to see if they have any association with vulnerability to political instability. Because the onset of instability is a complex process with diverse causal pathways, we originally expected that no simple model would have much success in identifying the factors associated with the onset of such crises. Rather, we expected that we would need to develop widely different models to identify the factors associated with instability onset for different regions, and for different kinds of events. Moreover, we assumed these models would have to be complex, relying on many independent variables, reflecting both their levels and rates of change, and their interaction in varied combinations. It was to our considerable surprise that these expectations turned out to be wrong. The Task Force's analysis has identified some differences across regions and types of instability, but these differences have generally proved minor.

Even more surprising, we have found that relatively simple models, involving just a handful of variables and no complex interactions, accurately classify 80% or more of the instability onsets and stable countries in the historical data. This is perhaps the most significant general finding of the Task Force's research: relatively simple models can identify the factors associated with a broad range of political violence and instability events around the world.

(Goldstone et al. 2005, 10)

Having (1) conducted extensive and intensive studies regarding the precursive structural conditions and social dynamics characterizing the risks of state failure events, (2) developed and refined data inputs, (3) designed multiple comparable models using various specifications and methodologies, (4) tested those models against both "in-sample" and "out-of-sample" case sets, (5) "unpacked" and "drilled down" to gain a more "fine-grained" understanding of the risk factors and the particular contexts in which those risk factors may be more or less likely to trigger event onsets and, consequently, having (6) "re-contextualized" their statistical findings into narrative form to examine the veracity of the risk factors in accordance with expert knowledge and analysis of country-specific observations, the PITF selects a single representative global model that is empirically robust, analytically sound, and theoretically grounded and which encompasses what the Task Force consensus considers to be its most prescient findings.[22] The PITF global model uses a triple-matched, case-control methodology and a conditional logistic regression statistical application to specify key precursive factors that characterize the imminent risk of the onset of a political instability (state failure) condition in any of 163 countries in the world (for a detailed specification of the model, see Goldstone et al. 2010).[23] The most recent specification of the PITF global model for the initial onset of a political instability condition contains five indicators: basic regime type, (polar) "factionalism," (high) infant mortality rate, state-led (ethnic) discrimination, and "armed conflict in [four or more] bordering states."[24] In our opinion, the principle findings of the PITF global modeling effort can be summarized in seven points:

first, the principal risk factors of political instability included in the global model are only five and these risk factors are common to all countries and all specified (initial) forms of instability (no additional risk factors have been found that, when added to the global model, substantially improved the performance of the model);

second, poorer and lesser-developed states are, perhaps inherently, the most highly prone to experience political instability onset;

third, multi-ethnic societies are at higher risk of instability only when the state institutionalizes discriminatory practices targeting any of its constituent groups;

fourth, autocratic governance—while diminished dramatically since its global peak in the mid-1970s—has been strongly associated with onsets of armed violence and the collapse of central authority, whereas incomplete democratization is susceptible to "autocratic backsliding," thereby, at least temporarily, raising the risks of armed violence in those countries;

fifth, societal polarization or "factionalism" is the principle observable dynamic factor leading directly to higher risks of political instability; this oppositional mobilization process takes time and, so, provides opportunities for both recognition of risk and prevention of instability onset (i.e., effective conflict management);

sixth, there is a spatial or systemic "neighborhood" component that compounds (bad) or alleviates (good) the risks of political instability;[25] and

seventh, the condition of political instability, whether regime instability or outbreak of serious armed conflict, has been identified as the precursive risk condition for inhumanity and the escalation of political violence to include its most extreme forms: genocide or politicide (i.e., the intentional targeting of lethal violence against distinct civilian/non-combatant populations).

Conclusion

Perhaps the most profound difference between the "self-help" system of the "old world order" and the "globalizing" system characterizing a "new world order" lies in the fundamental attitude of states toward one another. In the "old world order," the national interest of powerful states was focused on establishing and maintaining an advantage in "relative capabilities" *vis-á-vis* neighboring, competing, or coveted "others"; this outlook often drove states to actively weaken or undermine the viability of its real, perceived, or potential rivals. The "problem" of the "old world order" was associated with "state power." In the emerging "new world order," the nature of the "problem" is increasingly understood and conceptualized as "state failure." The security threats posed by powerful states in a self-help system are clear: the use of force in violation of a state's sovereignty or for control of contested interests. The security threats posed by failed states in a dynamic, integrated, and complex system of states cannot be fully understood in traditional (direct) "invasive," or even (indirect) "spillover," terms. The real security threat posed by the failure of individual components in an integrated system lies in the degradation of system potential and the absolute diminution of "relative opportunities" for all units within the system. The constriction of systemic well-being and entrepreneurial opportunities increases tensions and rivalries among units within the system, further degrading the system. The prevention of conflict within a societal-system, then, can be seen as tantamount to proactively improving compliance with systemic imperatives and effectively managing sustainable system performance. Developing a better understanding of why, how, and when components fail in complex societal-systems is essential to inform effective conflict management and will require a broader and more systematic approach to the accumulation of knowledge.

Notes

1 The PITF is a collaborative, unclassified (open source) research effort involving a core group of the country's leading research scholars. The effort is funded by the US Central Intelligence Agency; however, its analyses are not based on intelligence reporting nor does the work represent the official view of the US government but, rather, the personal views of the researchers themselves.

2 Both the terms "politicide" and "genocide" refer to the intentional and systematic targeting of civilian population groups with lethal repression by agents acting within the authority of the state; politicides target political groups and genocides target ethnic groups. The PITF research found that these two forms of extreme violence are "second-order" forms of political violence that occur only with or following the onset of a major armed conflict event or an "adverse regime change." Politicide and genocide have consequently been dropped from the Task Force's operational definition of state failure/political instability. "Autocratic backsliding" may be viewed as an attempt by regime authorities to "crack down" on political opposition in order to enforce and preserve the status quo.

3 The name and terminology of the PITF was changed in 2003 in recognition of the pejorative connotation of the term "failure" and in recognition of the fact that lesser forms of instability, and the disturbance they cause, are the main concern of foreign policy.

4 Ziaja and Mata (2010) offer a comprehensive survey of state fragility and failure metrics. As they note, the SFI is the only fragility metric that offers backdated data to allow for time-series analysis of fragility and failure dynamics.

5 Soon after completing their report on "state weakness," Susan Rice became one of Barak Obama's principal foreign policy advisors. Following Obama's election as president, Rice was appointed United States Ambassador to the United Nations and the "Index of State Weakness" has not been updated since its initial offering.

6 The Fund for Peace "automated coding" algorithms and software are derived from its Conflict Assessment System Tool (CAST), originally developed by its former president Pauline Baker.

7 For a more detailed treatment and analysis of the various measurement schemes, see Marshall (2008).

8 See Waltz (1979) for a succinct delineation of the anarchic "self-help" world system. The principle of non-interference is codified in the 1945 Charter of the United Nations (chap.I, art.1, par.7).

9 A project similar to the PITF macro-level (i.e., structural and institutional behavior data) risk-modeling effort within the US government is the Integrated Crisis Early Warning System (ICEWS) micro-level (i.e., coded events data) predictive-modeling effort supported since 2007 by the Defense Advanced Research Projects Agency (DARPA) initiative of the Department of Defense (O'Brien 2010).

10 The notion that "failed states" can be viewed as "threats to U.S. Interests" first entered official policy with President Clinton's "A National Security Strategy for a New Century," promulgated in October 1998. That document recognized that serious spillover effects from failed states "can threaten U.S. interests and citizens" (7). Following the September 11, 2001, al Qaeda attacks on US national territory directed by its leadership in Afghanistan, President Bush announced in his September 2002 National Security Strategy (NSS) that "America is now threatened less by conquering states than we are by failing ones." He goes on to argue that "The United States has long maintained the option of preemptive actions to counter [such] a sufficient threat to our national security" (15). President Obama's May 2010 NSS states clearly that "Failing states breed conflict and endanger regional and global security" (8).

11 "High casualty terrorist bombings" include single bomb, or coordinated multiple-bomb, attacks on non-combatant targets that result in fifteen or more reported deaths.

12 These figures include inactive non-governmental organizations that comprise about 30–40 percent of the total number. As such organizations become active or inactive according to issue salience at any point in time, the distinction between active and inactive may be temporal. Figures are from Table 3.1, posted on the Internet at www.uia.be/sites/uia.be/files/statistics/organizations/types-2004.pdf (accessed July 26, 2011).

13 Sources of data on the United States' organizations are posted on the Internet: National Center for Charitable Statistics for not-for-profit organizations (nccsdataweb.urban.org/PubApps/profile1.php); U.S. Census Bureau for business firms (www.census.gov/econ/smallbus.html); and U.S. Department of Labor, Bureau of Labor Statistics for advocacy organizations (www.bls.gov/iag/tgs/iag813.htm); all three sites were accessed on July 26, 2011.

14 The figure for not-for-profit organizations in India comes from a study commissioned by the government of India and referenced on the Internet by OneWorld South Asia; southasia.oneworld.net/todaysheadlines/india-more-ngos-than-schools-and-health-centres (accessed July 26, 2011).

15 As this section focuses on Task Force work, it is appropriate to repeat the caveat that the work of the Task Force is not based on intelligence reporting nor does it represent the official view of the US government, the US intelligence community, or the CIA, but rather the views of the individual Task Force members and, in this particular application, the views of the authors.

16 The Task Force's periodic reports provide some indication of the expanding nature and scope of the global modeling effort: the Phase I report comprises 100 pages; the reports have continued to grow in length such that the Phase IV report filled 400 pages. Since the Phase IV report, the Task Force has abandoned the comprehensive report in favor of shorter reports on specific aspects or topics of the project.

17 Several countries, principally the upper- and middle-income states, compile detailed records for sub-state administrative units which allow for analysis of spatial variations within those states. As part of its Phase IV research, the PITF modeled the onset of "sub-national" violent conflicts in India using federal state and district-level data drawn from the India central government's *Census of India* and *Crime in India* publications (Bates et al. 2003).

18 An important factor in the selection process is an assessment of the relative quality (accuracy and reliability) of the data resource.

19 The 2010 version of the PITF public data dictionary lists more than 2600 variables drawn from about 100 different sources covering 164 countries with annual data for the period 1955 to present.

20 As the Task Force is a US government project, all members of the Task Force are US citizens.

21 The PITF does not include classic interstate behaviors, such as wars, militarized disputes, and crises, within its research mandate. The systemic dimensions include such factors as military and economic interventions, foreign assistance and investment, trade flows, and neighborhood effects.

22 The PITF has examined and modeled various subsets of country and types of instability event to augment and inform its global modeling effort; these have included subset models for sub-Saharan Africa, Muslim countries, and autocracies, and topical models for ethnic war, revolutionary war, ethnic and revolutionary war, genocide and politicide, mass killings, and regime transitions.

23 The PITF global research and modeling effort includes all independent countries in the world, except the United States, that have reached a total population of 500,000 or more in the most recent year (i.e., 167 countries in 2014); the United States is not included owing to policy constraints. The political instability (state failure) condition used as the dependent variable in the global model is the "consolidated case," which is defined by the initial onset of any of the four categories of political instability events

and lasts until there is no ongoing event or additional onset in a particular country for a period of five years. Control cases are matched by year and region with problem cases.

24 "'Factionalism' refers to an advanced, macro-systemic stage of group polarization that transforms political behavior in distinct ways that are both systematic and sustained. Factionalism transforms the conventional politics of deliberation to the unconventional 'anti-system' politics of disruption" (Marshall and Cole 2008b, 7). The factionalism condition in societal politics is observed as contentious political behavior in ruling and non-ruling sectors over an accumulation of unresolved and/or unresolvable issues, a condition similar to that noted by Diamond (2005) and Acemoglu and Robinson (2012) to explain state failure and collapse. The "armed conflict in 4+ bordering states" indicator represents systemic/spatial factors affecting the onset of political instability.

25 The "neighborhood" component includes not only the "good" and "bad" circumstantial clustering and influence network systemic effects but also such spatial effects as large land area (large countries tend to be the most ethnically diverse and logistically more difficult to manage and administer) and land-locked countries (more logistically challenged, more dependent on neighboring countries, more remote from systemic influence and exchange networks).

12

GENOCIDE AND POLITICAL MASS MURDER

Definitions, Theories, Analyses

Barbara Harff

"Between the 1950s and 1980s the term 'genocide' languished almost unused by scholars" (Jones 2011, 15). The Holocaust dominated the literature, researchers were by and large historians and social-scientific studies were all but absent. During the later 1980s and 1990s genocide studies began to emerge as an interdisciplinary field focusing on man-made disasters that did not fit the definitions found in the existing conflict literature. Early data suggested that genocide phenomena were quite similar to the Holocaust and were neither rare nor absent from the later twentieth century. As I argued later, no lessons were learned from the Holocaust (see Harff 1994; Fein 1994).

Comparative Research on Genocides: the 1970s

Genocide scholars in the 1970s were rarely labeled as such. Most focused on individual cases, foremost of course the Holocaust, which was widely considered a unique event defying comparison. The Armenian genocide was mainly the province of ethnic Armenians, who, when some brave souls compared their genocide to the Holocaust, were chastised by the advocates of uniqueness. To some, comparison was sacrilegious, because the Holocaust was unique in its focus on the annihilation of the Jewish peoples and the efficiency by which its millions of victims were put to death. But there were other, more intellectual reasons; essentially, comparison of just two cases made little sense for the behavioral crowd. If one sought to establish patterns and seek explanations, there had to be a larger universe of cases. It took time and persuasion of the genocide pioneers to gather information on other historical cases that eventually established the legitimacy of large-n comparative research on genocide.

The contributors to this process included people from different disciplines, countries, and intellectual backgrounds who together established the foundations of an emerging discipline. Some were honored in a compilation of life stories in *Pioneers of Genocide Studies* (Totten and Jacobs 2002). Although the book omits some important contributors, it is representative of approaches and findings. Scholars who contributed case studies, theory, data, and empirical analyses in the early years include Irving Louis Horowitz, Leo Kuper, Helen Fein, Kurt Jonassohn, Roger Smith, Frank Chalk, Robert Melson, Israel Charny, Rudolph Rummel, and myself. Without the many area specialists, including Armenian scholars, comparative work would have floundered. Here I am thinking especially of Robert Conquest, Gerard Chaliand and Yves Ternon, Vahakn Dadrian, Gerard Prunier, Alison Des Forges, Ben Kiernan, Richard Hovannisian, James Mace, and A. M. Nekrich. Of the many Holocaust scholars who changed their mind about the uniqueness issues and became vocal advocates of comparative studies of genocidal violence and its prevention, I give special credit again to Yehuda Bauer, who now, in his late eighties, puts many younger scholars to shame with his enthusiasm for the cause and his tireless dedication to alerting policymakers, journalists, and anyone else who will listen that we must be proactive in preventing future genocides.

Definitional Issues

Raphael Lemkin (1944), a Polish jurist who immigrated to the US in 1941, coined the term that by today's standards means the intentional killing of groups of people by the state. His tireless lobbying of the newly formed UN eventually earned the respect of powerful supporters. In 1948 genocide became a crime under international law during war and peacetime. The Convention defines genocide in Article II as

> Acts committed with intent to destroy, in whole or part, a national, ethnical, racial or religious group as such: (a) Killing members of the group; (b) Causing serious bodily or mental harm to members of the group; (c) Deliberately inflicting on the group conditions of life calculated to bring about its physical destruction in whole or part; (d) Imposing measures intended to prevent birth within the group; (e) Forcibly transferring children of the group to another group.
>
> *(UN General Assembly 1948)*

There are major flaws in this wording, as discussed below. Aside from the definitional problems, there were major issues of concern to those who aim to prevent future genocides. First and foremost, there was no real enforcement mechanism that held offenders responsible and no sanctions attached to the crime of genocide. Nearly fifty genocides that I have identified since World War II have been committed by states, which, according to the Convention, are responsible for policing themselves (for the initial list see Harff and Gurr 1987; the most recent is Harff 2005). Typically the perpetrators are agents of the state or the state is otherwise complicit or directly responsible. Thus, unless there is regime change, or unless other states intervene, perpetrators get away with mass murder. The Convention did not establish special courts to try perpetrators, and there was no mechanism that would provide accusers with the legal means to adjudicate cases of genocide. The International Court of Justice, after all, needed to have the agreement of both parties to function effectively.

One can only guess at the rationales of the drafters or of states that ratified the Convention. Arguably, signing on to the Convention meant that the international community of nation-states would police itself. And, if this should fail, reasoning in light of the fiasco of the League of Nations between the two world wars, a more powerful UN would sanction violators. Furthermore, the wrong of genocide as established by the Convention would simultaneously produce new norms and set boundaries on what would be considered acceptable state behavior, which might also deter would-be perpetrators. In retrospect one can readily understand the glaring omissions. After all, in the late 1940s the USSR was a major violator of human rights and should have come under increased scrutiny. The Cold War was emerging and Germany was well on its way to becoming a needed member of the Western alliance, thus prompting an end to major war-crime trials. And, just possibly, after the birth of the state of Israel, which both the US and the USSR rushed to recognize, guilty consciences were satisfied. Whatever the reasons, very few scholars tackled the thorniest issue of it all: Why and how could another Holocaust occur, and what could or should be done to forestall it? By the 1970s dozens of other episodes of genocidal violence had taken place, but with little or no recognition by either the academic or policy community. Why?

Problems with Applying the Definition

The UN Genocide Convention was clearly informed by the Holocaust. Although Lemkin based his definition of what constitutes genocide on other historical cases, including the 1915 Armenian genocide, the killings of American Indians, and the massacres of rebellious Hereros by German colonial forces in south-west Africa (1904–7), most scholars used the Holocaust as the archetypal case.

The word genocide has two specific meanings: *cide* means killing and *genos* refers to specific types of peoples, not the killing of cultures or the oppression of or discrimination against peoples. And by people Lemkin meant identifiable groups based on ethnicity, race, religion, or nationhood. Political groups did not become part of the definition, largely but not exclusively because membership in political groups was fluid, i.e. one could move in and out of a political group, by contrast to ethnic and racial or religious groups. Given the lack of debate in the 1940s about what constitutes an ethnic or national group, such imprecision was understandable. In addition, some states were reluctant to embrace the idea that potentially subversive political groups could claim to be victims of genocide.

Another major hurdle was the clause that there had to be intent to destroy a group in whole or part. How to prove intent? It was relatively easy to explain motive using the Nazi example. Nazi ideologues clearly enunciated a message about what they hoped to achieve and why. Foremost was the goal to Germanize Europe, the rationale being that Germans were members of a superior race and thus would bring advanced culture to lesser races. Those perceived as being outside the circle of acceptable races based on imagined bloodlines, such as Slavs and Jews, were either to be annihilated (Jews) or decimated over time (Slavs).

Intent can be more difficult to decipher, although the Nazi case is straightforward since the goals were often accompanied with specific instructions on how to achieve the desired outcome. Thus, Jews were to be "resettled" (killed) or, in the case of half or quarter Jews, either enslaved or, in exceptional cases, barely tolerated. In the case of Slavs, starvation, sterilization, or, if possible, Germanization (if their features were sufficiently "Aryan") was made policy. The bureaucratic apparatus was combined with security and special forces, and sometime-collaboration with the military made it possible to implement genocidal policy decisions smoothly. Perhaps it was easier to commit genocide in authoritarian societies in which individual opposition was costly because of the fear of retribution. Or was it that indifference to the plight of others became the norm—thus, following orders and not questioning authorities was socially and psychologically rewarding behavior? Cultural cohesion, furthermore, made it easier to recognize "others," especially with the help of relentless propaganda, thus paving the way for indifference to the plight of victims. Today, we know that many post-Holocaust genocides and political mass murders have been carried out by authoritarian regimes that espouse such exclusionary ideologies.

Contemporary researchers, especially those concerned with preventing future cases, have the difficult task of detecting intent. This is problematic on two counts. One, most often we find clear evidence only after the genocide is well underway. And, two, intent is sometimes confused with motive and more often not easily discovered. I think we could help ourselves by clarifying what we mean by intent and thus eliminate the need to wait until genocide is on its way before declaring it as such. The situation in Darfur (Sudan) was a case in point for the latter argument. Early warning models developed by this author and by observers such as Eric Reeves led to the conclusion that this was indeed a genocide long before the UN-sponsored investigation that declared it a case of something resembling a genocide. Darfur is a glaring example of what is wrong with our understanding of intent. In the simplest way, intent has to do with how to implement motive. It is the process, mechanism, and actions by which the desired end goals are achieved.

The Current Definitional Debate

Essentially the debate is moot, in the sense that most scholars agree on the basic issues, with some differences on the margins. Definitions most commonly used are those by Israel Charny (1982), Leo Kuper (1981), Frank Chalk and Kurt Jonassohn (1990), Helen Fein (1979; 1993b) and Barbara Harff (1987; 2003).

Charny broadens the victim definition by including all groups based on whatever identity they share. Fein (1993b), Kuper (1981), and Harff (2003) include political groups as potential victims, although Kuper uses the term genocidal massacres, Fein uses the term ideological massacres, and Harff politicides. Chalk and Jonassohn (1990) include non-state actors in their definition of potential perpetrators, an extension later accepted by Harff and Fein. Dadrian (1974), a key expert on the Armenian genocide, talks about dominant authorities capable of committing genocide, a phrase that became part of a key explanatory variable in our understanding of which elites are most likely to use genocidal means to suppress potential opponents.

Some Key Issues and Possible Solutions

First, who should be included in the groups that are considered victims of genocide? Second, can non-state actors be considered perpetrators? Third, is proof of intent necessary to consider crimes against humanity genocide? And, lastly, how do we differentiate among terrorism, war, genocide, civil war, and revolution? The above problems become less of an issue when one looks at past and potential cases. In most cases since World War II, political and class victims have been targets of genocidal violence. Their identity was based on membership in parties or denunciation by regime sympathizers, or they were identified by the regime as enemies of the state. Occasionally victims have no clear identity to objective observers, and all that is known is that the genocidal regime assigned them characteristics that made victimization possible (for example, the Khmer Rouge targeting all intellectuals during their reign of terror). Of course, they are victims of politicide (political mass murder).

Can non-state actors be perpetrators? The answer has to be yes, given experiences in Bosnia and Congo–Kinshasa, where rebel groups and other non-state actors became the primary perpetrators. These situations emerge when there is no effective state authority, characterized by contending authorities in cases of civil war or revolutionary upheavals. As a matter of fact, most cases of genocide took place during or immediately after internal wars. This brings up another issue, which is how to differentiate among different types of conflict. There is an abundance of literature on what constitutes a civil war or revolution, thus there is no need to elaborate here. What one needs to consider are the distinguishing features of genocide. There are three. One is the systematic and intentional nature of the crime, in a manner similar to the way that homicide is separate from manslaughter. Second is the collective identity of the victims. Third is the disproportionate power of the perpetrators vis-à-vis victims. The latter may be rebels or resisters, but they face overwhelming odds.

Social Science Explanations of Genocide

No social scientist is satisfied with merely describing phenomena or collecting information. In all cases we seek general explanations. In the 1970s that was somewhat problematic because there was no known universe of cases other than the very few agreed-upon twentieth-century cases. As a political scientist I could not envision looking at antiquity to explain the Holocaust and other recent cases. The twentieth century, with its mechanized warfare and capabilities of mass destruction, combined with a state system that was at once enduring and ever changing owing to decolonization, proved to be a formidable obstacle to explanations rooted in the past. For example, how does one account for genocide committed by the Crusaders in the name of Christianity? Who was responsible? Was it the Pope in Rome or European rulers whose powers were easily undermined by the Holy See?

Particular problems emerged when sociologists, political scientists, and psychologists disagreed on how to merge different levels of analysis into one cohesive explanation. Though most scholars agreed that factors such as empire building, culture, elite characteristics, power drives, group cohesion, and interpersonal dynamics all combined to explain why genocide, which were the most important factors that triggered genocidal behavior? Given the complexity of today's world and the lack of formal testing of earlier theories, much work needed to be done. Foremost, we needed to identify cases post-Holocaust, which I thought of as the logical starting point—not only because the Holocaust became the case that prompted the Genocide Convention and showed to the extreme the dimensions of such a tragedy but also because the world, through decolonization and the redrawing of borders, became a different place post–World War II. Were there enough cases to test general explanations and how many were enough?

My early contribution was identifying and collecting information on forty-six cases since World War II, some of which were later discarded owing to more precise criteria or better information; others were added owing to emerging situations. Both Helen Fein and Rudolph Rummel did independent work on cases. Rummel's documentation of cases of "democide" includes not only cases of genocide but also warfare and egregious cases of human rights violations (1995). But, all in all, we now had a universe of cases to test our theories.

From an empirical perspective, an explanation is one that is tested using objective information. During the 1990s and the early twenty-first century of the empirically minded scholars only three—Fein (1990), Krain (1997), and Harff (2003)—have systematically tested competing theories. Others retested Harff's findings and added new variables to test new questions (see below for citations).

Fein and Harff's theoretical premises were remarkably similar and have been substantiated in empirical tests, yet offer plenty of opportunities for improvement. Scholars less empirically inclined also offer many valuable contributions and insights that cannot necessarily be captured by parsimonious empirical explanations. Often explanations emphasize cultural factors that contribute to the development of genocide or focus on the nature of individual or group characteristics (for example, Staub 1989), factors that cannot be necessarily captured through the construction of macro-variables and indicators. My focus here is on structural factors that have been empirically tested across substantial numbers of cases.

Levels of Analyses and Theory Development

Many scholars in different disciplines have contributed to the development of theories on why genocides occur, but disciplinary boundaries have stood in the way of a comprehensive framework or general theory that incorporates all aspects of genocide development. Helen Fein has written an excellent overview of earlier theories, *Genocide: a Sociological Perspective* (1990 and 1993b), and thus little elaboration is needed here. We both agree that explanations of genocide were subsumed under general conflict studies, treating genocide as one extreme outcome of interethnic competition for scarce resources. Alternatively, genocide occurs more often in stratified societies in which elites establish dominance by singling out other peoples for elimination. Neither approach helps to answer more specific questions about genocide. Why do some elites choose genocide over other forms of political violence? Why, indeed, was the destruction of peoples considered a logical choice by state actors? Fein and Harff are both skeptical about a purely biological or psychological approach to explaining genocidal phenomena. Whereas some theorists start from the premise that peoples are predisposed to aggression or altruism, the premise has not been empirically tested, nor can it necessarily be observed in cases of genocide (see Van den Berghe 1981; Charny 1982). Others broaden their emphasis to include intergroup conflict or cultural preconditions (Staub 1989; Waller 2007).

Of the early pioneers in our field both Fein and Kuper emphasize comprehensive explanations for why particular peoples are victimized. Both view ethnically divided or stratified societies as necessary conditions to theories of human destructiveness. Harff and Fein use the concept of communal groups, which focuses on a more broadly defined set of victims, including political groups, as potential targets of genocide. Fein adds a further necessary condition, that of dehumanization, to our arsenal of theoretical premises. She argues that excluding the victim groups from the universe of obligation makes it easier to implement their annihilation. Chalk and Jonassohn (1990) build on the well-established notion of a gap perception and the notion of an out-group that makes it easier to apply different standards of treatment to people designated as members of the out-group. Most of us agree that genocide is a purposeful action "related both to the interests of the state and leading social classes and elites" (Fein 1993b, 38). Ted Robert Gurr, who contributed to the cases compiled by Harff in part through his Minorities at Risk dataset, is well within the domain of general explanations of genocide by stressing group conflict histories and state-led discrimination as potential factors leading to the repression and victimization of minorities (Gurr 2000, chapter 3). He treats genocide as the most severe form of state repression (see 2000, 128). However, as mentioned above, there are many state elites that discriminate against peoples but do not try to annihilate whole groups. Here both Fein and Harff focus on the role of ideology, which designates certain peoples as undesirable outsiders. In many cases of genocide ideology was a driving factor in developing policies that systematically deprived future victims of rights. In addition, as part of my empirical exercise of collecting information on cases, it became readily apparent that many cases were imbedded in other conflicts, such as *civil war, revolution,* or *international wars.* It was hypothesized that insecure elites perceived oppositional activities as a threat to their continued dominance and thus chose to eliminate rival groups. Thus, the term "national upheaval," used by both Harff and Fein in earlier works, was added to our theoretical propositions in need of testing.

In designing the empirical analyses described below I came back over and over to the contributions of social psychologists. Most of us have never stopped asking how it was possible to overcome personal scruples to kill others without remorse or lasting psychological damage. But with some regret I realized that individual- and group-based theories using the individual as the unit of analysis could not be incorporated into a study that dealt primarily with state- and group-level characteristics. But let me re-emphasize the contributions of Charny, Lifton, Staub, Waller, and others who have done such work. They propose dichotomized aspects of individual and societal behavior, such as life denial versus affirmation (Charny quoted in Fein 1993b, 46); or fear of death; or treat historic and cultural crises as illness (Lifton 1986) whose cure depends on eradicating the unwanted. On the critical side none seems to capture the role of conscious, rational processes, or for that matter the dynamics of intergroup behavior, or the role of structures, ideology, or elites, and their contribution to why genocides occur with some regularity. Although scholars such as Staub and later Charny have gone beyond emphasis on the individual to embrace more general explanations, emphasis on particular levels of analysis is inherently unsatisfactory. However, this is not to diminish their contributions. Despite current empirical findings that allow us to do global risk assessment and to track current crises through early warning models (see below), no explanation is complete without assessing or taking into consideration psychological or cultural factors; thus, we need to be reminded of their contributions and recognize that much empirical work remains to be done.

Empirical Research

As mentioned above, Fein (1993a) and Krain (1997) had tested various hypotheses about why genocides occur. Arguably the most comprehensive study to date was published by this author in the *American Political Science Review* in February 2003, the first time this journal had published on the evolution of genocide. The study was carried out as part of the research program of the State Failure (later Political Instability) Task Force, established and funded by the US government (as described in Goldstone et al. 2002). The analysis of geno/politicide, described in detail below, proceeded by testing a wide range of hypotheses proposed in the literature, given the limits mentioned above in the levels of analysis discussion. When no data were available on key variables, we coded it. Thus, I was responsible for coding elite characteristics and exclusionary ideology for annual data for all states from 1955 onwards. An independent team recoded the variables and inconsistencies were resolved. The published article describes in detail the best-fit model, estimated using a case-control research design, but also reports briefly on alternative models. In designing the study we drew the net wide by incorporating hypotheses found in the ethnic conflict literature and the generic conflict literature, finding—as expected—that in some respects genocide phenomena are linked to other conflict phenomena.

Operational Definition

My operational definition has benefited from the input of others, especially Fein and Chalk and Jonassohn: *Genocides and politicides are the promotion, execution, and/or implied consent of sustained policies by governing elites or their agents—or in the case of civil war, either of the contending authorities—that are intended to destroy, in whole or part, a communal, political, or politicized ethnic group.* In genocides and politicides killings are never accidental, nor are they acts by individuals. They are intentional acts carried out by state authorities, or those claiming authority. Victims are members of an identifiable group, though in rare cases identity can be construed by potential perpetrators. There is no particular threshold of number of victims that must be reached in order to call an event genocide, nor is it necessary to destroy all members of a group. What matters is intent. In the case of group survival, it may be enough to kill a few members to endanger group survival—in other words, genocide occurs when perpetrators take the life out of a group. Cases abound: in Kosovo ethnic cleansing was the crux of genocidal policies; in Darfur death through privation and resettlement became the norm; and both had their antecedents in the gulag of the former Soviet empire. Death through induced starvation was both a precursor and accepted policy during the Holocaust and later in Biafra, and many other cases show similar patterns, either as genocidal patterns evolve or as part of such policies.

Testing Hypotheses: Ideology and Retribution[1]

Ideology is an essential variable, as proposed above. Fein focuses on exclusionary ideologies, defined as "hegemonic myths identifying the victims as outside the sanctioned universe of obligation" (Fein 1984, 18). The status of the victims is evident in the labels applied to them, such as "class enemies," "counter-revolutionaries," or "heretics." Examples of *ideologically inspired geno/politicide* occurred in China during the Cultural Revolution of 1966–75; in Marxist Ethiopia in the late 1970s; in Chile after the overthrow of the leftist Allende regime in 1973; and in Iran after the revolution.

Whereas ideological genocides can be thought of as outcomes of elite succession struggles, *retributive geno/politicides* are strategies forged during and in the immediate aftermath of civil wars. Case studies suggest that the more intense the prior struggle for power and the greater the perceived threat the excluded group poses to the new regime the more likely they are to become victims of geno/politicide. Some geno/politicides occur during a protracted internal war—whether ethnic or revolutionary or both—when one party, usually the government, systematically seeks to destroy its opponent's support base. Examples occurred in South Vietnam in the 1960s and early 1970s; during both phases of the Sudanese civil war; in East Timor after 1975; and in Guatemala, Angola, and Sri Lanka. Some retributive episodes occur after a rebel challenge has been militarily defeated. In Indonesia in 1965–66, for example, a coup attempt supposedly inspired by Communists led to country-wide massacres of party members and other civilians.

Since geno/politicides almost always occur in the context of violent political conflict and regime change, can they be explained in the framework of theories of revolutionary or ethnic conflict, or of political instability in general? Not directly, because the puzzle addressed here is why some such conflicts lead to episodes of mass murder whereas most do not. Theories of the etiology of civil conflict, such as Goldstone et al. (1991) on revolutions, Horowitz (1985) on ethnic conflict, and Tilly (1978) on political mobilization, do not address this question. There is no index entry for genocide in any of these books, nor in the 1980 edition of the *Handbook of Political Conflict* (Gurr 1980). More relevant are analyses of the causes of state repression and the maintenance of social order (see Lichbach 1987; 1998).

The approach taken here focuses on factors that affect the decision calculus of authorities in conflict situations, in particular the circumstances that lead to decisions to eliminate rather than accommodate rival groups. Several scholars propose that the greater the threat posed by challengers, the greater the likelihood that regimes will choose massive repression (Fein 1993b; Gurr 1986a; 1986b; Harff 1987). They also argue for the importance of habituation: successful uses of violence to seize or maintain power establish agencies and dispositions to rely on repression in future conflicts. Krain (1997, 332–37), among others, proposes that regime changes, including those that follow revolutions, open up opportunities for elites to eliminate groups that might challenge them. Numerous researchers point out that democratic norms and political structures constrain elite decisions about the use of repression against their citizens, whereas autocratic elites are not so constrained (Gurr 1986a; 1986b; Henderson 1991; Rummel 1995). Others suggest that the international environment is a major source of both incentives and constraints on elites' use of repression. Thus, a country's peripheral status in the international system can be a permissive condition (Harff 1987). International war can provide a cover (Melson 1992), whereas international engagement and condemnation can constrain repression. Each of the general factors below is interpreted in terms of its likely effects on authorities' choices about whether to resort to mass killings in conflict situations.

Political Upheaval: The Necessary Precondition for Genocide and Politicide

The beginning point for general theory is *political upheaval*, a concept that captures the essence of the structural crises and societal pressures that are preconditions for authorities' efforts to eliminate entire groups (Harff 1987; Melson 1992). Political upheaval is defined as *an abrupt change in the political community caused by the formation of a state or regime through violent conflict, redrawing of state boundaries, or defeat in international war.* Types of political upheaval include defeat in international war, revolutions, anti-colonial rebellions, separatist wars, coups, and regime transitions that result in the ascendancy of political elites who embrace extremist ideologies.

Empirically, all but one of the thirty-seven genocides and politicides that began between 1955 and 1998 occurred during or immediately after political upheavals, as determined from the State Failure Task Force's roster of ethnic and revolutionary wars and adverse regime changes:[2] twenty-four coincided with ethnic wars; fourteen coincided with revolutionary wars; and fourteen followed the occurrence of adverse regime changes. As these numbers imply, several geno/politicides began after multiple state failures of different types. In addition, four of the thirty-seven sequences of state failure followed the establishment of an independent state, through either decolonization or the breakup of an existing state.

A key variable in the analysis is the magnitude of political upheaval; the argument is that the greater the extent of violent conflict and adverse regime change, the greater the likelihood that geno/politicide will occur. There are two rationales: first, the more intense and persistent conflict has been, the more threatened and the more willing to take extreme measures authorities are likely to be. Second, following Krain (1997), the greater the extent of political disruption, the greater the opportunities for authorities to seek a "final solution" to present and potential future challenges.

Prior Genocides: Habituation to Mass Killings?

We observed that ten countries had multiple episodes of geno/politicide in the last half-century. Events that began four or more years after the end of a prior event were treated as separate cases in the analyses reported here. I am mindful of Fein's observation (1993a) that perpetrators of genocide are often repeat offenders, because elites and security forces may become habituated to mass killing as a strategic response to challenges to state security, and also because targeted groups are rarely destroyed in their entirety. To test for "repeat offender" effects, a binary indicator—whether or not a previous genocide had occurred in the country since 1955—was used.

Political Systems: Exclusionary Ideologies and Autocratic Rule

Political upheaval is a necessary but not sufficient condition for geno/politicide. Between 1955 and 1996 more than ninety state failures did not lead to geno/politicide within four years of their onset. Two characteristics of political governance have vital intervening effects—the ideological commitments of elites and the extent of democratic constraints on their actions. Contending elites usually have many strategic and tactical options for defeating or neutralizing opposition groups. Elite ideologies are crucial determinants of their choices. The theoretical argument for exclusionary ideology is summarized above.

Most geno/politicides are carried out by autocracies. Democratic and quasi-democratic regimes have institutional checks on executive power that constrain elites from carrying out deadly attacks on citizens, as noted above. Moreover, the democratic norms of most contemporary societies favor the protection of minority rights and the inclusion of political opponents, while competitive elections minimize chances for adherents of exclusionary ideologies to be elected to high office. This is the domestic equivalent of the "democratic peace" argument (see Davenport 1999; Hegre et al. 2001). There are, however, historical and contemporary instances of geno/politicide being carried out by governments with a semblance of democratic institutions. Ideologies that excluded indigenous peoples from the universe of obligation and justified their destruction coexisted with democratic institutions for white majorities in nineteenth-century Australia and the US. Sri Lanka's democratic government carried out a politicide against supporters of the radical Marxist Janathā Vimukthi Peramuṇa (JVP) at a time when the governing elite was seriously challenged. These exceptions aside, the general proposition is that a state that maintains democratic governance in the face of state failure is much less likely to commit geno/politicide than is an autocratic regime.

Ethnic and Religious Cleavages

Ethnic and religious divisions are often identified as preconditions of civil conflict in general (Rabushka and Shepsle 1972), ethnic conflict (Kuper 1981; Gurr 2000), and geno/politicide specifically (Kuper 1981; Chalk and Jonassohn 1990). We have reported that violent ethnic conflict was a precursor to nearly two-thirds (twenty-four of thirty-seven) of the geno/politicides of the last half-century (Harff and Gurr 1998). But what are the most direct linkages? One possibility is sheer diversity: the greater the ethnic and religious diversity, the greater the likelihood that communal identity will lead to mobilization and, if conflict is protracted, prompt elite decisions to eliminate the group basis of actual or potential challenges. A plausible alternative is that small minorities in otherwise homogenous societies are at risk, especially when a regime is committed to an exclusionary ideology. A discussion of the human rights consequences of cultural diversity and an analysis of alternative indicators is Walker and Poe (2002). To test these and similar arguments, indicators of diversity were constructed from a cultural dataset that records the size of ethnic, linguistic, and religious groups for each state from 1820 through the 1990s, compiled by Philip Shafer of the Correlates of War (COW) project.

A second and more complex connection begins with differential treatment of some groups. Discrimination against a communal (religious or ethnic) minority is likely to increase the salience of group identity and its mobilization for political action (Gurr 2000, 66–72). If political action takes the form of persistent communal rebellion, regimes are likely to respond with repression which, when other predisposing structural variables are present, can escalate into campaigns to eliminate the group. A country-level binary indicator of active discrimination was constructed for the State Failure project from group-level data collected by the Minorities at Risk project: if any group in a country was subject to active political or economic discrimination as a matter of public policy in a given year the country received a positive score.

A third possible connection is the ethnic and religious composition of the political elite. If the elite disproportionately represents one segment in a heterogenous society, two consequences follow that may lead to genocidal outcomes. Under-represented groups are likely to challenge the elite's unrepresentativeness, and elites fearing such challenges are likely to define their interests and security in communal terms, by, for example, designing policies of racial exclusion, such as the Afrikaner elite in South Africa, or advocating exclusive nationalism, such as Serbs and Croats in the Yugoslav successor states. The narrower the ethnic base of a regime, the greater the risks of conflict that escalates to genocidal levels.

Low Economic Development

The State Failure project has consistently found that armed conflicts and adverse regime changes are more likely to occur in poor countries. This is true globally and for sub-Saharan Africa, for Muslim countries, and for countries with ethnic wars (Goldstone et al. 2002; 2010). The fact that most geno/politicides of the last fifty years occurred in Africa and Asia suggests that a similar relationship should be included in this structural model. The hypothesis is tested using an indicator of infant mortality: reported deaths to infants under one year per 1000 live births. Extensive validation analyses by the Task Force suggest that infant mortality rates are a good surrogate for a wide range of indicators of material standard of living and quality-of-life. They have greater reliability and give somewhat better empirical results in models of risks of state failure than indicators of GDP/GNP.

International Context: Economic and Political Interdependence

International context matters for geno/politicides. Shifting global alliances such as those that followed the end of the Cold War decreased the predictability of international responses to instability and gross human rights violations. Post-Cold War international responses to genocidal situations have become more immediate and forceful, but it seems that Bosnian Serb nationalists and Rwandan militants, among others, concluded early in the 1990s that mass killings were not likely to have costly international repercussions.

It is also evident that both during and after the Cold War major powers and the UN system were selective about the humanitarian crises in which to engage. There was very little international concern with genocides in Uganda, Rwanda, and Burundi in the 1970s and 1980s—countries of low economic status in which the security interests of the major powers were not threatened. At the other end of the scale, many international actors were concerned about persistent crises in Tibet and Kashmir but lacked means of effective engagement. In the middle were Cold War-linked conflicts with genocidal consequences—in Vietnam, Cambodia, Afghanistan, Angola, and Central America—in which international rivalries trumped humanitarian concerns.

One underlying principle encompasses the specifics mentioned above: the greater the degree to which a country is interdependent with others, the less likely its leaders are to attempt geno/politicides. The converse is that leaders of isolated states are more likely to calculate that they can eliminate unwanted groups without international repercussions. Interdependency has two dimensions, economic and political. The State Failure studies have consistently shown that countries with a high degree of trade openness—indexed by exports plus imports as a percentage of GDP—have been less likely to experience state failures. The relationship holds when controlling for population size and density and for productivity indicators. It also has the same effect at the global and regional levels. Moreover, trade openness is weakly correlated with other economic and trade variables. The interpretation is that trade openness serves as a highly sensitive indicator of state and elite willingness to maintain the rules of law and fair practices in the economic sphere. In the political sphere a high degree of trade openness implies that a country has more resources for averting and managing political crises (Goldstone et al. 2002; 2010).

An indicator of political interdependence is a country's memberships in regional and intercontinental organizations. Countries with greater-than-average memberships in such organizations should be subject to greater influence, and receive more political support, when facing internal challenges, and their regimes should be less likely to resort to geno/politicide. Analysis of the preconditions of ethnic war—a common precursor of geno/politicide—shows that countries with below-average numbers of regional memberships are three times more likely to have ethnic wars than countries with above-average numbers of memberships (Goldstone et al. 2002; 2010).

Estimating a Structural Model of Genocides and Politicides

The empirical work reported here was undertaken in the context of the State Failure project, which uses a case-control research design common in epidemiological research but rare in empirical social science (an exception is King and

Zeng 2001b). The basic procedure is to match problem cases—people (or countries) affected by a disorder—to a set of controls that do not have the disorder (see Breslow and Day 1980; Schlesselman 1982). The State Failure project's researchers selected a set of controls by matching each problem case, in the year it began, with three countries that did not experience failures that year or in the preceding or ensuing several years. In effect, cases are selected on the dependent variable: those experiencing failure are matched with otherwise-similar cases that did not experience failure. Logistic regression is then used to analyze data on conditions in "problem" countries shortly before the onset of state failure with conditions in the controls.[3] The results are expressed in regression coefficients and in odds ratios that approximate the relative risks associated with each factor.

The task here is to distinguish countries where state failures led to genocides from those where they did not. The case-control method was adapted to the estimation of a structural model of geno/politicide in this manner. First, the universe of analysis consists of all countries already in state failure. The dependent variable represents the conditional probability that a genocide or politicide will begin one year later in a country already experiencing failure. This avoids the problem of comparing risks of genocide in Rwanda and Sudan with, say, the negligible risks in France and Canada. Instead, the objective is to examine countries experiencing episodes of internal wars and regime collapse and determine why geno/politicide occurred during such events in Rwanda and Sudan but not, say, in Liberia or Mali. Second, the model is estimated using as cases all geno/politicides since 1955, including multiple episodes that occurred in the same country. Two of the thirty-seven episodes were not sufficiently separated in time to be considered distinct incidents for analytic purposes.

Results: The Final Structural Model

The general procedure was to estimate a best-fit model that included a limited set of theoretically important variables, then to seek to improve it by testing the effects of adding other variables and alternative indicators. The six-variable model is the culmination of a long process of model estimation and indicator validation. All six variables have significant effects at the 0.10 probability level; three have significant effects at the 0.5 level.

Political Upheaval

Consistent with the theoretical argument, the greater the magnitude of previous internal wars and regime crises, summed over the preceding fifteen years, the more likely that a new state failure will lead to geno/politicide. When the magnitude of past upheaval was divided between high and low, in high-magnitude cases the risks of geno/politicides were nearly two times greater. Similar results were obtained using other indicators of upheaval, such as the magnitudes of armed conflict within states.

Prior Genocides

Arguments about the recurrence of geno/politicide are also supported. The risks of new episodes were more than three times greater when state failures occurred in countries that had prior geno/politicides. The effects of the magnitude of political upheaval were weaker than those of prior genocide—it appears that habituation to genocide adds more to the risks of future genocide than the magnitude of internal war and adverse regime change per se.

Elite Ideology and Regime Type

Theoretical arguments about the importance of elite ideologies and regime type are supported. Countries in which the ruling elite adhered to an exclusionary ideology were two and a half times as likely to have state failures leading to geno/politicide as those with no such ideology. Failures in states with autocratic regimes were three and a half times more likely to lead to geno/politicides than failures in democratic regimes. These events, if they occur in the context of other risk factors identified in the model, substantially raise the risks of massive human rights violations.

Ethnic and Religious Cleavages

Numerous indicators of ethnic and religious cleavages were evaluated but only one was significant in the final model. The risks of geno/politicide were two and a half times more likely in countries where the political elite was based mainly or entirely on an ethnic minority. But two other indicators of ethnic cleavage did correlate significantly (in bivariate analysis) with geno/politicide: active ethnic discrimination and salience of elite ethnicity. The results led us to two general conclusions. First, ethnic heterogeneity and salience of elite ethnicity are likely to lead to geno/politicide only if an ethnic minority dominates the elite. Second, ethnic discrimination makes a weak positive contribution to geno/politicide but not enough to add to the structural model. In later analyses, a more reliable indicator of active discrimination proved to have a more substantial effect. This is factored into my later annual assessment of countries at high risk of future genocide (posted at GPANet.org).

International Interdependences

Countries with low trade openness had two and a half times greater odds of having state failures culminate in geno/politicide. High trade openness (and the underlying economic and political conditions it taps) not only minimizes the risks of state failure in general, as shown in other State Failure analyses, but also reduces substantially the odds that failures, if they do occur, will lead to geno/politicides.

The results support arguments about the importance of a country's international economic linkages in inhibiting gross human rights violations.

We also tested the impact of indicators of country memberships in regional and intercontinental (i.e. global) organizations by adding them to the model in place of trade interdependence. Results were significantly weaker. This does not mean that political linkages are irrelevant to the analysis and prevention of geno/politicide. The critical question, in my view, is whether states and international organizations do in fact engage in preventive actions in the early stages. What counts is the political will to engage—and, as Samantha Power has shown (2002), major international actors have repeatedly chosen not to do so.

The overall accuracy of the model is shown in the summary statistics and notes in the 2003 article. The model correctly classifies 74 percent of all cases as genocides or non-genocides. Note that, since the analyses include all cases of state failure and all instances of geno/politicide, issues of sampling error do not arise. The probability of genocide for a country in failure with no risk factors is .028. If the country is an autocracy but has no other risk factors the probability is increased by .090. If the country has a minority elite but no other risk factors the probability is increased by .069.

The incremental effects of each risk factor are relatively small; their cumulative effect is large. Analysis of various combinations of risk factors shows that, if all risk factors are present in a failed state, the conditional probability of geno/politicide is 0.90 with a 95 percent confidence interval of .66 to .98. The only such country with all six factors in 2001 was Iraq. A hypothetical country with the following combination of four risk factors—high magnitude of past upheaval, minority elite, low trade openness, and autocracy—has a conditional geno/politicide probability of 0.52 (confidence interval .27 to .77). Sierra Leone is a contemporary example. If such a failed state also had a past genocide, the probability increases to 0.79 (confidence interval .43 to .95).

The information and data used to estimate the original geno/politicide model are posted on the GPAnet.org website. The dataset and dictionary for indicators used in the State Failure/Political Instability Task Force studies enable other researchers to apply other techniques and test alternative hypotheses and models; they are posted at the website of the Center for Systemic Peace (see note 2).

Two published studies retest Harff's model using different variables and methodologies that increase annual forecasting performance (Goldsmith et al. 2013; Wayman and Tago 2009). Also of note is Ulfelder and Valentino's empirical study of the correlates of a related phenomenon, mass atrocities (2008), which was carried out for the Political Instability Task Force. The dataset for their dependent variable includes most of Harff's genocides and politicides, plus a number of other mass killings that do not meet her criteria. Their findings are generally consistent with Harff's findings (2003). Also relevant is Valentino (2004).

Most recently Birger Heldt has collaborated with Barbara Harff and T. R. Gurr to update and correct many of the variables used in the 2003 studies. He has reanalyzed them using hazard models, applied to data on all country years, which show that autocracy, active discrimination, elite ethnicity, and exclusionary elite ideology all contribute significantly to risks of genocide and politicide, as in Harff's work. Table 12.1 shows hazards for two categories of high-risk countries as of 2013–14: countries already in failure (with ongoing internal wars or regime crises), and countries at high risk should they ever experience such events.

Comparison with genocide/politicide risk lists prepared using the previous model (posted at GPANet.org) show the usual suspects near the top of the lists. Hazard scores for countries with ongoing failures are well above average for Ethiopia, Syria (arguably already practicing genocide), and the Central African Republic. Hazard scores are even higher in eight or more countries not now in failure, including Saudi Arabia and Bahrain, followed by Cameroun, Uzbekistan, Mauritania, and Turkmenistan. If historical experience remains an accurate guide to future hazards, internal wars or regime crises in these countries would likely be followed by genocides or politicides.

Table entries show the specific variables that contribute to each country's hazards; the notes provide details about the analysis. There are two significant and yet unresolved differences from the 2003 results. Trade openness is not significant in the hazard analysis and past genocides seem to inoculate states from resorting to it again, though we suspect this may be an artifact of the analytic design. The results of this analysis were presented to a meeting of the International Association of Genocide Scholars in Winnipeg, Canada in July 2014. They have not yet been published elsewhere, or posted. However, they do give us a solid empirical basis for assessing the short- and medium-term risks of future genocides.

From Risk Assessment to Early Warning and Prevention

Risk assessment identifies countries and situations with substantial potential for genocide and/or political mass murder. It does not tell us when an episode is likely to occur, only that the structural conditions for it are present. Whereas risk assessment buys time, early warning holds the key to short-term planning. Often these two distinct approaches are used interchangeably; the differences need to be addressed. Our current ability to provide global risk assessment annually or whenever needed is a major advance over area experts' judgments about what is happening in country X at a specific point in time.

Early warning aims to identify the warning flags that tell us a genocide is in the making within the very near future. This means specifying the sequences and frequency of political actions that either propel or disrupt escalation of conflict. Under my direction, early warning efforts were carried out after 2000 with support from the US intelligence community. We tracked, on a daily basis, countries at risk for several years in near-real time. The model used was complex, including nearly seventy indicators. An early version of an events-based model was published in the *Journal of Peace Research* (Harff and Gurr 1998). A newer version,

TABLE 12.1 Risks of new onsets of genocide and politicide in 2013–14: a new hazards analysis

Hazards in countries with ongoing state failures

Countries and 2013 hazard score[a]	Recent changes in geno/pol hazards	Current instability	Contention re elite ethnicity[b] hazard ratio: 1.62	Regime type 2012[c] hazard ratio: 0.905	Targets of systematic discrimination[d] hazard ratio: 2.185	Exclusionary ideology hazard ratio: 2.16	Past geno/politicides hazard ratio: 0.35
Ethiopia 3.202	No significant change in last decade	Regional rebellion since 2006	Yes: Tigrean minority dominates	Partial autocracy	Oromo, Anuak	No	Yes: 1976–79
Syria 3.151	Very high since 1958, no change since 1982	Civil war since 2011	Yes: Alawite minority dominates	Full autocracy	Islamists, Alawites, Kurds+2	No	Yes: 1981–82
Sudan 1.207	Slight decline after 2009	Civil war, genocides since 1982	No	Partial autocracy	Darfuri, Nuba, Kordofan peoples	Yes: Islamist	Yes: 1956–72, 1983–present
Russia 0.635	Slight increase after 2006	Chechen rebellions since 1994	No	Partial democracy	None	No	Yes: 1920s, 1930s
Turkey 0.606	Significant decline after 2008	Kurdish rebellion since 1979	No	Full democracy	Kurds	No	No
Myanmar 0.590	Major decline after 2010	Regional wars since 1950s	Yes: Burman majority dominates	Partial democracy	Karen, Kachin, Royhinga Muslims	Yes: Burman nationalism	Yes: 1978
Yemen 0.426	Slight decline after 2011	Civil wars since 2004	No	Weak partial democracy	None	Yes: Islamist	No
DR Congo 0.471	Substantial decline after 2001	Regional rebellions since 1962	No	Partial democracy	Tutsis, Batwa/Bambuti	No	Yes: 1964–5, 1977, 1999
Libya 0.366	Major decline after 2011	Violent contestation for power since 2011	No	No effective regime	None	No	No

(Continued)

TABLE 12.1 (continued)

Countries with high risks of genocide and politicide if they should have major conflicts or state failures[e]

Countries and 2013 hazard score	Recent changes in hazards	Current instability	Contention re elite ethnicity	Regime type 2012	Targets of discrimination	Exclusionary ideology	Past geno/ politicides
Saudi Arabia 9.286	Persistently high	None	*Yes: Sunni majority, Sudairi clan dominates	Full autocracy	Shi'i	Yes: Wahhabism	None
Bahrain 6.478	Sharp increase after 2010	Mass protests by Shi'i majority	Yes: Sunni Al-Khalifa clan dominates	Full autocracy	Shi'i	No	None
Cameroun 3.541	No change since 1992	None	Majority ethnic elite: Christian southerners	Partial autocracy	Westerners, Bamileke, Bakassi	No	None
Uzbekistan 3.229	No change since 1992	Low-level Islamist terrorism	No	Full autocracy	Tajiks, Islamists	Yes: Uzbek nationalism	None
Mauritania 2.895	No change since 2009	Islamist terrorism	Minority ethnic elite: Beydane (White Moors)	Partial autocracy	Kewri, Black Moors	No	No
Turkmenistan 2.351	No change since 2003	None	No	Full autocracy	Uzbeks, Baloch, Russians	None	None

(Continued)

TABLE 12.1 (continued)

Countries with high risks of genocide and politicide if they should have major conflicts or state failures[e]

Countries and 2013 hazard score	Recent changes in hazards	Current instability	Contention re elite ethnicity	Regime type 2012	Targets of discrimination	Exclusionary ideology	Past geno/ politicides
North Korea 2.262	No change since 1994	None	No	Full autocracy	None	Communism	None
People's Rep. of China 1.996	No change since 1990	Low-level terrorism in Xinjiang	Majority ethnic elite: Han	Full autocracy	Tibetans, Uyghers, Falun Gong	Communism	Yes: 1950–51, 1959, 1956–75

[a] A hazard ratio of 2.16 shows that the country in question is 116 percent more likely to experience onset of genocide in a given year of state failure than the scenario where all variables are held at zero: a hazard ratio of 0.35 shows that the country is 65 percent less likely. These ratios are calculated based on results of an analysis of the hazards of onset of genocide or politicide in all years in which all countries were in state failure from 1955 to 2012. State failure is defined using the Political Instability Task Force's operational definition: it includes countries with ethnic or revolutionary wars underway and those with rapid, abrupt changes in regime. Birger Heldt carried out the analyses using new and updated data on all variables from previous risk assessments by Barbara Harff. The last five columns in the table show the variables that are strongly significant in predicting to the onset of genocides and politicides. Trade openness, used in previous analyses, is not significant in the statistical analyses used here. Past genocides seem to inoculate states from resorting to it again, according to new results.

[b] A three-category code is used: if the ethnicity (or religion) of the elite is politically contentious, the country is coded 1. If the elite in power represents a minority, such as Alawites in Syria, the country is coded 2. Otherwise the country year is 0.

[c] The Polity scale is used in the statistical analysis, converted so that a fully autocratic regime is 0 and a fully democratic regime is 20. The table here uses descriptive labels for polity types rather than reporting the numeric scores.

[d] From the Minorities at Risk project survey of groups subject to state-led discrimination (through 2006, www.cidcm.umd.edu.mar/) updated using information from the Minorities Rights Group's 2011 report on other groups subject to widespread discrimination, and additional reports.

[e] Countries that are not now experiencing failures—civil wars or regime instability—also have some of the factors that predict to the onset of geno/politicide. The countries listed here are the non-failure states with the highest hazards for geno/politicide, if state failure were to occur.

using twelve variables, each measured by three or more weighted indicators and operationalized as events, was used later. The findings were of interest to and were used by policymakers, but were not available for the scholarly community. However, a published version using interpretation rather than formal analysis was published in 2001 (Harff 2001). The results were useful in the sense that the findings potentially helped to develop better response scenarios.

The goal of every genocide scholar is to prevent future genocides and political mass murders. Many of us came full circle from first writing on prevention to case studies and data collection, only to return to identifying means and tools that work in particular high-risk situations. As mentioned above, much ink has been spilled on the pros and cons of humanitarian intervention, including a monograph and an annotated bibliography that includes over 100 entries (see Harff 1984; Harff and Kader 1991). Humanitarian intervention typically refers to military action that should be used in situations in which genocide is already well underway. This was the case in Rwanda, when UN inaction, despite General Romeo Dallaire's request for support and new marching orders, made the genocide possible. We need to focus on mediation, diplomacy, coercion, and inducements, actions short of military intervention that can prevent escalation of conflict into genocide. *The key question, however, is what kinds of action work in which situations at what point in time?*

But sorely missing are informed discussions on what individual states, regional organizations, or the UN can realistically do to prevent conflict escalation. Obviously countries such as Sweden and Switzerland are bound to respond in a different fashion than the US. It is not just a question of political will, but more so of capacity and national interest, history, law, and public pressure.

Finally, we need to look at the latest failure of the international community to prevent a man-made disaster in Syria, which was very high on or at the top of our risk lists one or two years prior to the outbreak of internal strife, which led in turn to genocidal massacres.

Conclusion

Lack of coordinated action is a recipe for disaster. Incentives for negotiations, security assurances, mediation, credible threats backed by action, protection of refugees, monitoring camps for infiltration of potential agitators, stopping hate propaganda—any and all of these may work. How naïve to assume that leaders such as Assad are reasonable, given the history of a regime (led by his father) that committed genocide in 1981–82 against the Muslim Brotherhood and civilians. Syria is riddled with sectarian strife; its clans and tribal leaders plot against each other, and the state is run by Alawites, a widely feared minority religious sect. It has an intelligence apparatus run by Assad relatives and other Alawites that was and is extremely repressive. It is a socialist country indebted to the Soviet Union, and now to Russia, armed by a theocratic state (Iran) and fighting for ascendency, or now survival, in the Mideast. It is in cahoots with terrorist organizations such as Hizbollah, Hamas, and other radical Palestinian factions, and is a middleman for Iranian interests. Its economy is riddled with corruption and ineptitude. Arming rebels who may prove to be the next ISIS members and allies is clearly not the answer.

It may be strange to end here. But we will never run out of potential genocides unless the world community heeds the lessons not just of the Holocaust and the Armenian genocide but also of the many other cases since 1945, such as Cambodia, Rwanda, Burundi, Sudan, and Syria, as well as many lesser-known episodes. When looking at our risk lists dating back to 2003, we find that almost every high-risk country either committed genocide or was on the verge of doing so.

Notes

1 The following pages are adapted, with revisions, from Harff (2003, 61–8).
2 The State Failure project's lists of ethnic and revolutionary wars and adverse regime changes are posted at www.systemicpeace.org/inscr/PITF%20Consolidated%20Case%20 List%202014.pdf. Coding profiles of each episode were carried out; the codebook is at http://globalpolicy.gmu.edu/documents/PITF/PITFProbSetCodebook2008.pdf. The one geno/politicide that did not coincide with a failure is the 1981–82 Syrian case, in which the Muslim Brotherhood was targeted because its revolutionary objectives were a threat to the regime. The Brotherhood's rebellion is below the threshold of revolutionary war used in the State Failure dataset. Since it fits the larger pattern of retributive geno/politicides it is included in the count of episodes that coincided with revolutionary war.
3 In logistic regression binary indicators are used. In practice the 2003 analyses reported here use a mixed strategy in which most indicators—including state failures—are binary, but others—magnitudes of upheaval, trade openness, and shared memberships— are analyzed as continuous variables.

13

TRANSNATIONAL CONFLICT

Normative Struggles and Globalization: The Case of Indigenous Peoples in Bolivia and Ecuador

Pamela Martin and Franke Wilmer

Struggles that were previously confined to remote localities, limited to action and reaction between indigenous peoples and their governments, and barely visible (if at all) to the outside world, are now the subject of worldwide coverage in mass and social media, amplification by large and influential NGOs, and consideration in international governmental fora. The international system consists of networks that enhance, and those that threaten, the interests of indigenous peoples. This chapter explores how these struggles impact indigenous peoples, and how the struggles of those people affect international and civil conflict.

Since the 1990s the indigenous rights movement has catapulted from resource-poor local activists to global activists. The rise of transnational indigenous rights movements has paralleled and interfaced with significant structural developments at the international and state-systemic level, raising questions about the interplay between global and local politics—especially conflict—as arenas of social change. States are increasingly open, and transnational networks facilitated by non-governmental and intergovernmental organizations are proliferating. Accelerating neoliberal reforms have entrenched the indigenous movement in conflicts over natural resource use and extraction. The opening of political spaces in which indigenous peoples are more influential in local, transnational, and global political processes is evident in political outcomes including constitutional reform and increased governmental representation that, in turn, have further empowered indigenous movements.

"Indigenous" refers to those peoples descended from the original inhabitants of a place where state institutions not of their own making assert jurisdiction over them, and who, as a consequence of colonization by European settlers, do not now control their own political destinies. Their very activism exposes and contests the normative basis both for the world system and the state as the primary institutional mechanism through which the values and resources of the world system are allocated (Wilmer 1993). Since indigenous peoples' social organizations predate the capitalist world system (Hall and Fenelon 2004), indigenous social movements provide a lens through which to view civil society resistance from a group with communally held property conceptions and non-capitalist systemic roots. Broadly speaking, indigenous peoples' activism advances a claim to exercise sovereign control over resources sufficient to sustain their cultural and physical existence as a right.

The path of normative conflict and norm transmission instigated by indigenous activism is not a case where norms arising from international consensus are diffused "downward" into domestic state environments as it is with issues involving human rights and humanitarian intervention (Finnemore and Sikkink 1998; Kowert and Legro 1996; Klotz 1995).[1] Instead, indigenous rights and the norms on which they rest arise from the "bottom" and are asserted "upward" in order to mobilize an international consensus, which in turn can be marshaled in support of indigenous peoples against state and transnational power. These aspirations represent a fundamental challenge (a) to what have been arguably the most impenetrable normative underpinnings of the present state system, and (b) to how the entitlements associated with either sovereignty or self-determination have thus far been allocated.

Making Connections from the Global to the Local and Vice Versa

To trace the transnational networks to the articulation of norms supportive of indigenous claims and the interplay between local and global political processes, we examine two cases of transnational indigenous activism and domestic responses in the Andean region of South America. We are particularly interested in whether the additional dimension of domestic and transnational mobilization that first contests existing international norms, and then seeks to diffuse normative changes at both the domestic and international levels, provides new insight about norm formation, transformation, and diffusion in international politics.

Our approach draws on international relations, social movement, and conflict theories. Recent studies in international relations theory (Keck and Sikkink 1998; Risse and Sikkink 1999; Brysk 2000; Wapner 1996) point to the influence of non-state actors in the international system, while globalization studies (Held and McGrew 2002; Mittelman 1996; Scholte 2002; Guidry et al. 2000) show the interpenetration of non-state actors at multiple levels of the world system. Although much work on social movements (Tilly 1978; Tarrow 1994; McAdam et al. 1996) focuses on the state as the provider of political opportunity for social movements, increased transnational mobilization calls into question the pinnacle role of the state and emphasizes global coordination processes of movements at both domestic and transnational levels (see also Brysk 2000; Smith and Johnston 2002; Sklair 2002).

Keck and Sikkink (1998) originally described the process of transnational advocacy networks as having a boomerang effect in which domestic actors circumvent the state through transnational coordination. Subsequent analyses of the Argentinean human rights movement show that transnational coordination has its intended impact: an increase in political opportunity at the domestic level (Sikkink 2011). Therefore, once transnational movements succeed in opening local spaces for political influence, they begin "spiraling" down their activity to concentrate on domestic policy issues.[2] While Latin American indigenous rights actors have gained increasing access to domestic political institutions and governance, their transnational movement has at the same time broadened in resistance to neoliberal economic reforms, encroachment on their territories and resources, growth in transnational coalitions, increased accessibility of communications technology and channels, and an increased presence and activity within international intergovernmental organizations. Rather than refocusing attention to one level or another, indigenous peoples have mobilized and coordinated at local, regional, and global levels simultaneously.

The UN estimates that there are over 350 million indigenous peoples in the world, constituting approximately 8–15 percent of the global population, of which 40–55 million live in Latin America.[3] Since the massive indigenous uprisings in Bolivia and Ecuador of 1990 and the Quincentenary of Christopher Columbus in 1992, indigenous peoples throughout South America have actively engaged in mobilization for increased political and economic rights within their states, regions, and globally. While both Bolivia and Ecuador have high percentages of indigenous populations (60 percent in Bolivia and 40 percent in Ecuador), their movements have responded distinctly to transnational networks and norms, as well as to the impact of globalization. The following cases examine the parallels and differences between the indigenous movements of each country and their relationship to the transnational level, as well as their coordination.

From Dictatorship to "Bloody October" and Beyond: Bolivia's Indigenous Rights Movement

The poorest of South America's nations with the largest population of indigenous peoples—over 60 percent in a recent census—Bolivia has the second largest proven hydrocarbon reserves in South America (Daly 2012). Given their historical lack of resources and political representation, it is surprising that indigenous protestors were able to overthrow a president in 2003 and challenge the US, World Bank, and International Monetary Fund's neoliberal economic reforms and coca eradication campaign.

The Bolivian indigenous rights movement is framed not only by ethnic identity and increased political and economic autonomy but also as part of a larger, worldwide anti-globalization movement. It is not a simple case of mobilization by solely domestic or solely transnational means. Rather, indigenous activists have "spiraled" to include struggles at the local, state, and international levels. Indigenous organizations and leaders are not only respected and known on a state level but often appear in the reports of the UN Working Group on Indigenous Peoples, lists of NGO-sponsored workshop participants, and as hosts of international congresses.

Social, political, and economic discrimination against indigenous peoples has been evident throughout Bolivian history. Indigenous peoples maintain distinct communities that include the cultures, languages, and ethnic identities of the highland Aymara and Quechua, and the lowland Guarani and Arawak peoples. Division between highland and lowland indigenous organizations was mitigated by their unified political mobilization in 2003. Aymara Indians, politically active since the 1940s, make up nearly half of the indigenous population of the highland region. Their most important legacy was the Katarista movement, identified with the Aymara leader Tupac Katari, who led an anticolonial uprising in 1781 (Gurr and Burke 2000, 178–9). Indigenous leader Felipe Quishpe and his Pachakutik movement have recently used symbolic power effectively by harkening back to the Katarista separatist/revolutionary spirit.

The 1990–95 indigenous protests in Bolivia provided openings for effective indigenous political action, resulting in domestic victories including constitutional reform and a decentralization of political power. While neoliberal reforms touting the "Bolivian Miracle" initiated by former presidents Victor Paz Estenssoro and General Hugo Banzer in the 1980s infused loans and touted privatization, such adjustments were also supportive of the decentralization of the Bolivian state, increasing opportunities for indigenous peoples. The paradox of threat and opportunity marks the challenges for the indigenous rights movement throughout Latin America, particularly in Bolivia.

Transnational Network Developments

Though less internationalized than Ecuador, indigenous activism in Bolivia is still embedded in global neoliberal economic reform and fiercely opposed to it. The Aymara leader and president, Evo Morales, who said during his history-making first campaign "Long live coca, death to the gringos,"[4] met on several occasions with the Venezuelan president Hugo Chavez, touting the Bolivarian movement platform against "US imperialism." Such discourse not only aligns Bolivia with its Venezuelan neighbor but also adds to the transnational normative repertoire for indigenous peoples' organization as part of a larger *movimiento bolivariano*.

Although international mobilization is less apparent in the highlands, church-funded NGOs did support earlier grass-roots confederations in the 1950s, including the Centro de Investigacion y Promocion del Campesinado (CIPCA) and various Katarista movement organizations. But their identity was *campesino*, or peasant, rather than ethnically Indian or indigenous. This type of fluidity between the *campesino* and indigenous identity is not uncommon in Bolivia, where *campesino* activists are also primarily indigenous. Thus, Bolivia represents a case of a fluid relationship between class and indigenous identities.

Other international support for the indigenous movement of Bolivia, the Campesino Self-Development Project, was funded by the European Union in the Northern Oruro department. This project, which funded local community development in the form of *ayllus*, or the traditional Andean political and social/ community structure, preceded a similar effort by Oxfam America in the mid to late 1980s (Andolina 2001). The *ayllu* organization projects linked Oxfam representatives, indigenous leaders and communities, and local NGOs, and, in conjunction with the political reforms of 1994–95, greatly strengthened indigenous movements throughout the Andes.

In addition to Oxfam, the Danish NGO IBIS has worked with Bolivian indigenous organizations for over twenty years, aiding in the coordination of the 1990 "March for Territory and Dignity" and actively supporting the lowland organization CIDOB (Confederación de Pueblos Indígenas de Bolivia (The Confederation of Indigenous Peoples of Bolivia)). Since the 1990s IBIS has supported the national *ayllu* organization, CONAMAQ (National Council of Ayllus and Markas of Qullasuyu (Consejo Nacional de Ayllus y Markas del Qullasuyu)), and its development in conjunction with Oxfam and DANIDA (Danish International Development Agency), another Danish NGO. In a recent program evaluation and goals agenda IBIS notes fractures among indigenous organizations over economic models and political institutions. The plan to initiate various forums of "political dialogue" included a new Indigenous Leadership School aimed at "creating a space for political analysis and strategy definition as well as promoting women leaders."[5] IBIS plans to monitor the progress of such projects through the goals and desire set forth by local indigenous organizations and communities.

In this case, the norms have come from indigenous actors from below with the aid of implementation from transnational actors. Additionally, as Robert Andolina (2001) observes, the funding flows in Bolivia have changed since the 1970s organization with the Catholic Church and funding to the *ayllu* organizations is being directly received, rather than through state or NGO mediators. This direct funding not only infuses local organizations and movements but also directly empowers them on a local–global level. Therefore, the Bolivian movement is no longer one in which local organizations receive direction from a national organization, but rather one in which the local and the global are intertwined. Andolina (2001) notes that the World Bank is also analyzing the *ayllu* form of organization and considering funding projects. The decentralization of funding, coupled with possible cooperation with the World Bank, presents opportunities for local organizational development and threats of friction among organizations and between the local- and state-level organizations.

Bloody October and the Gas Wars: Turmoil in the Andes

In 1993 an advisor to President Sanchez de Lozada declared that Bolivia needed to "get away from the rigid centralized system that had been in place" (Ho 2004, 10). Ironically, Sanchez de Lozada decentralized the Bolivian state throughout the late 1990s and empowered many of the *ayllu* systems in place under the Popular Participation Law of 1994. However, Sanchez de Lozada was ousted by the same indigenous peoples who were benefiting from decentralization in October 2003 in one of Bolivia's most violent protests. It is estimated that between 80 and 120 people were killed when the Bolivian military forcefully responded to six days of protest in La Paz, including the dynamiting of bridges and burning of roads. On October 17, 2003 the president, Gonzalo Sanchez de Lozada, fled the country via helicopter, resigning from his presidential post and fearing for his life among the angry crowds of primarily indigenous activists.

Following protests against the US-backed coca eradication plan and the 2002 protests against the privatization of water by Bechtel Corporation in Cochabamba, a Quechua city, the announced proposal to export gas to the US and Mexico through a pipeline across Chilean territory outraged indigenous peoples throughout the country. Two significant indigenous leaders emerged united against such plans: Evo Morales[6] of the Movement Toward Socialism (MAS) and Felipe Quishpe of the Pachakutik Indigenous Movement (MIP). Both leaders organized against the privatization of Bolivia's natural gas resources in favor of a more nationalized plan that would provide resources to the Bolivian peoples. From the dust of the violence the vice-president, Carlos Mesa, assumed power and pledged to hold a popular referendum on the natural gas pipeline project, led by Sempra Energy of California and Shell Oil Company.

On July 18, 2004, the referendum was held. It included five questions that asked whether citizens wanted natural gas nationalized, a restoration of the state company Yacimientos Petrolíferos Fiscales Bolivianos (YPFB), access to the Pacific Coast through leveraging natural gas, and a tax on companies for the production of oil and gas in Bolivia. All questions received a resounding Yes answer (Weinberg 2004a).[7] In the process of the referendum and its votes, violence again emerged among indigenous protestors who differed over the exact form of nationalization, including division between Morales and Quishpe and their organizations. While Morales sought nationalization without absolute state ownership, Quishpe called for absolute ownership of the natural resources of *Pachamama* (mother earth).[8]

Domestic Outcomes and Transnational Norms— Democratization or Fragmentation?

Violence escalated in the Bolivian case after the October 2003 protests. Felipe Quishpe called for indigenous peoples to "take up arms," as strikes and marches no longer seemed effective (Weinberg 2004b). In Achacachi two public officials who had jailed indigenous activists were killed, and Quishpe referred to then-President Mesa as a "bearded conquistador." Moreover, July 12–16, 2004 witnessed continued indigenous protests and blockages against natural gas fields in Santa Cruz, Chaco, and El Alto.

While Evo Morales's MAS party held the second largest majority in the Congress on December 5, 2004, by 2006 his party had won 140 of the 157 seats in the Congress and Morales was inaugurated as the first indigenous president of the country on January 22, 2006. However, indigenous peoples are still not without fragmentation. Felipe Quishpe's MIP movement is calling for a radical change in Bolivian society away from capitalism toward the *ayllu* form of governance. While the CIDOB, the national indigenous organization, is still intact, leadership is increasingly divided among local, municipal, or *ayllu* lines. It was unclear in 2006 whether indigenous peoples in Bolivia would be able to agree on a path of reform in the wake of Morales's inauguration.

The process of reform to decentralize and democratize reached new heights with the election of Morales and the MAS party, culminating in the constitutional referendum of February 2009, approved by just over 61 percent of voters with 90.2 percent participation. The coalition and convergence of interests represented by coca growers and indigenous voters that brought Morales and MAS to power would be tested by new constitutional provisions allowing for autonomy at the municipal and regional levels as well as for indigenous communities. Since some 60–70 percent of the population identifies as indigenous, the movement for greater and more kinds of subnational autonomy presents the greatest political challenge to the new government under the 2009 Constitution. Some critics fear that indigenous autonomy, modeled after the principles and provisions hammered out in the United Nations over the past several decades and now embodied in the Declaration on the Rights of Indigenous Peoples, is weakened by its co-existence with old (departmental) and new (municipal) forms of autonomy (Thies 2010). In this view indigenous autonomy, in other words, ought to be distinct from other "subnational" autonomies. This is somewhat analogous to the ambiguous legal status of indigenous or tribal sovereignty in the US federal system, which Vine Deloria, Jr. characterized as less than federal but greater than state sovereignty (Deloria and Lyttle 1998).

While Donna Lee Van Cott (2004) sees constitutional and legal reforms as providing increased access to indigenous peoples and Deborah Yashar (1999) views neoliberal economic policies as threats to indigenous organizations, we anticipate mixed results for the indigenous peoples in Bolivia. Clearly, their representation has increased at the local level, as evidenced by the Popular Participation Law and the more than 420 indigenous organizations that participated in the election of December 5, 2004. However, it is not clear that this decentralization will create a united mobilization on a national level for the indigenous movement. As noted by Robert Andolina (2001), direct funding from NGOs has provided a local–global network that may divert leadership attention from the national movement. Alternatively, such fragmentation may be the inception of a new kind of mobilization of the movement: one that is localized, yet empowered via transnational networks and funding mechanisms. The delicate balance between necessary economic development and investment and indigenous concerns for environmental and social justice policies will be the continued basis of threat and opportunity in Bolivia.

The 2009 Constitution articulates the most comprehensive indigenous rights at a constitutional level in the world, recognizing and protecting the cultural identities and customs of thirty-six indigenous groups, providing for their collective land ownership, greater autonomy, and the right to adjudicate offenses under their own legal systems (Watson 2014). President Morales was elected to a second term in 2009, winning 62.4 percent of the vote—almost 10 percent more than at his first election. His second term was marked by both an extraordinary improvement in economic conditions for most Bolivians, with annual per capita GDP growing from $1000 in 2006 to $2700 in 2013, and increasing discontent and opposition from environmental and indigenous groups (Schipani 2014a; 2014b; Shahriari 2011). Growing tensions over resource development—the key to Morales's ability to generously fund social programs, redistributive policies, and infrastructure projects—and indigenous and environmental priorities erupted into open confrontation and protests increasingly characterized by low-intensity civil conflict in 2011 over a proposed highway through the TIPNIS (Territorio Indígena Parque Nacional Isiboro Sécure) national park (Shahriari 2011; Achtenberg 2015). As of July 2015 the plans were back on track, with some indigenous and union groups in support and others opposed (Achtenberg 2015).

Two other developments are relevant to an assessment of the impact indigenous political empowerment embodied in the first-ever indigenous presidency and the coalition of indigenous social movements that brought to power a democratic socialist majority party (MAS) at a historical point characterized by mounting pressures for the development/exploitation of Bolivia's substantial natural resources by external agents of global capitalism.

One is growing unrest and violent protests that draw increasingly violent responses from the government over declining employment and stagnant wages in the mining sector, especially in the area of Potosi, where Japanese- and Indian-owned mining operations dominate the silver, zinc, and lead mining industries. A miners' strike in July 2015 turned violent when protesters threw dynamite at the police, who responded with the use of tear gas. Declining mineral prices drastically affected the economy there and, after several weeks and the violent turn of the protests, President Morales floated the idea of creating new jobs by investing in building a cement factory. Some observers suspect that right-wing opponents of Morales have tried to infiltrate and obstruct the negotiation process (TeleSUR 2015). This signals the continuing tension between Morales as the president of a broad-based union–indigenous–*campesino* coalition and as a president who funds anti-poverty and social development programs with government profits from the extractive industries.

The other important development is what thus far has to be deemed a socialist economic success, though whether it will be sustained, co-opted, or eventually undermined by pressures already creating fissures in the Morales coalition remains to be seen. Bolivia's economy has tripled since Morales's first election, with higher per capita GDP due primarily to cash redistribution policies and infrastructure funded by profits from the nationalized oil and gas industries. The 2013 commodity boom fueled a 6.5 percent growth rate due mainly to Bolivia's abundant mineral and hydrocarbon resources. In spite of a drop in mineral prices, the economy in the first five months of 2015 showed a steady and vigorous growth rate of 5 percent, according to the Global Index of Economic Activity (World Bank 2016). The International Monetary Fund (IMF) and World Bank have praised Bolivia for the current government's macroeconomic policies, maintenance of economic stability, and cautious approach to debt and financing. This success is not always viewed positively in Bolivia, as indigenous and environmental critics claim that the president has two faces—one that is pro-indigenous and pro-environmental abroad but fails to respect indigenous rights and engages in environmentally destructive projects on their lands at home. The president's critics see praise from international institutions of global capitalism as an affirmation of their worst suspicions (The Conversation 2015).

Evo Morales was elected to a third term in October 2014. Although he had vowed in 2008 not to run in 2014, the Bolivian Supreme Court ruled in 2013 that, since his first term was served before the adoption of the 2009 Constitution, he could run for another term. This time he and his party won 61.36 percent of the vote—less than at his second election but still much higher than at the first.

The central challenge for President Morales continues to be granting the demands of his indigenous constituents for (1) an alternative model to neoliberal reform, (2) an end to the coca eradication policy, and (3) the nationalization of natural gas. Will he be constrained by his own position of leadership within a state system that does not promote those norms?

When Transnational Networks and Allies Matter: The Indigenous Rights Movement of Ecuador

While the case of Bolivia has its origins in a strong indigenous identity with the Katarista movement and an antipathy for transnational actors, the case of Ecuador demonstrates the impacts of transnational networks and actors on an indigenous movement that has become one of the most successful in Latin America. The Confederation of Indigenous Nationalities of Ecuador (CONAIE), its national indigenous organization, unites the lowland, highland, and coastal indigenous organizations under one umbrella and has successfully connected with other non-indigenous actors within Ecuadorian civil society. Furthermore, the CONAIE's leaders have become well known on the world stage as what Sidney Tarrow terms "rooted cosmopolitan" leaders, hosting international conferences in Quito, such as the Indigenous Continental Congress and a Global Day of Action against the World Trade Organization regional meeting for Latin America in Quito. Indigenous leaders not only have become savvy participants in the International Non-Governmental Organizations (INGO) world but have successfully negotiated agreements with Trans National Corporations (TNCs), primarily oil companies, in the Amazonian region, and more recently have united the frames of human rights and the environment in legal lawsuits within the Organization of American States

Inter American Commission on Human Rights in conjunction with Earthrights International. Most significantly, the strategies of the indigenous rights movement of Ecuador have been dynamic throughout their mobilization period (since 1989–90): not only reacting to national and global issues but also taking a proactive stance.

Historical Underpinnings

Ecuador has a population of about 12 million, 40–45 percent of whom claim an indigenous identity.[9] The largest indigenous group in Ecuador is Quichua in the highlands, including peoples from Otavalo, Caranqui, Salasaca, Saraguro, Chibuleo, Chimbu, and Canari. The Amazonian region is inhabited by the Cofán, Secoya, Siona, Huaorani, lowland Quichua, Shuar, Achuar, Shiwiar, and Zápara nationalities. The Awa-Coaquier, Chachi/Cayapa, Epera, Tsáchila, and Huancavilca nationalities live in the coastal region. Regional differences do exist among the indigenous nationalities in Ecuador, as in Bolivia. The Amazonian region of Ecuador was not exposed to outside development or peoples for a significantly longer period of time than were the highlands. Additionally, the highland experience is historically one of agrarian issues, hacienda servitude and systems, and direct influence of European elites from the colonization period. While Amazonian Indians have focused on the issues of oil extraction and logging (coastal Indians are also focused on natural resource extraction, particularly logging), Sierra Indians have focused on issues of agrarian reform and agro-industry. Mining, while prevalent as an issue in the highlands previously (i.e., the Intag and Quichua communities), has re-emerged as a significant issue in all regions of the country. However, such differences have been mutually supported by the regional indigenous organizations within the country.

Indigenous organization, as in Bolivia, began in the 1940s in response to leftist political party organizations. In 1944 the Ecuadorian Indigenous Federation (FEI) was founded and protested government distribution of land. The organization of most historical significance is ECUARUNARI (Movement of the Indigenous People of Ecuador), the Sierra indigenous organization, whose inception began with funds from the Catholic Church, although it has since abandoned this connection. In 1980 the Amazonian indigenous confederation CONFENIAE (Confederation of Indigenous Nationalities of the Ecuadorian Amazon) was founded under Shuar and Quichua leadership. Today, the CONFENIAE represents all ethnic groups in the Amazon, which numbers near 200,000 peoples. Also in 1980 CONFENIAE and ECUARUNARI joined forces in a national organization, the CONAIE (The Confederation of Indigenous Nationalities of Ecuador). This unification inspired the coastal indigenous groups to form COICE (Coordinator of Indigenous Organizations of the Ecuadorian Coast) and join the national organization as well. Thus, Ecuador's indigenous movement has a strong history of regional organization that is unified and coordinated under a national organization (Martin 2003).

The CONAIE's leadership, however, extends from local, municipal levels to the global arena. Its transnational networks include local NGOs and INGOs that provide funding and technical assistance, as well as assistance from the World Bank and other IGOs (International Governmental Organizations). While state funding to the CONAIE is nonexistent, it maintains its level of power through outside funds, or, as Alison Brysk states, "foreign aid as a counterweight" (Brysk 2000, 120). An example of such a counterweight is the money provided to the CONAIE by the Danish NGO IBIS: $1 million for bilingual education programs and $35,000 annually for its operating budget (Brysk 2000, 121). Moreover, Oxfam American, Amazon Alliance, Rainforest Action Network (RAN), Earthrights International, the Inter-American Foundation, and the UN Development Program's Global Environmental Fund, in addition to IBIS Denmark, have all contributed to a plethora of programs in the Sierra and the Amazon in which funds have been directed to both the local indigenous organizations and the CONAIE (Martin 2003).

In June 2004 the World Bank announced that it had awarded a $34 million loan to support the development of indigenous and Afro-descendent communities in Ecuador. This grant will be facilitated through the Indigenous and Afro-Ecuadorian Peoples Development Project (PRODEPINE) with the purpose of strengthening indigenous and Afro-Ecuadorian membership in social organizations; promoting educational and cultural initiatives; increasing control over land and natural resources; and enhancing the government of Ecuador's capacity to formulate intercultural policies giving consideration to indigenous and Afro-descendent peoples. While not a grant directed specifically to the CONAIE, it certainly carries great impact for that organization and other local and regional organizations. Furthermore, it presents the dual threat and opportunity of funding by international financial institutions: such institutions encourage decentralization and direct funding for projects, yet also restructure national economic policies, which may counter indigenous peoples' needs and demands.

This dilemma was presented to the indigenous rights movement in 2003, when President Lucio Gutierrez signed a new agreement with the IMF. The then-president of the CONAIE, Leonidas Iza, rejected the agreement as showing a lack of "credibility" on the part of the president. However, Marcelino Chumpi, the executive secretary of the Council on the Development of Nationalities and Peoples (Condenpe—directed by the CONAIE), noted that the IMF agreement provided important resources for projects in indigenous communities and included over $50 million from the World Bank, the Inter-American Development Bank for Agriculture, the European Union, and the Spanish government (*El Comercio*, February 24, 2003). This situation illustrates the conflicts that neoliberal economic policies present to the coordinated mobilization of social movements and in particular to the indigenous organizations of Ecuador.

While the CONAIE was consolidating power domestically throughout the 1990s (including national protests in 1992, 1993, 1994, 1996, and 1997), it was also active in the anti-globalization protests of 1999, or the Battle of Seattle. On one level the CONAIE protested the WTO (World Trade Organization) in Seattle, yet it was also readying itself for another battle at home with then-President Jamil Mahuad, who was planning to dollarize the economy through the help of $900 million in international loans. By January 21, 2000 the Mahuad administration had been toppled by a massive social movement organization protest throughout the country and a rare collaboration between Antonio Vargas of the CONAIE and members of the military (including the current president, Lucio Gutierrez). This event sparked both empowerment and division within the indigenous movement, as transnational allies[10] became uncomfortable with state takeovers and military leadership (Rohter 2000). Although the takeover lasted only one day and the vice-president Jaime Noboa assumed the presidency, this event crystallized the authority of the CONAIE and Ecuador's indigenous movement both locally and globally. Furthermore, the CONAIE's frame had expanded from solely indigenous issues to those of anti-globalization and social justice issues.

Insiders or Outsiders? The Election of 2002 and Its Impacts

The election of 2002 seemingly brought great success to the indigenous rights movement of Ecuador. While it was previously known in municipalities, the national Congress, and international organizations, it had never been officially politically recognized at the national level. However, through an alliance with the indigenous political party Pachakutik, Lucio Gutierrez won the presidency in 2002 and appointed former CONAIE leader and attorney Nina Pacari as minister of foreign affairs and former (and current) CONAIE president Luis Macas as minister of agriculture. These once outsider activists were now part of the status quo government of the state, yet were promised true reform on behalf of the indigenous population.

Within the first six months of the Gutierrez administration the president announced natural gas price increases and new petroleum concessions for the Amazon (including those in Block 23 of Sarayacu). These policies placed Macas and Pacari in direct opposition (as government leaders) to their movement counterparts in the CONAIE. Additionally, President Gutierrez signed a $600 million loan with the IMF, which called for a reduction in spending on social equity programs. The then-president of the CONAIE, Leonidas Iza, called for opposition of indigenous communities to these new economic policies of the administration, which also implied opposition to his former colleagues Macas and Pacari. At the same time, Pacari traveled to a UN Forum on "Maintaining Indigenous Identity against Globalization," complicating her role as activist and government official (*El Comercio*, May 15, 2003). To further embroil the polemic, the CONAIE called for resignations of indigenous leaders in the government, yet Pachakutik leader Miguel Lluco called for indigenous leaders to remain in office, thus resigning his position in Pachakutik (*El Hoy*, July 6, 2003). Finally, both Macas and Pacari resigned their ministerial-level positions after a little over 200 days in office in protest of the anti-indigenous policies of the Gutierrez administration.

Following their resignation, Macas and Pacari worked to reunite the CONAIE and Pachakutik against the social and economic policies of the Gutierrez regime. In October 2003 (just after the Bolivian overthrow of Sanchez de Lozada), the Bolivian Felipe Quishpe attended an international indigenous workshop in Quito, where he hailed the international coordination of the CONAIE and called for strengthened indigenous networks in the region (*El Comercio*, November 18, 2003). By 2004 the CONAIE was actively opposing Ecuador's participation in the Free Trade of the Americas Act (FTAA), thus adding the frame of social justice to its menu of strategies.

In typical transnational style, the CONAIE called for another nation-wide uprising against the free trade and neoliberal policies of the Gutierrez regime on June 6–8, 2004—coinciding with the Organization of American States Assembly in Quito. While the protest did take place in concentrated areas of the Sierra (Cuenca, Carchi, Ibarra, Ambato, Riobamba), it did not extend throughout the nation, nor did it attract the non-indigenous sectors, as in previous campaigns. By June 8 the CONAIE disbanded the protest and Pachakutik leader Jorge Guaman publicly admitted to "fractures" among indigenous leaders (*El Comercio*, June 6, 2004).

Although the elections of Luis Macas and Humberto Cholango as presidents of the CONAIE have signaled attempted unification, the CONAIE remains fragmented and ruptures have taken place with popular leaders such as Otavalan mayor Mario Conejo from Pachakutik. This separation of an internationally recognized indigenous leader from the national indigenous movement calls into question internal organization and national identification with the CONAIE and with the political party Pachakutik.

Supported by Pachakutik and the CONAIE in the second round of voting, President Rafael Correa, a socialist, anti-neoliberal economic policy economist, was elected and assumed office in January 2007. President Correa's ideas of constitutional reform and anti-free trade policies, including the nationalization of Ecuador's petroleum industry, were strongly supported by Pachakutik, the CONAIE, and other regional indigenous organizations within the country. The indigenous social movement norms of global social justice and deeper democratic national representation of its peoples, plus respect for their lands and territories, were debated in the 2008 Constituent Assembly appointed by President Correa to ultimately revise the 1998 Constitution (*The Economist*, March 15, 2007). In September 2008 the Constitution, written in Montecristi, Ecuador, passed with nearly 64 percent approval.

The 2008 Ecuadorian Constitution is the first in the world to grant rights to nature and specifies the indigenous concept of wellbeing, or *sumak kawsay*, as a goal for the entire country. *Sumak kawsay* roughly translates as living in harmony with nature and respecting the individual and collective rights of citizens in a diverse country. In the Preamble to the Constitution, Mother Earth (*Pachamama*) is formally recognized as a vital part of human existence. Members of the Constituent Assembly worked with the Community Environmental and Legal Defense Fund (CELDF), a US-based NGO, on the inclusion of rights to nature in the Constitution. The inclusion of indigenous leadership and norms in the 2008 Constitution, in addition to the transnational network with CELDF, points to the continued global–local mobilization of Ecuadorian indigenous peoples.

While the strong statement of indigenous rights and rights of nature in the Constitution might signal a strengthened relationship with the Correa regime for indigenous peoples, in fact division has been heightened between the two. As of this time of writing in 2011, the CONAIE has placed various lawsuits against the government in response to a new mining law that will open the mining industry in the southern provinces of the country, particularly Zamora Chinchipe in the Amazonian region (*El Universo* 2013). Although the Correa administration boldly moved to keep oil underground in the Ishpingo-Tambococha-Tiputini (ITT) block of Yasuní National Park in the Amazon and created a pioneering global trust fund to do so, it also opened new oil and mining explorations in the southern blocks of this region and cancelled the pioneering intiative in August 2013. This inconsistency not only countered Article 407 in the Constitution that prohibits natural resource extraction in protected areas without prior informed consent and a national referendum, but it also ruptured the previously friendly relationship between President Correa's regime and indigenous communities (Martin 2011; 2015).

This tension was also highlighted by the national referendum of May 7, 2011 in which ten questions were asked of Ecuadorian citizens. President Correa proposed the referendum after an attempted coup on September 30, 2010 as a means of demonstrating continued popular support. The CONAIE and local indigenous organizations mobilized against the referendum, which ultimately passed by a small margin. In many indigenous provinces the majority voted against the referendum overwhelmingly, most particularly in the Amazon, where anti-natural resource extraction campaigns have been growing (Saavedra 2011).

The cancellation of the Yasuní ITT Proposal in 2013 ignited tensions over natural resource extraction between indigenous groups and the Correa regime. Ecuadorians (indigenous and non-indigenous) have protested in the streets, mobilized internationally, and called for a national referendum to keep the oil of the ITT block in the ground. The president of the CONAIE, Humberto Cholango, has denounced the new round of oil concessions as "illegitimate" and called for the rights of nature that are guaranteed in Ecuador's constitution. In response to the increased pressure to extract and expand into new areas, protests have surged against the Chinese consulates in various countries, including in Paris, France. Indigenous leaders in Canada have allied with Ecuadorians to protest in Calgary and NGOs such as Avaaz, Amazon Watch, and Planete Amazone have organized protests against the Ecuadorian government in Paris, Houston, and Calgary.[11]

In October 2013 women from various indigenous communities in the Amazon marched eight days from their villages to Quito to present a proposal against extraction to President Correa and the National Assembly. While the president and others did not receive them, other indigenous leaders and environmental activists met in California at the same time to collaborate on broader transnational activism to support their initiative and oppose this new round of drilling, based on the rights of nature and the spiritual and cultural norm of *Kawsak Sacha*, meaning living jungle.[12]

Despite the closing of the trust fund, mass global and national support for keeping oil in the ground remains, as shown by, for example, a petition to the Inter-American Commission of Human Rights (IACHR) (not recognized by Ecuador) requesting that the Ecuadorian state be held responsible for violating the civil and political rights of hundreds of thousands of Ecuadorians. Guided by Yasunidos (the non-governmental organization (NGO) that organized to keep oil in the ground in the ITT block), Ecuadoran citizens organized a petition drive in which 757,623 Ecuadorian citizens signed in favor of a referendum on whether or not to exploit Yasuní-ITT (Princen et al. 2015).[13] Most significantly, indigenous groups living in voluntary isolation live in the ITT block and many fear for their health and safety, as well as their existence, given the new extractive expansion. This sheds light on an under-analyzed area of research: the rights of indigenous peoples who have asked to be left in isolation against the rights of the state to extract natural resources for reasons of national security (as per the Ecuadorian Constitution). Thus, for now, Chinese interests in ITT oil have trumped local and indigenous rights in Ecuador.

And these rights, as documented by Human Rights Watch, the US State Department, and Amnesty International, have been declining. Reports of violent clashes with the police during protests and the jailing of indigenous leaders have occurred more frequently since 2010.[14] In December 2013 the Ecuadorian government closed the office of Fundacion Pachamama, an organization dedicated to indigenous rights. An international campaign to free Manuela Picq, partner of the leader of the highland indigenous organization ECUARUNARI, Cesar Perez Guartambel, from ninety hours of detention ignited renewed clashes between indigenous leaders and the Correa government during the August 2015 indigenous-led protests.[15]

In response to pressures of extraction and threats to natural and indigenous areas, the CONAIE, indigenous organizations, environmental NGOs, and their global counterparts formed a Global Alliance for the Rights of Nature. Joining this effort were Bolivian indigenous and environmental organizations, including a World Peoples Conference on Climate Change and Rights of Mother Earth in Cochabamba, Bolivia, in April 2010. This global alliance, led by Ecuadorian and Bolivian organizations with local and global NGOs, has proposed a Universal Declaration on the Rights of Nature in the United Nations through the United Nations Working Group on Indigenous Rights (Global Alliance for Rights of Nature 2011). Hence, the transnational struggle for normative change from indigenous peoples has only strengthened in light of new threats to their lands and ways of life.

Domestic Outcomes and Transnational Networks

The indigenous rights movement of Ecuador is a strong case of a movement spiraling its needs to respond to both local and global issues and demands simultaneously.

While, at the transnational level, indigenous organizations have gained resources and bargaining power with NGOs, IGOs, and TNCs, at the domestic level they have gained political power and access. For example, after the 2000 uprisings Pachakutik obtained nearly 15 percent of the electoral vote at the congressional and mayoral levels (Garcia Serrano 2003, 207). Furthermore, the CONAIE led a constitutional reformation in 1998 and its members were part of the Constituent Assembly that wrote the 2008 Constitution, which guarantees rights to indigenous and other communities, protects their collective identities and forms of organization, and grants them rights of prior informed consent in cases of natural resource extraction (Articles 56 and 57). Significantly, the 2008 Constitution marks as the state goal *sumak kawsay*, or wellbeing—living in harmony with nature, and guarantees rights to nature. Lastly, indigenous leaders Macas and Pacari did assume levels of national political authority, albeit briefly. Most significantly, Pachakutik is a major political party now in Ecuador that is allying with other parties in the Congress, including President Correa's new social movement/party Alianza País (although this alliance has since ruptured). None of these accomplishments or opportunities existed twenty years ago.

With regard to transnational norms, the CONAIE has been a trendsetter among indigenous movements. They have sponsored the Continental Summits of Indigenous Peoples and Nations of Abya Yala in Quito. Leaders there declared their collective rights to their territorial areas and countered the neoliberal reforms of the IMF, World Bank, and Inter American Development Bank (IADB) (Norrell 2004). Thus, CONAIE plays a key role in the anti-globalization coordination among indigenous peoples. Furthermore, the funding and coordination of activities with its coalition NGO partners has created a space for indigenous peoples at the transnational level not only within NGOs and IGOs but also with TNC executive boards. While such transnational mobilization has certainly gained CONAIE access to political representation and power, it remains to be seen whether it has also caused fragmentation among leaders who are competing for funds from the same transnational allies.

Case Comparison and Lessons Learned

As Hall and Fenelon (2004) find, when indigenous autonomy is contested or bounded (levels 3 and 4 in their typology) there is opportunity for indigenous mobilization yet also the possibility of increased contestation and violence over dominant capitalist system commodities, such as mineral, natural gas, and petroleum rights. They attribute this systemic conflict to the state's position within the hegemonic world system and its role within the global economy. This study has found that indigenous organizations and their non-governmental allies within the transnational social movement organizations (TSMOs) are part of the larger global economy and, thus, work within the world system, while at the same time contesting its very foundations and seeking (struggling for) alternatives. However, they too find themselves bounded by the rules within which they mobilize. These include (a) necessary resources for mobilization from larger NGOs generally from the North, (b) a reliance on representation from and with NGOs from the North, and (c) necessary negotiations within capitalist structures, such as compromises with multinational oil companies and nationalized natural gas extraction plans. While not at all co-opted by the dominant capitalist system, indigenous peoples certainly work within it for change and policy outcomes at all systemic levels.

As Hall and Fenelon (2004) note signs of long-term change toward the inclusion of indigenous values within the world system, this study also finds normative change exemplified in recent elections and constitutions in both countries. While, at the date of writing, no larger systemic changes have occurred, nationally both countries are reviewing the implementation of their new constitutions for issues of social justice, altering their economic systems to include more equitable distribution of wealth, and both are seeking forms to more deeply include indigenous peoples and their *cosmovisión* in the democratic structures of their political systems.

Whereas diffusion models ask: What are the conditions "under which international human rights ideas and norms contribute to domestic political change [?]", our case studies suggest slightly different questions: (How) does domestic transnational mobilization affect norm formation, transformation, and diffusion by (1) advocating norm formation, adaptation, and diffusion, and/or (2) contesting existing norms, at both international and national levels? Indigenous political activism in both national and international arenas does not attempt to mobilize international actors (human rights organizations and Western powers) to bring pressure to bear on domestic politics to incorporate or conform with existing international human rights norms. Instead, it seeks to validate normative claims that either have not been widely recognized internationally in the past (such as land rights and cultural rights), or that require an adaptation (or expansion) of existing norms (adding indigenous self-determination rights to human rights, or including rights of nature), or that actually contest existing non-human rights (norms such as neoliberalism and globalization). Indigenous rights are also distinctly shaped by a worldview that in broad strokes significantly differs from the capitalist worldview spread over the "*longue durée*" of Western capitalist development. Although diversity across indigenous cultures should not be overlooked or diminished, international indigenous rights, which informed the articulation of those rights in the Bolivian Constitution, are grounded in two assertions. One is that indigenous cultures and communities predate those of the settler states formed as a result of imperialism; the other is that indigenous peoples retain the right to pursue their own cultural evolution with the sovereignty and resources necessary to do so. Their cultural worldviews consistently focus on a balance between purely materialistic or economic needs and spiritual needs premised on the interconnectedness between human beings and the natural resource systems on which they depend for survival. Thus, assertions of indigenous rights also often constitute a critique of Western capitalism or neoliberalism. Under the new constitutional eras in Bolivia and Ecuador, this is evident in their assertion of uniquely indigenous norms calling for recognition of this interconnectedness—in Bolivia called *suma qamaña* and in Ecuador *bien vivir*. Thus, these cases offer the opportunity to gain insight into an area of international norms as "principled ideas" not otherwise addressed by diffusion models, which focuses on existing norms widely supported by rich, democratized, Western states, and attenuated by the entrance of non-Western ideas into the communication space of norm formation and diffusion.

Before offering some concluding observations about these issues, we should note that these cases highlight some factors that may influence the strategies and effectiveness of indigenous transnational coalitions (TCs) and TSMOs not explicitly taken into account here. They might, however, warrant further study, particularly when compared with some cases involving the rich and democratic "settler" states in North America and Australasia. These factors include:

(1) The proportion of the population that is indigenous (in Ecuador 45 percent, Bolivia 60 percent, Mexico 12–15 percent, US 1.5 percent);
(2) The degree to which neoliberalism is perceived to be a contestable versus an entrenched norm within the domestic environment;
(3) The relationship between indigenous groups and other regional and domestic actors, such as labor unions, political parties, international regional organizations, and NGOs;
(4) The cohesiveness of indigenous group(s) within the setting of domestic politics;
(5) Whether indigenous claims are advanced primarily through TC or TSMO or both;
(6) The coincidence of agendas advocated by different indigenous groups; the relationships between the groups;
(7) The domestic contexts in which indigenous political organization took place;
(8) Whether indigenous leaders hold national office and, if so, whether they represent indigenous interests and perspectives in national politics.

The advantage of studying these two cases is their similarity in terms of a number of these issues, including: their high proportion of indigenous populations; their similar situation vis-à-vis the diffusion of neoliberalism through globalization; the involvement of indigenous groups with regional and transnational ties as well as links with domestic political parties; evidence of some success in unifying indigenous peoples *as indigenous peoples* (as well as periods alternating between unification and fragmentation); having recently emerged from a long period of undemocratic government; and having had some experience and success in participating in national politics. There are also differences (some a matter of degree with respect to the characteristics above), which are summarized in Table 13.1.

Although the inclusion of indigenous rights issues within the framework of international human rights has been the subject of international activism by TSMOs (and TCs) and on the agenda of regional and international IGOs for the past three

TABLE 13.1 Characteristics of indigenous movements compared

	Bolivia	Ecuador
Identity	Strong on national level Weaker on transnational level	Strong on national level Stronger on transnational level
Leadership	Less cosmopolitan leaders	More cosmopolitan leaders
Organization	Historically weaker unification of national movement	Historically stronger national movement
	Base groups indigenous	Base groups non-indigenous and indigenous
Resources	Less transnational funding	More transnational funding
Issues	Indigenous cultural rights, coca growing, nationalization of gas pipeline, *ayllu* governance	(anti-)neoliberalism/globalization, oil development, mineral extraction, social equity
Strategies	Protest, direct action	Protest, direct action
	Alliance with political parties	Political party formation
	Anti-US and anti-World Bank	Willing to coordinate and compromise with US and multilateral financial institutions
	More Marxist, willing to use violence (influence of Quishpe?)	Less violent (but militarization in Sarayacu and assasination attempt on CONAIE President Iza)
Outcomes	Indigenous leader elected VP, Constitutional recognition, education reform, decentralization with *ayllu* empowerment and governance; representation increased but fragmentation/weakening of indigenous unity	15% electoral vote in mayoral and congressional elections; constitutional reform, strengthening of indigenous political party; rise of Ecuadorian indigenous groups to transnational leadership

decades, progress toward international recognition in the terms advocated by indigenous activists has been slow and uneven. This is unquestionably because the rights advocated by indigenous TSMOs and by national indigenous activists are in conflict with norms deriving from both neoliberalism and state sovereignty as practiced over the past several centuries. These conflicts, however, have centered on the powerful and influential settler states of North America and Australasia in general, and in particular (and often most vociferously) on the US.

In light of this record, the cases here represent an interesting departure from the cases evaluated by Risse and Sikkink (1999) for three reasons. One is the ways in which they deviate from the "spiral model." Neither Ecuador nor Bolivia was a major target of international criticism for violating or denying indigenous rights. This was in part because of the weak relationship between indigenous rights and human rights, but also possibly because indigenous peoples represented substantial proportions of the population and, in turn, were able to (or were perceived to be able to) advance their claims by participation in "normal" politics (elections, party formation, alliances with political parties). In neither case did governments respond to what criticism was targeted at them with "denial," which is the second phase of the spiral model. But they did, as the fourth phase of the model suggests, institutionalize norms pertaining to indigenous rights within their constitutions and, by appropriating some of the language and symbolism of indigenous peoples, one could say that both also engaged in discursive practices that acknowledged the validity of indigenous rights norms.

Other theoretical work on TSMOs focuses on institutional mediation (Tarrow 2005). The case studies examined here point to the importance of states as mediating institutions functioning in a kind of Janus-faced dual role, both disseminating norms as well as facilitating international mobilization around certain norms. Indigenous movements are also at least as engaged in political practice as a means of changing actual power relations as they are with articulating, diffusing, or strengthening norms. They are, in other words, practical. To those who play down the role of the state, the Bolivian case confounds, or at least complicates, this claim.

These cases also implicate a more important role for coercion than prevailing models of norm-diffusion acknowledge (Risse and Sikkink 1999, 35–6). Coercive power is implicated here in two ways. The first is that indigenous activists in these cases deployed coercive power both nonviolently through mass protest, and even by threatening, using, or provoking violent tactics. The other is implied, but not directly involved, in these cases and that is that the ability of, for example, the US to resist precisely the kinds of change Ecuador and Bolivia were compelled to make in large part because power enables the US to resist or ignore international normative pressures. At the same time, the small proportion of the population represented by indigenous peoples in the US and most other states diminishes their own coercive power. The role of coercive power must therefore be taken into account when explaining the successes and failures of indigenous rights activists in ways that do not figure so prominently into the diffusion of more well-established and less controversial international human rights norms. When indigenous peoples assert norms that conflict with those at the core of the globalization of capitalism (or neoliberalism), size matters: that is, the size of the indigenous sector as a political force matters.

Ecuador and Bolivia provide interesting cases through which to evaluate the role of modernization in norm diffusion. It seems that democratization does coincide with greater responsiveness on the part of new governments in these cases, but also with the new governments' incorporation of policies favorable to the globalization of neoliberalism. However, in the case of indigenous rights "modernization" just as often (or more often) threatens, rather than supports or promotes, indigenous rights, particularly when indigenous rights are asserted over territory and material resources, and, most of all, when that includes *energy* resources such as natural gas or oil. Like other human rights activists, indigenous activists tend to be somewhat cosmopolitan (more so in Ecuador than Bolivia). At the same time, policies that appear to produce an improvement in aggregate socio-economic conditions are also often the very policies that do so at the expense of indigenous peoples' claims to self-determination. This is particularly true when doing so obstructs various kinds of "modernization" projects that are deemed necessary to the globalization of neoliberalism, such as oil and gas exploitation or the appropriation of territory for infrastructure development (highways and hydroelectric power, for example). In these cases, indigenous activists formed alliances with other groups who either opposed or sought to mediate the infiltration of neoliberalism into their domestic arenas. One lesson illustrated in these cases is that their ability to influence national policies can be enhanced by forming alliances with labor unions, environmental groups, and others who share some kind of "anti-globalization" agenda.

Conclusion

What do these cases tell us about conflict and transnational actors? Non-state actors or TSMOs not only promote improvement in their domestic political circumstances when they appeal to international and transnational norms and actors but engage in norm-making, or at least norm-shaping, by doing so. This is perhaps nowhere better demonstrated than by TSMOs whose normative objectives contest or seek to adapt pre-existing and well-established international norms, such as neoliberalism, or a framework for human rights that emphasizes individual rights and only weakly promotes or takes into account collective or group rights. The successful elections of Evo Morales in Bolivia and Rafael Correa in Ecuador, based in large part on a transnational norm of anti-globalization and community equality, demonstrates a resonance of these norms. The significant question is whether *el movimiento bolivariano* will truly deepen the democratic representation of indigenous peoples and provide normative space within national and international institutions for alternative visions of the globe.

Notes

1 A "top-down" model of norm diffusion has also been applied to genocide in the case of Rwanda. See Lee Ann Fujii, "The diffusion of a genocidal norm in Rwanda," paper prepared for the Annual Convention of the International Studies Association, New Orleans, LA, March 24–27, 2002.
2 McAdam et al. (2001, 331–2) refer to this as a "downward scale shift."
3 See Minority Rights.org, "Indigenous Peoples and Poverty: The Cases of Bolivia, Guatemala, Honduras, and Nicaragua." http://minorityrights.org/wp-content/uploads/old-site-downloads/download-77-Indigenous-Peoples-and-Poverty-The-Cases-of-Bolivia-Guatemala-Honduras-and-Nicaragua.pdf (accessed December 19, 2016).
4 Quoted in Brysk (2000, 119).
5 IBIS Denmark (2004–07).
6 Morales lost the 2002 bid for the presidency by 1.5 points.
7 For specific referendum results, see Electionguide.org at http://209.50.195.230/eguide/resultsum/bolivia_ref04.htm (accessed December 19, 2016). It is also noted that spoiled and null votes made up 20 percent of the results.
8 See Weinberg (2004b).
9 It should be noted that official Ecuadorian government statistics claim that indigenous peoples are 25 percent of the total population. However, indigenous peoples boycotted this census and, therefore, claim that the data is inaccurate. CONAIE and other state-indigenous agencies claim that the figure is closer to 45 percent of the total population.
10 The Organization of American States (OAS), which was investigating human rights abuses of indigenous peoples in Ecuador, criticized Vargas's role in the military takeover.
11 *Associated Press*, February 16, 2013.
12 Interview with Franco Viteri, leader of the Government of the Original Nations of the Ecuadorian Amazon, at the Stillheart Institute, California, October 21, 2013.
13 *Summary of the Yasunidos Petition to the IACHR*, October 2014, e-mail communication.
14 Human Rights Watch. 2015. *World Report 2015: Ecuador*, www.hrw.org/world-report/2015/country-chapters/ecuador (accessed December 19, 2016); Amnesty International. 2015. *State of the World 2014–15*, www.amnesty.org/en/documents/pol10/0001/2015/en/ (accessed December 19, 2016); US Department of State. 2013. *Ecuador 2013 Human Rights Report*, www.state.gov/documents/organization/220651.pdf (accessed December 19, 2016).
15 *El Universo*, 2015. "Fui Secuestrada por el Estado." August 18, 2015, www.eluniverso.com/noticias/2015/08/18/nota/5074445/manuela-picq-fui-secuestrada-estado.

14

WARS, CIVIL WARS, AND ARMED CONFLICT

Patterns, Trends, and Analytic Paradigms

Peter Wallensteen

Wars, civil wars, and armed conflict are eternal subjects in discussions on peace, humankind, and the world's future. By now we know that violence is not uniform. It varies across time and space, and thus requires other explanations beyond that of unchanging human nature or the work of particular individuals or powers. As the frequency, intensity, and diffusion vary so does the dominant perspective on violence. Both the phenomenon as such and its perception require solid analysis. There have been significant advances in knowledge relating to violence in the post–Cold War period and the study of war and other forms of armed conflict has been broadened in significant ways. In this chapter these recent trends in the studies of war are analyzed and needs for future research suggested. In the process, it is important to analyze the predominant perspectives on wars. It is argued here that there is a paradigmatic shift associated with the end of the Cold War affecting scholarly work and policy action. It is also important to ask whether there is a discernable (objective) change as recorded in major compilations of conflict data. The shift, furthermore, may relate to the way data is collected, which also needs to be observed. In addition, this leads to discussions on trends in the frequency and intensity of armed conflicts as well as to new possible explanations. These are the issues that will be dealt with, one by one, in this chapter.

It is safe to say that during the Cold War the strategic concerns of the major powers led to an internationalization of local armed conflict. The global confrontation between East and West provided a frame of reference that colored the analysis of inter-state wars as well as of civil wars. During the Cold War the attitudes towards "distant" or "close" wars were formed by potential or strategic consequences for the major powers. In that perspective, wars were seen as one of the legitimate and necessary "instruments" to be used against the other side. This, furthermore, became the approach of other actors. Wars were described as part of a general, existential struggle, be it against Soviet communism, Western imperialism, European colonialism, fascism (apartheid), secularism, fundamentalism, or other broad issues. This also implied that the termination of the underlying conflicts stemmed not primarily from negotiations and compromises between the opposing sides but from conquest and the victory of one side over the other. There was a strong attitudinal and behavioral polarization. The world was divided in a Manichean way. For external sponsors and supporters of war, internal conflicts were regarded as elements in the larger struggle. They were perceived as expressions of actual or potential expansions of influence by the opposing side. For those interested in peace and worried about nuclear war, the dangers of escalation into major conflagrations were a major concern. The Cuban Missile Crisis displayed a scenario that generated fear, as did the nuclear alert during the October War of 1973 and other incidents affecting nuclear preparedness. The needs of arms control and disarmament, particularly in the field of weapons of mass destruction, were central. This resulted, for instance, in the creation of the Stockholm International Peace Research Institute (SIPRI) in Sweden in 1966. Its original aim was to independently collect data on weapons developments in the major powers from open sources. The public discourse was often stymied by the prevailing analytical approaches, which emphasized confrontation, balance of power, and strategic preponderance. Peace research emerged as an intellectual challenge to such approaches, and could make itself heard in periods of détente and negotiations, and with a greater voice in countries outside the main lines of confrontation.

The end of the Cold War changed this perspective in a remarkably swift and profound way. It deserves the label of paradigmatic shift. The many civil wars that occurred as the Cold War was winding down turned into challenges for a more cooperative major power approach. When armed conflicts no longer could be read as elements in a major conflagration they were increasingly seen as localized struggles that required differentiated analysis. The wars were now understood as humanitarian calamities, resulting from conflicts driven by concerns alien to the major powers. They were "ethnic," "religious," or "sectarian" conflicts, with potential implications for the local populations and possibly for neighbors. Only in a complicated chain of events would they be important to major decision-making centers, for instance, as sources of terrorism, nuclear proliferation, or anti-Western sentiment. The dominant approach became one of seeing these situations as state failure requiring early warning and prevention, negotiations, peacemaking, peacebuilding, and peacekeeping. The agenda changed into one more appreciative of the variation in causes of conflict, and thus also of conflict resolution.

In retrospect, one may wonder why such measures were not seen as equally valid during the Cold War. Many of the conflicts were actually the same and they continued in the same locations also after 1989. The conflicts in the Congo in the early 1960s were understood in terms of their potential of dividing the country along Cold War lines. When the same issues came back in the late 1990s the reading was different. The civil war in Angola was seen as a matter of Cold War strategy in the 1970s and 1980s, but in the 1990s as a local war requiring solution through concerted international action. The politicide in Cambodia in the 1970s was neglected in the West, as the presence of Vietnamese troops was more important, only for the perspective to change in the late 1980s. The fact that some of the actors were understood to be aligned to the Soviet Union (Lumumba in the Congo, Movimento Popular de Libertação de Angola (People's Movement for the Liberation of Angola (MPLA)) and Cuba in the Angola case, Vietnam in the third example) or to the United States (Mobutu in the first case, União Nacional para a Independência Total de Angola (National Union for the Total Independence of Angola (UNITA)) and South Africa in the second, the Pol Pot regime and China in the third) was more important than the actual disagreements on the ground. Such secondary actors were of primary interest for analysts and policymakers, although the warring parties themselves may have pursued their own agendas and only made arrangements of convenience by labeling themselves in terms that could be appreciated by their external supporters.

The only way a different perspective could be infused was through the perspective of preventing escalation to another Cold War conflagration. That is what stimulated UN Secretary-General Dag Hammarskjöld to organize a peacekeeping mission in the Congo in 1960. The non-aligned movement was formed as a way for countries to withdraw from Cold War dynamics. But that did not challenge the basic paradigm of the time.

So how did the discourse change? The intellectual agenda changed as strategic analysis no longer seemed to fit with the facts. Thus, the dominant paradigm gave way to an undercurrent that emphasized local nuances and alternative ways of action. The declining validity of classical game theory, as the actors were many more and less entrenched than the superpowers, provided space for the peace research agenda. Politically, strategic discourse gave way to the humanitarian imperative. Force that had been seen as an absolute necessity for political action became a problem to control in order to reduce suffering, or even for humanitarian purposes.

This newly developed understanding of war among researchers and policymakers required new reliable sources for conflict information. It also made it necessary to draw lines between wars and riots, insurrections, revolutions, and military coups. The research agenda for peace studies changed as the security concerns changed. It was a profound shift. It even seemed to make work done before 1989 irrelevant. This would go too far, however, but this chapter points to the new puzzles that have come to dominate research on the causes of war. This includes matters of economics (poverty, trade, natural resource), identity (ethnic, religious, nationalist fundamentalism), geography (terrain, location), and weapons (access to small arms, security sector set-up). Certainly, the classic concerns with victory and military strength, the Realpolitik, or the Geopolitik that surrounded particular strategic locales, were not obsolete, but they had a reduced role. The concerns with economic development (Kapitalpolitik) and legitimate governance (Idealpolitik) stepped forward (these notions are elaborated in Wallensteen 2011).

Only in the mid-2010s did strategic analysis again surface, in dealing with the crises that followed on from Russia's annexation of Crimea and its support for separatism in Ukraine. But it still did not have the dominance it once enjoyed.

Does this change in perspective also have support in the "objective" world of armed conflict? The Correlates of War (COW) project is the only source that generates comparable information for a longer period of time, covering wars since 1816 (Sarkees and Wayman 2010). Thus, by using its information we can generate a long-term approach to armed political conflict in our times. When we come closer to our own period, however, there is a need to focus on a different set of events, making other data sources more significant. Let us see what the long-term data tells us and then proceed to more contemporary data collections.

The Present Era in Perspective

During the Cold War the focus on inter-state conflict came from a concern with the relations between the two dominant actors at the time, the United States and the Soviet Union. The two blocks confronted each other in an almost symmetrical way disturbed in its simplicity only by the increasing autonomy of the People's Republic of China. Interactions appeared to take place between different and independent decision-making centers, minimizing the role of interdependence and even history. It was the ideal case for game theory (Schelling 1960; Rapoport 1960). There was, for instance, no history of war between the two chief protagonists. For both, the main concern was with each other and possible challenges that might again rise from defeated Germany (chiefly a Soviet concern) or subjugated Japan (chiefly a United States interest). Thus, the data that was significant concerned not armed conflicts but rather armaments, nuclear weapons, and military expenditures. Such information was prominent in the studies of the Cold War era. The idea behind such data collections was not only to demonstrate dangers in trends but also to point to the opportunity costs: resources could have been spent differently, for tax reductions, for private spending, for investments in more worthwhile projects, or for collective welfare. In the post-Cold War period the gains from ending wars and serious societal tensions may have been obvious. The concept of peacebuilding after war today captures what was earlier described as "a peace dividend" and "disarmament-development links."

This is not the only point where there might be convergence. The focus on intra-state conflict in the post-Cold War era is obvious, but the amount of intra-state conflict too was actually high earlier. Table 14.1 demonstrates this by dividing the years 1816–2007 into four distinct periods that have gained recognition as particularly salient to the workings of the international system. Largely, they follow the relations between the leading powers in the period, demonstrating European dominance during the 1800s, followed by a period where non-European states also become important (at least regionally), then the first post-World War II period, with its global confrontation, and finally our present time.

TABLE 14.1 Historical systems, two types of war Correlates of War data, 1816–2007

System	Time	Length of period, years	Number of inter-state wars	Number of intra-state wars	Intra-state war of all wars (%)
Eurocentric	1816–1895	80	27	103	79.2
Interregional	1896–1944	49	30	59	66.3
Global	1945–1989	45	29	111	79.3
Post-Cold War	1990–2007	18	9	61	87.1

Notes: The column to the right includes all intra-state war as percentage of all intra- and inter-state wars for each period. The totals for inter-state wars are 95 and for intra-state wars 334.

Sources: Wallensteen (2012, 263); Sarkees and Wayman (2010).

Table 14.1 gives rise to a number of reflections. One arises from the sixth column: namely, that intra-state conflict always has been more frequent than inter-state conflicts, even using the high threshold of the COW project, requiring more than 1000 battle-related deaths. However, when examining battle-related deaths it could plausibly be argued that inter-state conflicts are more devastating than intra-state ones in sheer numbers killed. The Interregional period had the fewest intra-state conflicts, but it included, without doubt, the highest war-related casualties, as it includes the two world wars. Equally, the period following World War II saw a series of highly destructive inter-state conflicts (for example, the Korean War, the Vietnam War, the war between Iran and Iraq). Thus, even if the inter-state conflicts may be fewer in numbers, once they become large they also are more likely to turn into very intense conflagrations. The escalation potential of inter-state conflicts may be higher than for intra-state conflicts. When two (or more) states confront each other they may be able to mobilize resources in an unmatched way. They may also be able to involve allies and thus spread the dispute. The fact that there are comparatively few inter-state conflicts in the post-Cold War period could, in fact, mean that key allies and major powers have been unwilling to contribute to escalation. Without sustained international support, inter-state conflicts may be more difficult to escalate. Indeed, the developments in Ukraine in 2014 bear testimony to this. The rapid escalation of this conflict was largely unexpected, even as the events unfolded on Maidan Square in the capital of Kiev in November 2013. Once Russia decided to get involved, matters intensified quickly from February 2014, resulting in action by Russian separatists equipped by Russia. By the end of the year Ukraine was de facto divided into three parts (Ukraine, Eastern Ukraine, and Crimea, annexed into the Russian Federation). Typically, intra-state conflicts driven only by internal actors do not intensify this quickly.

These considerations notwithstanding, the post-Cold War period has the lowest number of inter-state conflicts than any period since 1816. Almost nine-tenths of all conflicts in this period were internal, by COW definitions. Table 14.1 underlines the paradigmatic shift in research and policy agendas.

However, the agenda may have changed in a different way as well. Calculating the frequency of inter-state and intra-state wars and taking into consideration the length of the period, a disturbing picture emerges, as can be observed in the column to the far right in Table 14.1. The period with the highest frequency of conflict is the most recent one, with an average of close to four wars occurring every year, compared to 1.6 for the first period, 1.8 for the second one, and 3.1 for the third. This is using two categories of the COW project. Even if we consider the third category of conflicts used by the project, extra-state conflicts, the pattern is almost the same, although the differences between the periods are reduced: the annual frequency of war is 2.9 for the first period, followed by 2.7, 3.5, and 4.2 for the most recent one. The post–Cold War period, in other words, has seen more wars than comparable periods in history and has been marked by intra-state conflict. This certainly is a challenge to the international community of researchers as well as to opinion-leaders and decision-makers. It makes the peace research agenda all the more relevant.

The humanitarian imperative may also drive action. Once the strategic concerns of the Cold War and earlier periods yielded, actual human suffering from war could be observed. To a world that wanted to believe in democracy and human rights, the many intra-state wars were a challenge. This was expressed in many ways: the creation of more humanitarian organizations; new civil society actors pushing human agendas; consensus on negotiations as the way to end conflicts; the development of comprehensive peacekeeping operations; the interests in dealing with war crimes; the setting up of the international criminal court (ICC). A remarkable feature of the post–Cold War period was not only the amount of conflict but also the many efforts at preventing, containing, and solving the conflicts. The number of peace agreements is an indicator. The Uppsala conflict database contains 213 peace agreements for the period 1975–2010. Of these, twenty-eight were in the period 1975–88 (that is, the last fourteen years of the Cold War) and 185 in the period 1989–2010 (that is, the twenty-two years after the post–Cold War) (UCDP customized report, www.ucdp.uu.se). Thus, there was a discernable trend of fewer armed conflicts as the period progressed. The total of forty-nine and fifty armed conflicts in 1990 and 1991 respectively fell to thirty-two in 2012, only to rise again to forty in 2014 (Pettersson and Wallensteen 2015). The end of Cold War dynamics, in other words, did not bring an end to armed conflict and war. Instead, there were twenty-five years with an unusually high number of armed conflicts, albeit few of them as destructive as many of the Cold War period. The fatalities, even in the largest post–Cold War conflicts, were lower than those from the corresponding conflicts in the years 1946–89.

The Rise in Conflict Data Resources

The change of object following the end of the Cold War also made it more important to have more systematic information on war, political violence, and conflict.

The use of data for research as well as policy has gained traction. Previously only a few datasets on conflicts were available. These included the classical works associated with names such as Sorokin (1937), Richardson (1960), and Wright (1942). These were path-breaking efforts that demonstrated that war could be compared across time. This was done most daringly by Sorokin, who included Ancient Greece and Rome in his work, not just Europe (the center for Wright's investigation). Wright in particular saw the importance of strict definitions for achieving comparability. Richardson, with a background in meteorology, was the first to work with formal models. These were efforts that did not have the political impact the authors may have hoped, but still pointed to the future importance of data and statistics in addition to theory and analysis. They helped in bringing forth the systematic study of war and its causes.

During the Cold War there were data efforts connecting to the pioneers, most strongly by a few researchers, notably J. David Singer (Lear et al. 2012) and Ted R. Gurr (1970). The recent emergence of the Internet and electronic sources revolutionized the field, as have the refining of statistical methods and comparative studies. New data sources have mushroomed in all fields, and the study of political conflict has been in the lead. Those dealing specifically with wars still remain few, however. Much research has been connected to particular projects where the data archives have not been maintained once the project was competed (Eck 2005). For the specific field of conflict analysis there are presently four projects that have records of sustained efforts over decades, combined with scholarly significance and provision of data for the entire planet.

First, there is the seminal COW project, the mother of all modern conflict data projects, started by J. David Singer and Melvin Small in the mid-1960s (Lear et al. 2012, 57–128). It builds on the idea of the inter-state system as the most important aspect for capturing causes of war and conflict, particularly when focusing on inter-state conflict (Geller and Singer 1998; Vasquez 2000). It covers wars since 1816, and the most recent update contains wars until 2007. As we have seen above, it includes inter-state, intra-state, extra-state, and non-state wars (Sarkees and Wayman 2010). Most updated are its data on militarized inter-state disputes. The data is retrievable from the COW data page (www.correlatesofwar.org). For 1816–2007 COW has located ninety-five inter-state, 163 extra-state, 335 intra-state, and sixty-two non-state wars (Sarkees and Wayman 2010, 75–7, 193–7, 337–46, 485–7), giving a total of 655 wars. Other projects cover only a fraction of these conflicts, as they focus on shorter time periods. Thus, COW is helpful in providing a perspective on our present period (as exemplified by Table 14.1).

Second, there is the "local war" approach, developed by Istvan Kende in Budapest, Hungary, in the late 1960s and now pursued by Die Arbeitsgemeinschaft Kriegsursachenforschung (AKUF) at the University of Hamburg. It is based on the idea of armed conflict as a result of European domination and the elimination of traditional forms of social relations world-wide (Schreiber 2011, personal communication). It covers local wars since 1945 and is annually updated (Gantzel and

Schwinghammer 2000; Schreiber 2009). For 2014 the project recorded thirty-one wars and armed conflicts, according to a press release of January 2015.[1]

Third, there is the Uppsala Conflict Data Program (UCDP), which adds conflict incompatibility as well as aspects of conflict resolution to its concern. Its data collection covers armed conflicts since 1945. Its database has particularly detailed information on all armed conflicts after 1975. UCDP also has information on non-state armed conflicts and one-sided violence since 1989. It was initiated by the present author in the late 1970s (Wallensteen 2011) and is continuously updated (Wallensteen 2015a, chapters 1–4). Recently UCDP has released the geographical locations of conflicts in Africa and Asia. For 2014 UCDP recorded forty armed conflicts of which eleven were wars. For the full periods since 1946 it has identified 259 armed conflicts (Pettersson and Wallensteen 2015).[2]

Fourth, there is the Conflict Barometer from the Heidelberg Institute of International Conflict (HIIK). Its research provides a broader spectrum of political conflict and includes, for instance, non-violent conflicts, a category not available in the other three data compilations. With this definition the project reports 424 conflicts in one year, 2014, of which forty-six were classified as highly violent, including twenty-one wars. This width distinguishes the project from the others. The project's information is not yet available in a form that can be easily used for systematic and statistical analysis.

In addition, there are more specific projects which have resulted in significant contributions to the understanding of war and politically motivated violence. Some have dealt with the complicated issue of minorities and ethnic groups. The first one was the Minorities at Risk project at the University of Maryland, which collected information on ethnic minorities around the world (Gurr 1993a; 2000). It is undergoing substantial and significant revisions, emerging as a form that includes minorities whether under threat or not, labeled A-MAR for "all" minorities at risk (Birnir et al. 2012). A new dataset tackling the same problem in a novel way is the EPR data from Zurich, with a focus on "ethnic power relations," which carries data from 1946 until 2010 (Wimmer et al. 2009; Wimmer 2015).[3]

Crisis behavior data dealing with relations between states has been collected and analyzed (Brecher 1993) and has recently been updated until 2007. It now includes 455 international crises, thirty-five protracted conflicts, and 1000 crisis actors from the end of World War I through 2007.[4]

There is also increasingly more data on interventions into conflicts. For instance, data on mediation has been published by Bercovitch et al. (1991), while UCDP has data on conflict prevention as well as on peace agreements and conflict termination (Harbom et al. 2006; Kreutz 2010; Melander et al. 2009). Recently Karl DeRouen has presented new data on third-party mediation (DeRouen et al. 2011; Lindgren et al. 2010). The field of military coups and interventions was first explored by Tillema (1989) and additional data was published by Powell and Thyne (2011). Repression and genocides are now also subject to more systematic research (Harff and Gurr 1989; Davenport and Ball 2002, as well as, in the UCDP one-sided violence category, Eck and Hultman 2007). The diversity of conflict data sources also gives rise to a need to go deeper into the utility of different datasets as well as to the issue of data quality (Eck 2005; 2008; Öberg and Sollenberg 2011; Forsberg et al. 2012).

These projects all meet crucial criteria for systematic research. Their definitions of conflict and war are not dependent on a particular period, geographical entity, or type of conflict. They provide information that is open for many forms of analysis. Of the projects with a focus on war, information from COW and UCDP are the only ones presently and directly available for statistical uses to the international research community. They have a central role in this field of research. However, these sources will have to be complemented with the others that are rapidly evolving into useful and reliable data sources. It is safe to say that the field of inquiry is likely to be radically transformed in the coming decade.

Furthermore, these projects provide data for analysis beyond inter-state events, which otherwise are those that are most easily approached (in terms of game theory and data generation). This is supported by the shared ambition to be as comprehensive as possible and to include all the conflicts that fit the definition. Of great importance is that their definitions are precise enough to allow for reliable, simple data collection. They include conflict beginnings and endings, and ways in which to separate one violent event from another taking place at the same time and within the same locality. To be credible, finally, the data must rely on open sources and be accessible to any researcher interested in the information, for scrutiny, use, or adding on other types of data. In addition, COW and UCDP keep datasets for statistical treatment of conflict data. This makes the projects unique (Dixon 2009).

COW, AKUF, and UCDP have different epistemologies, which explains their varying emphasis. The COW definitions depart from an international system made up by states, being the constituted system members. This focus leads to a challenge to typical realist ideas notably about the concentration of power as a way to measure the balance of power and deterrence, as indicated in military expenditures or other strategic resources. This focus has been enlarged with the new categories now included, but many of the newer categories have been subject to little analysis by COW researchers.

The AKUF perspective is radically different. AKUF researchers see the world's present conflict situation as a result of the marginalization of traditional social relations and societies by Western domination. This means that the central conflicts are found in asymmetric relations between dominant Western or Western-supported local parties. In the AKUF perspective, the international system is not one of states acting independently towards each other (as in COW) but one of domination, imposition, and increasing conformity. It could be that the states are the visible actors, but they are not necessarily the "real" ones. The positions of government are controlled by someone, notably particular groups, but more difficult to identify, classify, and compare across time and space. Clearly stemming from this, AKUF wants to capture conflicts that are more continuous. For instance, there is no threshold of a particular number of deaths. This means that AKUF covers a broader set of cases than COW. The project has data on all wars since 1945. For the period to 2007, the project reported 238 wars.[5] For the same period, COW documents 179 wars when adding its categories. Many armed conflicts reported by AKUF are below the COW threshold of 1000 battle-related deaths.

The two projects are different from the Uppsala program (UCDP), which uses the concept of "armed conflict" rather than "war" and also has an emphasis on conflict resolution. UCDP is concerned with the use of violence, no matter between what actors. Like the other two, its original work focused on conflicts with at least one state or government as a party. This has now been developed into separate data collections where violence between non-state actors is also included, as is one-sided violence again unarmed civilians.[6] As does COW, it applies a threshold, but a much lower one—twenty-five battle-related deaths in a conflict in a year.

For a long time the Uppsala project was alone in identifying an explicit issue of political contention, as it defines conflict as a "contested incompatibility." This also means drawing a clear line between political and non-political violence. To be included by UCDP the incompatibility has to deal with control over government or territory, also defined as an exclusive category at a moment in time. Conflict theory suggests that parties act for particular purposes. Thus, the goals need to be taken at face value and the project separates between power/government issues and territorial ones. This approach receives interesting support, for instance, by Holsti (1991) and several investigations by Vasquez and associates (Vasquez 2000; 2012; Vasquez and Henehan 2001). The COW project focuses on behavior and searches for structural explanations, not motives. Interestingly, the project now separates intra-state conflict for control of the central government from intra-state conflict over local or regional interests (Sarkees and Wayman 2010, 339). This terminology is close to the Uppsala project. Similarly, HIIK now also categorizes the issues in conflict (Heidelberg Institute for International Conflict Research 2014, 8–10). As this discussion makes clear, the projects capture slightly different dimensions of the same phenomenon of war and armed conflict.

The UCDP provides data on the number of conflicts going on each year, information which is also contained in the other projects, although it is more difficult to retrieve. Thus, the Uppsala data provides a quick introduction to the development of armed conflicts during the period since World War II. That is reproduced in Figure 14.1, where the armed conflicts are categorized as either war or minor armed conflict.

Given the discussion of wars, the lower area of Figure 14.1 is most interesting to follow. The trends are not linear. During the Cold War period there was a constant increase in overall conflict frequency. The number of about twenty ongoing wars also parallels what is reported by the COW project for these years. By the middle of the 1990s the total numbers as well as the number of wars declined

FIGURE 14.1 Armed conflicts by intensity, 1946–2011

Source: Uppsala Conflict Data Program.

somewhat. Several wars were brought to a halt or settled by peace agreements. However, by the late 1990s the number of severe conflicts was again rising, in a gradual increase in later years. UCDP recorded a marked surge in the most recent years, particularly for 2014. Neither AKUF nor HIIK has yet reported a similar change. However, the UCDP data has considerable face validity. Whether this is a new trend or just within the range of ordinary long-term variations, as a comparison over the entire period since 1816 may suggest (Sarkees and Wayman 2010, 562–9), is debatable, and that bring us to the next section of this chapter.

The Declining War Thesis

In the past years there has been scholarly discussion on whether wars are declining or not. Again, this can be said to reflect the paradigmatic shift. During the Cold War continued conflict was taken for granted and the prospect of the Soviet Union disintegrating peacefully was not serious entertained. Thus, this discussion belongs to the new era. The waning-war thesis originated with the provocative and elegant writings of John Mueller (1989) and was the topic of a conference at the University of Notre Dame in 2001 (Väyrynen 2006). The shock of September 11, 2001 quelled the discussion for a while, but the Human Security Report of 2005 (Human Security Centre 2005) brought it back and five years later it gained new attention with the works of Pinker (2011), Goldstein (2011), and Gleditsch (2013).

There are a number of dimensions in this debate. There may be less controversy around the trend, particularly if one thinks of the number of people that are killed in battles and relates this to the global population. The number of inhabitants on Earth has increased more rapidly than those killed in wars. Thus, in general the likelihood of individuals dying in war today is lower. However, this is not necessarily true for all regions in the world. Since 2011 the Middle East has found itself in an especially turbulent period. So far, two-thirds of the twenty-two member-states of the Arab League have been involved in an armed conflict in the region, either as intervener or as the location of such a conflict. Indeed, the number of refugees from this region reached record levels by 2015. However, the global trend may still persist, as other regions may fare better.

There are various plausible explanations for the global decline in wars and armed conflicts. Realpolitik explanations focus on major power relations and the lack of rivalries between such powers in recent decades. The end of the Cold War seemed to mark the end of global contention. Some described the post-1989 period as a unipolar world centered on the United States. Others would portray the situation as one of multipolarity, where no longer just two states mattered (the United States and USSR, as it were): emerging centers included, notably, China, India, and Brazil, in addition to the older ones: Russia, Western European states (individually as well as in the form of the EU), Japan, and possibly others. The post-1989 ability of major powers to cooperate marked a change, also indicated by a decline in the use of the veto in the Security Council of the United Nations. Still, there has been speculation about potential rivalries between the United States and certain states in East Asia. With the 2014 crisis over Ukraine as well as the protracted war in Syria (which pitted the West and Russia against each other) theories of rivalry returned, and a continued declining trend seemed less certain. Even so, these tensions did not amount to the dramas of the Cold War. Nor were they reminiscent of the major powers' interventions before World War I. Something may have happened to make a global decline in wars explainable and to suggest that it has traits that may make it more lasting. It may not simply be the result of opportunistic power calculation, but have a basis in supporting societal change.

For instance, the decline cannot easily be explained by pointing to a traditional factor such as nuclear deterrence. Nuclear weapons existed also during the Cold War. Indeed, the rise of conflicts during the Cold War, as demonstrated in Figure 14.1, runs parallel to a rise in the number of nuclear weapons. The decline in wars and armed conflict after the Cold War actually parallels a reduction in nuclear weapons, suggesting that a reduced reliance on nuclear strategies actually is more able to generate peace efforts.

Some explanations emphasize a declining willingness of major powers to be engaged in major war owing to internal considerations (Mueller 1989), normative changes (Pinker 2011), or increased gender equality (Melander 2005a). The argument is that the general public is normally not willing to pursue military options and that sentiment is more easily communicated in democracies. There will, for instance, be a preference for welfare expenditure, economic expansion, and general tolerance than for war adventures. Similar logics of changed national priorities, furthermore, could also predominate in authoritarian regimes, reflecting an unrepresented public sentiment. The argument would predict fewer major power interventions and a preference for limited war fighting: that is, a reduction in battle-related deaths. There is such a trend, and the United States actions in Iraq may reflect this: a democracy fighting a war, but giving that war limited resources compared with other wars in which the United States has been involved. Most importantly, in this case, the United States tried to isolate its own public from the impact of the war (economically as well as militarily). Thus, major democracies will not always abstain from military intervention, but will use more "economical" and "publically acceptable" military options, notably drones controlled from a distance (Cortright et al. 2015).

A further possibility is that there is a shift in types of war, and that inter-state wars are particularly unlikely since the end of the Cold War, no matter which actors are involved (i.e., also lesser powers). There has been a set of inter-state conflicts since then and in sheer number they may not be fewer than before, but it is noteworthy that major powers have acted to prevent them from spreading, rather than taking sides and resourcing the wars (Ecuador–Peru, Ethiopia–Eritrea, India–Pakistan, Sudan–South Sudan). In the immediate post-Cold War period the interest in exploiting such tensions declined. With increasing pressure on major powers in the 2010s, however, that may come to change. It may also have given space for action by neighbors. Thus, UCDP reports a strong increase in "internationalized civil wars" by 2014, constituting one-third of all conflicts. This refers to increased involvement by global and regional actors dispatching their own troops into the domestic affairs of other states (Pettersson and Wallensteen 2015, 537). A disconcerting aspect is that such interventions historically have been associated with an increased duration of conflicts (Regan 2000a).

An alternative explanation is that internal affairs have become the central subject of analysis. Thus, the declining trend might reflect a spread of democracies or regimes, which are more transparent and willing to accommodate peaceful changes when facing widespread internal dissatisfaction. Certainly, civil wars have constituted the bulk of the armed conflicts, particularly since 1989 (Table 14.1). In addition, the Cold War saw a number of such conflicts, but they were almost always exposed to heavy international involvement. The internal conflicts in, for instance, Angola, Cambodia, Central America, the Horn of Africa, the Middle East, and Southeast Asia were all interpreted through their (potential or actual) linkages to the Cold War parties. Since 1989 this has no longer been the case, and the conflicts have been attended to in their own right. Internationally stimulated peace efforts have focused on such situations, and possibly with increasing efficacy. However, it seems also that peace processes became more protracted and many setbacks were reported—in, for instance, Syria, Libya, South Sudan, and Yemen, where power-sharing deals were suggested or difficult to implement.

There were also profound changes in the way the international community was organized after the end of the Cold War. This might impact on the frequency and intensity of war. There was more space for international organizations, there was an activated international public opinion (as seen in a proliferation of NGOs), there was an obvious globalization of national economies, and personal communication was made easier through the advent of social media. All this served to alert the decision-makers to the possibilities and dangers of war in seemingly distant places. In fact, as transportation costs have declined, no place is "distant" any longer. Nonetheless, armed conflicts still continue to occur. The changes in the international system mean that more capacity and willingness is now available for preventing escalation to war. There are advances in mediation, conflict resolution, and conflict prevention. A closer scrutiny of the two curves in Figure 14.1 shows that there is a widening gap between them, which may indicate an ability to prevent more conflicts from becoming wars. Thus, it is not surprising to find that the use of peacekeeping is seen by some as a particularly important factor in the declining use of war (Goldstein 2011). Others might point to the ability to settle conflicts, particularly the territorial ones (Gibler 2007; 2014; Vasquez 2012).

These observations indicate that the ability of the international community to act may be central. Clearly the end of the Cold War released pent-up energy, unleashing tensions that had been held back by the Cold War confrontations and solutions that had similarly been defined as outside the scope of practical political strategies. Thus, the period since 1989 saw a considerable explosion of creative energy, for constructive as well as destructive reasons. The net effect was that the number and intensity of wars both declined. The developments in 2014 may be a trend breaker, but that is not possible to determine at this juncture. If they result in lasting tensions between the West and Russia, it may not bode well for the areas immediately affected. On the other hand, a speedy and agreed ending to some of the wars in Syria could positively affect the rest of the Middle East. The more this is based on concomitant changes in society the more the chance of lasting peace increases. If the normative expectation since the end of the Cold War is to support non-war strategies, the chances increase that this would reduce the overall risk of major wars. The way world power is distributed, however, still makes it difficult to create other checks and balances than those that can be developed in the domestic affairs of those states with huge military resources.

The Rise of Competing Theories

The new period has also led to a vigorous debate about the general causes of conflict and war, whether between or within states, beyond the issue of a possible decline in wars. In fact, there are now competing theories to explain non-war conditions in inter-state as well as intra-state relations, supported by statistical analysis and with the use of the new data sources. The traditional Realpolitik considerations have been challenged in an unprecedented way. Table 14.1 also demonstrates that civil wars have been more common than inter-state wars. This is something that has come to the forefront in the post-1989 period, but there is no general theory that can explain both these phenomena. The one that comes closest is that of the democratic peace. It started as an explanation of the absence of war in inter-state relations. It has also been used to understand intra-state conditions. The "original" democratic peace theorem (Maoz and Abdolali 1989;

Maoz and Russett 1993; Russett 1993; Russett and Oneal 2001; assessed in Ungerer 2012) deals with regimes and regime types in explaining inter-state war. Such variables had previously been dismissed. They have now returned, as the focus was on the dyad—that is, the relations between two states, not just the individual state and its war-proneness (the monadic dimension). This became an important topic during the 1990s. It would suggest that Idealpolitik is significant for international affairs, not just the postulated, strategic calculations made by leaders in perfect control over the societies they dominated. The strongest evidence still resides with inter-state war data, but there are also applications to domestic conditions, supporting the notion that mature democracies are indeed less war-prone in internal affairs (Hegre et al. 2001). It has now become a standard procedure to control for regime type when suggesting new factors.

Still there have been challenges with considerable statistical support, notably Kapitalpolitik considerations, as seen in the concept of the "capitalist peace" (Gartzke 2007; Gartzke and Hewitt 2010) pointing to the importance of economic integration in particular spheres as important. There is also a more classical Geopolitik approach, developing ideas on what has been labeled "territorial peace" (Gibler 2007; 2014) and emphasizing the importance of settling territorial disputes before a reduction in violence can take place. Recently the possibility of what we may call a concept of "welfare peace" has appeared (Taydas and Peksen 2012). The explanations tend also to become increasingly complex, particularly when gender variables are introduced and demonstrated to have strong support (Tickner 1992; Caprioli 2005; Melander 2005a; 2005b). Much of the support for notions of welfare and equality relates to civil wars and internal conditions, rather than inter-state conditions.

However, with increasing complexity one might also ask how general the findings supporting the theories actually are. For instance, democracy, territorial accords, capitalism, welfare, and gender equality may have a strong connection or correlation: that is, we may be facing a problem of endogeneity. They may say something about the same societies—namely, comparatively rich westernized countries in North America, Australasia, and Europe. If other regions in the world build up peaceful systems that could be a challenge to the dominant theories. For instance, Tønnesson has emphasized that East Asia has seen a long period without war, beginning around 1980 (Tønnesson et al. 2013). The region does not fit any of the notions that have so far been suggested as explanations for the absence of war in inter-state relations or within states. The societies remain fairly authoritarian, their economies are state-controlled, territorial disputes abound and flare up at times, and gender inequality remains strong. Would this example suggest that the "East Asian Peace" is only a temporary pause in conflict, only a temporary state of affairs without the underpinnings of "peace" found in other places? Or does it suggest that there are additional frameworks that have to be considered? The clear decline in inter-state and civil wars in South America points to other factors, such as democratization, retrenchment of military establishments, and a tolerance of territorial ambiguity (as many territorial disputes remain unsolved). The project on "Latin Peace" remains to be started. By the mid-2010s there were two war-torn states in this region, Colombia and Mexico, with a protracted peace process going on in the former. At the same time many societies were plagued by gang violence, partly resulting from previous war experiences.

This actually brings the discussion one step further. If there are regional variations we can also ask how comparable the different types of conflict actually are. Civil wars, country experts often say, are "unique" and "not comparable" to each other. The systematic research reviewed here presupposes that the societies involved actually are sufficiently—although not completely—comparable. This is what allows for general conclusions. For instance, international linkages, such as exports, imports, and investments, are likely to be similar and to have parallel effects. Many countries have highly comparable international relations, created by European colonialism. Many countries thus will now be subject to a comparable post-colonial legacy, seen, for instance, in a heavy reliance on raw material exports. They remain equally exposed to commodity prices, investment requirements, and the outflow of capital. For Africa there seems to be strong evidence for a connection between commodity exports and armed conflict (Collier and Hoeffler 2004; Fearon 2005). The findings support a conclusion that international dependence is analogous across regions and cases, and thus that international causes of conflicts could be the same.

What, then, about the internal affairs of nations? How can societies, for instance, handle their international dependences and what will that say to us about their comparability? There are countries, also in Africa, that are not on the conflict list although they are dependent on commodity exports, notably Botswana and Namibia (Brosché and Höglund 2015). Are they able to "buy off" opposition and thus use their resources to gain stability by corruption (Fjelde 2009)? There are also countries that are not dependent on such commodity exports, thus not generating such wealth, notably Mozambique and Benin, that have still remained remarkably peaceful, open, and non-corrupt (Wantchekon 1999).

National governance has been a factor that previously was considered to lack comparability. However, there is an increasing attention to shared aspects, such as corruption (measured by the Quality of Governance Institute, QOG), constitutional aspects (as measured by the Comparative Constitutions Project, CPP), and electoral aspects (as covered by the Constituency-Level Elections Archive, CLEA). These projects have drawn interest not least because of the experience of low-quality government, mostly noticeable after the end of the Cold War. State failure emerged as a new concept; it was often applied to states in Africa, but the same phenomenon could be studied in Afghanistan, Cambodia, East Timor, and other parts of the world. Thus, the notion of good governance has also been opened for cross-sectional analysis. Certainly there could be special forms of corruption, depending on a state's resources, the actors involved, and its experience of war and colonialism. On this front there is likely to be headway in the coming years, deepening our understanding of governance issues. It is clearly not only a matter of democratic institutions but more pointedly matters of the control of the executive branch, the recruitment of the state administration, and corruption (Öberg and Melander 2009; Rothstein 2011).

Even so, there could be an argument for regional variations. The state structures in many African states appear weak compared with those in West, South, and Southeast Asia, which may be more robust, entrenched, and with more loyal military apparatuses. State legitimacy and resources vary between these two conflictual regions. The Arab Spring is an important case. In the first wave of revolutions in 2011 it appeared that monocracies crumbled, rather than monarchies. Possibly this was because of their inability to build durable legitimacy, which monarchies had had more time to develop (Allansson et al. 2012), a result corroborated by general findings (Charron and Lapuente 2011).

However, entrenched regimes could also face challenges. Even if an authoritarian government could quell a democratic capital-centered opposition it might have difficulties in controlling regional or ethnic groups in more remote parts of the country (Wallensteen et al. 2009). This may eventually unravel the entire regime and contribute to a fragmentation of the society, once the central regime is weakened. Even federal solutions can turn into devastating wars (Regan and Wallensteen 2013). This is the story of the end of the Soviet and Yugoslav empires, but also a challenge faced by the post-Suharto regime in Indonesia and a post-military government in Burma/Myanmar.

Regional dynamics need to be part of the picture. War in one country is likely to affect relations in the entire region. Efforts of containment, peacemaking, and peacebuilding will have to be regional in order to be effective. Diffusion effects, furthermore, are likely to be regional rather than global. But the phenomenon as such could repeat itself across the globe. Regional variations need to be on the agenda (Wallensteen and Bjurner 2015). The combinations that result in war may vary in an important way, as the examples should have made clear.

Researchers on the causes of war face new opportunities in the coming years. New sources and an improved ability to incorporate findings both from interstate and intra-state war will enrich this direction of research. What other challenges are there?

Conclusion

The study of the causes of war has received a remarkable injection following the end of the Cold War. The Realpolitik notions that guided Cold War dynamics have taken a back seat. The explanations for the many wars as well as the changes in war frequency and intensity have been located elsewhere, notably in national governance, international relations, economic integration, gender inequality, and willingness to solve disputes in constructive ways. This amounts to a paradigmatic shift, where even the perspective on war itself moved, from being a legitimate instrument to a humanitarian challenge that needed to be contained. The questions asked by researchers as well as by political leaders became dramatically different.

Still, the questions are many. A vision in the original study of the causes of war was developing an *integrated* theory of war, including both inter- and intra-state conflicts. Data sources that provide integrated definitions have emerged (UCDP, AKUF, HIIK), but still studies tend to be done either on inter-state or on intra-state conflicts. The possible communalities constitute challenges for the future.

There is also a clear move in intellectual as well as political interest away from state-based and state-dominated violence to *other forms of violence*. The challenges to data collection and systematic analysis by sexual and domestic violence are dramatic and require methodological innovation. There are theoretical challenges in finding explanations, where a parallel between power structures in society and family may generate hypotheses of importance. This may even extend to family access to weapons, which is tolerated in only a few countries, notably the United States and Iraq, both of which exhibit high levels of domestic violence.

Recent developments also suggest *new possible causal connections* not investigated earlier. The financial crisis since 2008 has demonstrated that external debt and financial problems can bring down governments (Greece, Italy) and generate tensions and violence. It is not farfetched to suggest that this may eventually lead to repression and armed conflict in countries that have otherwise been spared such events. The connections between external debt and domestic conflict have not been systematically studied, but may now come to the fore.

The advances in data collection are rapid. The next generation of conflict data from UCDP is *geo-coded* down to the level of events. Similar ambitions exist in other global or regional projects. This raises an entirely new set of questions on conflict dynamics, for instance, concerning the location of conflicts, their effects on local populations, and the way they can spread across borders. It also gives impetus to peace studies, notably for peacekeeping (where should such troops actually be located?), sanctions (which borders are to be controlled to maintain an arms embargo?), and mediation (where are there good places to meet, with secure access for the warring parties?).

There are also *new datasets* emerging on phenomena that are difficult to capture, notably ethnic relations (as collected by the Ethnic Power Relations project, Wimmer et al. 2009) and repression. There are new sources, including leaks from governments and new ways to enter into archives. Even the concept of *peace* receives new challenges. In recent years it has been put on the agenda of leading research associations, notably the Peace Science Society and the International Studies Association. In addition, peace needs to be defined and measured, which requires new ways of making scales and indexes (Klein et al. 2008; Vision of Humanity 2015). It also means moving towards a broader understanding of peace, not least the qualities required for sustaining a solution after war (Wallensteen 2015b).

The creativity unleashed by the end of the Cold War was not stifled by the events of September 11, 2001, although it made conflicts relating to terrorism more difficult to negotiate. It also spurred others to find solutions to their conflicts. The real challenges may be those that have resulted from the nightmares that followed the Arab Spring of 2011 (Syria, Libya, Yemen, Egypt, Iraq) as well as the renewed tensions between Western states and Russia (Georgia, Ukraine). The number of conflicts and casualties has increased (Pettersson and Wallensteen 2015). Hopefully the achievements in research and politics in the past twenty-five years will not be undone, but instead built upon. The study of war and conflict has made considerable headway. At the same time the message is clear: Much more remains to be done.

Notes

1   www.wiso.uni-hamburg.de/fileadmin/sowi/akuf/Text_2010/AKUF-Pressemitteilung-2014.pdf (accessed December 20, 2016). See www.akuf.de (accessed December 20, 2016), where the conflicts are listed but information is not provided in a form that can easily be used in statistical studies.
2   For more, see www.ucdp.uu.se (accessed December 20, 2016), where there is both a conflict encyclopedia for descriptive information and a dataset page for statistical studies.
3   www.epr.ucla.edu/ (accessed December 20, 2016).
4   www.cidcm.umd.edu/icb/ (accessed August 28, 2015).
5   www.akuf.de (accessed August 8, 2011).
6   www.ucdp.uu.se (accessed December 20, 2016).

Conclusion

15

THE FUTURE OF CONFLICT STUDIES[1]

Ted Robert Gurr

A half-century ago, when I began writing about violent political conflict, the comparative literature consisted of a few isolated clusters of work on revolutions and terrorism. Scholars, notably Harry Eckstein (1964), recognized that there were larger universes of phenomena—internal wars in Harry's case—that needed systematic comparative research. There has been an explosion of analytic literature on terrorism; a recent handbook lists about 4,000 items, most published since 2000 (Schmid 2011, chapter 9). My own work on *Why Men Rebel* (1970; 2010) was an analysis of the motivations and circumstances that lead people to participate in the risky business of protest and violence against state authorities—a broader question that prompted a British critic to imply that I might as well have tried to develop a theory of holes (MacIntyre 1971, 260).

The essays in this book are evidence of a sweeping transformation of the field of study. First, the scope has expanded vastly to encompass state repression, genocide and mass political killings, and crime, seen as microcosmic conflict (see Grabosky, Chapter 8 in this book) or as a means to finance political violence (see Mincheva and Gurr 2013). Second, researchers take a much broader view of contributing causes, notably international factors such as the regional diffusion of armed conflict and insecurity (Marshall 1999) and the structure and dynamics of the international system (Shaw 2013). In the emerging research agenda on conflict and climate change, analysis begins with environmental issues and traces through their impact on conflict behavior—an approach that I advocated many years ago (Gurr 1985), but never followed through in my own empirical work.

This chapter is not so much a conclusion as a commentary on issues. First is the interaction of political events and policy concerns on our agenda. In the next two sections I discuss foci for future research and highlight some fundamental issues of contention within and among countries that I think will drive future waves of violent conflict. Fourth, I sketch two paradigmatic research projects: first my own work on ethnopolitical conflict, then a strategy to understand the sources of jihadist and Salafist movements. The final section focuses on some general issues about research design and repeats my contention, and practice, that we should do both large-n empirical research and comparative case studies. Throughout I refer to the need for more analytic knowledge about the ideologies and generalized beliefs that are the essential links between people's grievances and their political actions.

New Conflict Challenges: How to Understand, How to Respond

Much of the expansion of analytic work on political conflict has been driven by concerns among scholars and analysts about new and dramatic manifestations of conflict behavior. My own work on motivations for rebellion was prompted by outbreaks of political instability in post-colonial Africa, though its immediate professional impact was due to its relevance for explaining mass protest and riots in the US in the late 1960s. The comparative study of political terrorism was spurred by episodic campaigns by the radical left and separatists in Western Europe (1970s), Marxists in Latin America (1980s), and then and now the Middle East. Self-determination movements became a hot research topic in the aftermath of the dissolution of the USSR and the Yugoslav Federation, and the proliferation of separatists who followed their examples on other continents. Researchers have come to see that climate change poses a global set of challenges in the form of migration, local and regional conflict, and instability. And others are returning to the age-old issue of how inequalities motivate conflict—not just inequalities within countries but among them.

So, driven by real-world policy concerns, does the accumulation of empirical evidence in conflict studies have much impact on state and international policies? The record is decidedly mixed, especially but not only because the research is usually a belated response to crises, often after immediate responses have failed. A case in point was the US government's reaction following the 1994 genocide in Rwanda. Empirical research on the causes and dynamics of genocide was in its infancy, but Vice President Gore charged the government-sponsored State Failure (later Political Instability) Task Force with designing empirical research that could anticipate future episodes—along with the other episodes of political instability that were already on the Task Force's agenda. The connection between event, feckless international responses, and the initiation of policy-relevant empirical research was obvious (Power 2002; see Harff, Chapter 12 in this book on the research that followed). This raises an important general question for the future, not for the first time. Since we are learning so much about the dynamics of past and ongoing conflicts, does this knowledge give us or policy-makers tools to anticipate future conflicts? And, if so, when and how do they use them?

The future of conflict studies will continue to be reshaped by real-world events and concerns. The internationalization of conflict and responses to it has been one major set of developments in the last fifty years. The signaling effects of successful movements of resistance to repressive regimes, demands for indigenous rights, and now fundamentalist religious revivals have reshaped the world of conflict and refocused scholarship. Rebels take lessons and confidence from others. They also redefine their identities, no longer just local but as part of imagined international communities of the oppressed. Ease of travel and especially communications and the spread of social media amplify this process.

Perhaps less recognized, authorities also learn from one another. Reform and incorporation by democratic regimes has had a moderating effect on many political conflicts and given impetus to the global trend toward democratization. That trend seems stalled because it has encountered the obdurate resistance of political cultures and deeply rooted authoritarian systems that for now resist further change. Whether democratization per se has positive or negative impacts on conflict and instability, and why and how, remains a major research issue, as demonstrated by Marshall and Cole (Chapter 11 in this book) and by Jaggers (Chapter 5). International organizations have similarly acquired and tried to implement "lessons learned" about conflict management. The next handbook on conflict studies might well expand its focus: What has been learned that can be, and is being, used for prevention and mediation, and with what effects?

Foci for Future Research: Issues, Motives, and Ideologies

If I were to begin my own research on "why people rebel" in politically organized societies now, knowing what's been learned thus far, I likely would start with a historically grounded general framework that took account of both international and local contexts. The first step would be to generalize about the kinds of issue that lead to protest and rebellion. Second would be analysis of the grievances and motives of potential rebels that are shaped by these issues. Third, I would focus on the content and uses of generalized beliefs and ideologies that channel people's energies into collective action. These shared mental constructs are the foundations on which competing leaders mobilize and formulate strategies for remediation. Charles Tilly rightly observed that there are pockets of discontent or grievances in every society, but concluded that analysis should begin with how they are mobilized. My own view is that we cannot understand successful mobilization or strategies of political action without an accounting of the issues, grievances, and beliefs on which mobilization is built. A promising framework for this kind of analysis is Sanin and Wood (2014). And, like a generation of recent scholarship, this kind of analysis needs to be done in the context of authority structures and political events, domestic and international, that shape opportunities for political action.

Issues

The wellsprings of political protest and rebellion against the political order since the French Revolution (if not earlier) can be reduced to four general issues, sometimes alone, usually in combination. This is in effect a way of categorizing and analyzing grievances along with their structural or situational sources. They are:

1. *Resistance to repression* by authorities, public or private: that is, the fundamental grievance is anger about the controls and coercion used by authorities to maintain an oppressive political, economic, or social order.
2. *Stratified inequalities*, in which classes or categories of people resent and aim to dismantle social systems that systematically restrict their access to politics and material well-being. This is often coupled with resistance to repression, but is nonetheless analytically separate and often has different manifestations.
3. *Collective autonomy*, the desire by collectivities—defined by some combination of ethnicity, belief, region of residence, or other bases of shared identity—for control of their own collective existence. The demand may be intensified or justified by grievances about the repression used to suppress their autonomy, or to maintain the group's subordination, but is analytically separate from its structural causes.
4. *Identity*, a collectivity's quest for purity of culture or belief. Identities based on cultural traits can be recognized, protected, and coexist with others: they are not necessarily exclusive. But religious belief is a more potent source of conflict because of its exclusive nature. Coexistence with people practicing different faiths is morally offensive and a challenge to the faithful and has been the source of persecution, religious wars, crusades, and jihads for centuries. It is intrinsically inconsistent with coexistence, secularism, and most strategies of reform.

These issues are often intertwined. For purposes of conflict management, or resolution, some are more easily moderated than others. Inequalities can be lessened by advantaged groups and governments, given the political will and capacity to act. Repression can be relaxed by a variety of strategies and reforms short of revolution. Recognition and autonomy can be extended by the modification of existing authority structures, if those in power are prepared to compromise. Religious purity, though, can be an intractable demand. Following David Laitin (1998), people can speak multiple languages and inhabit shared space with peoples of different identities, but they cannot be both Roman Catholic and Shi'i or Buddhists and Muslims at the same time.

Motives

I no longer think it is useful to make a sharp analytic distinction between rational and non-rational motives for political action. Mark Lichbach (1995) has demonstrated that many political acts that I attributed to non-rational anger can equally well be explained by the logic of rational action. Ganor, in his analysis of the rationality of Islamist and jihadist terrorism, summarizes the argument succinctly:

> The terrorist's cost–benefit analysis and the choice it dictates are … the result of subjective judgment, which is influenced by the background of the decision maker who is making that judgment—that is, his culture, religious beliefs, ideology, experiences, and values. The relative cost or benefit that a terrorist assigns to his various alternatives will depend on this background, the morals it dictates—and his personality.
>
> *(Ganor 2015, 101)*

This means that in any analysis of political action it is necessary not only to deconstruct motives but also to analyze the situation and experiences of the actors.

But what do we know empirically, rather than surmise, about decision-making by militant strategists? Some intensive and in-depth interviews with "retired" militant leaders may be the most convincing way to approach this question. I continue to think that political actors and actions are motivated by innate senti-ments as well as calculation. Maybe most important among innate sentiments is solidarity with others—intimates, co-ethnics, neighbors, co-workers. So motives need careful dissection among their sources, passionate and dispassionate. And we need the most direct possible evidence.

I suggested a long time ago that the mix of motives will vary across strata of movements as well as among them. Leaders and cadre are more likely to be moti-vated by ideology and situationally specific cost–benefit calculations, whereas grievances and solidarity are typically more important for followers and sympa-thizers. And one great set of challenges to those who would mobilize people for political action is how to frame appeals that maximize commitment within the resonant group.

Ideology

Collective beliefs are the most intangible of analytic topics. What are they, how pliable, how do they shape action—and how are they used to motivate and lead activists? A commonplace about contemporary jihadist movements is that their leaders use derivations of Islamic doctrine in the service of their political agendas— to topple corrupt rulers, create a just Islamic social order, establish a new caliphate, etc. But then why do these appeals attract followers in an increasingly modernized and interconnected world?

Sanin and Wood (2014) argue that ideology is an essential variable in the analysis of political action, but one we know too little about. Two studies that demonstrate possible empirical approaches are Smith et al. (2008), using thematic content analysis, and Asal et al. (2013), who use coded information on the gender (and other) ideologies of 104 minority-based organizations in the Middle East. From my perspective, here are a half-dozen key dimensions for comparative analysis:

1. To what imagined community do ideologies appeal? Workers, discriminated minorities, indigenous peoples, suppressed nationalities, fellow believers?
2. What issues do they address, and how plausible are they to the target audience? Which group(s) are in fact mobilized in significant numbers because of these appeals?
3. What large strategies of action do they lay out? How do they connect actors to those strategies?
4. What mix of individual and collective incentives do they offer? By joining a group, one can gain the respect of one's fellows; by leading, one can enjoy the perquisites of success, or risk martyrdom as the price of failure.
5. What are the long-term expectations of gains for the collectivity?
6. How plausible are expectations of gain in view of the situations of the potential actors? There are also instrumental bases of comparison. How are ideologies propagated? How important is the role of heroic, visible leaders in mobilizing members?

Most of these issues are likely to be addressed in ideographic analyses of specific political movements. What I am proposing here is explicit attention to the accumulation of comparative information on them. In a later section I suggest a strategy for comparative analysis of militant jihadist movements. And to what purpose? Not just academic understanding, but practical theory about how they can shape policies about the prevention and mitigation of violent political conflict.

Structures and Issues of Future Political Conflict

Two fundamental conflict-generating divides, or cleavages, in the early twenty-first century are cultural and economic. The essential cultural divide is between the societies and intellects who promote the values of individualism and personal freedom, protected and promoted by democratic states, versus those who advocate and maintain doctrines of communalism and self-discipline in the service of the collectivity—however defined. This is the basis of contention between Western societies and Salafists, and between Western democratic and Asian communist doctrines. This echoes and updates Huntington's clash-of-civilization thesis (1993). I criticized his thesis on empirical grounds in my 1994 presidential address to the International Studies Association (Gurr 1994). Looking back from 2015 I continue to think he was wrong on some specifics, but his larger view was correct.

The cultural cleavage is mainly transnational but also shows up within societies, for example in the Sunni–Shi'a contention in Middle Eastern countries. The economic divide, which is both societal and transnational, is material inequality between the beneficiaries of neoliberalism and the workers and lower-middle classes who are the basis, but not the main beneficiaries, of increasingly global capitalism (on inequalities in Europe and the US see Picketty 2014; Atkinson 2015). We usually associate this inequality with the way capitalist economics work in Europe and North American societies, yet it also flourishes now in China (probably also in Vietnam and other "liberalizing" late communist states), where it straddles the two lines of cleavage: prosperity for the rising entrepreneurs coupled to ideological demands that the new rich and middle class and workers remain committed to the Communist Party-directed collectivity which promotes the new materialist economies.

In the broadest sense the jihadist wars are based on resentments across both lines of cleavage: rejection of Western materialism and Western ascendency, cultural and political, in the heartland of Islam. Resentment about the inequalities engendered by neoliberalism have yet to find any shared expression, despite episodic campaigns of demonstrations against international capital and finance, the World Bank, Wall Street, and so on. Labor movements, which historically fought for the rights of disadvantaged workers, are now either weak and in decline—as in the US—or coopted by capitalist associations and governments (on the US labor movement see Fraser 2015).

I am not attempting a radical critique, rather pointing out where the evolving issues of conflict within and across international boundaries are most likely to generate new waves of protest and rebellion. These are potent drivers of future conflicts. What forms they will take are already foreshadowed by the confrontation between the West and militant Islam and divisions within Islamic societies. Political conflicts over inequality remain inchoate, though it is not likely that they will follow the traditions of the technophobic Luddites of early nineteenth-century England or the labor movements of Europe and North America in the 1870s to 1950s. Marxism, similarly, has lost its power to stimulate mass action. The demand to redress inequalities awaits a new Marx, or more likely will be dispersed across many distinct movements making different ideological and rational appeals.

Other more narrowly focused issues of violent political conflict will persist and be manifest in new and unpredictable ways. Ethnopolitical issues and Islamic jihad are discussed in greater detail in the next section. Here let me highlight four other important issues.

Resistance to Incompetent and Corrupt Governments

Transitions to democracy since the 1990s have generated high expectations in post-communist states and the Third World about the advent of competent and accountable governance. Those expectations have been widely and deeply disappointed. The responses include mass protest movements and revolutionary resistance to the incompetence and corruption of these governments. Jack Goldstone points out (personal correspondence) that there have been more revolutionary movements since 1989 than in the previous quarter-century. He includes the "color revolutions" of post-communist states as well as failed attempts to replicate them elsewhere. I have written about a related issue in African states whose leaders have failed to deliver on promises of public goods:

> What state socialism has come to mean in practice in African societies is a political system in which new elites use state power to command foreign assistance, expropriate private wealth, and extract rents from resources ... for their own and supporters' benefits, and to build a state apparatus strong enough to suppress resistance.
>
> *(Gurr 2015, 254)*

A similar critique, and a source of bitter resentment, fits many post-communist states, including Russia itself. Does this kind of resentment also underlie the anti-statist politics of the radical right in the US and the rise of right-wing political parties in the European Union? If so, it is thus far channeled into electoral politics rather than collective action.

Conflict–Crime Linkages

Thirty years ago James Adams thus concluded his comparative study of *The Financing of Terrorism* (1986, 237–8):

> to survive terrorist groups need to cross an economic divide that separates those who live a hand-to-mouth existence from those who can actually plan ahead .... [G]ood financial planning means having enough cash to buy and keep support, to pay for arms and to build a propaganda base among the people that the organization claims to represent.

This is equally true of all durable campaigns of violent political activism, then and now. Some kinds of fund-raising are better than others. Contributions from a popular support base are more reliable than, say, armed robbery. Trafficking in drugs is more lucrative than kidnappings for ransom. And many militant organizations have gone into criminal business, either on their own or in alliance with international criminal networks (for case studies see Mincheva and Gurr 2013; also Napoleoni 2005 and Grabosky and Stohl 2010).

A symbiotic relationship often develops between militant movements and crime. Leaders of violent ethnonational wars may become criminals or officials in corrupt post-war governments. Anti-terror strategies of the major powers and international organizations aim at interdicting money transfers to and from militant organizations. This is often a catch-up game because of militant networks' criminal and economic adaptability. So this is a continuing, major topic for policy research: understanding how militant organizations finance their activities and connections with international crime, and how to disrupt the economic activities and transactions that sustain them.

Refugees and Immigrants

Civil wars and state failures in the global South send hundreds of thousands of refugees to more stable and prosperous countries. They, along with economic migrants, pose a host of challenges for conflict analysis. The risks of mass population movements help motivate international efforts at containing and mediating internal wars in poor countries. International interventions aimed at regime change in Iraq and Libya, though, inadvertently helped create massive refugee problems for neighboring countries and for Europe. Ironically, the lack of international intervention in the early stages of Syria's civil war had the same results. So here is one major set of research topics: how to design international policies toward potential internal wars that can minimize the immediate and longer-run risks of human disasters. This pushes the research agenda back one step further. Conflict researchers need to generate systematic assessment of risks of instability and mass atrocities by country and region, assessments that help identify workable preventive strategies. And policy-makers need to be persuaded that empirical assessments need to be taken seriously.

At the receiving end of cross-boundary and transcontinental population movements are a different set of challenges for conflict studies. How can countries assist and incorporate new arrivals? There are two separable issues here. First, states need to be able to accommodate refugees and immigrants without stimulating resistance by their own citizens. Second is a security issue: preventing the newcomers from hosting violent militants and replicating in their host countries the conflicts that set the refugees in motion in the first place.

Gender and Conflict

Much is being written now about the victimization of women in Third World civil wars, in which rape and enslavement are both tactics and incidental consequences of warfare. We also think we understand why this happens, especially in Islamist wars, where it is justified by medieval Arab custom and contemporary jihadist doctrine. The subject of women's roles as activists and resistors is less well studied. *Why Men Rebel* (1970) was written before the gender revolution, after which "men" was no longer an acceptable synonym for "people." More than terminology or political correctness is at issue here. Women rarely had a significant role in violent conflict before the 1970s. Bernadine Dohrn, a leader of the Weather Underground from 1969 onward, was a pioneer in this respect. In 1970 Gudrun Ensslin and Ulrike Meinhof were among the founders of Germany's terrorist Red Army Faction. Other examples might be cited but the point remains: they were very few in proportion to men. A suggestive comparative account is Joanne Gilbert's *Women of*

Valor: Polish Resisters to the Third Reich (2014), based on late-in-life interviews with four Jewish women who, as teenagers, had the courage to actively oppose Nazi rule and the skills and luck to survive. Gilbert is a genealogist and biographer, not a conflict researcher, but a more systematic application of her approach could lead to the cumulation of micro-data on women's roles in violent conflict.

A larger issue for empirical research is what impact women have had on the evolution of the forms and issues of conflict over the last half-century. Not enough is known of the role of women as activists and resistors, with the obvious exception of their leadership of movements for women's equality. These movements have relied almost exclusively on nonviolent tactics. Some women have taken visible and effective roles in other mass movements in Western societies, especially those concerned with human rights issues. How numerous are they among the leaders of these movements by comparison with men? Or by comparison with the proportions of women in legislatures, or corporate positions? And does it matter? Do women leaders in mass protest movements prefer different strategies and tactics than men, do they lead to differences in outcomes?

Two Research Projects

These next sketches show, in the first instance, how I went about the Minorities at Risk project and what lessons it suggests for how to do long-term projects on specific kinds or issues of conflict. Second is an outline of research that should contribute to better analytic understanding of Islamic State and similar jihadist movements.

Explaining Ethnopolitical Conflict[2]

Ethnic conflict is an uneasy marriage of two concepts, each of which is in turn ambiguous and contested. It does not define a more objective universe of analysis like the concepts "the state" or "elections" or "internal war." Thus, researchers need to specify more precisely what is meant by "ethnicity" in different social contexts and circumstances. It is equally important to narrow the concept of conflict to observable kinds of action: usually physical contestation among groups, or between groups and states, over issues of power, resources, and status. My approach in the Minorities at Risk project, from the late 1980s onward,[3] was to focus in on the more specific concept of *ethnopolitical conflict*, defined as political contestation in which one or more parties mobilizes support based on appeals to communal identity and aims to protect or improve the group's status vis-à-vis the state or other groups (Gurr 1993a; 2000). Among the questions that motivated the project are these:

1.   Under what circumstances, internal and external to an identity group, do the interests of a collectivity lead to political action either in defense or promotion of group interests?

2. What are the roles of shared grievances, leadership, ideology, opportunities, and external threats in mobilizing a group for political action?
3. What kinds of political strategy are chosen by mobilized identity groups, and why?
4. Once an organization based on the claims of an identity group does engage in political action, what determines the outcomes? What are the relative importance of group strategies, domestic and international political context, and regime ideology and resources in determining whether a group's actions have positive or negative consequences?
5. What strategies of negotiation, incorporation, and electoral representation can minimize the risks and costs of violent ethnopolitical conflict?
6. What is the impact of international factors on ethnopolitical conflicts, among them regional power shifts, the ascendance of ideologies about national self-determination and group rights, economic globalization, and international mediation and peace-keeping?

What have we learned? The necessary precondition for systematic knowledge about the causes and processes of ethnopolitical conflict has been the development of global and regional datasets. We know a great deal about the universe of ethnopolitical groups, based on the Minorities at Risk (MAR) project's profiles of the structural characteristics, status, and actions of some 300 identity groups that are or recently have been either politically active or subject to systematic discrimination (Gurr 1993a; www.cidcm.umd.edu/mar/). Johanna Birnir's selection bias project has identified a larger universe of some 900 identifiable ethnic groups (called A-MAR) to permit systematic comparisons between non-politicized and politically active ethnic groups (Birnir et al. 2011). Some studies, including mine, have included religiously based identity groups such as Muslim minorities in non-Muslim countries and Shi'a in Sunni-dominated societies. Jonathan Fox has adapted the MAR approach in a series of global studies that identify organized religious entities and codes their relationship with states (Fox 2008; 2015).

As a consequence of many quantitative analyses of these datasets, it is possible to answer some important general questions sketched above, such as the relative importance of grievances and different structural and opportunity factors that lead to ethnopolitical protest and rebellion (see Asal and Deloughery, Chapter 2 in this book). Some comparative research has focused on specific types of groups—for example, indigenous peoples, communal contenders, or trans-state ethnonationalists. Other research has examined the dynamics of ethnopolitical conflict in particular world regions, notably the post-communist states and the Middle East. We also have gained some understanding about the political systems in which ethnopolitical action is most likely to take the form of protest rather than rebellion, and the longer-range consequences of both strategies.

There is a substantial body of comparative research, quantitative and qualitative, on the causes, dynamics, and outcomes of self-determination and secessionist movement (for example, Gurr 2000, chapter 6; Saideman and Ayres 2008; and a recent summary by Toft 2012b). Other quantitative studies have helped pinpoint the structural conditions that are associated with, and differentiate between, civil wars that aim at revolution versus secession. A post-Cold War decline in the global incidence of ethnopolitical wars and a commensurate increase in international mediation and peace-keeping efforts have been convincingly documented. The circumstances in which terrorism is used by ethnopolitical groups have been examined with the new Minorities at Risk Organizational Behavior (MAROB) dataset developed at the University of Maryland (Asal et al. 2008; Asal et al. 2015a).

There is also a large and growing set of studies about the processes and institutional arrangements that can contain or prevent ethnopolitical conflict. Some use quantitative research strategies, others comparative case studies. Examples of good studies that happen to be on my shelves as I write: Birnir on ethnicity and electoral politics (2007) and Oberschall on conflict and peace-building in divided societies (2007).

Many other case and small-n comparative studies are relevant to the general questions identified above, far too many on which to comment. Suffice to say that the cumulative effect of qualitative case studies on our understanding is as great as what has been learned from quantitative research. The difference is not merely methodological. Qualitative research makes it possible to deal with subjective and micro-issues, such as how group identities and intergroup boundaries are formed and change in salience, leaders' decision-making, processes of mobilization, and how specific settlements are negotiated. The multiple research strategies, at different levels of analysis, are or should be seen as complementary. My sense, though, is that scholars working in one mode give too little attention to the work done in the others.

Let me provide one specific example. In a recent comparative study of terrorism and crime networks that are based on trans-boundary identity groups, Lyubov Mincheva and I did in-depth studies of the Kurds, Kosovar Albanians, Serbian nationalists, and Bosnian and Algerian Muslims, among others. There is a substantial social science and historical literature on each of these groups and we were able to draw on it, with our theoretical questions in mind, to do case studies in ways that would have been impossible based on existing quantitative studies. For instance, the salience of Bosniaks' Muslim identity greatly increased because of civil war with Serbian and Croat nationalists, so much so that non-militant Islam is now the basis of Bosniak national identity. Maybe less well known, during the civil war the Bosnian government made creative political uses of Islamic appeals to mobilize domestic support and attract international support from Islamists, then later acted to contain external efforts at propagating Wahhabist influence in what remains a mainly secular society (Mincheva and Gurr 2013, chapter 4).

The development of large-n datasets on identity groups and religious groups has been a major advance in conflict studies. Theoretical advances include a shift away from the assumption that ethnies are primordial social entities—a view more common in the media and foreign policy circles than among scholars— toward the recognition that group identities vary in salience across time and among individuals, and can change depending on multiple circumstances within and among groups. Studies of the framing and boundaries of communal identities thus are a major contribution to our understanding (see Murer's review, 2012). I also think it is commonly recognized that "the salience of ethnocultural identity depends on how much difference it makes in peoples' lives" (Gurr 2000, 67). Thus, threats to a group, such as attacks on the Alawite-dominated regime in Syria, and opportunities for ethnonational gain, such as the deconstruction of the USSR and the Yugoslav Federation, both sharpen group boundaries and activate mobilization for political action, or, in the case of Syria, genocidal defense of the Assad regime.

Another kind of development is the use of data and insights from studies of ethnopolitical conflict in other research fields. For example, the US government's rebadged Political Instability Task Force used various ethnicity variables in developing its global and regional models, including indicators of countries' ethnic diversity and group discrimination. Both were among the handful of variables that survived an extensive empirical winnowing process and were included in final models (Goldstone et al. 2010). Barbara Harff's final postdictive model for genocides and politicides included a MAR variable, the existence of state-led discrimination against ethnies, and her country-specific risk assessments use MAR data on politically active and endangered groups (Harff 2003 for the model; GPANet.org for annual updates of the risk list; Harff Chapter 12 in this book).

Explaining Islamic State[4]

With all our theories and empirical analyses, what can we say about the rise of Islamic State, aka Daesh, ISIS, or ISIL? An explosion of new studies examines its origins and dynamics (for example, Cockburn 2015; Filiu 2015; Weiss and Hassan 2015). These writings are enormously informative about how Islamic State capitalized on Sunni resentment against Shiite domination (in Iraq) and state repression (in Syria). Its historical roots and the jihadist and Salafist bases of its operating doctrine are increasingly well understood. Journalist Abdel Bari Atwan, in *Islamic State: The Digital Caliphate*, "draws a convincing picture of Islamic State as a well-run organization that combines bureaucratic efficiency and military expertise with a sophisticated use of information technology" (Ruthven 2015, 74). Hugh Roberts (2015) shows how international engagement, or meddling, has confounded efforts to promote negotiations between the Assad regime and its non-jihadist opposition, thus giving more space for IS to expand its control.

These provide an in-depth case study understanding of IS, not a nomothetic one. And here is a great opportunity for a comparative case study, because the

Islamic State is not unique. It is one of at least five violent jihadist efforts to establish a militant, geographically grounded Islamic state in the last two decades. First was the Pashtun-based Taliban, which did precisely that by taking power in 1996 and governing as the Islamic Emirate of Afghanistan until it was ousted from power by its local ethnopolitical rivals, with US backing, in 2001. Next, in point of time, was the Algerian Salafist Group for Preaching and Combat (GSPC), which in 2006 formally aligned with al-Qaida and rebadged as al-Qaida in the Maghreb (AQIM). In response to Algerian counterinsurgency tactics the GSPC/AQIM retreated into the Sahara and established a large if amorphous area of operation that included parts of Mali, Mauritania, and Niger. In 2012 a revolt by Tuareg nationalists, in temporary alliance with the Algerians, gave it temporary control of a substantial part of Mali and threatened to overthrow the coup- and corruption-weakened Malian regime.

Next is Somalia, where the jihadist Islamic Courts movement in the mid-2010s established control of significant areas. Marginalized by Ethiopian and other intervening military forces, they were succeeded by Al-Shabaab, an even more militant Islamist movement that by 2011 controlled most of southern Somalia, including the environs of Mogadishu. Fourth is the Boko Haram movement of northern Nigeria, led by a stridently fundamentalist young preacher from Bornu. By 2015 it was firmly based in north-east Nigeria, had murdered an estimated 23,000 people in establishing its hegemony by terror—some Christian victims but many of them Muslims who rejected the movement—and announced its allegiance to Islamic State (a recent study is Smith 2015).

A new background report on global terrorism in 2014 by the National Consortium for the Study of Terrorism and Responses to Terrorism (START 2015) identifies the total numbers of attacks and fatalities by each major perpetrator organization. The most deadly perpetrators globally are four of the above five jihadist organizations: Islamic State (9,596 fatalities), the Taliban (4,914), Al-Shabaab (1,783), and Boko Haram (7,112). AQIM is the only one of the five that is not among the top twenty on the 2014 terrorist hit parade.

A comparative study of these five cases could begin by pointing out that all took advantage of geopolitical opportunities: they established themselves in badly and weakly governed areas of existing states or, in IS's case, contested areas of two adjacent states. Their jihadist doctrines justified rebellions against grossly corrupt governments and regional impoverishment—north-east Nigeria is the poorest of the country's regions. IS had the additional advantage that it came to represent Sunnis who were marginalized by the Iraqi government. Poverty and communal resentments provided a stream of recruits from the region and elsewhere. Coercion through terror cowed some observers and compelled others to support the movements. IS probably would be judged to have the most effective military. Disaffected Sunni officers from Iraq, some who had served Saddam Hussein, are said to have been instrumental. Hoards of US-supplied military equipment, abandoned by the Iraqi army, provided material means for rapid conquest.

One important characteristic of both the Taliban and Islamic State is that they restored governance in chaotically ungoverned regions. This could also be the basis of their growing appeal in Libya and Yemen. Islamic State is said to be "putting in place the kinds of measures associated with governance: Issuing identification cards for residents, promulgating fishing guidelines to preserve stocks, requiring that cars carry tool kits for emergencies" (Arango 2015). The Taliban earlier gained widespread acquiescence in Afghanistan because it also ended corruption and established predictable order, albeit based on harshly implemented, traditional Islamic law. Stephen Walt has recently argued that by establishing order out of chaos IS may be accepted by many people under its control. Journalists' accounts of conversations with IS subjects lead to the same conclusion. Acceptance of a stable government may well prove more enduring than resentment against the terror used to promote its cause and to establish order. In short, Islamic State is in fact a state in becoming, not an ephemeral and easily defeated jihadist movement (Walt 2015).

None of this fully explains the essential role of jihadist and Salafist ideology in fueling these five movements, which is one of the issues for comparative analysis. Al-Shabaab's fight against international military interventions, and its celebration of Salafist doctrines and rule, attracted some recruits from overseas, especially young Somali expats. Police work prevented some volunteers and financial aid from reaching AQIM from continental Europe. IS has been by far the most successful in recruiting supporters from abroad, thanks in good part to its sophisticated use of social media. Not lightly does Atwan characterize it as "the digital caliphate" (the subtitle of his 2015 book).

Comparative analysis of the five movements should contribute to a general understanding of why and how they emerge, organize, and command or lose support. The Taliban and Islamic State stand out from Boko Haram and AQIM in their ability to establish systems of governance. Of particular concern should be the role of ideology and ideological manipulation in inspiring and sustaining the movements. The studies also should provide insights into the success (and failures) of international strategies, thus far mostly military ones, in containing the movements. GSPC/AQIM has been marginalized—not eliminated—by the defection of its onetime Tuareg allies and by French and other international military engagement. Boko Haram is now the target of joint military action by a reinvigorated Nigerian military in coalition with forces from Niger, Chad, and Cameroon, all of which had suffered from the rebels' incursions. The outcomes are unknown. But it is certainly reasonable to think that government offensives will not succeed in the longer run if they fail to deal with the two main grievances that provide the combustible fuel for these movements: pervasive poverty, and corrupt, incompetent, and repressive government.

To varying degrees these and other jihadist movements use the tactic of suicide bombing. A long-term comparative study by Robert Pape and his colleagues at the University of Chicago identified one other major grievance.

They have studied the phenomenon at two levels, strategic and individual. In-depth analysis of the seven most deadly campaigns of suicide terrorism from the 1980s through 2009—six of them by Islamic groups—were responses to the presence and influence of foreign forces, military and political, in the attackers' homelands. The militants directing these suicide campaigns say they use the strategy because it is an effective means for inducing the occupiers—for example, the US in Iraq and Afghanistan, Israelis in Lebanon, Gaza, and the West Bank—to withdraw. The testimony of suiciders, and interviews with their friends and families, repeatedly say that martyrdom was a way to attack hated occupiers of their lands. Sometimes there were also personal motives of revenge because friends and family members had been killed by occupying forces, events that precipitated conversion to jihadist ideology and their willingness to sacrifice their lives to its cause (Pape and Feldman 2012; on the more general issue of strategic choices of terror versus other conflict tactics see, among others, Crenshaw 1998 and Ganor 2015).

Conclusion: Some Suggestions for Future Conflict Analysis

A linear logic underlies almost all systematic conflict analysis. The first step is to specify the structures and settings in which political conflict arises. The second is to identify the issues in dispute. Third is analysis of the issues, ideologies, and motives of the actors who engage in conflict. Next is specification of the organizations, or the basis of mobilization, at the disposal of the principal actors. Fifth are the collective actions themselves, violent and nonviolent, by which the actors pursue their objectives. Last is assessment of the outcomes—who wins or loses, and with what results for themselves and their societies.

Researchers make choices about where to begin their analyses. Examples of foci include the consequences of inequalities along class or ethnic lines (structures), how collectivities organize for action (mobilization), "why people rebel" (motives), the incidence of military coups in new states (collective actions), or the outcomes of revolutionary movements. This logic is inherent in studies of repression as well as of resistance. States, and other agents of repression, have structures, norms, and agencies that shape political decisions about whether and when to use force against subjects and violence against opponents.

The assumption of linearity should not detract from interest in feedback effects. Outcomes may reshape structures, as they do in successful revolutions. The process of mobilization often leads to the redefinition of conflict issues and motives. Ideologies, and widely held beliefs that violence is justified and functional in particular situations, help identify issues, mobilize collectivities, and specify preferred forms of collective action (see Gurr 1970, chapter 6).

Ideology tells people why they are aggrieved, who is responsible, and—when articulated by clever strategists—what to do about it. And while we know a great deal about the content of specific ideologies, from Marxism to nationalism to

Salafism, I suggested above that we do not yet have much generalizable knowledge about how conflict is shaped by ideology, or generalized beliefs, or what Charles Tilly (1978) called repertoires of collective action. This is, I agree with Sanin and Wood (2014), a particular challenge for future empirical research, not just comparative studies of jihadist movements. Some questions may have nomothetic answers: In what settings do militant ideologies arise? Which are more effective in creating solidarity among believers? What determines how widely they attract adherents? What is the relative importance of shared grievances, group identity, cultural resonance, or any of a dozen other factors that may determine why individuals respond to particular ideological appeals? These are questions that may seem most suitable to ideographic accounts of particular movements. Yet they may also be susceptible to empirical research, from the micro level (like the interview studies described in Pape and Feldman 2012) to the macro (comparative case studies).

This brings me to the question of appropriate research strategies. In my own work I have alternated between large-n empirical research and comparative case studies (eg. Goldstone et al. 1991; Mincheva and Gurr 2013). Macro research designs of conflict behavior then draw and test causal links across the stages identified above, conceived of as bundles of variables. I have done such studies to test cross-national hypotheses about magnitudes of political violence (Gurr 1968) and the extent of ethnopolitical protest and rebellion (Gurr 1993b). Threads of research have followed in which others have focused on the same (or similar) explananda, testing other hypotheses, or using new data, or employing the latest statistical methodologies.

Good comparative case studies use a common theoretical framework for analysis and aim at explaining the network of interactions that lead to a common outcome. What they lack in generalizability they make up in depth of understanding. And they may be the best way to deal with less tangible issues such as the questions I posed above about radical ideology, and more complex issues such as the impact of international engagement on conflict dynamics. This research strategy is as close as we can come to answering a common criticism of empirical conflict research: it is disconnected from the lives, and emotions and sufferings, of its actors. But these are the domains of the participant observer, not least the journalist and diarist and novelist. We sacrifice this level of *verstehen* in the hope of gaining understanding of patterns and sequences.

No conventional conclusion is possible for this chapter, or the book as a whole, because the phenomena we study are not static. Of course there are continuities, but issues, beliefs, mobilization, and forms of political action are changeable. So are government and international responses. New issues and strategies of political conflict will provoke new waves of research. New datasets and methodologies will provide attractive means to explore research questions in greater depth. And the results of new research will suggest new puzzles. Of all the subjects of comparative analysis, political conflict, like its subject matter, is the most protean and unpredictable.

Notes

1 With thanks to the editors of this book for their comments on a draft of this chapter.
2 This section is extracted from an essay written in 2013 that will be included in a forth-coming special issue of the journal *Ethnopolitics*.
3 James Scarritt inadvertently set the project in motion when he asked me in 1986 to collaborate on a paper that inventoried minorities subject to discrimination (Gurr and Scarritt 1989). Barbara Harff encouraged me to use the project's information to iden-tify groups that were potential victims of genocide. Monty Marshall was the earliest research assistant on the ever-expanding project and continued to work on it for nearly two decades. A great many graduate assistants and research associates contributed to the project over the years, too many to list here. After I retired the project remained at the Center for International Development and Conflict Management, directed first by Jonathan Wilkenfeld and now by Johanna Birnir.
4 I mentioned this essay project to my friend Jonathan Reid, a former biology instructor and now successful attorney, and asked what he as a layman might expect to find here. This section sketches how comparative conflict analyses might answer his question: Can we explain Islamic State?

INDEX

Note: Tables are indicated in bold; figures in italics.